T0211982

Lecture Notes in Computer Science 11721

More information about this series at http://www.springer.com/series/7410

Vijay Gadepally · Timothy Mattson ·
Michael Stonebraker · Fusheng Wang ·
Gang Luo · Yanhui Laing ·
Alevtina Dubovitskaya (Eds.)

Heterogeneous Data Management, Polystores, and Analytics for Healthcare

VLDB 2019 Workshops, Poly and DMAH
Los Angeles, CA, USA, August 30, 2019
Revised Selected Papers

 Springer

Editors
Vijay Gadepally
Massachusetts Institute
of Technology
Lexington, MA, USA

Michael Stonebraker
Massachusetts Institute
of Technology
Cambridge, MA, USA

Gang Luo
University of Washington
Seattle, WA, USA

Alevtina Dubovitskaya
Lucerne University
of Applied Sciences
Rotkreuz, Switzerland

Timothy Mattson
Intel Corporation
Portland, OR, USA

Fusheng Wang
Stony Brook University
Stony Brook, NY, USA

Yanhui Laing
Google
Mountain View, CA, USA

ISSN 0302-9743   ISSN 1611-3349 (electronic)
Lecture Notes in Computer Science
ISBN 978-3-030-33751-3   ISBN 978-3-030-33752-0 (eBook)
https://doi.org/10.1007/978-3-030-33752-0

LNCS Sublibrary: SL4 – Security and Cryptology

This Springer imprint is published by the registered company Springer Nature Switzerland AG
The registered company address is: Gewerbestrasse 11, 6330 Cham, Switzerland

Preface

In this volume we present the accepted contributions for the VLDB conference workshops entitled Towards Polystores that Manage Multiple Databases, Privacy, Security and/or Policy Issues for Heterogenous Data (Poly 2019) and the 5th International Workshop on Data Management and Analytics for Medicine and Healthcare (DMAH 2019) held in Los-Angeles, California, with the 45th International Conference on Very Large Data Bases during August 26–30, 2019.

Poly 2019 Overview

Enterprises are routinely divided into independent business units to support agile operation. However, this leads to "siloed" information systems. Such silos generate a host of problems, such as:

- *Discovery* of relevant data to a problem at hand. For example, organizations may have 4000 (+/-) relational databases, a data lake, large numbers of files, and an interest in public data from the Web. Finding relevant data in this sea of information can be a challenge.
- *Integrating* the discovered data. Independently constructed schemes are never compatible.
- *Cleaning* the resulting data. A good figure of merit is that 10% of all data is missing or wrong.
- *Ensuring Efficient Access* to resulting data. Scale operations must be performed "in situ", and a good polystore system is required.

It is often said that data scientists spent 80% (or more) of their time on these tasks, and it is crucial to have better solutions. In addition, the EU has recently enacted GDPR that will force enterprises to assuredly delete personal data on request. This "right to be forgotten" is one of several requirements of GDPR, and it is likely that GDPR-like requirements will spread to other locations, for example California. In addition, privacy and security issues are increasingly, an issue for large internet platforms. In enterprises, these issues will be front and center in the distributed information systems in place today. Lastly, enterprise access to data in practice will require queries constructed from a variety of programming models. A "one size fits all" mentality just won't work in these cases.

Poly 2019 focuses on research and practice in developing tools that address and/or mitigate the challenges presented above.

DMAH 2019 Overview

The goal of the workshop is to bring together researchers from the cross-cutting domains of research including information management and biomedical informatics. The workshop aims to foster exchange of information and discussions on innovative data management and analytics technologies. We encourage topics that highlight the end-to-end applications, systems, and methods addressing problems in healthcare, public health, and everyday wellness; integration with clinical, physiological, imaging, behavioral, environmental, and "omics" data, as well as the data from social media and the Web. Our hope for this workshop is to provide a unique opportunity for mutually benefiting and informative interaction between information management and biomedical researchers from the interdisciplinary fields.

Organization

POLY 2019

Workshop Chairs

Vijay Gadepally   Massachusetts Institute of Technology, USA
Timothy Mattson   Intel Corporation, USA
Michael Stonebraker   Massachusetts Institute of Technology, USA

Program Committee Members

Edmon Begoli   Oak Ridge National Laboratory, USA
Kajal Claypool   MIT, USA
Michael Gubanov   Florida State University, USA
Amarnath Gupta   University of California, San Diego, USA
Jeremy Kepner   Massachusetts Institute of Technology, USA
Dimitris Kolovos   University of York, UK
Tim Kraska   Massachusetts Institute of Technology, USA
Samuel Madden   Massachusetts Institute of Technology, USA
Ratnesh Sahay   AstraZeneca, UK
Nesime Tatbul   Massachusetts Institute of Technology, Intel, USA
Daniel Weitzner   MIT Internet Policy Research Initiative, USA

DMAH 2019

Workshop Chairs

Fusheng Wang   Stony Brook University, USA
Gang Luo   University of Washington, USA
Yanhui Liang   Google, USA
Alevtina Dubovitskaya Lucerne University of Applied Sciences and Arts,
                          Swisscom, Switzerland

Program Committee Members

Jesús B. Alonso-Hernández   Universidad de Las Palmas de Gran Canaria, Spain
Edmon Begoli   Oak Ridge National Laboratory, USA
Thomas Brettin   Argonne National Laboratory, USA
J. Blair Christian   Oak Ridge National Laboratory, USA
Dejing Dou   University of Oregon, USA
Alevtina Dubovitskaya   École polytechnique fédérale de Lausanne, Switzerland
Peter Elkin   University at Buffalo, USA
Zhe He   Florida State University, USA
Maristela Holanda   Universidade de Brasília, Brazil
Guoqian Jiang   Mayo Clinic, USA

Contents

DMAH 2019: Database Enabled Biomedical Research

DMAH 2019: AI for Healthcare

DMAH 2019: Knowledge Discovery from Unstructured Biomedical Data

DMAH 2019: Blockchain and Privacy-Preserving Data Management

Keynotes

POLY 2019: Privacy, Security and/or Policy Issues for Heterogenous Data

Data Capsule: A New Paradigm for Automatic Compliance with Data Privacy Regulations

Lun Wang[2(✉)], Joseph P. Near[1], Neel Somani[2], Peng Gao[2], Andrew Low[2], David Dao[3], and Dawn Song[2]

[1] University of Vermont, Burlington, USA
[2] University of California, Berkeley, USA
wanglun@berkeley.edu
[3] ETH Zurich, Zurich, Switzerland

Abstract. The increasing pace of data collection has led to increasing awareness of privacy risks, resulting in new data privacy regulations like General data Protection Regulation (GDPR). Such regulations are an important step, but automatic compliance checking is challenging. In this work, we present a new paradigm, *Data Capsule*, for automatic compliance checking of data privacy regulations in heterogeneous data processing infrastructures. Our key insight is to pair up a data subject's data with a policy governing how the data is processed. Specified in our formal policy language: PRIVPOLICY, the policy is created and provided by the data subject alongside the data, and is associated with the data throughout the life-cycle of data processing (e.g., data transformation by data processing systems, data aggregation of multiple data subjects' data). We introduce a solution for static enforcement of privacy policies based on the concept of residual policies, and present a novel algorithm based on abstract interpretation for deriving residual policies in PRIVPOLICY. Our solution ensures compliance automatically, and is designed for deployment alongside existing infrastructure. We also design and develop PRIVGUARD, a reference data capsule manager that implements all the functionalities of *Data Capsule* paradigm.

Keywords: Data privacy · GDPR · Formalism of privacy regulations · Compliance of privacy regulations

1 Introduction

The big data revolution has triggered an explosion in the collection and processing of our personal data, leading to numerous societal benefits and sparking brand-new fields of research. At the same time, this trend of ever-increasing data collection raises new concerns about data privacy. The prevalence of data breaches [1,2], insider attacks [3], and organizational abuses of collected data [4] indicates that these concerns are well-founded. Data privacy has thus become one of the foundational challenges of today's technology landscape.

© Springer Nature Switzerland AG 2019
V. Gadepally et al. (Eds.): DMAH 2019/Poly 2019, LNCS 11721, pp. 3–23, 2019.
https://doi.org/10.1007/978-3-030-33752-0_1

To address this growing challenge, governments have begun crafting data privacy regulations to protect us (the *data subjects*) from those who collect and process our personal data. Recent examples include the European Union's *General Data Protection Regulation* (GDPR) [5], the *California Consumer Privacy Act* (CCPA) [6], the *Family Educational Rights & Privacy Act* [7], and the *Health Insurance Portability and Accountability Act* [8].

Unfortunately, compliance with data privacy regulations is extremely challenging with current data processing systems. The regulations are written in natural language, and thus are difficult to formalize for automatic enforcement. In addition, some of the systems currently used for data processing were designed and deployed before the existence of these privacy regulations, and their designs make the compliance even more difficult. For example, many existing data processing systems do not provide an option to delete data, since it was assumed that organizations would want to keep data forever [9]—but GDPR requires that a subject's data be deleted on request. Even if the deletion is possible, its enforcement can be challenging: organizations often make multiple copies of data, without no systematic record of the copies, because each data processing platform requires its own data format; as a result, an organization may not even be able to *locate* all of the copies of a data subject's data for deletion.

Compliance with data privacy regulations is therefore costly or impossible for many organizations. These challenges reduce the rate of compliance, resulting in harm to data subjects via privacy violations. Moreover, the cost of implementing compliance acts as a barrier to entry for small organizations, and serves to protect large organizations from new competition. Paradoxically, new data privacy regulations may actually *help* the large corporations whose abuses of data originally motivated those regulations.

This paper presents a new paradigm for *automatic compliance* with data privacy regulations in heterogeneous data processing infrastructures. Our approach is based on a new concept called the *data capsule*, which pairs up a data subject's data with a *policy* governing how the data may be processed. The policy follows the data subject's data *forever*, even when it is copied from one data processing system to another or mixed with data from other subjects. Our solution is designed for deployment *alongside* existing infrastructure, and requires only minimal changes to existing data processing systems. The approach is *automatic*, enabling compliance with minimal additional cost to organizations.

The Data Capsule Paradigm. We propose a new paradigm for collecting, managing, and processing sensitive personal data, called the Data Capsule Paradigm, which *automates* compliance with data privacy regulations. Our paradigm consists of three major components:

1. **Data capsule**, which contains sensitive personal data, a *policy* restricting how the data may be processed, and *metadata* relevant for data privacy concerns.
2. **Data capsule graph**, which tracks all data capsules, including data collected from data subjects and data derived (via processing) from the collected data.

3. **Data capsule manager**, which maintains the data capsule graph, registers new data capsules, enforces each capsule's policy, and propagates metadata through the graph.

Principles of Data Privacy. To reach the design requirements for our solution, we examine four existing data privacy regulations (GDPR, CCPA, HIPAA, and FERPA). We propose five *principles of data privacy* which accurately represent common trends across these regulations: *transparency & auditing, consent, processing control, data portability,* and *guarantee against re-identification.* Our principles are designed to be flexible. A solution targeting these principles can be made compliant with current data privacy regulations, and is also capable of being extended to new regulations which may be proposed in the future.

PRIVPOLICY: A Formal Privacy Policy Language. To enforce the five principles of data privacy outlined above, we introduce PRIVPOLICY: a novel *formal policy language* designed around these principles, and capable of encoding the formalizable subset of recent data privacy regulations. By formalizable subset, we filter out requirements like "legitimate business purpose" in GDPR, which is almost impossible to formalize and have to rely on auditing to enforce requirements like this. We demonstrate the flexibility of PRIVPOLICY by encoding GDPR, CCPA, HIPAA, and FERPA.

PRIVPOLICY has a formal semantics, enabling a sound analysis to check whether a data processing program complies with the policy. To enforce these policies, we present a novel static analysis based on abstract interpretation. The data capsule graph enables *pipelines* of analysis programs which together satisfy a given policy. To enforce policies on these pipelines in a compositional way, we propose an approach which statically infers a *residual policy* based on an analysis program and an input policy; the residual policy encodes the policy requirements which remain to be satisfied by later programs in the pipeline, and is attached to the output data capsule of the program.

Our approach for policy enforcement is entirely static. It scales to datasets of arbitrary size, and is performed as a pre-processing step (independent of the *execution* of analysis programs). Our approach is therefore well-suited to the heterogeneous data processing infrastructures used in practice.

PRIVGUARD: A Data Capsule Manager. We design and implement PRIVGUARD, a reference data capsule manager. PRIVGUARD consists of components that manage the data capsule graph and perform static analysis of *analysis programs* which process data capsules. PRIVGUARD is designed to work with real data processing systems and introduces negligible performance overhead. Importantly, PRIVGUARD makes no changes to the format in which data is stored or the systems used to process it. Its static analysis occurs as a separate step from the processing itself, and can be performed in parallel. In a case study involving medical data, we demonstrate the use of PRIVGUARD to enforce HIPAA in the context of analysis programs for a research study.

Contributions. In summary, we make the following contributions.

- We propose five *principles of data privacy* which encompass the requirements of major data privacy regulations.
- We introduce PRIVPOLICY: a new and expressive formal language for privacy policies, which is capable of encoding policies for compliance with the formalizable subset of data privacy regulations.
- We propose the data capsule paradigm, an approach for ensuring compliance with privacy regulations encoded using PRIVPOLICY, and formalize the major components of the approach.
- We present the encoding of GDPR in PRIVPOLICY.
- We introduce a solution for static enforcement of privacy policies based on the concept of *residual policies*, and present a novel algorithm based on abstract interpretation for deriving residual policies in PRIVPOLICY.
- We design and develop PRIVGUARD, a reference data capsule manager that implements all the functionalities of data capsule paradigm.

2   Requirements of Data Privacy Regulations

Recent years have seen new efforts towards regulating data privacy, resulting in regulations like the European Union's *General Data Protection Regulation* (GDPR). It joins more traditional regulations like the *Health Insurance Portability and Accountability Act* (HIPAA) and the *Family Educational Rights and Privacy Act* (FERPA).

2.1   Principles of Data Privacy

Historically, organizations have collected as much personal data as possible, and have not generally considered data privacy to be a high priority. The recent adoption of GDPR has forced a much wider set of organizations to consider solutions for ensuring compliance with data privacy regulations. Complying with regulations like GDPR is extremely difficult using existing systems, which generally are designed for *easy access to data* instead of strong data privacy protections. These regulations are even more difficult to satisfy when data is shared between organizational units or with third parties—yet the regulatory requirements apply even in these cases.

To address this challenge, we considered the *commonalities* between the three major data privacy regulations mentioned above to develop five *principles of data privacy*. These principles expose and generalize the fundamental ideas shared between regulations, and therefore are likely to also apply to future regulations. As described in Sect. 3, these five principles form the design criteria for our proposed data capsule paradigm.

In describing the five principles of data privacy, we use terminology from the GDPR. The term *data subject* refers to individuals whose data is being collected and processed, and the term *data controller* refers to organizations which collect and process data from data subjects. Briefly summarized, the five principles of data privacy are:

1. **Transparency & Auditing:** The data subject should be made aware of who has their data and how it is being processed.
2. **Consent:** The data subject should give explicit consent for the collection and processing of their data.
3. **Processing Control:** The data subject should have control over what types of processing are applied to their data.
4. **Data Portability:** The data subject should be able to obtain a copy of any data related to them.
5. **Guarantee Against Re-identification:** When possible, the results of processing should not permit the re-identification of any individual data subject.

2.2   Applying the Principles

The five principles described above represent the design criteria for our data capsule paradigm. They are specified specifically to be *at least as strong as* the requirements of existing privacy regulations, to ensure that our approach is capable of expressing all such requirements, and are general enough to apply to future regulations as well. This section demonstrates how our five principles describe and subsume the requirements of the four major privacy regulations.

GDPR. The major pillars of GDPR fall squarely into the five requirement categories described by our principles. Articles 13 and 14 describe *transparency & auditing* requirements: the data controller must inform the data subject about the data being collected and who it is shared with. Article 4, 7 and 29WP requires *consent*: the controller must generally obtain consent from the data subject to collect or process their data. Note that there are also cases in GDPR when personal data can be used without consent, where some other "lawful basis for processing" applies, such as public interest, legal obligation, contract or the legitimate interest of the controller. However, these purposes are almost impossible to formalize so we have to rely on auditing to enforce them and omit them in the system. Articles 18 and 22 ensure *processing control*: the data subject may allow or disallow certain types of processing. Articles 15, 16, 17, and 20 require *data portability*: the data subject may obtain a copy of their data, fix errors in it, and request that it be deleted. Finally, Recital 26 and Article 29WP describes a *guarantee against re-identification*: data controllers are required to take steps to prevent the re-identification of data subjects.

CCPA. CCPA is broadly similar to GDPR, with some differences in the specifics. Like GDPR, the requirements of CCPA align well with our five principles of data privacy. Unlike GDPR, CCPA's *consent* requirements focus on the

sale of data, rather than its original collection. Its *access & portability* requirements focus on data deletion, and are more limited than those of GDPR. Like
GDPR, CCPA ensures a *guarantee against re-identification* by allowing data
subjects to sue if they are re-identified.

HIPAA. The HIPAA regulation is older than GDPR, and reflects a contempo-
raneously limited understanding of data privacy risks. HIPAA requires the data
subject to be notified when their data is collected (*transparency & auditing*),
and requires *consent* in some (but not all) cases. HIPAA requires organizations
to store data in a way that prevents its unintentional release (partly ensuring
a *guarantee against re-identification*), and its "safe harbor" provision specifies a
specific set of data attributes which must be redacted before data is shared with
other organizations (an attempt to ensure a *guarantee against re-identification*).
HIPAA has only limited *processing control* and *data portability* requirements.

FERPA. The *Family Educational Rights and Privacy Act of 1974* (FERPA) is
a federal law in the United States that protects the privacy of student education records. FERPA requires *consent* before a post-secondary institution shares
information from a student's education record. It also requires *access & portability*: students may inspect and review their records, and request amendments.
In other respects, FERPA has fewer requirements than the other regulations
described above.

3   The Data Capsule Paradigm

This section introduces the *data capsule paradigm*, an approach for addressing
the five principles of data privacy described earlier. The data capsule paradigm
comprises four major concepts:

- *Data capsules* combine sensitive data contributed by a data subject (or
  derived from such data) with a *policy* governing its use and *metadata* describing its properties.
- *Analysis programs* process the data stored inside data capsules; the input of
  an analysis program is a set of data capsules, and its output is a new data
  capsule.
- The *data capsule graph* tracks all data capsules and analysis programs, and
  contains edges between data capsules and the analysis programs which process
  them.
- The *data capsule manager* maintains the data capsule graph, propagates policies and metadata within the graph, and controls access to the data within
  each data capsule to ensure that capsule policies are never violated.

In Sect. 3.3, we demonstrate how these concepts are used to satisfy our five
principles of data privacy. Section 4 describes PRIVGUARD, our proof-of-concept
data capsule manager which implements the paradigm.

3.1 Life Cycle of a Data Capsule

The life cycle of a data capsule includes four phases:

1. **Data Ingestion.** *Data subjects* construct data capsules from their sensitive data via the *ingestion* process, which pairs the data with the policy which will govern its use. In our setting, the data subject is the original data owner, whose privacy we would like to protect.

2. **Analysis Program Submission.** *Analysts* who would like to process the data contained in data capsules may submit *analysis programs*, which are standard data analytics programs augmented with API calls to the data capsule manager to obtain raw data for processing.

3. **Data Processing.** Periodically, or at a time decided by the analyst, the data capsule manager may run an analysis program. At this time, the data capsule manager statically determines the set of input data capsules to the program, and performs static analysis to verify that the program would not violate the policies of any of its inputs. As part of this process, the data capsule manager computes a *residual policy*, which is the new policy to be attached to the program's output. The data capsule manager then runs the program, and constructs a new data capsule by pairing up the program's output with the residual policy computed earlier.

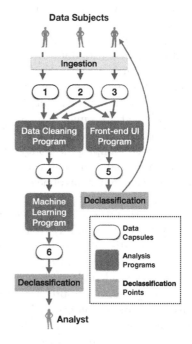

Fig. 1. Example Data capsule graph

4. **Declassification.** A data capsule whose policy has been satisfied completely may be viewed by the analyst in a process called *declassification*. When an analyst requests that the data capsule manager declassify a particular data capsule, the manager verifies that its policy has been satisfied, and that the analyst has the appropriate role, then sends the raw data to the analyst. Declassification is the only process by which data stored in a data capsule can be divorced from its policy.

3.2 The Data Capsule Manager

The data capsule life cycle is supported by a system implementing the functionality of the data capsule manager. The primary responsibility of the data capsule manager is to maintain the data capsule graph and maintain its invariants—namely, that no data capsule's policy is violated, that new data capsules resulting from analysis programs have the right policies, and that metadata is propagated correctly. We describe our reference implementation, PRIVGUARD, in Sect. 4.

Figure 1 contains a global view of an example data capsule graph. This graph contains two different organizations representing data controllers, and data subjects associated with each one. Both organizations use analysis programs which combine and clean data from multiple data subjects into a single data capsule; a third analyst uses data capsules from *both* organizations to perform marketing research. Such a situation is allowed under privacy regulations like GDPR, as long as the policies specified by the data subjects allow it. This example therefore demonstrates the ability of the data capsule paradigm to break down data silos while at the same time maintaining privacy for data subjects—a key benefit of the paradigm.

In this example, the policy attached to each data subject's capsule is likely to be a formal representation of GDPR. The data capsule paradigm requires a formal encoding of policies with the ability to efficiently compute residual policies; we describe our solution to this challenge in Sect. 5.

Note that the data capsules containing the data subjects' combined data (capsules 1, 2, 3, and 4) cannot be viewed by *anyone*, since their policies have not been satisfied. This is a common situation in the data capsule paradigm, and it allows implementing useful patterns such as extract-transform-load (ETL) style pipelines [10]. In such cases, analysts may submit analysis programs whose primary purpose is to prepare data for *other* analysis programs; after being processed by some (potentially long) pipeline of analysis programs, the final output has satisfied all of the input policies and may be declassified. The intermediate results of such pipelines can never be viewed by the analyst.

3.3 Satisfying the Principles of Data Privacy

The data capsule paradigm is designed specifically to enable systems which satisfy the principles of data privacy laid out in Sect. 2.

Transparency and Auditing. The data capsule manager satisfies transparency & auditing by consulting the data capsule graph. The global view of the graph (as seen in Fig. 1) can be restricted to contain only the elements reachable from the ingested data capsules of a single data subject, and the resulting sub-graph represents all of the data collected about or derived from the subject, plus all of the processing tasks performed on that data.

Consent. The data capsule manager tracks consent given by the data subject as metadata for each data capsule. Data subjects can be prompted to give consent when new analysis programs are submitted, or when they are executed.

Processing Control. The formal policies attached to data capsules can restrict the processing of the data stored in those capsules. These policies typically encode the restrictions present in data privacy regulations, and the data capsule manager employs a static analysis to verify that submitted analysis programs do not violate the relevant policies. This process is described in Sect. 5.

Data Portability. To satisfy the data portability principle, the data capsule manager allows each data subject to download his or her data capsules. The data capsule manager can also provide data capsules *derived* from the subject's capsules, since these are reachable capsules in the data capsule graph. However, the derived data returned to the data subject must *not* include data derived from the capsules of *other subjects*, so a one-to-one mapping must exist between rows in the input and output capsules for each analysis program involved. We formalize this process in Sect. 5.

The same mechanism is used for data deletion. When a data subject wishes to delete a capsule, the set of capsules derived from that capsule is calculated, and these derived capsules are re-computed *without* the deleted capsule included in the input.

Guarantee Against Re-identification. To provide a robust formal guarantee against re-identification, the data capsule manager supports the use of various techniques for anonymization, including both informal techniques (e.g. removing "personal health information" to satisfy HIPAA) and formal techniques (e.g. k-anonymity, ℓ-diversity, and differential privacy). A data capsule's policy may require that analysis programs apply one of these techniques to protect against re-identification attacks.

4   PrivGuard: A Data Capsule Manager

We have designed and implemented a reference data capsule manager, called PrivGuard. The PrivGuard system manages the data capsule graph, propagates policies and metadata, and uses static analysis to calculate residual policies on analysis programs.

Figure 2 summarizes the architecture of PrivGuard. The two major components of the system are the data capsule manager itself, which maintains the data capsule graph, and the static analyzer, which analyzes policies and analysis programs to compute residual policies. We describe the data capsule manager here, and formalize the static analyzer in Sect. 5.

Finally, outputCapsule defines an output data capsule of the analysis program. The analyst specifies a dataframe containing the output data, and PrivGuard automatically attaches the correct residual policy. This process is formalized in Sect. 5.

Deployment and Integration. The data capsule paradigm is intended to be integrated with existing heterogeneous data processing infrastructures, like the ones already in place for data analysis at many organizations, and PRIVGUARD is designed to facilitate such deployments. These infrastructures leverage a variety of data stores, including SQL databases [11], key-/value stores like MongoDB [12], distributed filesystems like HDFS [13], and short-term publish/subscribe systems like Cassandra [14]. They employ many different techniques for processing the data, includ-

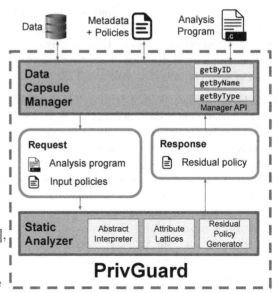

Fig. 2. The Architecture of PRIVGUARD.

ing SQL engines and distributed systems like MapReduce [15], Hadoop [13], and Spark [16].

To work successfully in such a heterogeneous environment, PRIVGUARD is deployed *alongside* the existing infrastructure. As shown in Fig. 2, policies and metadata are stored separately from the data itself, and the data can remain in the most efficient format for processing (e.g. stored in CSV files, in HDFS, or in a SQL database).

Similarly, PRIVGUARD's static analyzer uses a common representation to encode the semantics of many different kinds of analysis programs, so it works for many programming languages and platforms. The only platform-specific code is the small PRIVGUARD API, which allows analysis programs to interact with the data capsule manager. Our static analysis is based on abstract interpretation, a concept which extends to all common programming paradigms. Section 5 formalizes the analysis for dataflow-based systems which are close to relational algebra (e.g. SQL, Pandas, Hadoop, Spark); extending it to functional programs or traditional imperative or object-oriented programs is straightforward.

5   Policies and Policy Enforcement

This section describes our formal language for specifying policies on data capsules, and our static approach for enforcing these policies when an analytics program is registered with the system. We describe each of the four major components of this approach:

- Our policy specification language: PRIVPOLICY (Sect. 5.1).
- A set of attribute definitions suitable for encoding policies like GDPR and HIPAA, which are more expressive than the corresponding attributes proposed in previous work (Sect. 5.2).
- A flexible approach for deriving the *policy effects* of an analysis program via abstract interpretation (Sect. 5.3).
- A formal procedure for determining the *residual policy* on the output of an analysis program (Sect. 5.4).

5.1 PRIVPOLICY: Policy Specification Language

$A \in$ attribute $::= attrName\ attrValue$
$C \in$ policy clause $::= A \mid A$ AND $C \mid A$ OR C
$P \in$ policy $::=$ (ALLOW $C)^+$

$A ::= attrName\ attrValue$
$C_{DNF} \subseteq \mathcal{P}(A)$
$P_{DNF} \subseteq \mathcal{P}(C_{DNF})$

(1) PRIVPOLICY surface syntax.   (2) PRIVPOLICY disjunctive normal form.

Fig. 3. Surface syntax & Normal form.

Our policy specification language: PRIVPOLICY is inspired by the LEGALEASE language [17], with small changes to surface syntax to account for our more expressive attribute lattices and ability to compute residual policies.

```
1  ALLOW SCHEMA NotPII
2    AND NOTIFICATION_REQUIRED
3    AND (ROLE $user_id
4        OR (CONSENT_REQUIRED
5            AND DECLASS DP 1 0.000001))
```

Fig. 4. A subset of GDPR using PRIVPOLICY.

The grammar for the surface syntax of PRIVPOLICY is given in Fig. 3 (1). The language allows specifying an arbitrary number of *clauses*, each of which encodes a formula containing conjunctions and disjunctions over attribute values. Effectively, each clause of a policy in our language encodes one way to satisfy the overall policy.

Example. Figure 4 specifies a subset of GDPR using PRIVPOLICY. Each **ALLOW** keyword denotes a clause of the policy, and *SCHEMA, NOTIFICATION_REQUIRED , ROLE, CONSENT_REQUIRED*, and *DECLASS* are attributes. This subset includes only a single clause, which says that information which is not personally identifiable may be processed by the data controller, as long as the data subject is notified, and either the results are only viewed by the data subject, or the data subject gives consent and differential privacy is used to prevent re-identification based on the results.

Conversion to Disjunctive Normal Form. Our first step in policy enforcement is to convert the policy to *disjunctive normal form* (DNF), a common conversion in constraint solving. Conversion to DNF requires removing OR expressions from each clause of the

{{*SCHEMA* NotPII, *NOTIFICATION_REQUIRED*,
    ROLE $user_id}
  {*SCHEMA* NotPII, *NOTIFICATION_REQUIRED*,
    CONSENT_REQUIRED, *DECLASS* DP(1.0)}}

Fig. 5. Disjunctive normal form of the example policy.

policy; we accomplish this by distributing conjunction over disjunction and then splitting the top-level disjuncts within each clause into separate clauses. After converting to DNF, we can eliminate the explicit uses of **AND** and **OR**, and represent the policy as a *set of clauses*, each of which is a *set of attributes* as shown in Fig. 3 (2). The disjunctive normal form of our running example policy is shown in Fig. 5. Note that the disjunctive normal form of our example contains two clauses, due to the use of **OR** in the original policy.

5.2 Policy Attributes

LEGALEASE [17] organizes attribute values into *concept lattices* [18], and these lattices give policies their semantics. Instead of concept lattices, PRIVPOLICY leverages *abstract domains* inspired by work on abstract interpretation of programs [19]. This novel approach enables more expressive attributes (for example, the *FILTER* attribute) and also formalizes the connection between the semantics of policies and the semantics of analysis programs.

We require each attribute domain to define the standard lattice operations required of an abstract domain: a partial order ($\sqsubseteq$), join ($\sqcup$), and meet ($\sqcap$), as well as top and bottom elements $\top$ and $\bot$. Many of these can be defined in terms of the corresponding operations of an existing abstract domain from the abstract interpretation literature.

Filter Attributes. One example of our expressive attribute domains is the one for the *FILTER* attribute, which filters data based on integer-valued fields. The attribute domain for *FILTER* is defined in terms of an *interval* abstract domain [19]. We say filter : $f : i$ when the value of column f lies in the interval i. Then, we define the following operations on *FILTER* attributes, completing its attribute domain:

$$\text{filter} : f : i_1 \sqcup \text{filter} : f : i_2 = \text{filter} : f : i_1 \sqcup i_2$$
$$\text{filter} : f : i_1 \sqcap \text{filter} : f : i_2 = \text{filter} : f : i_1 \sqcap i_2$$
$$\text{filter} : f : i_1 \sqsubseteq \text{filter} : f : i_2 = : i_1 \sqsubseteq i_2$$

Schema Attributes. The schema attribute leverages a *set* abstract domain, in which containment is defined in terms of an underlying (finite) lattice of datatypes:

$$\text{schema} : S_1 \sqcup \text{schema} : S_2 = \text{schema} : \{s' \mid s_1 \in S_1 \wedge s_2 \in S_2 \wedge s' = s_1 \sqcup s_2\}$$
$$\text{schema} : S_1 \sqcap \text{schema} : S_2 = \text{schema} : \{s' \mid s_1 \in S_1 \wedge s_2 \in S_2 \wedge s' = s_1 \sqcap s_2\}$$
$$\text{schema} : S_1 \sqsubseteq \text{schema} : S_2 = \forall s_1 \in S_1, s_2 \in S_2 . s_1 \sqsubseteq s_2$$

Other Attributes. In PRIVPOLICY, as in LEGALEASE, the partial ordering for analyst roles is typically finite. It encodes the important properties of each analyst (e.g. for GDPR, the government typically has more authority to analyze data than members of the public). The role, declass, and redact attributes are defined by finite lattices. We omit the details here.

5.3 Abstract Interpretation of Analysis Programs

$$f \in \text{field} \quad m \in \text{int} \quad s \in \text{schema} \quad x \in \text{data capsules}$$

$$\delta \in \text{filter} \qquad ::= f < m \mid f > m$$
$$e \in \text{expression} ::= \text{getDC}(x) \mid \text{filter}(\varphi, e) \mid \text{project}(s, e) \mid \text{redact}(a, e)$$
$$\mid \text{join}(e, e) \mid \text{union}(e, e) \mid \text{dpCount}(\epsilon, \delta, e)$$

Fig. 6. Program surface syntax

We next describe the use of abstract interpretation to determine the *policy effect* of an analysis program. We introduce this concept using a simple dataflow-oriented language, similar to relational algebra, Pandas, or Spark, presented in Fig. 6. We write an abstract data capsule with schema s and policy effect ψ as $\mathbb{D}[s, \psi]$. A data capsule environment Δ maps data capsule IDs to their schemas (i.e. $\Delta : id \rightarrow s$).

$$\frac{\Delta(id) = s}{\Delta \vdash \text{getDC}(id) : \mathbb{D}[s, \emptyset]} \text{ GETDC} \qquad \frac{\Delta \vdash e : \mathbb{D}[s, \psi] \quad \varphi \leadsto_s a : v}{\Delta \vdash \text{filter}(\varphi, e) : \mathbb{D}[s, \psi + \text{filter} : a : v]} \text{ FILTER}$$

$$\frac{\Delta \vdash e : \mathbb{D}[s, \psi] \quad s' \subseteq s}{\Delta \vdash \text{project}(s', e) : \mathbb{D}[s', \psi + \text{schema} : s']} \text{ PROJECT} \qquad \frac{\Delta \vdash e : \mathbb{D}[s, \psi] \quad a \in s \quad e_r \leadsto_s v}{\Delta \vdash \text{redact}(a, e_r, e) : \mathbb{D}[s, \psi + \text{redact} : a : v]} \text{ REDACT}$$

$$\frac{\Delta \vdash e_1 : \mathbb{D}[s_1, \psi_1] \quad \Delta \vdash e_2 : \mathbb{D}[s_2, \psi_2]}{\Delta \vdash \text{join}(e_1, e_2) : \mathbb{D}[s_1 \cup s_2, \psi_1 \cup \psi_2]} \text{ JOIN} \qquad \frac{\Delta \vdash e_1 : \mathbb{D}[s, \psi_1] \quad \Delta \vdash e_2 : \mathbb{D}[s, \psi_2]}{\Delta \vdash \text{union}(e_1, e_2) : \mathbb{D}[s, \emptyset]} \text{ UNION}$$

$$\frac{\Delta \vdash e : \mathbb{D}[s, \psi]}{\Delta \vdash \text{dpCount}(\epsilon, \delta, e) : \mathbb{D}[s, \psi + \text{declass} : DP(\epsilon, \delta)]} \text{ DPCOUNT}$$

Fig. 7. Sample collecting semantics for the data capsule expressions in the language presented in Fig. 6.

We present the *collecting semantics* [19] for PRIVPOLICY in Fig. 7. The collecting semantics represents an abstract interpretation of programs in this language to determine their policy effects. If we can use the semantics to build a derivation tree of the form $\Delta \vdash e : \mathbb{D}[s, \psi]$, then we know that the program is guaranteed to satisfy the policy clause ψ (or any clause which is less restrictive than ψ).

5.4   Computing Residual Policies

Let $\Upsilon(id)$ be the policy of the data capsule with ID id. The free variables of a program e, written $fv(e)$, are the data capsule IDs it uses.

We define the *input policy* of a program e to be the least upper bound of the policies of its free variables:

$$\Upsilon_{\mathsf{in}(e)} = \bigsqcup_{id \in fv(e)} \{\Upsilon(id)\}$$

This semantics means that the input policy will be *at least as restrictive* as the *most restrictive* policy on an input data capsule. It is computable as follows, because the disjunctive normal form of a policy is a set of sets:

$$p_1 \sqcup p_2 = \{c_1 \cup c_2 \mid c_1 \in p_1 \wedge c_2 \in p_2\}$$

The *residual policy* applied to the output data capsule is computed by considering each clause in the input policy, and computing its residual based on the policy effect of the program. The residual policy is computed using the following rule:

$$\frac{\vdash e : \mathbb{D}[s, \psi]}{\Upsilon_{\mathsf{out}(e)} = \{c' \mid c \in \Upsilon_{\mathsf{in}(e)} \wedge residual(c, \psi) = c'\}} \; \text{RP}$$

where

$$residual(c, \psi) = c - \{k : p \mid k : p \in c \wedge \text{satisfies}(k : p, \psi)\}$$
$$satisfies(k : p, \psi) = \exists k : p' \in \psi.p \sqsubseteq p'$$

Here, the *satisfies* relation holds for an attribute $k : p$ in the policy when there exists an attribute $k : p'$ in the policy effect of the program, such that p (from the policy) is less restrictive than p' (the guarantee made by the program). Essentially, we compute the residual policy from the input policy by *removing* all attributes for which *satisfies* holds.

6   Formally Encoding GDPR

This section describes our formal encodings of GDPR. We are in the process of developing similar encodings for other regulations, including HIPAA, FERPA.

Figure 8 contains a full formal encoding of the requirements of GDPR. The first clause (lines 1–5) allows the use of data for

```
1   ALLOW SCHEMA NotPII
2     AND NOTIFICATION_REQUIRED
3     AND (ROLE $user_id
4       OR (CONSENT_REQUIRED
5         AND DECLASS DifferentialPrivacy 1 0.000001))
6
7   # Definitions mainly given in Article 6. Also Article 4, 25, 32
8   ALLOW SCHEMA PersonalInformation (Article 9)
9     AND CONSENT_REQUIRED (Article 4, 6)
10
11  ALLOW SCHEMA PersonalInformation (Article 9)
12    AND ROLE UserAffiliatedOrganizations($user_id)
13    AND SCHEMA HasAppropriateSafeguards (article 25, 32, 46)
14
15  ALLOW SCHEMA PersonalInformation
16    AND ROLE SupervisoryAuthority OR ROLE
           HealthcareOrganization
17    AND PURPOSE PublicInterest LegalObligation PublicHealth
18
19  ALLOW SCHEMA PersonalInformation
20    AND ROLE LegalAuthority
21    AND PURPOSE PublicInterest ForJudicialPurposes
```

Fig. 8. Formal encoding of GDPR.

any purpose, as long as it is protected against re-identification and subject to consent by the data subject. The third clause (lines 11–13) allows the use of personal information by organizations affiliated with the data subject—a relationship which we encode as a metafunction. The final two clauses specify specific public interest exceptions, for public health (lines 15–17) and for judicial purposes (lines 19–21).

GDPR is designed specifically to be simple and easy for users to understand, and its requirements are well-aligned with our five principles of data privacy. Our formal encoding is therefore correspondingly simple. We expect that most uses of data will fall under the third clause (for "business uses" of data, e.g. displaying Tweets to a Twitter user) or the first clause (for other purposes, e.g. marketing).

Data subjects who wish to modify this policy will generally specify more rigorous settings for the technologies used to prevent their re-identification. For example, a privacy-conscious data subject may require differential privacy in the first clause, instead of allowing any available de-identification approach.

7   Performance Evaluation

Recall that one of the goals of PRIVGUARD is to easily work with existing heterogeneous data processing systems and incur smallest additional overhead to the analysis itself. In order to achieve this goal, PRIVGUARD must have good scalability when the number of users are large. In this section, we first conduct an end-to-end evaluation to figure the bottleneck of the system scalability. Then we conduct several experimental evaluation to test the scalability of the bottleneck component. Specifically, we want to answer the following question: how is the scalability of PRIVGUARD and how much overhead PRIVGUARD will incur into the original data processing system.

7.1   Experimental Design and Setup

We first conduct an end-to-end evaluation to determine the sources of overhead when PRIVGUARD is used in a complete analysis. We then focus on the performance of policy ingestion as described in Sect. 3.1, which turns out to be the largest source of overhead in PRIVGUARD. We vary the number of data capsules from 2 to 1024 (with a log interval 2) and the policies are random subset of GDPR, HIPAA, FERPA or CCPA following a Gaussian distribution. The experiments are run on a single thread on top of an Ubuntu 16.04 LTS server with 32 AMD Opteron Processors. The experiments are run for 10 iterations to reach relatively stable results. Performance of PRIVGUARD does not depend on the data, so a real deployment will behave just like the simulation if the policies are similar.

7.2   Evaluation Results

In the following, we show and summarize the experiment results. In addition, we discuss and analyze the reasons for our findings.

End-to-End Evaluation. We first conduct an end-to-end evaluation to figure out the most time-consuming component in the execution path of PRIVGUARD. We evaluate the time of each component in the execution path in an system with 1024 clients with random subsets of HIPAA.

The results are summarized in 1. The "Parsing" column represents the time parsing the analysis program. The "Ingestion" column represents the time ingesting the input policies. The "Residual Policy" column represents the time computing residual policy given the ingested input policy and the analysis

Table 1. End-to-end evaluation

Operation	Parsing	Ingestion	Residual Policy
Time (ms)	83	9769	11

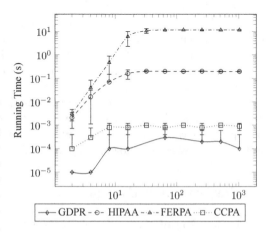

GDPR — HIPAA — FERPA — CCPA

Fig. 9. Scalability of policy analysis: ingestion operation.

program. Note that the input policy ingestion take up almost all of the running time, which indicates this operation as the bottleneck of the system.

The results demonstrate that the performance overhead of PRIVGUARD is negligible for these programs when the policy guard approach is used, and the bottleneck of PRIVGUARD is the ingestion operation.

Policy Ingestion Evaluation: Next, we perform a targeted microbenchmark to evaluate the scalability of the policy ingestion operation. Figure 9 contains the results. As we can observe in the figure, the running time exhibits a polynomial growth (recall that both the x-axis and y-axis are in log scale) at first and then keep stable after the policy number reaches some threshold. The reason is that the ingestion is implemeted using a least upper bound (LUB) operation, and the LUB operation in PRIVGUARD is composed of two sub-operations: (1) unique with $\mathbb{O}(n \log n)$ complexity, and (2) reduce with $\mathbb{O}(n')$ complexity (n' is the number of policies after unique operation). Because policies are a random subset of some complete policy (GDPR, HIPPA, FERPA and CCPA in this case), if the number of policies are large enough, n' will become a constant. Furthermore the unique operation is $\mathbb{O}(n \log n)$ with a small coefficient so this part is negligible compared to the reduce operation. All these factors result in the trend we observe in Fig. 9. This indicates excellent scalability of PRIVGUARD in terms of the number of data capsules.

8   Related Work

Recently, there are some research efforts on bootstrapping privacy compliance in big data systems. Technically, the works in this area can be categorized into two directions - (1) summarize the issues in privacy regulations to guide deployment; (2) formalise privacy regulations in a strict programming language flavor; (3) enforce privacy policies in data processing systems. Our work falls into all three categories. In the following, we briefly describe these research works and discuss why these existing approaches do not fully solve the problems in our setting.

Issues in Deploying Privacy Regulations. Gruschka et al. [20] summarize privacy issues in GDPR. Renaud et al. [21] synthesize the GDPR requirements into a checklist-type format, derive a list of usability design guidelines and providing a usable and GDPR-compliant privacy policy template for the benefit of policy writers. Politou et al. [22] review all controversies around the new stringent definitions of consent revocation and the right to be forgotten in GDPR and evaluate existing methods, architectures and state-of-the-art technologies in terms of fulfilling the technical practicalities for the implementation and effective integration of the new requirements into current computing infrastructures. Tom et al. [23] present the current state of a model of the GDPR that provides a concise visual overview of the associations between entities defined in the legislation and their constraints. In this work, our research goal is to summarize and formalize general-purpose privacy principles and design a lightweight paradigm for easy deployment in heterogeneous data processing systems. As a result, these discussions can serve as a good guidance to our work but not actually solve the problem we aim to tackle.

Privacy Regulation Formalism. In [24], Hanson et al. present a data-purpose algebra that can be used to model these kinds of restrictions in various different domains. To formalise purpose restrictions in privacy policies, Tschantz et al. [25] provide a semantics using a formalism based on planning modeled using a modified version of Markov Decision Processes. Chowdhury [26] present a policy specification language based on a restricted subset of first order temporal logic (FOTL) which can capture the privacy requirements of HIPAA. Lam et al. [27] prove that for any privacy policy that conforms to patterns evident in HIPAA, there exists a finite representative hospital database that illustrates how the law applies in all possible hospitals. However, because of these works' specific focus on purpose restriction or HIPAA, the above two approaches do not generalize to other regulations like GDPR. Gerl et al. [28] introduce LPL, an extensible Layered Privacy Language that allows to express and enforce these new privacy properties such as personal privacy, user consent, data provenance, and retention management. Sen et al. introduce LEGALEASE [17], a language composed of (alternating) ALLOW and DENY clauses where each clause relaxes or constricts the enclosing clause. LEGALEASE is compositional and specifies formal semantics in attribute lattices. These characteristics are useful in general-purpose description of privacy regulations and are inherited in PRIVPOLICY. However, compared with LEGALEASE, PRIVPOLICY supports much more expressive attributes to represent abstract domains for static analysis which allows us to encode more complicated privacy regulations. Other work (e.g. Becker et al. [14]) focuses on the access control issues related to compliance with data privacy regulations, but such approaches do not restrict *how* the data is processed—a key component of recent regulations like GDPR.

Privacy Regulation Compliance Enforcement. Going beyond formalism of privacy regulations, recent research also explores techniques to enforce these formalised privacy regulations in real-world data processing systems. Chowdhury et al. [29] propose to use temporal model-checking for run-time monitoring of privacy policies. While Chowdhury demonstrates the effectiveness of this approach in online monitoring of privacy policies, it does not provide the capability of static analysis to decide if a analytic program satisfies a privacy policy and can only report privacy violation after it happens. Sen et al. [17] introduce GROK, a data inventory for Map-Reduce-like big data systems. Although working perfectly in Map-Reduce-like systems, GROK lacks adaptability to non-Map-Reduce-like data processing systems.

9   Conclusion and Future Work

In this paper, we have proposed the data capsule paradigm, a new paradigm for collecting, managing, and processing sensitive personal data. The data capsule paradigm has the potential to break down data silos and make data more useful, while at the same time reducing the prevalence of data privacy violations and making compliance with privacy regulations easier for organizations. We implemented PRIVGUARD, a reference platform for the new paradigm.

We are currently in the preliminary stages of a collaborative case study to apply the data capsule paradigm to enforce HIPAA in a medical study of menstrual data collected via mobile app. The goal of this study [30] and similar work [31,32] is to demonstrate the use of mobile apps to assess menstrual health and fertility. Data capsules will allow study participants to submit their sensitive data in the context of a policy which protects its use. As part of this effort, we are in the process of encoding the requirements of HIPAA using PRIVPOL-ICY and applying PRIVGUARD to the analysis programs written by the study's designers.

References

1. The 18 biggest data breaches of the 21st century (2019). https://www.csoonline.com/article/2130877/the-biggest-data-breaches-of-the-21st-century.html. Accessed 23 May 2019
2. Solove, D.J., Citron, D.K.: Risk and anxiety: a theory of data-breach harms. Tex. L. Rev. **96**, 737 (2017)
3. Insider threat 2018 report (2019). https://www.ca.com/content/dam/ca/us/files/ebook/insider-threat-report.pdf. Accessed 23 May 2019
4. Murdock, L.E.: The use and abuse of computerized information: striking a balance between personal privacy interests and organizational information needs. Alb. L. Rev. **44**, 589 (1979)
5. The EU general data protection regulation (GDPR) (2019). https://eugdpr.org/. Accessed 16 Apr 2019
6. California consumer privacy act (CCPA) (2019). https://www.caprivacy.org/. Accessed 16 Apr 2019
7. The family educational rights and privacy act of 1974 (FERPA) (2019). https://www.colorado.edu/registrar/students/records/ferpa. Accessed 16 Apr 2019
8. Health insurance portability and accountability act (HIPAA) (2109). https://searchhealthit.techtarget.com/definition/HIPAA. Accessed 16 Apr 2019
9. Google keeps your data forever - unlocking the future transparency of your past (2019). www.siliconvalleywatcher.com/google-keeps-your-data-forever--unlocking-the-future-transparency-of-your-past/. Accessed 30 May 2019
10. Extract, transform, load (2019). https://en.wikipedia.org/wiki/Extract,_transform,_load. Accessed 30 May 2019
11. Codd, E.F.: A relational model of data for large shared data banks. Commun. ACM **13**(6), 377–387 (1970)
12. Chodorow, K.: MongoDB: the definitive guide: powerful and scalable data storage. O'Reilly Media, Inc. (2013)
13. Shvachko, K., Kuang, H., Radia, S., Chansler, R., et al.: The hadoop distributed file system. In: MSST, vol. 10, pp. 1–10 (2010)
14. Lakshman, A., Malik, P.: Cassandra: a decentralized structured storage system. ACM SIGOPS Oper. Syst. Rev. **44**(2), 35–40 (2010)

15. Dean, J., Ghemawat, S.: Mapreduce: simplified data processing on large clusters. Commun. ACM **51**(1), 107–113 (2008)
16. Zaharia, M., Chowdhury, M., Franklin, M.J., Shenker, S., Stoica, I.: Spark: Cluster computing with working sets. HotCloud **10**(10–10), 95 (2010)
17. Sen, S., Guha, S., Datta, A., Rajamani, S.K., Tsai, J., Wing, J.M.: Bootstrapping privacy compliance in big data systems. In: 2014 IEEE Symposium on Security and Privacy, pp. 327–342. IEEE (2014)
18. Formal concept analysis (2019). https://en.wikipedia.org/wiki/Formal_concept_ analysis. Accessed 30 May 2019
19. Nielson, F., Nielson, H.R., Hankin, C.: Principles of Program Analysis. Springer, Heidelberg (2015)
20. Gruschka, N., Mavroeidis, V., Vishi, K., Jensen, M.: Privacy issues and data protection in big data: a case study analysis under GDPR. In: 2018 IEEE International Conference on Big Data (Big Data), pp. 5027–5033. IEEE (2018)
21. Renaud, K., Shepherd, L.A.: How to make privacy policies both GDPR-compliant and usable. In: 2018 International Conference on Cyber Situational Awareness, Data Analytics And Assessment (Cyber SA), pp. 1–8. IEEE (2018)
22. Politou, E., Alepis, E., Patsakis, C.: Forgetting personal data and revoking consent under the GDPR: challenges and proposed solutions. J. Cybersecur. **4**(1), tyy001 (2018)
23. Tom, J., Sing, E., Matulevičius, R.: Conceptual representation of the GDPR: model and application directions. In: Zdravkovic, J., Grabis, J., Nurcan, S., Stirna, J. (eds.) BIR 2018. LNBIP, vol. 330, pp. 18–28. Springer, Cham (2018). https://doi. org/10.1007/978-3-319-99951-7_2
24. Hanson, C., Berners-Lee, T., Kagal, L., Sussman, G.J., Weitzner, D.: Data-purpose algebra: modeling data usage policies. In: Eighth IEEE International Workshop on Policies for Distributed Systems and Networks (POLICY 2007), pp. 173–177. IEEE (2007)
25. Tschantz, M.C., Datta, A., Wing, J.M.: Formalizing and enforcing purpose restrictions in privacy policies. In: 2012 IEEE Symposium on Security and Privacy, pp. 176–190. IEEE (2012)
26. Chowdhury, O., et al.: Privacy promises that can be kept: a policy analysis method with application to the hipaa privacy rule. In: Proceedings of the 18th ACM Symposium on Access Control Models and Technologies, pp. 3–14. ACM (2013)
27. Lam, P.E., Mitchell, J.C., Scedrov, A., Sundaram, S., Wang, F.: Declarative privacy policy: finite models and attribute-based encryption. In: Proceedings of the 2nd ACM SIGHIT International Health Informatics Symposium, pp. 323–332. ACM (2012)
28. Gerl, A., Bennani, N., Kosch, H., Brunie, L.: LPL, towards a GDPR-compliant privacy language: formal definition and usage. In: Hameurlain, A., Wagner, R. (eds.) Transactions on Large-Scale Data- and Knowledge-Centered Systems XXXVII. LNCS, vol. 10940, pp. 41–80. Springer, Heidelberg (2018). https://doi.org/10.1007/ 978-3-662-57932-9_2
29. Chowdhury, O., Jia, L., Garg, D., Datta, A.: Temporal mode-checking for runtime monitoring of privacy policies. In: Biere, A., Bloem, R. (eds.) CAV 2014. LNCS, vol. 8559, pp. 131–149. Springer, Cham (2014). https://doi.org/10.1007/978-3-319- 08867-9_9
30. Symul, L., Wac, K., Hillard, P., Salathe, M.: Assessment of menstrual health status and evolution through mobile apps for fertility awareness, bioRxiv (2019). https:// www.biorxiv.org/content/early/2019/01/28/385054

31. Liu, B.: Predicting pregnancy using large-scale data from a women's health tracking mobile application. arXiv preprint arXiv:1812.02222 (2018)
32. Alvergne, A., Vlajic Wheeler, M., Högqvist Tabor, V.: Do sexually transmitted infections exacerbate negative premenstrual symptoms? Insights from digital health. In: Evolution, Medicine, and Public Health, vol. 2018, no. 1, pp. 138–150, July 2018. https://doi.org/10.1093/emph/eoy018

SCHENGENDB: A Data Protection Database Proposal

Tim Kraska, Michael Stonebraker, Michael Brodie, Sacha Servan-Schreiber[(✉)], and Daniel Weitzner

MIT CSAIL, Cambridge, USA
`3s@mit.edu`

Abstract. GDPR in Europe and similar regulations, such as the California CCPA, require new levels of privacy support for consumers. Most challenging to IT departments is the "right to be forgotten". Hence, an enterprise must ensure that ALL information about a specific consumer be deleted from enterprise storage, when requested. Since enterprises are internally heavily "siloed", sharing of information is usually accomplished by copying data between systems. This makes finding and deleting all copies of data on a particular consumer difficult.

GDPR also requires the notion of purposes, which is an access control model orthogonal to the one customarily in SQL. Herein, we sketch an implementation of purposes and show how it fits within a conventional access control framework.

We then propose two solutions to supporting GDPR in a DBMS. When a "green field" environment is present, we propose a solution which directly supports the process of ensuring GDPR compliance at enterprise-scale. Specifically, it is designed to store every fact about a consumer exactly once. Therefore, the right to be forgotten is readily supported by deleting that fact. On the other hand, when dealing with legacy systems in the enterprise, we propose a second solution which tracks all copies of personal information, so they can be deleted on request. Of course, this solution entails additional overhead in the DBMS.

Once data leaves the DBMS, it is in some application. We propose "sandboxing" applications in a novel way that will prevent them from leaking data to the outside world when inappropriate. Lastly, we discuss the challenges associated with auditing and logging of data. This paper sketches the design of the above GDPR compliant facilities, which we collectively term SCHENGENDB.

1 Introduction

The General Data Protection Regulation (GDPR) took effect on May 25, 2018, affecting all enterprises operating within the European Union (EU) and the European Economic Area (EEA) [1]. The GDPR is the leading example of a new generation of privacy laws around the world that impose a strict and more comprehensive set of requirements on all systems that "process" personal data.

V. Gadepally et al. (Eds.): DMAH 2019/Poly 2019, LNCS 11721, pp. 24–38, 2019.
https://doi.org/10.1007/978-3-030-33752-0_2

In particular, the GDPR now mandates that no personal data may be "processed" at all without an adequate "legal basis." This legal attitude with respect to personal data stands in sharp contrast to other legal systems, including that in force in the United States, in which companies can do whatever they choose with personal data unless there is a specific legal prohibition against a specific type of processing. Nevertheless, today the United States, and a number of other countries, are actively debating new privacy laws, many of which would entail similar requirements as imposed by the EU GDPR.

The requirement to keep personal data "under control" at all times imposes several important new conditions on enterprises processing personal data. We do not describe all of those here but rather concentrate on the new technology necessary to enable fundamental parts of GDPR compliance. We define two broad requirements for database implementation of GDPR rules. First, enterprises must now keep track of the legal basis under which data is allowed to be processed, and assure that applications, services, and analysis driven by enterprise data bases systems adhere to those legal restrictions. Second, enterprises also must keep data "under control" such that when an individual (aka. a "data subject" in GDPR parlance) requests that their data be "erased" or "forgotten", that such request is honored throughout the enterprise's own systems.

The GDPR mandates that a "legal basis" is required in order to permit any processing of personal data. That means that whenever a company collects, stores, analyzes, shares, publishes, or takes any other action on personal data it must point to a specific legal authority defined by the GDPR as the "legal basis" for such processing. Personal data must be kept under control by database systems so that enterprises can verify that when data is processed, that processing is permitted based on the relevant legal basis, effectively a permission (GDPR Art. 6). Contrary to popular misunderstanding of the GDPR, however, consent of the data subject is only one of several specific legal bases for processing. For clarity, we summarize the several legal bases for processing available under the GDPR. Data may be processed based on one of the following six legal conditions:

- **Consent:** An individual agrees to have their personal data processed for some specific purpose.
- **Contract:** The individual and the enterprise have entered into a contract providing the enterprise with the right to process personal data.
- **Legal obligation:** The enterprise can process data to comply with a legal obligation binding on that enterprise.
- **Vital interests:** The enterprise can process personal data to protect vital interests of the user or another person.
- **Public interest:** The enterprise can process, including disclose, personal data when it is in the public interest, generally as directed by a government authority.
- **Legitimate interest:** The enterprise can process data for purposes that are necessary to the legitimate interest of the enterprise, provided such interest is not overridden by the fundamental rights of the individual.

Every step taken to process personal data must conform to one of these legal conditions. So while there are circumstances in which personal data can be processed without consent, it must always be processed under the control of some legal authority. Consider two motivating scenarios to understand how the GDPR operates and what requirements are placed on database systems:

Scenario 1: A company collects phone numbers for user authentication purposes (two factor authentication) but data subjects agree to provide their phone number only for that purpose. The company now has a database containing phone numbers but no explicit purpose associated with them. The company's marketing department decides to use the phone numbers for product promotion purposes without the knowledge that the phone numbers were collected only for the purpose of authentication, thus violating GDPR requirements.

Scenario 2: A company is running a study and would like to obtain a list of users that opted-in while excluding those that opted-out of participation in analytics. Users of the data must have tools to respect the preferences and purposes agreed to by the data subjects. To achieve this today, the company must redesign the database schema to incorporate all possible GDPR-related data usage purposes for every user which hinders the company's ability to gain insight from their data.

The above circumstances give rise to the following three requirements of systems that store personal data inside the EU (see also [9]):

- **Controlled storage and access:** The storage system must store the legal basis on which access is allowed, including specific purpose limitations.
- **Queries:** All queries of personal data must be associated with a purpose, which defines the data allowed to be accessed.
- **System wide erasure:** A data subject has the right to request that ALL of their personal data be erased, in which case the request will be honored throughout the enterprise. We adopt a modification of this requirement which states that personal data must be deleted to the extent technically practical or "placed beyond use" if full erasure is not possible.

Besides increasing interest in GDPR from database and cloud providers [4,5,7,8], as of June 2019, we are unaware of any end-to-end system solution to manage personal data within the confines of GDPR. Hence, we present a data management system, SCHENGENDB, that can implement these restrictions efficiently. Our solution focuses on managing compliance within an enterprise, not between enterprises. Furthermore, we do not attempt to protect against malicious employees but rather protect and limit misuse through direct support for privacy requirements. Our solution has multiple parts. In Sect. 2, we describe a system that supports the definition of purposes and ensures that only personal data authorized for a given purpose is released to applications with that purpose.

Then Sects. 3 deals with supporting GDPR within the DBMS. Primarily, we show how to support the right to be forgotten. First, we present a solution appropriate for new applications being constructed. In this case, we can force a logical data base design that stores each fact exactly once. Deleting this fact will thereby perform the appropriate "right to be forgotten". The second solution is appropriate for existing DBMS schemas, which often employ data redundancy. In this case, we need to track all personal data as the DBMS updates multiple copies and constructs derived information through new tables and materialized views.

Once personal data leaves the DBMS, it resides in an application. In Sect. 4, we outline how "sandboxing", the use of virtual containers, can be used to disallow leaks. If that is too onerous, then we propose a second solution that trusts the owner of the sandbox to "do the right thing" when data leaks. Lastly, in Sect. 5 we discuss implementation issues dealing with audit and logging.

In summary, we make the following contributions:

- We propose SCHENGENDB, a database management system that helps enterprises comply with GDPR, through two different implementations of the right to be forgotten.
- SCHENGENDB's novel data purpose protection ensures that personal data can be used only for specific purposes for which the user gave explicit permission.
- SCHENGENDB's novel sandboxing helps ensure that applications do not leak personal data.
- SCHENGENDB provides efficient auditing procedures which facilitate the burden of proving enterprise-wide GDPR compliance and guaranteed data deletion.

2   Purpose-Based Access Control

One of the biggest changes brought by GDPR and related regulations is that personal data cannot be used within an enterprise for an arbitrary purpose. For example, as outlined in the introduction, a phone number might be usable only for authentication and not for direct marketing (e.g., by calling the phone number) or even indirect marketing (e.g., to infer the person's location). Thus, we propose a "purpose" based access control model. Unlike the existing database security model [2], purposes are associated with personal data in a fine-grained manner (e.g., different attributes of a record in a table can have different allowed purposes), and are "carried along" when the personal data is processed. In this section, we formalize the notion of purposes and describe our solution.

2.1   Data and Access Model

In our model, database users can define arbitrary purposes describing how they intend to use personal data. For example, a member of the marketing team can associate his team with the purpose "marketing" which will restrict their access to personal data that has the associated "marketing" purpose. Who is authorized to define purposes and how they get the consent of data subjects are administrative tasks beyond the scope of this paper. However, we assume that each data subject can opt-out or opt-in for each purpose.

It is important to note that purposes restrict system users to a logical subset of personal data in the DBMS. SQL access control has a similar function,

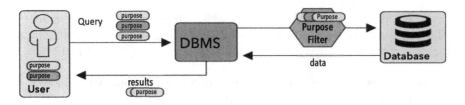

Fig. 1. Example of purpose usage of personal data in queries. The client has two associated purposes and issues a query with a third purpose. SCHENGENDB queries the database and returns the filtered results to the client.

but there are important differences between purposes and SQL access control. First, SQL deals with system users not with applications. Second, SQL protects relational views, so all rows of data are treated uniformly. Purposes may define so-called "ragged" tables. Lastly, each data subject must be able to opt-in or opt-out of each purpose. Hence, access is defined individual-by-individual. On the other hand, SQL protects logical subsets of the data (so called views). Hence, the definition facility is totally different. It is certainly possible to modify SQL access control to deal with these differences. However, in the following we present a direct implementation.

Tables and columns that contain personal data must be declared and are designated with a schema-level notation. A purpose is defined by a documented use and by the queries and applications that are used to implement that purpose. From this information, tables and columns that contain personal data can be deduced. This activates personal data checking for all accesses to that table and column.

Each cell in a personal data column can indicate if the user agreed to, or opted-out of, any of the purposes. GDPR requires that the default value be "opt-out". In principle, the query processor simply skips "opt-out" cells.

Purposes are designed, developed, documented, and maintained by an individual who is responsible for that purpose. Each query and application that accesses personal data must be associated with at least one purpose. To add, delete, or modify a purpose, the responsible individual works with trusted database administrators (DBAs) who authenticate, verify, and implement the purpose. Legal verification may be required.

For management purposes, and to reassure data subjects of authorized control, the use of purposes can be restricted to specific users or roles. Hence, processing a database access to personal data involves mutually applying the purposes of the database access, the user, and the user's role, as illustrated in Fig. 1.

This system does not replace the current SQL access control system. Instead, it is implemented in addition to the current system. Specifically, a system user must have SQL access to a datum in addition to purpose access. In the following, we focus on purpose access, as SQL access is well understood.

2.2   Execution Model

Given a query with a purpose, SCHENGENDB checks if the system user is allowed to access the specified tables and columns given the indicated purpose. Assuming the system user is allowed to proceed with the query, the execution engine returns all personal data that matches the query except for the records which do not permit the purpose specified in the query. As a result, a query may give different answers based on the purpose associated with the query. In addition to the result, the database indicates how many items were omitted due to a purpose violation. This latter feature is useful for debugging and for endowing the system with operational transparency.

2.3   Implementation and Optimization

Macro-level purposes (database, table, column purposes) involve minimal storage overhead and can be safely ignored in the present discussion. Hence, we focus on row and cell level purposes.

Our first (naive) solution stores row and cell purposes as a bit vector. Given N rows and C columns, we require N bit vectors for the rows and N * C bit vectors for the cells. We focus herein only on the cell-level overhead. Given a set of purposes T that require cell level specification, and given the assumption that a fraction α of cells have a non-default purpose then the overhead is:

$$O(\alpha * N * C * T) \qquad (1)$$

To illustrate the overhead, consider a table of 1 Billion rows with 100 columns and 50 purpose bits where 5% of the cells have cell-specific bits. The overhead is $(0.05 * 10^9 * 100 * 50)$ bits which is more than 30 GB of storage. If 10% of the cells have cell-specific bit vectors then the overhead jumps to almost 70 GB. This could represent as much as 20% of the size of the table. There are both benefits and drawbacks to the naive solution.

Pros: such a purpose storage solution would allow very efficient query processing (simply check the correct bit in the bit vector).

Cons: storage overhead is linear in the number of purposes. This may be acceptable when the number of purposes is small or when a very small percentage of cells require cell-specific purposes. In general, we need a more efficient solution.

Consider the worst case for which a set of purposes is defined for every cell in a table. This requires $O(N * C * T)$ storage. Suppose purposes are not randomly assigned to cells but follow some distribution (e.g., exponential). In this case, we can efficiently compress purposes using a variant of Huffman encoding [3]. Such an encoding can be used in conjunction with a bit vector representations to minimize storage for frequent combination of purposes found in the database while leaving infrequent combinations as-is.

A second mechanism for cell purpose encoding assumes that the number of purpose combinations follows some distribution. Hence, most cells in the table have some combination A_i of tags, for example:

$$A_1 = (marketing, analytics, support)$$

and a less frequent combination,

$$A_2 = (marketing, support)$$

and so on, for some combination A_n, which is the nth most frequent combination of purposes in the database.

Arrange these combinations in sorted order $A_1, A_2, A_3, ..., A_n$. Purpose bit vectors can then be stored with $O(logn)$ overhead by intelligently encoding them using a compression scheme. However, such encoding can introduce bottlenecks at query time because combinations must be decoded and matched against query specified purposes. Additionally, such encodings do not easily support updates to the database.

It is conceivable that the compression is efficient enough (i.e., a large enough fraction of cells in the database have the same combinations of purposes) that querying with purposes can be achieved by first scanning the purpose combinations to determine which compressed representations must be included. The remaining elements can be matched using bit vectors as in the naive solution. It is likewise reasonable to assume that changes to the database will follow a similar purpose distribution. However, in the case that a certain percentage of the database has purposes that are no longer "optimally" encoded, a re-encoding procedure may be necessary. Moreover, adding a new purpose can be done using the compressed representation and does not require re-encoding.

3   DBMS Support for GDPR

In the previous section, we explained how to ensure that personal data will be returned only for personal data with an opt-in value for the purpose associated with a query. In this section, we turn to the "right to be forgotten". To address this issue in SCHENGENDB, we need a reliable way to identify all personal data for a single user and to delete it efficiently. In this section, we propose two solutions, one for a "Green Field" application and another which deals with an existing schema. First we explore support within a single database and then we show how to support this requirement across systems.

3.1   Green Field Within a Single System

The key idea is to disallow duplicate or derived data to be stored. To do so, we propose to enforce an entity-relationship (E-R) model on the data. This data model requires data to be stored as:

Entities: these are features that have independent existence. Hence, they have a unique identifier and can only be inserted and deleted. Entities can have attributes that describe the entity. For example, an entity might be an employee with e-id as its identifier and attributes birthday, home address, etc.

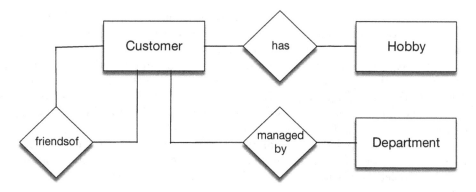

Fig. 2. Customer contains data about each customer, for example, address, birth_date and date_of_first_service. Department is an entity showing departments in the enterprise. The Hobby entity has hobby-specific data. The enterprise collects information that links customers to other entities. The three relationships indicate what department manages the customer, what hobbies they has, and who their friends are.

Relationships: entities can participate in relationships. For example, the entities employee and department may have a relationship, works-in, that indicates that an employee works in a specified department. Entities are often represented graphically as boxes with relationships indicated as arcs between the boxes. Relationships are usually further specified as 1-N or M-N to indicate allowed participation, but that feature is not needed in our discussion. Hence, we require a DBA to construct an E-R model for the data using standard E-R modelling techniques, which are discussed in any undergraduate text on database concepts.

Standard E-R practice requires that each entity have a primary key, which uniquely identifies the entity. In addition, we require every entity to have an additional "surrogate key". For example, although Customer name may be a unique identifier, we require that the Customer entity also have a surrogate key, which we require to be a random set of bits. Hence, the relational schema for the data of Fig. 2 is shown in Listing 1.

```
1  Customer (cname, c-surrogate-key, other-fields)
2  Department (dname, d-surrogate key, other-fields)
3  Hobby (hname, h-surrogate-key, other-fields)
4
5  friendsof (c1-surrogate-key, c2-surrogate-key, other-fields)
6  managedby (c-surrogate-key, d-surrogate-key, other-fields)
7  has (h-surrogate-key, c-surrogate-key, other-fields)
```

Listing 1. The Relational Schema for Fig. 2

There is a table for each entity type and one for each relationship that contains the surrogate keys for the pairs of records in that relationship. Although 1-N relationships can be optimized as additional fields in one of the entity tables, we do not pursue this improvement herein.

Hence, the information base for an enterprise is an E-R diagram, which is a graph of entities interconnected by relationship edges, together with a relational implementation of this structure, with surrogate keys defining the relationships.

There are a few constraints we impose on accessing and updating this structure. Since all the relationship data uses surrogate keys, SCHENGENDB can lazily delete "dead" relationship data as circumstances permit, through a background process the finds "dead" surrogates. To support lazy deletion, the following restrictions must be put in place:

Materialized views must be prohibited. Otherwise, there are data copies elsewhere in the database, which would have to be discovered and an appropriate additional delete performed. To avoid this error-prone and costly operation, we disallow materialized views.

Second, surrogate keys must be hidden from users. Hence, every query to the database must be expressed in E-R form and must begin by referencing an entity. Therefore, queries which directly access a relationship such as:

```
SELECT . . . FROM . . . WHERE surrogate_key = value
```

must be disallowed. This restriction is required to ensure that surrogate keys are not seen by a user. Were that true, then users could query (and store in user code) surrogate keys. In this case, lazy deletion of surrogate keys would leak information.

With these restrictions, the implementation of deletes is straightforward. To delete an entity, the appropriate record in the appropriate entity table is found and removed. This makes all surrogate keys "dangling" and unusable for generating query results. Over time, a background process can find and delete "dead" relationship data. Of course, one could also implement an "eager delete" system which would not need surrogate keys, but would require all references to an entity to be found and removed, which would increase the response time for deletes.

3.2   Existing Schema Within a Single System

While the "Green Field" solution has compelling advantages, in most cases it requires a complete redesign of the schema and the application, which can be a huge cost factor. As such, it is appropriate for new applications, but we need another solution for existing schemas.

To handle this case, we propose fine-grained tracking of changes. Every insert into SCHENGENDB has to be done on behalf of a specific data subject, i.e., owner of the personal data (as before). Thus, every inserted record belongs to one (or conceivably more) person. Furthermore, every derived record (think materialized view) automatically inherits the owners of the records from which it was derived. If the enterprise is concerned about the aggregation of information, then many owners will have to be recorded. This information can be stored using standard lineage techniques [3,6,11]. Although this may result in onerous overhead, there is no other way to track all the personal data as it is spread around the database.

This allows SCHENGENDB to track all records related to a specific data subject and delete them when asked. We now turn to the copying of personal data information between systems.

3.3   Across Systems in the Enterprise

In a large enterprise there may be hundreds to thousands of separate databases. When a system user needs information from multiple databases, a prevalent practice is to copy needed information from the primary copy to a secondary one. Otherwise, a federated query must be performed, which is much slower than the same query to a single database.

To achieve this functionally in a Green Field schema, an application will request some entities from one database and then copy them into a second database. To support this operation in a GDPR-compliant way, we require that entity identifiers be global to the enterprise. For example, there must be single global notions of Customer, Hobby, and Department. If there is not a single notion of Customer, then GDPR will be impossible to implement because it is impossible to tell if, for example, Mike Stonebraker, M.R. Stonebraker, and Michael Stonebraker are 1, 2, or 3 entities. Hence, the enterprise must engage in a data integration project for GDPR compliant entities to ensure global uniqueness of these entities.

All the purposes attached to an entity record must be carried over from the first system to the second system. This requires purposes to be unique across the enterprise. In addition, we need to record in a global entity catalog that an entity has been copied into system 2 from system 1. We call this catalog the Data Management Server (DMS), which will also be used in the next section. Notice that DMS records information that happens outside the DBMS. In this case, when a GDPR compliant entity is deleted from either system, a trigger must be run to delete all copies of the entity.

In an existing schema, there may be no E-R schema associated with the data. In that case, a data copy to a second system must preserve the owners of records from the first system. Obviously, owners (i.e., data subjects) must be global to the enterprise. Hence, the DMS must record and manage all data subjects. With this caveat, the same trigger processing will work for existing schemas.

4   Application Support for Purposes

In decision support environments it is common practice (and often essential) to copy data from the database in order to analyze it using separate tools such as Python, R, or Tableau. Moreover, such analysis often involves a pipeline of operations. In this case, personal data is outside the confines of the DBMS. Some might argue that application users are trustworthy, and therefore we do not need to worry about applications leaking. However, it seems clear that stringing together application systems can yield inadvertent leakage. This section describes a mechanism of protecting such pipelines from inadvertently leaking.

We propose a "sandboxing" approach, which monitors copies of personal data at a higher level which will prevent misuse. A sandbox is a virtual machine which allows unrestricted access and movement of data inside the sandbox, but controls interaction with other VMs. We propose a sandbox for every purpose. That sandbox contains all the applications that use that purpose in a query. If there are N purposes, then there are N VMs. The DBMS allows access only from this collection of VMs, so DBMS requests can come only from one of these sandboxes. Hence, pipelines of programs with the same purpose can freely exchange data. Otherwise, sandboxes cannot be allowed to communicate with each other, since if data is moved from a sandbox with a less restrictive purpose to one that is more restrictive, then a leak has occurred.

These restrictions can be enforced easily at the networking level without any changes to the applications. For example, in modern virtualized environments, it is possible to configure the environment so that certain VMs get special IP-ranges and that only those ip-ranges are allowed to access the database system, or one can restrict the privilege of opening a connection to the outside to a certain set of VMs. Furthermore, thanks to dockers and similar light-weight virtualization mechanisms, even hosting a large number of virtual machines no longer pose a technical challenge.

However, if an application has queries with multiple purposes, then it is placed in multiple sandboxes, wherein each sandbox can read a portion of the overall data. It is then likely that these VMs will have to communicate to get the overall task accomplished. To support such applications, we now propose a "loosey goosey" version. In this world, we point out potential violations instead of completely forbidding interaction between sandboxes. Since every communication between sandboxes is a potential violation, when a communication occurs we alert the owner of the sandbox, who is the owner of the purpose associated with the sandbox. Their VM is assumed to be non-compliant. It is up to them to figure out how to bring the VM into compliance. This will likely mean deleting offending personal data. To ensure compliance, we use a timeout mechanism for the communication operation. At the end of the timeout the VM owner has either brought the VM into compliance or we terminate the VM. Of course, this requires us to trust the owner of the purpose to "do the right thing". The strategy of reply on *ex ante* compliance checking, as opposed to *a priori* compliance guarantees is recognized as a necessary strategy involving privacy rules for complex information systems, as it is often simply impossible to detect all violations with certainty in advance of processing [10]. As noted in Sect. 5, we can rely on the auditing system to discover violations after the fact, and to hold employees accountable.

We turn now to the last matter dealing with applications. When a delete of personal data is requested by a data subject, the DBMS will perform the actions specified in the previous section. However, personal data may be present at the application level. In this case, we assume that the DMS logs, at the application level, every query to the DBMS for every sandbox. Every permitted communication between sandboxes is similarly logged. When a person requests to be forgotten, we can determine which sandboxes may have the relevant personal data (or data derived from that personal data) by reading the log. We alert the owner of the sandbox to this potential violation who can then take action, as described above.

So far, the tracking and the deactivation are pessimistic and might cause false positives, i.e., unjustified warnings to sandbox owners and terminations of VMs that are, in fact, compliant. For example, a sandbox might read data from SCHENGENDB but then does not store the data within the sandbox or a sandbox does an aggregate query such as SELECT COUNT(*) FROM Customer which requires a scan of all data but does not extract any user-specific data. Both cases will cause warnings for non-existing violations after a request from a person to delete their personal data.

Fortunately, a wide variety of optimizations are possible to reduce the number of false positives. For example, privacy-preserving analysis could be used to determine that data derived from SELECT COUNT(*) FROM Customer do not contain GDPR violations. Furthermore, we could provide annotations to indicate that a sandbox is stateless, transient, or has a specific time-to-live. Similarly, a data warehouse dashboard might be in violation, but if the data warehouse is refreshed every day, the violation will resolve itself after a time-to-live.

We could provide additional annotations to provide sandbox owners more fine-grained control. For example, if a sandbox is used to build a machine-learning model and the model is then deployed in a service, according to the previous section the entire model might be in violation. However, if the developer considers the model to be GDPR compliant, they could annotate that the model does not contain GDPR violations and mark the data transfer between the sandboxes as safe.

5 The Audit Process

The audit process consists of two components, one within SCHENGENDB and one at the application level.

5.1 Audit Within SCHENGENDB

The fundamental auditing technology in SCHENGENDB is the DBMS log. Log processing is well understood by the DBMS community and is implemented in all commercial DBMSs. Specifically, all operations which alter the database are logged, typically on a record-by-record basis, with the before image of the record (so the change can be backed out if the application running the transaction fails to commit) and the after image (to restore the change if there is a crash or other unforeseen event). To support GDPR compliance, we must also log all reads, together with the query invoked and its purposes. A similar statement applies to updates. Obviously, this will slow down log processing; however, in current systems the log is highly optimized and does not consume excessive resources. Hence, an audit merely entails inspecting the log to ensure that the purposes allowed by the enterprise are enforced. If SCHENGENDB is operating correctly, there should be no violations. In the unlikely event of a violation, the offending user and request can be quickly discovered and dealt with accordingly.

As stated in the introduction, we assume that enterprise employees are not malicious. Hence, users with a legitimate access to data are assumed not to share it outside the SCHENGENDB system, for example by copying a result into an e-mail message and sending it to an unauthorized user. Dealing with such inadvertent or purposeful leaks is outside the scope of this paper. A similar comment applies to the DBA of a SCHENGENDB database, which has unfettered access to everything.

However, the presence of the log raises the following question. If person X asserts their right to erasure, then a sequence of updates will occur in SCHENGENDB. Such updates are logged and contain the before images of deleted records.

Hence, the information about X has been deleted from the database, but not from the log. In the case of the GDPR, we understand that it is still an open question whether respect for the right to erasure requires deleting personal data from DBMS logs along with the accessible instance of the database. For reasons explained below, from a technical perspective, there are reasons to exclude the log from the scope of the right to erasure. In theory, log files can be purged after a sufficient delay, thereby deleting records for X. However, we would caution against this strategy. To deal with application errors, for example a buggy app inadvertently gives a raise to Y, the database is typically "rewound" to a time before the errant app, and then the log is replayed forward. Hence, the log must be retained for a period of time. In addition, legal requirements often require the log to be retained much longer. Removing log files is therefore not recommended. Also, logs are write-once and are never updated. Hence, updating the log to remove X's log records is not recommended. This would allow an errant log updater to wreck real havoc.

The net-net is to trust DBAs (who are the only people with access to the log) to do their job and not be malicious. After all, they can easily leak tax returns and/or financial records of important individuals, which will be far more damaging than the issues we are discussing in this section.

5.2   Application Audit

In contrast to the audit of SCHENGENDB itself, the audit process between sandboxes is more involved and less automatic. The data rights sandboxing approach relies on the trustworthiness of its sandbox owners. For example, the system user needs to be trusted if they declares that a GDPR violation was manually resolved. Similar, they needs to be trusted to provide the correct annotations or correct implementations of delete functions. Obviously, this can lead to violations if users make (un-)intentional mistakes.

While we do not believe it is possible to entirely avoid such violations, the SCHENGENDB framework can provide tools to make it easier to detect potential violations and allow an internal audit to detect potential problems, before an external audit might discover any problems. For example, the DMS could simulate a worst-case scenario for which it ignores all user-provided annotations and mistrusts all manually-resolved GDPR violations. This simulation could now be used to create a list of sandboxes and tables within SCHENGENDB that are potentially in violation of GDPR or in which owners made mistakes. It is also reasonable to assume, that the same simulation could be used to rank the risk of violation or mistakes. An internal auditor could then manually check some of the reported sandboxes.

Furthermore, it might be possible (with limitations of course) to scan the sandboxes for potential GDPR violations based on finger prints. For example, let's assume that we associate a random 256 bit key to every GDPR-related record. If the bit sequence is found for a deleted GDPR record within a sandbox it is a strong indication that the sandbox is in violation.

Finally, any communication with the outside (e.g., between an application running in a sandbox and the web) is impossible to audit. While it might be possible to log all such communication, it will be very hard to provide a full audit as these logs are not trivial to analyze, as they are usually much less structured than DBMS logs.

6   Conclusion

In this paper, we have presented SCHENGENDB, which provides the infrastructure to support GDPR and other possible future privacy regulations. It does so with modest overhead for purpose processing and expanded log processing. In addition, it suggests doing "clean" database design, which will benefit an organization in multiple downstream ways (easier application maintenance, easier security control, etc.). When this is not possible, then additional lineage information must be preserved. At the application level, we suggest "sandboxing" such modules that access personal data to ensure the security of this data.

References

1. Regulation (EU) 2016/679 of the European Parliament and of the council of 27 April 2016 on the protection of natural persons with regard to the processing of personal data and on the free movement of such data, and repealing directive 95/46/EC (General Data Protection Regulation). https://eur-lex.europa.eu/eli/reg/2016/679/oj. Accessed 25 May 2010
2. Chandramouli, R., Sandhu, R.: Role-based access control features in commercial database management systems. In: Proceedings of the 21st National Information Systems Security Conference (NISSC 1998) (1998)
3. Glavic, B., Alonso, G.: Perm: processing provenance and data on the same data model through query rewriting. In: 2009 IEEE 25th International Conference on Data Engineering, pp. 174–185, March 2009
4. Google: Google cloud and the GDPR, Technical report. https://cloud.google.com/security/gdpr/
5. Oracle: 5 perspectives on GDPR. https://www.oracle.com/applications/gdpr/

6. Psallidas, F., Wu, E.: Smoke: fine-grained lineage at interactive speed. PVLDB **11**(6), 719–732 (2018)

7. Rayani, A.: Safeguard individual privacy rights under GDPR with the Microsoft intelligent cloud. https://www.microsoft.com/en-us/microsoft-365/blog/2018/05/25/safeguard-individual-privacy-rights-under-gdpr-with-the-microsoft-intelligent-cloud/

8. Shah, A., Banakar, V., Shastri, S., Wasserman, M., Chidambaram, V.: Analyzing the impact of GDPR on storage systems. CoRR, abs/1903.04880 (2019)

9. Shastri, S., Wasserman, M., Chidambaram, V.: The seven sins of personal-data processing systems under GDPR. In: 11th USENIX Workshop on Hot Topics in Cloud Computing (HotCloud 2019), Renton, WA. USENIX Association (2019)

10. Weitzner, D.J., Abelson, H., Berners-Lee, T., Feigenbaum, J., Hendler, J., Sussman, G.J.: Information accountability. Commun. ACM **51**(6), 82 (2008)

11. Widom, J.: Trio: a system for integrated management of data, accuracy, and lineage, pp. 262–276, January 2005

Position: GDPR Compliance by Construction

Malte Schwarzkopf[1(✉)], Eddie Kohler[2], M. Frans Kaashoek[1], and Robert Morris[1]

[1] MIT CSAIL, Cambridge, USA
malte@csail.mit.edu
[2] Harvard University, Cambridge, USA

Abstract. New laws such as the European Union's General Data Protection Regulation (GDPR) grant users unprecedented control over personal data stored and processed by businesses. Compliance can require expensive manual labor or retrofitting of existing systems, *e.g.*, to handle data retrieval and removal requests. We argue for treating these new requirements as an opportunity for new system designs. These designs should make data ownership a first-class concern and achieve compliance with privacy legislation by construction. A *compliant-by-construction* system could build a shared database, with similar performance as current systems, from personal databases that let users contribute, audit, retrieve, and remove their personal data through easy-to-understand APIs. Realizing compliant-by-construction systems requires new cross-cutting abstractions that make data dependencies explicit and that augment classic data processing pipelines with ownership information.

We suggest what such abstractions might look like, and highlight existing technologies that we believe make compliant-by-construction systems feasible today. We believe that progress towards such systems is at hand, and highlight challenges for researchers to address to make them a reality.

1 Introduction

Many websites store and process customers' personal data in server-side systems. Companies operating these websites must comply with data protection laws and regulations, such as the EU's General Data Protection Regulation (GDPR) [9] and the California Consumer Privacy Act of 2018 [1], that grant individuals significant control of and powers regarding their own data. For example, the GDPR makes it mandatory for enterprises to promptly provide users with electronic copies of their personal data ("right of access"), and for enterprises to completely remove the user's personal data from its databases on request ("right of erasure"). Non-compliance with the GDPR can result in severe fines of up to 4% of annual turnover, and the EU has recently imposed fines of hundreds of millions of dollars on Mariott [28] and British Airways [27] for negligent handling

© Springer Nature Switzerland AG 2019
V. Gadepally et al. (Eds.): DMAH 2019/Poly 2019, LNCS 11721, pp. 39–53, 2019.
https://doi.org/10.1007/978-3-030-33752-0_3

of customer data. At one estimate, the cost of GDPR compliance is expected to exceed \$7.8bn for U.S. businesses alone [25].

In this paper, we survey the challenges that GDPR compliance creates for data storage and processing systems, and argue that the database and systems research communities ought to treat these challenges as an opportunity for new system designs. These new designs should broadly treat end-users' control over their personal information as a first-class design concern. Our vision is to align system designs closely with the reality of data ownership and legislative requirements such as those imposed by the GDPR. Concretely, systems should achieve compliance with GDPR-like legislation *by construction*, with significantly more help from databases than current systems can offer.

The GDPR differs from prior privacy legislation primarily in its comprehensiveness. The GDPR has an expansive interpretation of "personal data" that covers any information related to an identifiable natural person, the *data subject*. The legislation establishes data subjects' rights over the information that *data controllers* (*e.g.*, web services) collect and which *data processors* (*e.g.*, cloud providers) store and process.

This has wide-ranging implications, including for the relational backend databases that support web applications. To comply with the spirit of individual control over data and to guarantee the data subjects' rights, such databases should become *dynamic, temporally-changing federations of end-users' contributed data*, rather than one-way data ingestors and long-term storage repositories that indiscriminately mix different users' data.

To realize this ideal, a database must:

1. logically separate users' data, so that the association of ingested, unrefined "base" records with a data subject remains unambiguous;
2. model the fine-grained dependencies between derived records and the underlying base records; and
3. by appropriately adapting derived records, handle the removal of one user's data without breaking high-level application semantics.

More ambitious goals may include having the database attest the correctness of its ownership tracking and data removal procedures, or to synthesize such procedures from a high-level privacy policy.

Today's websites and applications rely on much more than databases, however: blob stores may store artifacts like photos, machine learning models may train on users' derived data, and long-term analytics pipelines may update aggregate statistics on dashboards. Consequently, implementing our vision in any single system is likely insufficient. Instead, *cross-cutting* abstractions that generalize across systems are needed.

We believe that one promising approach is to conceptualize web service backends—databases, blob stores, analytics pipelines, machine learning (ML) models, and other systems—as a large *dataflow computation*. In this model, a user "subscribes" and contributes her data into an exclusively-owned shard of the backend. This shard stores all data owned by this user. As data arrives into the shard, it streams into other systems for processing and storage, but remains associated with the contributing user. The user may at any point choose to withdraw her shard (and thus, her data) from the system. For example, a newly-uploaded picture will initially be associated with the uploader's shard (and logically, or perhaps even physically, stored with it). Subsequently, it may percolate into a blob store (for storing the binary image data), a database (for tracking the picture's metadata), a request log, and a notification service that pushes updates to the uploader's friends. Beyond the original, encrypted user shard, the picture is associated only with a pseudonymous identifier, a model that is GDPR-compliant by construction. If the uploading user decides to retrieve her data, the service merely needs to return her shard and all information it contains; if she demands erasure of her data, the service deletes the shard and streams revocation messages that remove derived data.

The dataflow architecture we sketched here crucially requires systems to track data origin, e.g., via explicit labels or well-defined relationships. In addition, all systems must support both data contribution and data revocation. We believe that efficient mechanisms for these purposes are within reach, and that developing mechanisms and systems that achieve compliance by construction constitutes a fruitful research direction for databases and privacy-aware and distributed datacenter systems.

2 Vision

We envision a compliant-by-construction web service backend that allows users to seamlessly introduce, retrieve, and remove their personal data without manual labor on the application developer's part. In the following, we focus how this vision addresses data subjects' rights to access, objection, erasure, and data portability under the GDPR. Existing techniques discussed in Sect. 4 are sufficient to provide data protection and security, and should compose with our proposal.

For concreteness, we center our discussion around relational databases, which are central to many web service backends. We first sketch the system design, and then explain how it facilitates key GDPR rights. Section 3 will discuss how to extend our design to include other systems, such as blob stores and model serving infrastructure.

2.1 System Design

Our key idea is for each user to have her own, structured shard of the storage backend (Fig. 1). This **user shard** stores all information about this user, such as profile information, posts, uploaded pictures, records of votes or "likes", or other application-specific information. Storing data in a user shard represents an association of control, or, for many data items, ownership. Therefore, a user shard never contains information related to other users, or derived information that combines multiple users' data. We expect that the data subject owning the user

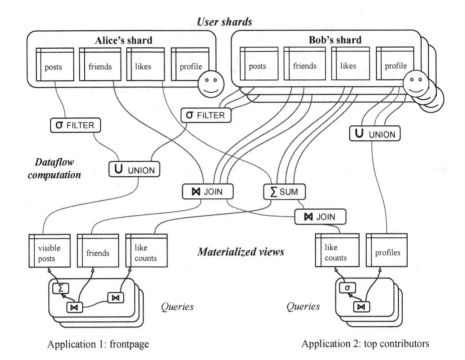

Fig. 1. Example of our architecture for a web service with two applications. Applications write new data to user shards *(top)*. The database processes changes through a dataflow *(middle, blue)* to update tables in the materialized views, which applications *(bottom)* query (Color figure online).

shard is often the primary contributor to it, although other entities—including data controllers—may also add data to the shard (consider, *e.g.*, doctors adding to a medical record).

To combine users' data, as most applications require, the backend builds **materialized views** over the user shards. These materialized views are what applications query, and different applications may define different views that suit their needs. For example, a microservice application for the personalized front page of a social application may define a view for the social graph, views that hold users' most recent and most-liked posts, and a view for posts with associated images.

We envision a highly dynamic user shard set. Users will continuously update their shards as they interact with the web service; new users will add shards, while other users remove their shards or withdraw parts of their data. Moreover, we would like a system based on dynamic user shards to enjoy the same performance as today's applications do with an optimized schema. Such optimized schemas often combine multiple users' data in tables that make sense for application semantics, such as a table containing all posts. This requires a system with support for a large number of materialized views (tens or hundreds of thousands with many users), with efficient dynamic view creation and destruction, and with excellent read and incremental update performance.

We believe that a key enabling technology for making this design efficient already exists. The **partially-stateful dataflow** model supports high-performance, dynamic, partially materialized, and incrementally-updated views over input data [11]. Using this model, we can build a streaming dataflow computation over the user shards, linking each user shard to the materialized views that changes to the shard will affect. Every write to a user shard then becomes a streamed update that flows through this dataflow to update the materialized views; the addition of new user shards becomes a set of batched updates introducing a large collection of new records; and the removal of a user shard becomes a set of batched updates that revoke previously-sent updates. The backend becomes a long-running, streaming dataflow computation with its ground-truth state federated over the user shards. The partially-stateful nature of the dataflow allows the system to proactively update some materialized views (or parts thereof), while reactively computing information in others by querying "backwards" through the dataflow.

Partially-stateful dataflow is a convenient abstraction for materialized views over federated user data for several reasons:

1. the dataflow implicitly represents dependencies between records, such as a post and the likes associated with it via a foreign key;
2. dataflow models (*e.g.*, differential dataflow [17]) allow processing additions, updates, and removals of user shards as incremental computations;
3. dataflow computations can be sharded, parallelized, and scaled with relative ease, making the architecture suitable for scaling to large web services; and
4. partially-stateful dataflow can selectively materialize only parts of downstream views, which keeps the space footprint manageable and allows applications to implement their own caching policies, such as keeping data only for active users, or only for the most popular entities.

The challenges in realizing our design lie in achieving high performance while still providing intuitive consistency semantics for complex applications. Specifically, the user shard structure will yield dataflows over thousands or millions of individual user shards. These dataflows will have extremely "wide" dependencies (*i.e.*, many incoming edges) at points where the computation combines data across users. Query evaluation of partially-stateful dataflow is likely to be slow for such dependencies, since an upwards query through the dataflow must contact many shards. But eager, forward update processing has no such limitation. Semantics of the dataflow execution also matter: in a distributed, streaming dataflow with many servers processing updates in parallel, updates derived from a particular change to a user shard may reach some materialized views before others. An application that writes to a user shard may expect to see its write reflected in subsequent reads, as it would when interacting with a classic database. But providing even this read-your-writes consistency over a large-scale dataflow will result in expensive and unscalable coordination if done naively. Finally, if the dataflow combined data from many user shards, several users may share ownership of derived records in the materialized views. The withdrawal of a user shard may affect these derived results, and the semantics of handling revocation of records that impacted such co-owned derived results need to be clear.

We believe that if it works, our dataflow design will yield a framework for building complex applications while granting users unprecedented control over their data.

2.2   Right to Access

Supplying a user with a copy of all her data stored and processed in the system, as required by the GDPR's "right to access" for data subjects (Article 15), is straightforward in a compliant-by-construction design like ours. To serve a data subject's access request, the system simply sends the data subject a copy of her user shard. This simplicity contrasts with post-hoc approaches that extract data using complex, manually-crafted queries or custom crawlers that identify data related to a subject for extraction and manual verification [8]. Achieving this simple compliance-by-construction with user shards imposes only two requirements: first, that the schema of the user shard is free of proprietary information—such as, *e.g.*, the data controller's or processor's backend architecture—and second, that the data subject is permitted see all data in her user shard. We therefore believe that compliance-by-construction systems should assume that a user shard and its structure are visible to the data subject in their entirety.

In addition to access to the raw data, the GDPR right of access also requires that the user be provided with information regarding "the purposes of processing" and "the existence of automated decision-making [. . . and] the logic involved" [9, Art. 15]. Compliance with these requirements is trickier to ensure by construction, since processing purpose and decision making happen—at least partly—in the application code. It might be possible, however, to analyze the dataflow below user shards and generate a description of all materialized views and applications that a given user's data can reach and thereby might affect. Such an analysis would provide an automated means of extracting the information required, and might also facilitate compliance with the GDPR's right to objection, which allows data subjects to reject certain types of processing (see Sect. 2.5).

2.3   Right to Erasure

The GDPR's Article 17 requires that users must be able to request erasure of their data "without undue delay". In a compliant-by-construction design, this involves removing a user shard from the system. Withdrawing a user shard effectively erases all data contained in it, and then remove or transform dependent downstream information in the dataflow and materialized views.

In principle, removing dependent downstream data is easy as long as the dataflow's operators understand revocations as well as insertions. For example, revoking a vote record for a post from a counting operator involves reducing the count by one, processing a revocation through a join produces revocations for all joining keys, etc. By sending a revocation update for all information contained in the withdrawn shard, the system ensures that all derived downstream information is removed. And since all materialized views queried by applications depend on the dataflow, which itself is a fault-tolerant, distributed computation, we can be assured that all derived information will indeed (eventually) be removed.

All common relational operators have complements compatible with this model, but more complex application semantics may require deeper system support for data removal. For example, consider Alice removing her account from a news aggregator website such as HackerNews or Lobste.rs[1]: removing the user shard in question will remove Alice's posts and votes. More insidiously, the revocation also covers information like invitations to the site that Alice issued, moderation decisions she made (if she's a moderator), and personal messages she sent to other users. Some of this information may need to persist—perhaps in anonymized form—even though Alice originally contributed it!

We believe that dataflow will work even in the presence of these complex application semantics, provided the application developer can express a policy for how each dataflow operator or materialized view handles record revocation. Instead of simply inverting the effect of the original record, the operators may e.g., re-attribute, anonymize, or otherwise transform the derived information.[2] However, the invariants of partially-stateful dataflow require that any materialized result must also be obtainable by executing a query over the base data. The dataflow system may meet this requirement by creating records that support the transformed derived data, and storing these records in a special shard for deleted users.

2.4 Right to Data Portability

Compliance with the right to data portability (GDPR Article 20) follows from the combination of the rights to access and erasure. To move data her data from one data controller to another, a user can simply retrieve her user shard from the current controller, withdraw it, and then introduce the retrieved shard to the new controller. All derived information at both controllers will update appropriately, assuming that there is a common data description standard for user shard schemas, or that the controllers know how to transform user shards to and from their respective schemas. This is admittedly a big assumption, but we believe that standardized formats or conversion tools will become available once user data is widely available in the "structured, commonly used and machine-readable format" [9, Art. 20] that the GDPR requires.

---

[1] https://lobste.rs.

[2] However, general-purpose "undoing" of computation that extends beyond relational operators can be hard [5,6]. Imagine, for example, a dataflow operator that trains an ML model on Alice's data: it is unclear how to "invert" the training and revoke Alice's information from the trained model. Section 3 describes ideas for how we might handle this situation.

2.5 Right to Objection

The GDPR also grants users the right to object "any time to processing of personal data concerning him or her" [9, Art. 21] for specific purposes (such as marketing), with some exceptions. With our design, exercising this right involves preventing the flow of data from a user shard into subgraphs of the dataflow that apply specific kinds of processing or which lead to materialized views for specific applications.

We believe that adding appropriate "guard" operators to the dataflow can make it feasible to enforce this right. These operators would check whether a user has objected to the use of her data for *e.g.*, marketing, and prevent any data from an objecting user's shard from affecting views used in marketing workflows. We envision that achieving compliance this way requires applications to augment their materialized view specifications with a declarative specification of each view's purpose, or a reason for overriding the right to objection and processing data without consent (as per GDPR Article 6). We believe that such a declarative specification is far simpler, easier to audit, and more likely to be enforced correctly than adding explicit checks for user objection in application code.

3   Challenges and Opportunities

Realizing our vision raises interesting research questions and its success requires overcoming several challenges.

Classes of Personal Data. The data associated with a data subject can be contributed directly by that subject into her user shard, but may also originate with other entities. For example, data controllers sometimes create data *about* a user: a government agency may create a birth certificate or tax information, a hospital may create and add to a medical record, or a network operators may collect metadata statistics about the user's network use. The GDPR grants that user the rights of a data subject for this content, requiring the system to store such content in the relevant user shard. This will require intuitive interfaces that allow applications to address the correct user shard on each database write, ideally without requiring intrusive application changes.

Even if the data subject contributed content directly, it may be subject to different policies. For example, a user may both browse and contribute articles to a news site. Browsing data is personal, unshared, and typically subject to strong GDPR protections; meanwhile, a contributed article may be subject to a contract giving the site permission to host the article indefinitely. Furthermore, in some cases, such as shared data, a user's withdrawal from a site might require application-specific anonymization rather than outright data removal. The presence of multiple classes of data in the same user shard could complicate some compliance mechanisms; however, user shards are inherently flexible, allowing such designs as *multiple* shards per user, one per data class.

Shared Data. Not all data is clearly owned by a single user. Should a private message on Facebook be associated with one user or both? If my friend deletes her copy of the message from Facebook's database, is my side of our conversation removed entirely, or should a possibly-anonymized ghost message persist in my user shard?

Access Control. Even though a user shard contains data associated with a particular data subject, this association may not imply unlimited control. For example, although you may be the data subject of tax records indicating what you owe, you certainly cannot change or remove them! This suggests that controls over the management of data in a user shard need to exist: some information will be immutable to the data subject, but mutable by data controllers; other information may need to persist even when the user removes her shard from the system. To realize the right to portability by retrieving a user shard (as per Sect. 2.4), we may need a form of trusted transfer between data controllers, or an assurance mechanism for immutable data if the data subject is part of the transfer. Perhaps the controllers could exchange hashes or signatures of the immutable content, and use these to validate the ported user shard after import.

Schemas. User shards will have a well-defined schema, but this schema may differ significantly from the schemas desired by applications, which often perform queries across groups of user data. The dataflow transformations that combine user shards into views convenient for application access may be complicated; their performance may benefit from insights from literature on partitioned in-memory databases [26].

Changing the user shard schema presents challenges and opportunities, as there will be as many user shards as there are users, or more. On the one hand, user shards represent natural boundaries for gradual schema change deployment; but on the other hand, completing a schema change may require migrating millions of logically- and physically-distinct databases.

Consistency. Current partially-stateful dataflow implementations provide only eventual consistency. This may suffice for some applications, or for many parts of some applications, but strong consistency is important for some parts of all applications. We see this as an opportunity to develop high-performance partially-stateful dataflow implementations that support stronger consistency, *e.g.*, through pervasive multiversioning.

Cross-system Abstractions. Our exposition in Sect. 2 focused on an RDBMS, but web services rely on many backend systems for storage and data processing. If user shards are the unified ground truth storage of all contributed data, the dataflow over them must feed not merely tabular materialized views, but also diverse endpoints like blob stores, MapReduce jobs, ML training and inference, and others. This creates an opportunity to define cross-cutting abstractions for dataflow between backend systems that augment current datacenter system

APIs. It also raises challenges: *e.g.*, how do we revoke training data from an already-trained ML model?

We envisage partially-stateful dataflows that feed data from user shards into consumer systems subject to policies over the interfaces. For example, a policy governing MapReduce jobs may require recording which user shards contributed to the job result, and have withdrawal of any such shard trigger re-execution. Systems might also specify a threshold on shard withdrawals below which the derived effects of data revocation are minimal or provably untraceable (*i.e.*, a notion of differential privacy is guaranteed). This might help, *e.g.*, with ML models trained on a data subject's information: if it is impossible to tell whether an inference came from a model trained with this data or from one trained without it, it is safe to avoid retraining when the subject withdraws her data.

Trust Model. In an ideal world, an end-user would never need to trust a data controller or data processor. A strong threat model provides hard guarantees, but often yields systems heavily rely on cryptography and have restrict functionality. Alternatively, we might presume that companies follow the law and faithfully implement laws like the GDPR, and that out-of-band enforcement mechanisms (such as fines) take care of exceptions.

In technical terms, this model shifts the focus from making it impossible to violate privacy laws to easing compliance with them. This can result in low-overhead systems that maintain the functionality users demand, but offers no absolute guarantees.

Specifying Privacy Policies. The GDPR codifies general responsibilities of a data processor, but leaves it to the data processor to provide specifics in a *privacy policy*. Privacy policy languages designed for computers rather than human lawyers could be a fruitful research direction to ease automated policy enforcement. For example, our proposed system would benefit from machine-parseable privacy policies that specify what dataflows to restrict, how to handle data erasure on shard withdrawal, and what views specific applications are permitted to define.

4   Related Work

The desire to give users control over their personal data has been the motivation for considerable existing research. This research addresses a wide variety of use cases, adversary models, and presupposes different standards and ideals for user data protection. The GDPR and similar comprehensive privacy legislation, by contrast, for the first time defined concrete standards that real-world companies must comply with.

Researchers have observed that retrofitting compliance with such wide-ranging regulation onto existing systems and processes is challenging: business models rely on combining data across services, modern machine learning (ML) algorithms violate rights to explanation of automated decisions, and pervasive caching and replication complicate data removal [24]. Minimally-invasive changes that make existing system compliant can substantially degrade their performance [23]. We believe that this inability to retrofit compliance motivates new system designs and new abstractions for inevitable interaction between systems.

4.1 Malicious or Negligent Data Controllers and Data Processors

Some prior work seeks to protect users against a malicious data processor, using sandboxes [12], by relying on decentralized storage with churn to effect self-destruction of data unless refreshed [10], or by using cryptographic constructs for oblivious computation [29,31] or computation over encrypted data [21,22]. These systems have seen limited uptake in practice, perhaps due to the high cost—in terms of overhead and restricted functionality—that strong, often cryptographic, guarantees impose.

Information flow control (IFC) can protect against data breaches by statically or dynamically verifying that it is impossible for specific system components or code to access private user data [7,14,34]; programming language techniques similarly ensure that applications handle user data in accordance with a privacy policy [20,32,33]. To the same end, multiverse databases [16] compute individualized materialized views for each end-user. These approaches help meet the GDPR's data security requirements, but they do not address other aspects, such as users' rights to access, object, erasure, or data portability, which our proposed design addresses by construction.

4.2 User Control over Data

Riverbed [30] allows end-users to define policies for their data and enforces them over entire web service stacks: using containers, Riverbed forks a complete stack for every new set of policies. This grants users control over their data, but prohibits and sharing across users with disjoint policy sets, which severely restricts functionality. W5 [13], by contrast, proposes to combine user data in a single platform and has users explicitly authorize access by applications running on this platform, relying IFC to enforce isolation. This achieves good performance, but requires laborious effort on users' part, and is incompatible with web services that may wish to avoid exposing their internal application structure.

Perhaps most similar to our dataflow design are the ideas of "standing queries" over distributed data in Amber [2] and Oort [3]. Structured as a publish-subscribe network, the their focus is to allow cloud applications to access data stored with multiple storage providers, and users are responsible for setting permissions on their data. This is akin to making our user shards held globally queryable; our design instead focuses on enforcing GDPR compliance over data stored within a single web service backend.

BStore [4] and DIY hosting [19] suggest to store users' data lives on cloud storage services (such as Amazon S3), which web applications access through a filesystem interface or serverless functions. Solid [15] and Databox [18] go one step further and have users run personal, physical or virtual, servers that host all data and execute all server-side application logic, combining user data on different "pods" or databoxes via well-defined APIs. These interfaces achieve user control over data, but lack support for the long-running, stateful services at the backbone of today's web services, which rely on computing and caching derived data. Our user shards are instead held on a web service's servers (*e.g.*, Google's), allowing for efficient stateful services, but we envisage APIs for the creation and withdrawal of user shards.

4.3   Data Revocation

Removing user data from server-side systems, and revoking its effects on derived information, is a challenging problem. Some prior systems, such as Vanish [10], seek to give users the ability to revoke data even if processed, cached, and stored online and on machines beyond their control. In Vanish, data "self-destructs" after some time unless it is actively refreshed, but revocation is all-or-nothing— *i.e.*, it is impossible to revoke only one of many records that impacted a piece of data stored in Vanish—and Vanish relies on cryptography and a peer-to-peer distributed hash table, making it hard to fit into today's established web service stacks. Undo computing [5,6], on the other hand, seeks to provide a general-purpose mechanism to undo only *specific* frontend requests and their derived side-effects. The use case is to undo malicious requests that exploited bugs in a web application, and any secondary effects or subsequent data modifications these requests applied, restoring a "clean" web service backend.

In a compliant-by-construction database, we trust the system (and the data processor who runs it) to faithfully execute shard revocation requests, and expect that fines under the GDPR are sufficient to discourage foul play. In our dataflow design, determinism simplifies undoing requests, as the dataflow's inherent dependency structure and known operator semantics capture much of the information that undo computing (which covers non-determinism) has to extract from logs.

5   Conclusions

In this position paper, we argued that recent privacy legislation such as the GDPR constitutes an exogenous change that necessitates new system designs, much like changing applications or hardware have in the past.

We proposed a new web service backend architecture that puts users in control of their data, and which aims to be GDPR-compliant by construction. Applied to an RDBMS, our design requires changes to classic schema design and query processing, but leaves the application development model unchanged.

While we believe our ideas indicate a promising direction, and efficient and generalizable implementation requires addressing several research challenges that span databases, distributed systems, programming languages, and security. We are excited to work on these challenges ourselves, and we encourage the community to take them up, as there is plenty of work to do.

Acknowledgments. We thank Jon Gjengset and the anonymous reviewers for helpful comments that substantially improved this paper. This work was funded through NSF awards CNS-1704172 and CNS-1704376.

References

1. California Legislature. The California Consumer Privacy Act of 2018, June 2018. https://leginfo.legislature.ca.gov/faces/billTextClient.xhtml?bill_id=201720 180AB375
2. Chajed, T., et al.: Amber: decoupling user data from web applications. In: Proceedings of the 15th Workshop on Hot Topics in Operating Systems (HotOS). Kartause Ittingen, Switzerland, May 2015
3. Chajed, T., Gjengset, J., Frans Kaashoek, M., Mickens, J., Morris, R., Zeldovich, N.: Oort: user-centric cloud storage with global queries. Technical report MIT-CSAIL-TR-2016-015. MIT Computer Science and Artificial Intelligence Laboratory, December 2016. https://dspace.mit.edu/bitstream/handle/1721.1/105802/MIT-CSAIL-TR-2016-015.pdf?sequence=1
4. Chandra, R., Gupta, P., Zeldovich, N.: Separating web applications from user data storage with BSTORE. In: Proceedings of the 2010 USENIX Conference on Web Application Development (WebApps), Boston, Massachusetts, USA, p. 1 (2010). http://dl.acm.org/citation.cfm?id=1863166.1863167
5. Chandra, R., Kim, T., Shah, M., Narula, N., Zeldovich, N.: Intrusion recovery for database-backed web applications. In: Proceedings of the 23rd ACM Symposium on Operating Systems Principles (SOSP), Cascais, Portugal, October 2011
6. Chen, H., Kim, T., Wang, X., Zeldovich, N., Kaashoek, M.F.: Identifying information disclosure in web applications with retroactive auditing. In: Proceedings of the 11th USENIX Symposium on Operating Systems Design and Implementation (OSDI), Broomfield, Colorado, USA, October 2014
7. Chlipala, A.: Static checking of dynamically-varying security policies in database-backed applications. In: Proceedings of the 9th USENIX Symposium on Operating Systems Design and Implementation (OSDI), Vancouver, British Columbia, Canada, October 2010. http://adam.chlipala.net/papers/UrFlowOSDI10/
8. Cresse, P.: The GDPR: Where Do You Begin? CloverDX Blog, August 2017. https://blog.cloverdx.com/gdpr-where-do-you-begin. Accessed July 17 2019
9. Regulation (EU) 2016/679 of the European Parliament and of the Council of 27 April 2016 on the protection of natural persons with regard to the processing of personal data and on the free movement of such data, and repealing Directive 95/46/EC (General Data Protection Regulation). In: Official Journal of the European Union L119, pp. 1–88, May 2016. http://eur-lex.europa.eu/legal-content/EN/TXT/?uri=OJ:L:2016:119:TOC
10. Geambasu, R., Kohno, T., Levy, A.A., Levy, H.M.: Vanish: increasing data privacy with self-destructing data. In: Proceedings of the 18th USENIX Security Symposium. Montreal, Canada, pp. 299–316 (2009). http://dl.acm.org/citation.cfm?id=1855768.1855787
11. Gjengset, J., Schwarzkopf, M., Behrens, J., et al.: Noria: dynamic, partially-stateful data-flow for high-performance web applications. In: Proceedings of the 13th USENIX Symposium on Operating Systems Design and Implementation (OSDI), Carlsbad, California, USA, pp. 213–231, October 2018

12. Hunt, T., Zhu, Z., Xu, Y., Peter, S., Witchel, E.: Ryoan: a distributed sandbox for untrusted computation on secret data. In: Proceedings of the 12th USENIX Conference on Operating Systems Design and Implementation (OSDI), Savannah, Georgia, USA, pp. 533–549 (2016). http://dl.acm.org/citation.cfm?id=3026877.3026919

13. Krohn, M., Yip, A., Brodsky, M., Morris, R., Walfish, M.: A world wide web without walls. In: Proceedings of the 6th Workshop on Hot Topics in Networks (HotNets), Atlanta, Georgia, USA, November 2007

14. Krohn, M., et al.: Information flow control for standard OS abstractions. In: Proceedings of the 21st ACM SIGOPS Symposium on Operating Systems Principles (SOSP), Stevenson, Washington, USA, pp. 321–334 (2007). https://doi.acm.org/10.1145/1294261.1294293

15. Mansour, E., Sambra, A.V., Hawke, S., et al.: A demonstration of the solid platform for social web applications. In: Proceedings of the 25th International Conference Companion on World Wide Web (WWW), Montréal, Québec, Canada, pp. 223–226 (2016). https://doi.org/10.1145/2872518.2890529

16. Marzoev, A., Araújo, L.T., Schwarzkopf, M., et al.: Towards multiverse databases. In: Proceedings of the 17th Workshop on Hot Topics in Operating Systems (HotOS), Bertinoro, Italy, pp. 88–95 (2019). https://doi.acm.org/10.1145/3317550.3321425

17. McSherry, F., Murray, D.G., Isaacs, R., Isard, M.: Differential dataflow. In: Proceedings of the 6th Biennial Conference on Innovative Data Systems Research (CIDR), Asilomar, California, USA, Janaury 2013

18. Mortier, R., Zhao, J., Crowcroft, J., et al.: Personal data management with the databox: what's inside the box? In: Proceedings of the 2016 ACM Workshop on Cloud-Assisted Networking (CAN), Irvine, California, USA, pp. 49–54 (2016). https://doi.acm.org/10.1145/3010079.3010082

19. Palkar, S., Zaharia, M.: DIY hosting for online privacy. In: Proceedings of the 16th ACM Workshop on Hot Topics in Networks (HotNets), Palo Alto, California, USA, pp. 1–7 (2017). https://doi.acm.org/10.1145/3152434.3152459

20. Polikarpova, N., Yang, J., Itzhaky, S., Solar-Lezama, A.: Type-driven repair for information flow security. CoRR abs/1607.03445 (2016). arXiv: 1607.03445

21. Popa, R.A., Redfield, C.M.S., Zeldovich, N., Balakrishnan, H.: CryptDB: protecting confidentiality with encrypted query processing. In: Proceedings of the 23rd ACM Symposium on Operating Systems Principles (SOSP), Cascais, Portugal, pp. 85–100 (2011). https://doi.acm.org/10.1145/2043556.2043566

22. Popa, R.A., et al.: Building web applications on top of encrypted data using mylar. In: Proceedings of the 11th USENIX Conference on Networked Systems Design and Implementation (NSDI), Seattle, Washington, USA, pp. 157–172 (2014). http://dl.acm.org/citation.cfm?id=2616448.2616464

23. Shah, A., Banakar, V., Shastri, S., Wasserman, M., Chidambaram, V.: Analyzing the impact of GDPR on storage systems. In: Proceedings of the 11th USENIX Workshop on Hot Topics in Storage and File Systems (HotStorage), July 2019

24. Shastri, S., Wasserman, M., Chidambaram, V.: How design, architecture, and operation of modern systems conflict with GDPR. In: Proceedings of the 11th USENIX Workshop on Hot Topics in Cloud Computing (Hot-Cloud), July 2019

25. Smith, O.: The GDPR racket: who's making money from this $9bn business shakedown, May 2018. https://www.forbes.com/sites/oliversmith/2018/05/02/the-gdpr-racket-whos-making-money-from-this-9bn-business-shakedown/

26. Stonebraker, M., Abadi, D.J., Batkin, A., et al.: C-store: a column oriented DBMS. In: Proceedings of the 31st International Conference on Very Large Data Bases (VLDB). VLDB Endowment, Trondheim, Norway, pp. 553–564 (2005). http://dl.acm.org/citation.cfm?id=1083592.1083658

27. Sweney, M.: BA faces £183m fine over passenger data breach. The Guardian, July 2019. https://www.theguardian.com/business/2019/jul/08/ba-fine-customer-data-breach-british-airways. Accessed July 17 2019

28. Sweney, M.: Marriott to be fined nearly £100m over GDPR breach. The Guardian, July 2019. https://www.theguardian.com/business/2019/jul/09/marriott-fined-over-gdpr-breach-ico. Accessed July 17 2019

29. Volgushev, N., Schwarzkopf, M., Getchell, B., Varia, M., Lapets, A., Bestavros, A.: Conclave: secure multi-party computation on big data. In: Proceedings of the 14th ACM EuroSys Conference on Computer Systems (EuroSys), Dresden, Germany, pp. 3:1–3:18, March 2019. https://doi.acm.org/10.1145/3302424.3303982

30. Wang, F., Ko, R., Mickens, J.: Riverbed: enforcing user-defined privacy constraints in distributed web services. In: Proceedings of the 16th USENIX Symposium on Networked Systems Design and Implementation (NSDI), Boston, Massachusetts, USA, pp. 615–630, February 2019. https://www.usenix.org/conference/nsdi19/presentation/wang-frank

31. Wang, F., Yun, C., Goldwasser, S., Vaikuntanathan, V., Zaharia, M.: Splinter: practical private queries on public data. In: Proceedings of the 14th USENIX Symposium on Networked Systems Design and Implementation (NSDI), Boston, Massachusetts, USA, pp. 299–313 (2017). http://www.usenix.org/conference/nsdi17/technical-sessions/presentation/wang-frank

32. Yang, J., Hance, T., Austin, T.H., Solar-Lezama, A., Flanagan, C., Chong, S.: Precise, dynamic information flow for database backed applications. In: Proceedings of the 37th ACM SIGPLAN Conference on Programming Language Design and Implementation (PLDI), Santa Barbara, California, USA, pp. 631–647, June 2016. https://doi.acm.org/10.1145/2908080.2908098

33. Yang, J., Yessenov, K., Solar-Lezama, A.: A language for automatically enforcing privacy policies. In: Proceedings of the 39th Annual ACM SIGPLAN-SIGACT Symposium on Principles of Programming Languages (POPL), Philadelphia, Pennsylvania, USA, pp. 85–96, January 2012. https://doi.acm.org/10.1145/2103656.2103669

34. Yip, A., Wang, X., Zeldovich, N., Frans Kaashoek, M.: Improving application security with data flow assertions. In: Proceedings of the ACM SIGOPS 22nd Symposium on Operating Systems Principles (OSDI), Big Sky, Montana, USA, pp. 291–304 (2009). https://doi.acm.org/10.1145/1629575.1629604

From Here to Provtopia

Thomas Pasquier[1](✉)(iD), David Eyers[2](iD), and Margo Seltzer[3](iD)

[1] University of Bristol, Bristol, UK
thomas.pasquier@bristol.ac.uk
[2] University of Otago, Dunedin, New Zealand
[3] University of British Columbia, Vancouver, Canada

Abstract. Valuable, sensitive, and regulated data flow freely through distributed systems. In such a world, how can systems plausibly comply with the regulations governing the collection, use, and management of such data? We claim that distributed data provenance, the directed acyclic graph documenting the origin and transformations of data holds the key. Provenance analysis has already been demonstrated in a wide range of applications: from intrusion detection to performance analysis. We describe how similar systems and analysis techniques are suitable both for implementing the complex policies that govern data and verifying compliance with regulatory mandates. We also highlight the challenges to be addressed to move provenance from research laboratories to production systems.

Keywords: Provenance · Distributed systems · Compliance

1 Vision

We live in an information economy. However, the goods on which that economy is based, i.e., the information itself, are of questionable quality. Individuals, corporations, and governments are overwhelmed with data, but the path from data to information is opaque. Imagine a different world, one we call Provtopia.

In Provtopia, the information we consume comes with a description of its composition, just as the food we buy comes with nutrition labels that alert us to allergens or additives or excessive amounts of some substance we wish to limit. Imagine that the next time you received a piece of spam, you could click on the `why` link and obtain a clear and concise explanation of why you received that email. Even better, imagine that clicking on the `never again` link ensured that you never received another piece of spam for that reason.

Now imagine that the programs and services with which we interact can also consume such labels, what will that enable? Your corporate firewall examines the labels of outgoing data and prohibits the flow of sensitive data. Or perhaps it checks to see if your customer data has been routed through a suitable aggregation mechanism, before being released to third parties. Maybe each service in your network checks the data it consumes to see if the owners of that data have authorized its use for the particular service.

V. Gadepally et al. (Eds.): DMAH 2019/Poly 2019, LNCS 11721, pp. 54–67, 2019.
https://doi.org/10.1007/978-3-030-33752-0_4

Finally, imagine that we can empower users of all sorts to ask, "Where has my data been used?" whereby a graphic, such as the one shown in Fig. 1, details the flow of their information. And just as easily, they can indicate places to which they do not want their information to flow, and all future uses are prevented. We do not yet live in Provtopia, but we could.

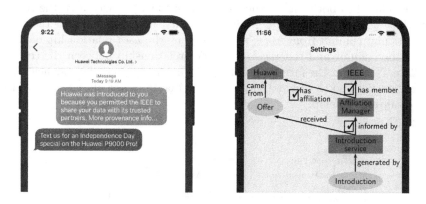

Fig. 1. In Provtopia, the path of information is tracked and can be managed.

Provtopia exists in millions of distributed computers, large and small, that comprise our cyberinfrastructure. The currency of Provtopia is data provenance.

We begin our journey to Provtopia with a brief introduction to data provenance in the next section. We then present examples of how provenance has enabled or could enable applications ranging from security to regulatory compliance in Sect. 3. Section 4 describes the technologies that exist today and form the foundation of Provtopia. In Sect. 5, we discuss the obstacles that lie between today's world and Provtopia, and in Sect. 6 we chart the path from here to there.

2   Provenance Explained

Digital provenance—or just *provenance* or *lineage* or *pedigree*—is metadata detailing the origin and history of a piece of data. It is typically represented formally as relationships (interactions) among entities (data), computational activities, and the agents responsible for the generation of information or the execution of actions [11]. Its representation frequently takes the form of a directed acyclic graph (DAG) as formalised by the W3C provenance working group [6], which is derived from earlier work on the open provenance model [35]. As an illustration, Fig. 2 depicts how the W3C provenance data model represents provenance information. It depicts a scenario reporting the outcome of a continuous integration (CI) result. We have three microservices, each implemented by a different company: git from *gitCo*, CI from *SquareCI*, and Flack from *FlackCo*. Each service is an activity, each company is an agent, and each service is related to the company that provides it via the *associated with* relationship. The diagram shows that the Flack service is responsible for monitoring the CI process. The CI process produces reports, represented here by the *wasGeneratedBy* relationship connecting the report entity to the CI activity. The Flack activity consumes those reports, represented via the *uses* relationship connecting Flack and the report. In this case, the report came from a CI run on a particular repository, which is related to both the CI and git services: the CI service *used* the repository, which *wasGeneratedBy* git. Additionally, that instance of git was the result of a particular commit from Alice, represented by the *used* relationship between git and the commit and the *wasAttributedTo* relationship between the commit and Alice. Note that the formal models of provenance express dependencies, not information flow, so the arrows in provenance diagrams are all instances of the *depends-on* relationship.

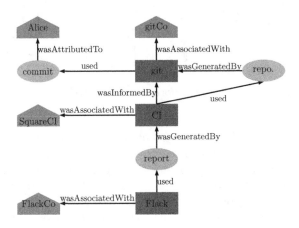

Fig. 2. A simple W3C PROV-DM provenance graph.

As a topic of research, digital provenance originated in the database community, where it provided a way to explain the results of relational database queries [8,9,12]. It later attracted attention as a means to enable reproducibility of scientific workflows, by providing a mechanism to reconstruct the computational environment from formal records of scientific computation [18,44,53,54]. Next, storage or operating system provenance emerged as a general purpose mechanism to document the transformation and flow of data within a single system [38]. Naturally, network extensions came next, and network provenance emerged as a way to debug network protocols [63]. More recently, the cybersecurity community has explored using provenance for explaining [31] and detecting system intrusions [23,24]. These applications use provenance both to explain the origin of data and to represent system execution in terms of information flow.

3 Use Cases

Some of the following provenance-based applications have been implemented in prior systems, frequently using data collection infrastructures designed specifically for the application; some of have been implemented using existing provenance capture systems; and some seem possible, but have not been implemented to the best of our knowledge. Ideally, these exemplar applications provide a glimpse of what is possible in Provtopia. As a practical matter, using provenance in these applications addresses two different challenges that arise in complex distributed systems: it replaces one-off custom collection infrastructures with a single general one, and it enables an interesting class of applications for explanation, documentation, auditing, and enforcement.

3.1 Performance Monitoring

Today's cloud applications are hosted on distributed systems that interact in complex ways. Performance monitoring of these systems is particularly challenging, because the root cause of an application slowdown frequently appears on a machine different from the one that reports anomalous behavior [34,59]. However, even in these complex situations, the interactions can be captured in a provenance graph. Since there must be an interaction of some sort between the faulty component and the component registering anomalous behavior, provenance can assist in being able to trace backwards along edges in the interaction graph to help pinpoint the root cause. We are aware of large cloud organizations such as eBay [57] already applying this sort of graph analysis to performance monitoring.

3.2 Debugging

Modern applications are composed of large numbers of interacting heterogeneous components (i.e., microservices). In these environments, managing the volume of diagnostic information itself becomes a challenge. Alvaro et al. [1] advocate for using provenance traces to help with such tasks, because they reveal the causal relationships buried in software system logs. Provenance data provides a consistent and systematic source of information that can expose correlated system behaviors. Automated analysis of such data has the potential to replace some of the manual debugging work that might otherwise be needed. For example, engineers debugging performance problems expend significant effort analyzing outlier events, trying to correlate them to behaviors in the software [17]. Once such outliers are detected, provenance graphs contain the necessary information to identify such correlations. While, to the best of our knowledge, no such automated tools yet exist, constructing them seems entirely feasible.

3.3 Causal Log Analysis

Provenance enables causal analysis of complex systems. Most such systems are assembled from pre-existing software components, e.g., databases and message queues, each of which may run on a different host. Such software components often already perform their own logging. However, because unexpected behavior can emerge from the interactions between such components, it is necessary to correlate data from these independent logging facilities.

Some modern provenance capture systems [42] allow information from separate software components' logs to be embedded directly into the provenance graph. The resulting provenance graph provides a qualitatively more complete view of system activity, highlighting the causal relationships between log entries that span different software components. This use case also illustrates one way that application-specific provenance (in the form of log records) can be integrated with system-level provenance to provide a complete and semantically meaningful representation of system behavior. One could imagine similar integration between multiple application-level provenance capture systems [28, 39, 56, 61] using system provenance.

A further benefit of this approach to causal log analysis is that provenance makes information about interrelationships readily available and explicit. Traditional log analysis techniques have instead tried to infer this sort of information *post hoc*, which is potentially computationally expensive and error-prone.

3.4   Intrusion Detection

Provenance also plays a crucial role in system security. The two main types of (complementary) intrusion detection system (IDS) are (a) network-based, and (b) host-based. Existing provenance-based work focuses on host-based IDS, as even in a distributed system, an intrusion begins at one or more hosts within the network. However, the approaches described here for host-based intrusion detection can potentially be made to work in a distributed setting given existing infrastructures that can transmit provenance to an external host in real time. If many such hosts export provenance to a single analysis engine, that engine is free to implement distributed system wide detection.

It has been common practice to design host-based IDS to analyze recorded traces of system calls. Recently, though, the approach of using traces of system calls has run into difficulty correlating complex chains of events across flat logs [23]. Whole-system provenance [5, 24, 42] provides a source of information richer than traces of system calls, because it explicitly captures the causal relationships between events. Provenance-based approaches have shown particular promise in their ability to detect advanced persistent threats (APTs). APTs often involve multi-phase attacks, and detecting them can be difficult, due to the phases of attack often being separated by long periods of time. Solutions to APTs using system call traces have been elusive due to the challenge of correlating related events over long time periods using existing forms of log files. However, provenance can provide a compact and long-lived record that facilitates connecting the key events that are causally related. Provenance approaches that filter data at run-time can further reduce the volume of data that needs to be maintained to analyze attacks within emerging, provenance-based IDS [26, 43].

3.5   Intrusion and Fault Reporting

Beyond *detecting* intrusions, or other software faults, provenance can also help visualize and explain these attacks and faults. Provenance may also help in assessing the extent of the damage caused by a leak. Such a capability may help in complying with GDPR article 33 [16], for example, which requires that users affected by breaches of personal data to be notified within a short time-window of the discovery of the breach.

Attack graphs [40,52,55], which represent computer exploits as a graph, are a common way to collect relevant information about chains of correlated activities within an attack. A provenance graph is an ideal source of data to be transformed into an attack graph to explain how an intrusion progressed and escalated.

Provenance can provide insight into the parts of the system that were affected in the process of a developing attack. The flexibility in how and what provenance data is recorded can lead to systems that capture additional context, which may help in identifying related weaknesses preemptively. These capabilities are useful in enabling system administrators to strengthen their systems, given a deeper understanding of the source of vulnerabilities.

3.6   Data Protection Compliance

The EU GDPR and similar regulations emerging in other jurisdictions place strong, enforceable protections on the use of personal data by software systems. Due to the wide-spread impact of the GDPR on existing cloud services, public attention has been drawn to both the regulation and its underlying motive— e.g., users of popular services have been notified that those services' terms and conditions have been updated both to effect the more direct simplicity and transparency required by the GDPR, and to get users' consent to use of their data.

However, there is little value in the users being given rights that they are unable to usefully exercise [41,47]. At present, most software systems that manipulate user data are largely opaque in their operations—sometimes even to experts. This makes it extremely unlikely that users will be able to fully understand where, how, when and why their data are being used.

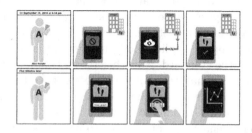

Fig. 3. Representing provenance as comic strips [51]. The comic show how Alice downloaded and visualized `fitbit` data.

Provenance can provide a useful means to explain the behavior of systems to end users, because it can provide both a high-level overview of the complete operation of a system and fine-grained details underlying each high-level operation. That said, transforming provenance into explanation, is a non-trivial task, requiring further research. Explanations from today's provenance systems are crude, presenting a user with multiple graphs and highlighting their differences or providing metrics that have no intuitive meaning to a user.

Nonetheless, promising approaches are emerging for making the behavior of distributed software systems more generally intelligible. For example, recent research demonstrated the approach of presenting data in comic-book form (see Fig. 3) [51]—not yet widely deployable, but a step in the right direction.

4   Existing Technologies

Provtopia from Sect. 1 and the use cases from Sect. 3 present a compelling vision of what is possible in a provenance-aware world. In this section, we outline existing technologies that can help realize this vision while Sect. 5 identifies the areas requiring further research.

Based on our experience developing many provenance-aware applications, including some of those discussed in Sect. 3, we propose that the key to large-scale distributed system analysis, management, and policy enforcement lies in pervasive use of whole-system provenance. First, system level provenance makes it possible to collect provenance without requiring the use of provenance-aware application and services. Second, in the presence of provenance-aware applications, system level provenance provides a mechanism to combine provenance from multiple applications in a manner that preserves causality. Third, system level provenance provides visibility into implicit interactions, for example, multiple applications that use the same data, but do not explicitly communicate. The greatest problem with system level provenance is that it does not capture application semantics. Deriving both the benefits of system level provenance and application semantics requires some form of cooperation or layering [37] among the different captures mechanisms. In Sect. 4.2, we discuss mechanisms to facilitate such integration.

The use of whole system provenance does not require agreement on any particular provenance capture system, but does require agreement on data representation. While a provenance standard exists [6], we have found it insufficiently expressive to support applications. Instead, we have had to create our own schema on top of the standard. Nonetheless, we believe better standardization is possible, but is premature until we have significantly more widespread adoption and use of provenance. In the absence of such standardization, it is still possible today for organizations to deploy and use provenance capture systems in their own data center, without having to negotiate standards with other organizations.

We begin this section with a brief overview of whole-system provenance capture, including its practicality and how such systems can provide guarantees of completeness. Next, we discuss how to integrate provenance from different capture mechanisms, whether they be the same mechanism running on different hosts or different mechanisms on a single host, but at different layers of abstraction. Finally, we discuss the state of the art in provenance analysis.

4.1   Whole-System Provenance Capture

Early whole-system provenance capture systems, such as PASS [38], implemented OS-level provenance capture via system call interception and extensive, manual, and non-portable instrumentation of an existing operating system. This architecture suffered from two serious problems. First, it was unmaintainable; each new operating system release required hundreds of person hours of porting effort, and in practice, PASS died as the version of Linux on which it was based aged. Second, the fundamental architecture of system call interception is prone to security vulnerabilities relating to concurrency issues [20,58].

Hi-Fi [49] provided a better approach that relied on the reference monitor implementation in Linux: the Linux Security Module framework (LSM) [60]. Using the reference monitor—a security construct that mediates the interactions between all applications and other objects within an operating system [2]— provides increased confidence in the quality of the provenance data captured.

CamFlow built upon Hi-Fi and PASS to provide a practical and maintainable implementation of the reference monitor approach. CamFlow modularized provenance-capture, isolating it from the rest of the kernel to reduce maintenance engineering cost [42]. While PASS and Hi-Fi where one-off efforts, CamFlow has been actively maintained since 2015, has been upgraded consistently and easily with new Linux versions, and is used in several research projects. Both Hi-Fi and CamFlow use LSM, for which mediation completeness has been discussed [15,19,21,30]. Pasquier et al. elaborate on how these mediation guarantees relate to provenance completeness [43]. Further, CamFlow represents temporal relationships directly in the graph structure, rather than through metadata, improving computational performance and easing data analysis [43].

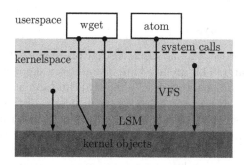

Fig. 4. Capturing provenance via the LSM framework.

Figure 4 shows how all interactions between processes and kernel objects (eg files, sockets, pipes or other processes) are mediated by the LSM framework. Details of the CamFlow implementation appear in prior work [10, 42, 46].

4.2 Integration of Capture Mechanisms

CamFlow neatly integrates with semantically rich information from applications in two ways. First, records from existing provenance capture mechanisms such as: "big data" analytics frameworks [29], Data Science programming languages [33], network communication [62], and databases [13] can simply inject provenance records into the provenance stream [42]. Second, as discussed in Sect. 3.3, CamFlow can incorporate application log records into its provenance stream. It connects a log event to the node representing the precise version of the thread of execution that generated it. It is then possible to correlate the surrounding graph structure to log content, enriching the system-level provenance with application-level semantics [42].

It is also possible to integrate CamFlow provenance from multiple hosts. Just as CamFlow allows applications to inject provenance records into the provenance stream, it can transmit its own system level provenance to the messaging middleware, enabling a single machine to coalesce provenance from multiple hosts. CamFlow identifies causal connections between the different hosts by analyzing the nodes representing network packets between them. This approach provides a relatively simple way to build and analyze provenance graphs that represent the execution of a distributed system [42]. We envision such a deployment within a single organization's data center. When traffic flows across multiple networks, packet labeling techniques can retain the provenance relationships (see [5]).

Summarizing the state of the art, capture mechanisms exist, they are efficient both in execution time, and storage requirements (via selective capture and storage), and system level provenance provides an easy way for them to interoperate, without requiring changes to existing infrastructure. Research-quality prototypes of all these systems exist; the only missing piece is a compelling application that convinces organizations to adopt the approach.

4.3 Provenance Analysis

Early provenance capture systems assumed that provenance data must be stored and then analyzed later. This architecture introduces a significant delay between provenance capture and analysis, precluding real time applications that can prevent data movement. However, through careful design of the provenance data and graph structures, we have demonstrated that efficient runtime analysis of provenance is possible [43]. As noted in Sect. 3, high-speed provenance analysis creates the opportunity for enforcement in addition to detection. The ability to decouple storage from analysis opens up new opportunities in the design of provenance storage as it can be removed from the critical path both of the system being monitored and the applications monitoring it.

5   From Vision to Reality

In this section we discuss areas of research into provenance systems that will support the achievement of our vision.

Machine Learning and Data Analytics: While provenance can be tracked within data analytics frameworks [29], understanding overall information flow is challenging when using algorithms that combine large amounts of data in relatively opaque ways. For example, it has been demonstrated that membership within a training dataset can be inferred from ML models [50]. Should this risk be presented to end-users? Are such dependencies still understandable across long chains of transformations? The interrelations between complex analytical techniques and data tracking need to be more thoroughly investigated.

Securing Provenance: Provenance security is fundamental to its use in almost all applications. Provenance security encompasses confidentiality, integrity, unforgeability, non-repudiation and availability. Securing provenance is particularly difficult as the stakeholder interested in auditing a particular application may differ from those administrating or using the application. Further, provenance and the data it describes may have different security requirements [7]. For example, in a conference review scenario, the reviews (the data) should be available to authors, but the provenance of those reviews (the reviewers) should not. Conversely, we may be allowed to know the authors of a confidential report (parts of its provenance), while we may not have access to the contents of the report (the data).

Techniques exist to verify that the provenance chain has not been broken [25], and we can use hardware root of trust techniques, such as TPM [3] or vTPM [48], and remote attestation techniques [14,22] to verify the integrity of the kernel containing the provenance capture mechanism and the user space elements that manage and capture provenance data [5]. While prior work has shown that LSM mediates all flows in the kernel, there is no proof that any capture mechanism correctly and completely captures the provenance.

Storing Provenance for Post-Hoc Analysis: Recording the entire provenance graph of the execution of large distributed systems remains a significant challenge. Moyer et al. show that even a relatively modest distributed system could generate several thousand graph elements per second per machine [36]. Relatively quickly, this means handling graphs containing billions of nodes. Several options exist to reduce graph size, such as identifying and tracking only sensitive data objects [4,45] or performing property-preserving graph compression [27]. We have demonstrated that runtime provenance processing can be used to extract critical information [43], but this might not be sufficient to support some provenance needs. To our knowledge no deployment at scale has yet been attempted to demonstrate the practicality of such provenance storage approaches.

Provenance Reduction: Generating high-level execution representations (see Figs. 1, 2 and 3) from low-level provenance capture at the system or language level requires that provenance be trimmed and summarized. A common technique that is applied is to identify meaningful repeating patterns that can be aggregated in a single node representing a set of actions [32]. Such summarization eases the conversion to graphical representations such as Fig. 3. Summarization may also reduce storage needs. However, potential data-loss needs to be considered carefully as important information for forensic investigations may be lost.

Provenance Across Administrative Domains: Managing and using provenance across administrative domains introduces myriad problems, including (1) semantic interoperability, (2) transmitting (trustworthy) provenance across domains, (3) long term provenance archival and access. Although provenance standards exist [6], they are too general to support most applications. This is a vital area of investigation to build a practical deployable solution that reaches beyond a single organization.

6   Conclusion

We have introduced Provtopia—a world in which the path from data to information is annotated so as to effect its careful management and curation. In Provtopia, users have clear visibility of, and control over the use of their data by commercial organizations and government agencies. Those organizations are confident that their distributed systems comply with data handling regulation.

Despite seeming far-fetched, Provtopia is more attainable than you might expect. The provenance technologies required are emerging rapidly from many research projects, today. We provide an overview of the technologies that we and others have developed that help support this vision and highlight a number of key research challenges that remain to be addressed.

References

1. Alvaro, P., Tymon, S.: Abstracting the geniuses away from failure testing. ACM Queue **15**, 29–53 (2017)
2. Anderson, J.P.: Computer security technology planning study. Technical report. ESD-TR-73-51, ESD/AFSC, Hanscom AFB, Bedford, MA, October 1972
3. Bajikar, S.: Trusted Platform Module (TPM) based security on notebook PCs-white paper. Mobile Platforms Group Intel Corporation, pp. 1–20 (2002)
4. Bates, A., Butler, K., Moyer, T.: Take only what you need: leveraging mandatory access control policy to reduce provenance storage costs. In: Workshop on Theory and Practice of Provenance (TaPP 2015), p. 7. USENIX (2015)
5. Bates, A.M., Tian, D., Butler, K.R., Moyer, T.: Trustworthy whole-system provenance for the Linux kernel. In: USENIX Security, pp. 319–334 (2015)
6. Belhajjame, K., et al.: PROV-DM: the PROV data model. Technical report, World Wide Web Consortium (W3C) (2013). https://www.w3.org/TR/prov-dm/
7. Braun, U., Shinnar, A., Seltzer, M.I.: Securing provenance. In: HotSec (2008)
8. Buneman, P., Chapman, A., Cheney, J.: Provenance management in curated databases. In: Proceedings of the 2006 ACM SIGMOD International Conference on Management of data, pp. 539–550. ACM (2006)

9. Buneman, P., Khanna, S., Wang-Chiew, T.: Why and where: a characterization of data provenance. In: Van den Bussche, J., Vianu, V. (eds.) ICDT 2001. LNCS, vol. 1973, pp. 316–330. Springer, Heidelberg (2001). https://doi.org/10.1007/3-540-44503-X_20

10. CamFlow. http://camflow.org/. Accessed 21 Sep 2019

11. Carata, L., et al.: A primer on provenance. Commun. ACM **57**(5), 52–60 (2014)

12. Cheney, J., Ahmed, A., Acar, U.A.: Provenance as dependency analysis. In: Arenas, M., Schwartzbach, M.I. (eds.) DBPL 2007. LNCS, vol. 4797, pp. 138–152. Springer, Heidelberg (2007). https://doi.org/10.1007/978-3-540-75987-4_10

13. Cheney, J., Chiticariu, L., Tan, W.C., et al.: Provenance in databases: why how and where. Found. Trends® Databases **1**(4), 379–474 (2009)

14. Coker, G.: Principles of remote attestation. Int. J. Inf. Secur. **10**(2), 63–81 (2011)

15. Edwards, A., Jaeger, T., Zhang, X.: Runtime verification of authorization hook placement for the Linux security modules framework. In: Conference on Computer and Communications Security (CCS 2002), pp. 225–234. ACM (2002)

16. General Data Protection Regulation. http://eur-lex.europa.eu/legal-content/EN/TXT/?uri=uriserv:OJ.L_.2016.119.01.0001.01.ENG&toc=OJ:L:2016:119:TOC

17. Fedorova, A., et al.: Performance comprehension at WiredTiger. In: Joint Meeting on European Software Engineering Conference and Symposium on the Foundations of Software Engineering, ESEC/FSE 2018, pp. 83–94. ACM (2018)

18. Freire, J., Koop, D., Santos, E., Silva, C.T.: Provenance for computational tasks: a survey. Comput. Sci. Eng. **10**(3), 11–21 (2008)

19. Ganapathy, V., Jaeger, T., Jha, S.: Automatic placement of authorization hooks in the Linux security modules framework. In: Conference on Computer and Communications Security (CCS 2005), pp. 330–339. ACM (2005)

20. Garfinkel, T., et al.: Traps and pitfalls: practical problems in system call interposition based security tools. NDSS **3**, 163–176 (2003)

21. Georget, L., Jaume, M., Tronel, F., Piolle, G., Tong, V.V.T.: Verifying the reliability of operating system-level information flow control systems in Linux. In: International Workshop on Formal Methods in Software Engineering (FormaliSE 2017), pp. 10–16. IEEE/ACM (2017)

22. Goldman, K., Perez, R., Sailer, R.: Linking remote attestation to secure tunnel endpoints. In: Workshop on Scalable Trusted Computing, pp. 21–24. ACM (2006)

23. Han, X., Pasquier, T., Seltzer, M.: Provenance-based intrusion detection: opportunities and challenges. In: Workshop on the Theory and Practice of Provenance (TaPP 2018). USENIX (2018)

24. Han, X., Pasquier, T., Ranjan, T., Goldstein, M., Seltzer, M.: FRAPpuccino: fault-detection through runtime analysis of provenance. In: Workshop on Hot Topics in Cloud Computing (HotCloud 2017). USENIX (2017)

25. Hasan, R., Sion, R., Winslett, M.: The case of the fake picasso: preventing history forgery with secure provenance. In: Conference on File and Storage Technologies (FAST 2009). USENIX (2009)

26. Hassan, W.U., Lemay, M., Aguse, N., Bates, A., Moyer, T.: Towards scalable cluster auditing through grammatical inference over provenance graphs. In: Network and Distributed Systems Security Symposium. Internet Society (2018)

27. Hossain, M.N., Wang, J., Sekar, R., Stoller, S.D.: Dependence-preserving data compaction for scalable forensic analysis. In: Security Symposium (USENIX Security 2018). USENIX Association (2018)

28. Huang, Y., Gottardo, R.: Comparability and reproducibility of biomedical data. Brief. Bioinform. **14**(4), 391–401 (2012)

29. Interlandi, M., et al.: Titian: data provenance support in Spark. Proc. VLDB Endowment **9**(3), 216–227 (2015)
30. Jaeger, T., Edwards, A., Zhang, X.: Consistency analysis of authorization hook placement in the Linux security modules framework. ACM Trans. Inf. Syst. Secur. (TISSEC) **7**(2), 175–205 (2004)
31. King, S.T., Chen, P.M.: Backtracking intrusions. ACM SIGOPS Oper. Syst. Rev. **37**(5), 223–236 (2003)
32. Lee, S., Niu, X., Ludäscher, B., Glavic, B.: Integrating approximate summarization with provenance capture. In: Workshop on the Theory and Practice of Provenance (TaPP 2017). USENIX (2017)
33. Lerner, B., Boose, E.: RDataTracker: collecting provenance in an interactive scripting environment. In: Workshop on the Theory and Practice of Provenance (TaPP 2014). USENIX (2014)
34. Li, J., et al.: PCatch: automatically detecting performance cascading bugs in cloud systems. In: EuroSys 2018, pp. 7:1–7:14. ACM (2018)
35. Moreau, L., et al.: The open provenance model core specification (v1.1). Future Gener. Comput. Syst. **27**(6), 743–756 (2011)
36. Moyer, T., Gadepally, V.: High-throughput ingest of data provenance records into Accumulo. In: High Performance Extreme Computing Conference (HPEC 2016), pp. 1–6. IEEE (2016)
37. Muniswamy-Reddy, K.K., et al.: Layering in provenance systems. In: USENIX Annual Technical Conference (ATC 2009) (2009)
38. Muniswamy-Reddy, K.K., Holland, D.A., Braun, U., Seltzer, M.I.: Provenance-aware storage systems. In: USENIX Annual Technical Conference (ATC 2006), pp. 43–56 (2006)
39. Oracle Corporation: Oracle Total Recall with Oracle Database 11g release 2 (2009). http://www.oracle.com/us/products/total-recall-whitepaper-171749.pdf
40. Ou, X., Boyer, W.F., McQueen, M.A.: A scalable approach to attack graph generation. In: Proceedings of the 13th ACM Conference on Computer and Communications Security, pp. 336–345. ACM (2006)
41. Pasquier, T., Eyers, D., Bacon, J.: Personal data and the Internet of Things. Commun. ACM **62**(6), 32–34 (2019)
42. Pasquier, T., et al.: Practical whole-system provenance capture. In: Symposium on Cloud Computing (SoCC 2017). ACM (2017)
43. Pasquier, T., et al.: Runtime analysis of whole-system provenance. In: Conference on Computer and Communications Security (CCS 2018). ACM (2018)
44. Pasquier, T., et al.: If these data could talk. Sci. Data **4** (2017). Article number: 170114. https://www.nature.com/articles/sdata2017114
45. Pasquier, T., Singh, J., Bacon, J., Eyers, D.: Information flow audit for PaaS clouds. In: IEEE International Conference on Cloud Engineering (IC2E), pp. 42–51. IEEE (2016)
46. Pasquier, T., Singh, J., Eyers, D., Bacon, J.: CamFlow: managed data-sharing for cloud services. IEEE Trans. Cloud Comput. **5**, 472–484 (2015)
47. Pasquier, T., Singh, J., Powles, J., Eyers, D., Seltzer, M., Bacon, J.: Data provenance to audit compliance with privacy policy in the Internet of Things. Pers. Ubiquit. Comput. **22**, 333–344 (2018)
48. Perez, R., Sailer, R., van Doorn, L., et al.: vTPM: virtualizing the trusted platform module. In: Proceedings of the 15th Conference on USENIX Security Symposium, pp. 305–320 (2006)

49. Pohly, D.J., McLaughlin, S., McDaniel, P., Butler, K.: Hi-Fi: collecting high-fidelity whole-system provenance. In: Annual Computer Security Applications Conference, pp. 259–268. ACM (2012)

50. Salem, A., Zhang, Y., Humbert, M., Berrang, P., Fritz, M., Backes, M.: ML-leaks: model and data independent membership inference attacks and defenses on machine learning models. arXiv preprint arXiv:1806.01246 (2018)

51. Schreiber, A., Struminski, R.: Tracing personal data using comics. In: Antona, M., Stephanidis, C. (eds.) UAHCI 2017. LNCS, vol. 10277, pp. 444–455. Springer, Cham (2017). https://doi.org/10.1007/978-3-319-58706-6_36

52. Sheyner, O., Haines, J., Jha, S., Lippmann, R., Wing, J.M.: Automated generation and analysis of attack graphs. In: Proceedings 2002 IEEE Symposium on Security and Privacy, pp. 273–284. IEEE (2002)

53. Simmhan, Y.L., Plale, B., Gannon, D.: A survey of data provenance techniques. Computer Science Department, Indiana University, 69 (2005)

54. Singh, G., et al.: A metadata catalog service for data intensive applications. In: ACM/IEEE Conference on Supercomputing, p. 33. IEEE (2003)

55. Swiler, L.P., Phillips, C., Ellis, D., Chakerian, S.: Computer-attack graph generation tool. In: Proceedings DARPA Information Survivability Conference and Exposition II. DISCEX 2001, vol. 2, pp. 307–321. IEEE (2001)

56. Tariq, D., Ali, M., Gehani, A.: Towards automated collection of application-level data provenance. In: Workshop on Theory and Practice of Provenance, TaPP 2012, p. 16. USENIX (2012)

57. Wang, H., et al.: GRANO: Interactive graph-based root cause analysis for cloud-native distributed data platform. In: Proceedings of the 45th International Conference on Very Large Data Bases (VLDB) (2019, to appear)

58. Watson, R.N.: Exploiting concurrency vulnerabilities in system call wrappers. WOOT 7, 1–8 (2007)

59. Whittaker, M., Alvaro, P., Teodoropol, C., Hellerstein, J.: Debugging distributed systems with why-across-time provenance. In: Symposium on Cloud Computing, SoCC 2018, pp. 333–346. ACM (2018)

60. Wright, C., Cowan, C., Morris, J., Smalley, S., Kroah-Hartman, G.: Linux security module framework. In: Ottawa Linux Symposium, vol. 8032, pp. 6–16 (2002)

61. Xu, S.C., Rogers, T., Fairweather, E., Glenn, A.P., Curran, J.P., Curcin, V.: Application of data provenance in healthcare analytics software: information visualisation of user activities. AMIA Jt. Summits Transl. Sci. Proc. 2018, 263–272 (2018)

62. Zhou, W., Fei, Q., Narayan, A., Haeberlen, A., Loo, B.T., Sherr, M.: Secure network provenance. In: Symposium on Operating Systems Principles (SOSP 2011), pp. 295–310. ACM (2011)

63. Zhou, W., Sherr, M., Tao, T., Li, X., Loo, B.T., Mao, Y.: Efficient querying and maintenance of network provenance at internet-scale. In: Proceedings of the 2010 ACM SIGMOD International Conference on Management of data, pp. 615–626. ACM (2010)

Privacy and Policy in Polystores: A Data Management Research Agenda

Joshua A. Kroll$^{(\boxtimes)}$, Nitin Kohli, and Paul Laskowski

U.C. Berkeley School of Information, Berkeley, USA
jkroll@jkroll.com

1   Introduction

Modern data-driven technologies are providing new capabilities for working with data across diverse storage architectures and analyzing it in unified frameworks to yield powerful insights. These new analysis capabilities, which rely on correlating data across sources and types and exploiting statistical structure, have challenged classical approaches to privacy, leading to a need for radical rethinking of the meaning of the term. In the area of federated database technologies, there is a growing recognition that new technologies like polystores must incorporate the mitigation of privacy risks into the design process.

While databases and privacy have always been connected, a number of trends are now providing new reasons for database architects to engage more directly with notions of privacy. The changing view of privacy by data analysts, based on the power of statistical inference, implies that privacy can no longer be addressed by traditional access control techniques. Federation of data sources increases the potential value of databases, but also the potential privacy harms from analysis and the use of such data in products. The law often requires system operators to address privacy concerns, but addressing these concerns cannot happen simply through choices in how technology is used; addressing privacy harms must become part of the design of these tools.

The success of new federated technologies, including polystores, will rest not only on their ability to extract information from data, but also on whether they are flexible enough to address the privacy concerns of end users and regulators. This is not to say that federated databases should be designed to prescribe a single privacy solution. Privacy is context-specific, subject to balancing acts, and complicated by the fact that even determining which values must be protected can be a point of debate [27]. Nevertheless, it is important for new systems to expose a set of metrics and parameters that privacy law and policy can leverage to the benefit of society.

New technologies have often triggered concerns about the privacy of individuals, dating back to the advent of publishing photographs in newspapers and even earlier [41]. The origin of modern data protection and privacy laws can be traced as far back as 1972, when the public learned that the U.S. government had been holding secret databases of information about citizens. In a formative report created in response to the episode [39], a study committee at the U.S. Department of Health, Education and Welfare articulated a set of core

© Springer Nature Switzerland AG 2019
V. Gadepally et al. (Eds.): DMAH 2019/Poly 2019, LNCS 11721, pp. 68–81, 2019.
https://doi.org/10.1007/978-3-030-33752-0_5

Fair Information Practices (FIPs) that have formed the basis of nearly every subsequent privacy and data protection law [16]. Attempting to mitigate these concerns and to operationalize protections around them has led to a rich field of privacy study across several disciplines.

This paper situates these concerns in light of research on polystores [9] and database federation more generally. While the correlation of data across stores presents significant new privacy risks, it also provides new opportunities for interventions and mitigations. Addressing the privacy needs of individuals represented in databases requires new ways of thinking, and interdisciplinary collaborations. This paper outlines the modern privacy situation and presents a research agenda for research in data privacy for the database community.

2   Traditional Approaches to Privacy in Databases

The study of privacy in computer science largely emerged from the broader study of information security, inheriting a focus on concepts like confidentiality. This section briefly surveys traditional approaches, while Sect. 3 describes ways in which they are insufficient to the task of protecting privacy.

Access Control. In databases, privacy-as-confidentiality has often meant assigning permissions and roles to database users [2]. Modern applications of this idea include *data tagging* systems, which maintain metadata about data items to enable access and query policies [5]. Together, these methods support the important goal of limiting who (or which processes) can access which data items in which contexts at which times. However, access control methods do not directly provide a way to protect the semantics of the underlying data items. Moreover, these methods are not tailored to limit what can be learned from data when access is allowed, for example to protect against misuse by insiders or against authorized-but-privacy-impinging uses.

Query and Result Filtering. To complement access control and enable more flexible policies, the database community has invested significant research effort in developing query auditing and result filtering systems [28]. Auditing provides two significant improvements over methods purely based on access control: First, auditing allows for flexible, detailed, and context-sensitive policies, as decisions can be based on arbitrary processing of query text, rather than a model based only on rows, columns, and user roles. Second, auditing decisions can be made in an online fashion, adapting to the history of prior queries based on estimates of the cumulative privacy risk. However, these systems generally define such risks in the frame of controlling individual pieces of data.

Anonymization. Another line of work considers how to render information in databases or outputs *anonymous*, meaning that rows of data cannot be associated to a particular individual. This extends the concept of privacy beyond information flow to the protection of individual *identities*. The question of what constitutes an identity is, however, difficult and its answers are hotly contested. Traditional approaches to anonymization focus on syntactic properties of data sets, such as the property that no query can return fewer than k individuals [37], or that any result set has at least ℓ distinct values for a protected sensitive attribute [24]. Many legal definitions of identity treat data as belonging to one of two categories: "personally identifiable information" (PII) and "not personally identifiable information". This separation is easy to implement in code; however, it elides an important fact (discussed in detail in Sect. 3: syntactic methods are insufficient to prevent the disclosure of attributes of individuals [30] and so have given way to more information-theoretic protections.

Differential Privacy. Over the last 15 years, a formal approach to privacy has emerged from a branch of computer science known as *differential privacy*. Researchers in this field design computer systems that employ randomness or noise to conceal information about individuals. Moreover, a mathematical proof characterizes the privacy loss that can befall any individual in the worst case.

The term differential privacy does not refer to a single technique, but rather a mathematical standard. It guarantees that the behavior of a computer system is very similar whether an individual is included in a database or removed [10, 11]. The degree of similarity is controlled by a parameter ϵ, which represents the maximum amount of information that an adversary can learn about an individual by studying the mechanism output. Conceptually, a smaller ϵ provides stronger privacy protection, but there is usually a cost in the form of greater noise and thus limited utility from queries. Many heuristics have been proposed to determine an appropriate value of ϵ [18, 21, 23, 29].

From a different angle, the parameter ϵ can be viewed as a *measure* of (worst-case) privacy loss for a given algorithm. A useful property of differential privacy is additive composition, meaning that when multiple queries are run in sequence, the individual ϵ's can be added together to yield a bound for the entire process [12]. This allows organizations to manage access using a *privacy budget*. Each time a query is run, the corresponding ϵ is subtracted from the budget. When the budget is exhausted, the data must be permanently retired to ensure the privacy guarantee holds.

3   Polystores as Privacy Risk

We have outlined a toolkit of existing privacy defenses, including access control, query and result filtering, anonymization, and differential privacy. These are all valuable tools, but each has limitations. In this section, we present three stylized facts to explain why existing approaches to privacy are insufficient to protect individuals, and why database federation only exacerbates the problem. To meet evolving risks to privacy, it will therefore be necessary to look beyond traditional technologies and develop new areas of research.

Statistical Inference Presents New Privacy Threats. Syntactic approaches to database anonymization – such as k-anonymity and ℓ-diversity preserve the structure of the data and the relationships between data elements. This structure can often be exploited, along with information outside the database, to "re-identify" or "de-anonymize" the database. Early efforts by Narayanan and Shmatikov demonstrated that this could be achieved at large scale [32]. Subsequent work has demonstrated an almost complete failure of anonymization techniques to protect individuals [30]. A corollary of this is that the legal notion of personally identifiable information (PII) (known in the GDPR as "personal data") should now be considered obsolete, and all data should be treated as if it is "personal" or "identifying" unless there is a strong case that it is not [31].

One reason for this is the ease of determining *functional identifiers* in large, rich data sets, or sets of attributes which are held by only one individual in that collection. Such identifiers "single out" individuals, implying a set of binary queries for which the individual has a unique set of answers [6]. Representationally, such queries could be treated as the bits of a numeric identifier, which would clearly qualify as personal and identifiable data under existing legal regimes (see Sect. 4) [33]. A curious corollary of this argument is that there exists a 33-bit functional identifier that would suffice to identify all humans on earth uniquely.[1] Thus, any reasonably rich data set should be considered to contain such functional identifiers.

Database Federation Presents New and Heightened Risks. A central motivation for the federation of disparate databases is the idea that cross-referencing the data across them will yield new and better insights. It is therefore natural that such cross-source correlation may enable the increased extraction of sensitive information about individuals, groups of people, or organizations. In fact, federated databases share several features that contribute to increased privacy risks. First, it is clear that cross-referencing data across many sources abstractly creates data items with more attributes, providing more free parameters for the construction of functional identifiers as described above. Second, it is often the case that these systems are built to enable downstream analytics processing or machine learning pipelines. Such processing naturally seeks to determine how to separate, cluster, and classify data items and so can be thought of as inherently and automatically constructing such identification schemes. Finally, consolidation of data across data sources risks undermining assumptions made during the policy establishment process when sources were not federated. Even properties as straightforward as access control or data permissions can be so subverted as to be totally violated when such assumptions change [2]. Relatedly, centralization of data access creates new and attractive points of attack for outside hackers or malicious insiders. Such "attacks" on privacy can also occur without malice, simply through the authorized realization that new insights are possible through analysis of newly combined data, undermining existing business logic.

---

[1] $2^{33} = 8,589,934,592$, compared to a world population of around 7.7 billion.

Differential Privacy Requires Design-Level Intervention. One might hope that we can take an arbitrary algorithm and make it differentially private. Unfortunately, this is not the case in general. As differentially private algorithms require noise to protect any possible input data value, sufficient noise must be introduced to mask the presence or absence of any input that possibly alters the output of an algorithm, even in the worst-case. This amount of noise can be unbounded, implying that an infinite amount of noise might be required to achieve this privacy definition. More generally, differential privacy is difficult to achieve for computations that are sensitive to the input of a single value over an unbounded domain, such as reporting the mean, the smallest and largest order statistics, and other non-robust statistics that operate over the entire real line. Without additional modifications of the problem statement, such as placing domain restrictions or bounds on the input space or by replacing a sensitive algorithm with a more statistically-robust one, we cannot ensure that any arbitrary algorithm can be made differentially private with a finite (let alone reasonable) amount of noise. While there are circumstances where such assumptions and modifications can be reasonably made in practice, we cannot immediately make use of differential privacy in every possible deployment scenario. It should be noted that this is not a bug in the differential privacy approach, but rather a feature, as it forces the algorithm designer to consider computational tools that are synergistic with the goal of not revealing "too much" about a single individual. It also suggests a need for thinking about privacy at the design stage and encourages the adoption of contextually relevant protection mechanisms.

4   The Policy Landscape

We briefly set forth provisions in a selection of applicable laws and policies which bear on how privacy requirements are set within practical data governance regimes as they concern the design, engineering, and operation of database systems; because we are from the U.S. context, our summary is very U.S.-focused. Policy generally operationalizes privacy as a broader set of *data protection* rights, which protect other equities including human dignity and autonomy and which, in some jurisdictions, are conceptualized as extensions of human rights frameworks.

GDPR. The European Union's new General Data Protection Regulation (GDPR) provides for a baseline standard of data protection and privacy that applies across all EU and European Economic Area (EEA) countries. The GDPR applies to all data about EU citizens, regardless of where in the world the data are collected or held, and violations carry maximum fines of €10 million or 4% of a company's global turnover. In addition to requiring traditional privacy notions based around confidentiality (e.g., collecting, storing, and processing only the data necessary to achieve some particular purpose and limiting processing only to claimed purposes), the GDPR provides a number of rights of interest to database design and operation. The general framework applies to "personal data", which is, broadly speaking, any data that can be tied to an individual person. While the law defines several classes of information which are affirmatively personal data, the question of whether functional identifiers should be treated as personal data remains unsettled [6]. Several special provisions apply to data processing defined as "profiling", which broadly covers any "automated processing of personal data" which "evaluate[s] certain personal aspects relating to a natural person".

Articles 9 and 10 restrict the processing of several classes of sensitive data for certain purposes, for example Article 9 stipulates that "racial or ethnic origin, political opinions, religious or philosophical beliefs, or trade union membership, and the processing of genetic data, biometric data for the purpose of uniquely identifying a natural person, data concerning health or data concerning a natural person's sex life or sexual orientation shall be prohibited" unless one of several conditions is met, such as the acquiring of affirmative consent. Article 10 prohibits processing based on criminal history except as allowed under the law of the relevant EU member state. But as noted above, the ease of inferring sensitive data makes it challenging to comply with these provisions, as covered personal data may be created or inferred during processing [40].

Articles 15–17 provide for *subject access, rectification, and erasure rights*, which enable subjects to demand all personal data about them, the ability to alter and correct those data, and the right to request that all such data be deleted. These rights apply whether data have been gathered from the subject directly or indirectly Implementing these processes efficiently represents a formidable engineering challenge in the era of large, distributed, federated databases. In particular, deletion may prove a challenge in systems where removing a single subject's data would prove costly or require denormalization or reindexing.

Article 20 provides for a right to data *portability*, which stipulates that subjects should be able to extract their data in open, machine-readable formats. This is more straightforward, but the nature of what formats are acceptable and the question of what constitutes a sufficiently "open format" could benefit from input by the database community.

Articles 18, 21, and 22 provide for rights of the data subject to object to processing in a number of situations, including the use of data for marketing purposes and situations where processing is "solely automated". An active scholarly and legal debate further asks whether these rights require that automated decisions be explained to data subjects and what that would require [36], although stronger explanatory rights may exist in Articles 13–15.

CCPA. The California Consumer Privacy Act (CCPA) is a new state law in California, which takes effect on 1 January 2020 and provides a number of new consumer rights to California residents, including the right to access, rectify, and delete data similar to the GDPR. Additionally, the CCPA provides for data breach notification and the right to object to the sale of personal information, as well as the right to know when data are transferred to or shared with third parties and to opt out of most data sharing. Once again, the problematic issue of determining when data are personal data and thus covered under the law remains open to interpretation by both by technologists and in courts.

HIPAA. The U.S. Health Insurance Portability and Accountability Act (HIPAA) governs the use of most medical and healthcare data in the United States. HIPAA provides a list of enumerated categories of "protected health information" (PHI) and a list of "covered entities" which must follow the rules, such as hospitals, insurance companies, and medical providers. The U.S. Department of Health and Human Services has created and administers the enforcement of a detailed HIPAA Security Rule, which defines exactly what data practices are and are not acceptable under the law. Broadly, however, HIPAA requires that patients give consent or receive notice for many uses of their data and that covered entities not share PHI without consent or to unauthorized other entities (covered or not).

The U.S. Federal Trade Commission. Another twin pair of privacy policy tools in the U.S. landscape is are the unfairness and deceptive practice doctrines of Sect. 5 of the FTC Act. While not a privacy law per se, the unfairness and deception doctrines have become a major part of the US privacy policy landscape by policing behavior in the marketplace that is detrimental to consumers' privacy interests [17]. These flexible pieces of policy can be applied to many different situations, entities, and technologies, as the law covers any practices "affecting commerce". Under Sect. 5, a business practice is deceptive if there exists a material representation, omission, or practice that is likely to mislead consumers acting reasonably under the circumstances [13], whereas unfairness describes practices that cause or are likely to cause substantial injury to consumers that are not outweighed by the benefits to consumers or competition and are not reasonably avoidable [14].

U.S. Sectoral Privacy Rules. Privacy regulation in the United States is highly sector-specific. In the finance industry, covering consumer credit, insurance, and banking, the Gramm-Leach-Bliley Act (GLBA) limits when a "financial institution" may disclose "nonpublic personal information" to unaffiliated third parties. GLBA also requires notice of data practices be given to customers, and the Federal Trade Commission has issued a "model privacy notice", which describes practices at a high level as well as when a consumer has the right to opt out of relevant practices; companies that follow the pattern of the model notice receive a limited safe harbor against enforcement under GLBA, leading nearly all financial institutions to give privacy disclosures in this format [7].

Other relevant U.S. laws include: educational privacy laws such as the Federal Educational Right to Privacy Act (FERPA), which limits data about students and gives rights to parents of minor students or to adult students themselves; the Children's Online Privacy Protection Act (COPPA), which requires certain additional consent be obtained from parents for children under the age of 13; the Video Privacy Protection Act (VPPA), which protects the disclosure of video rental records in nearly all cases; and more specific state laws such as the Illinois Biometric Privacy Act, which limits the use of biometric data to situations where subjects have given explicit, written consent.

Because federation of databases and cross-source data analysis has the power to reveal information which may be covered by one of these sector-specific laws, current U.S. privacy policy is somewhat unsuited to balancing meaningful protection with the development of new products and services, pointing to a need for regulatory innovation to match technological progress. This development of novel public policy approaches would benefit substantially from input by the database research community.

5   Polystores as Privacy Opportunity: A Research Agenda

We have identified a gap between traditional approaches to privacy protection in databases and the modern understanding of privacy risks, especially those based on statistical inference. By facilitating cross-referencing of data across stores and faster deployment of models, polystore technologies have the potential to extend analytical capabilities and widen this gap. At the same time, we believe that the current interest in new polystore architectures presents an opportunity to create technologies that improve privacy protection in a meaningful way.

There is a natural alignment between the goal of protecting privacy and a polystore architecture. We now understand that privacy is not a property of individual queries or even individual datastores. If we are to build any code that engages with privacy in a meaningful way, it will need the global visibility afforded by a polystore layer. As polystores enter operation, they will in turn provide a useful testbed for a range of privacy-preserving technologies

We identify three goals that make up a future-oriented research agenda for privacy in polystores. One is motivated by fair information practices and compliance with existing laws. The second and third are complementary responses to the advance of algorithms for inferring personal information.

5.1   Reconcile Legal Regimes with Algorithmic Capabilities

Our first research goal is motivated by the difficulty of mapping concepts from law onto the techniques of computer science. New privacy regulations like GDPR and the CCPA have created considerable uncertainty for companies, which have incurred significant expenditures in the hopes of being compliant without necessarily achieving confidence in their fidelity to legal requirements [20]. The meanings of many legal provisions are still being tested in courts, and may yet evolve in response to changing technologies. At the core of this issue are the very different languages used by the legal and computer science communities. Legal concepts like "singling out" are difficult to identify in technical architecture, and technical obstacles may conflict with the meaning anticipated in law [6].

Even more fundamentally, privacy itself is an essential contested concept [27], and this contestation often leads to difficulties in articulating exactly what needs to be protected.[2]

Whether legal requirements can or should be formalized, and whether such formalizations are better conceptualized as necessary (as in Cohen and Nissim [6]) or sufficient (as in Nissim et al. [34]) conditions that approximate legal requirements is an inherently contextual question, based on the application scenario and the particular law at issue. Computer scientists often attempt to separate "policy" from "mechanism" in abstractions and subsequently assume that policy is given and the job of a mechanism is to ensure fidelity to that policy. However, such an approach is impoverished in the many important situations where acceptable outcomes and unacceptable outcomes are difficult to separate *ex ante* but must instead be established via *oversight and review* [22].

Laws are often specified in terms of flexible standards or general principles, which are applicable in many contexts and at different levels of abstraction, rather than actionable rules [15]. Because standards and principles are evaluated according to the balancing of countervailing concerns and may hinge on vague concepts such as standards of "reasonableness", they are generally not amenable to encoding as system requirements. Legal requirements are rarely, if ever, specific enough to be formalizable directly in code.

To address this gap, we foresee the need for interdisciplinary research teams, rooted in both technology and law. Such teams will be well positioned to understand the interface between computer systems and legal requirements, designing guarantees that support legal needs or compliance goals by providing relevant information or establishing key properties that can be consumed by the non-software processes of litigation, assessment, or other oversight rather than attempting to guarantee consistency with the law up front. For example, while it may be difficult to establish up front to what extent the use of sensitive classes of data (e.g., gender, race, political affiliations, or correlates of such attributes) constitutes illegal discrimination, systems can maintain query logs that aggregate estimates of how influential such categories have been based on models of the population in a database [1,8]. To match legal language to the capabilities of polystores will require explicit collaboration with legal scholars, who can interpret not only what laws are relevant and what these laws require, but how best to support their actual operationalization in real systems.

Interesting open questions in this area, prompted by the existing policy landscape include: Prompted by deletion rights in GDPR and CCPA and by the "right to be forgotten" in the GDPR, if a system can undo deletions, for example by restoring from a crash log or by losing deletion lists for write-only or write-mostly backing stores (e.g., tape libraries), when can data be safely considered deleted? If we delete an individual's data from a database, what about downstream uses of those data - can we track what computations or models derived from these data now require updating? Do machine learning models based on deleted data fall under these legal erasure rights? (The last of these is largely a

---

[2] Frameworks have been proposed to grapple with the multi-dimensional nature of privacy. See Mulligan et. al.'s *privacy analytic.* [27].

legal question, but the database community must design in light of its uncertain answer.) Prompted by legal regimes that protect the use of sensitive data for significant computations (e.g., the GDPR) or which outlaw discrimination (several laws in many jurisdictions), must we carefully track the storage and use of data which can be used to make sensitive inferences, such as race, color, national origin, gender, religion, age, sexual activity and orientation, disability or health status, political affiliation, or genetic information? Additionally, prompted by subject access and correction rights in the GDPR, the CCPA, and sectoral laws in the US including HIPAA, FCRA, and ECOA, database systems should be prepared to answer queries that return all data about a particular individual and which allow these data to be corrected or deleted. Questions around schemata and workload support for such rights are important in practice.

5.2   Develop Accountability Mechanisms for Privacy Protection

Traditional privacy defenses, including access control, anonymization, as well as differentially private systems, can be viewed as preventative mechanisms. Like a fence or a moat, they are designed to foreclose the possibility of a privacy breach in advance, without the need for any active steps on the part of a system owner. Unfortunately, access control and anonymization are insufficient to counter modern attacks, and differentially private solutions may not be available for the vast majority of the computations that a typical company performs on data. The alternative to prevention, to borrow a term from the security literature, is accountability. An accountability system can be seen instead as akin to an alarm, a security camera, or a dye pack or ink tag: its purpose is not to prevent all privacy breaches in advance, but rather to make breaches detectable and attributable to individuals. Given the limitations of preventative systems, further research into accountability systems will be needed to provide privacy protection for many uses of databases in the future.

At its core, an accountability system for privacy needs the ability to measure the risk to individuals that arises from a given pattern of access. Such techniques can be used to monitor the overall level of protection for users, to flag suspicious query behavior, and to support systems of deterrence for insiders. For sequences of queries that pose unusual privacy risks to individuals, such measures could trigger automatic suppression of results, identify situations which require auditing or review, or assist firms in compliance efforts.

In certain cases, it may be appropriate to apply formal methods from differential privacy to measure risk in an accountability system. However, such methods are based on worst-case analysis and would lead to a conclusion of infinite privacy loss for many common database operations. To provide useful insight for these cases, new measurement techniques are required, which provide finite results in most cases, and are responsive to common human patterns of access that threaten privacy. Because such techniques will be based on a adversary model with limited capabilities, we will refer to them as *privacy heuristics*.

It is important to stress that privacy heuristics, by their nature, are not a perfect defense against the leaking of personal information. There is no limit to how clever a determined attacker may be in obfuscating an attempt to gain private information. Moreover, a higher standard of protection, including differential privacy, should be used for any output that is shared with the public. However, we believe that privacy heuristics have an important role to play in mitigating risks. It should be possible to recognize common patterns of behavior with high risks to individual privacy. Even in the case of a deliberate attack that aims to uncover an individual's secret, it may be possible to increase the cost to the attacker, or the probability of being discovered.

Future work on accountability systems for privacy can draw on diverse fields of study. New heuristics may be inspired by concepts from law, such as the GDPR's notion of "singling out." They may be informed by empirical studies of past privacy breaches, and responsive to particularly sensitive types of information. Search algorithms can be developed to detect when individual information can be extracted by differencing outputs across multiple queries or multiple islands. Finally, techniques from machine learning can be leveraged to recognize query patterns when an adversary deliberately obfuscates an attempt to gain private information. Taken together, we believe that these efforts can yield broad advances in how personal information is handled by firms and governments.

5.3   Incorporate Formal Privacy Techniques into Private Islands

As firms and governments seek to extract value from databases, they often encounter use cases for which informal protections based on accountability systems are insufficient. For some companies, it may be that sensitive data is accessed by too many employees to maintain a reasonable standard of accountability. At times, it may be necessary to present the results of an analysis to the public or to share data with outside collaborators.

To enable applications like these, we envision an effort to incorporate techniques from differential privacy into polystore systems. We note that the polystore layer is an appropriate place to deploy formally private algorithms, since it can maintain a view of what data is associated with individual units across various datastores. Algorithms can be naturally organized into formally private islands that accept a limited range of commands, and inject randomness into all output before it is returned to the user. To accommodate the possibility of multiple private islands, a centralized privacy accountant is required to maintain a privacy budget and allocate it across islands, users, and queries. This accountant can be based on the ϵ of differential privacy, but also on alternative measures rooted in information theory or statistical inference.

The differential privacy literature contains a number of algorithms that can be immediately deployed in formally private islands. One strand of research concerns formally private algorithms that are appropriate for relational databases. This vein includes the PINQ [25] system, which provides analyst with a limited "SQL-like" language, as well as the system used by Uber for internal data analytics [19]. Private SQL has also been explored within federated database environments. Shrinkwrap is a private data federation that allows users of a system to have a differentially private view of other user's data that is a robust against computationally bounded adversaries [3]. When deploying formally private systems, care must be taken so that practical constraints of computing do not interfere with the theoretical privacy guarantees. For example, floating point representations can lead to privacy losses [26].

Another active area of differential privacy research concerns private implementations of machine learning algorithms. For algorithms that rely on stochastic gradient descent, a "bolt-on" implementation of differentially private gradient descent has been designed specifically to scale well for modern analytics systems [42]. For more general machine learning tasks, differentially private models can be constructed using the PATE framework [35]. Within federated systems, research is underway on the development of private federated learning methods that aim to construct machine learning models without specifically requiring individual user's data at runtime in a centralized location [4,38].

These existing solutions provide an excellent starting point for incorporating formal privacy standards and techniques into polystore systems. The intersection of these fields suggests a number of directions for possible future research. For one thing, work is needed to shed light on the proper design of a privacy accountant. The accountant bears the central task of allocating privacy budgets across individuals and across queries. Significant gains can be found by performing this role intelligently, directing privacy budget to important queries that require greater accuracy. In another direction, an advanced privacy accountant may recognize when queries are similar across different islands, and utilize shared randomness to save on privacy budget. Finally, work is needed on the design of interfaces that enable analysts to consider the privacy implications of their work and adjust their workflows to balance utility with privacy risk. This last direction would benefit from collaborations between database experts, differential privacy practitioners, and researchers in human-computer interaction.

Acknowledgements. The work of authors Kroll and Kohli was supported in part by the National Security Agency (NSA). Any opinions, findings, and conclusions or recommendations expressed in this material are those of the authors and do not necessarily reflect the views of the NSA. Kroll was also supported by the Berkeley Center for Law and Technology at the University of California, Berkeley Law School. Author Laskowski was supported by the Center for Long Term Cybersecurity at the University of California, Berkeley.

References

1. Albarghouthi, A., D'Antoni, L., Drews, S., Nori, A.: Fairness as a program property. arXiv preprint arXiv:1610.06067 (2016)
2. Anderson, R.: Security Engineering. Wiley, New York (2008)
3. Bater, J., He, X., Ehrich, W., Machanavajjhala, A., Rogers, J.: Shrinkwrap: efficient SQL query processing in differentially private data federations. Proc. VLDB Endowment **12**(3), 307–320 (2018)
4. Bhowmick, A., Duchi, J., Freudiger, J., Kapoor, G., Rogers, R.: Protection against reconstruction and its applications in private federated learning. arXiv preprint arXiv:1812.00984 (2018)

5. Bruening, P.J., Waterman, K.K.: Data tagging for new information governance models. IEEE Secur. Priv. **8**(5), 64–68 (2010)
6. Cohen, A., Nissim, K.: Towards formalizing the GDPR notion of singling out. arXiv preprint arXiv:1904.06009 (2019)
7. Cranor, L.F., Idouchi, K., Leon, P.G., Sleeper, M., Ur, B.: Are they actually any different? Comparing thousands of financial institutions' privacy practices. In: Proceedings of the WEIS, vol. 13 (2013)
8. Datta, A., Sen, S., Zick, Y.: Algorithmic transparency via quantitative input influence: theory and experiments with learning systems. In: IEEE Symposium on Security and Privacy (SP), pp. 598–617. IEEE (2016)
9. Duggan, J., et al.: The BigDAWG polystore system. ACM Sigmod Rec. **44**(2), 11–16 (2015)
10. Dwork, C., Kenthapadi, K., McSherry, F., Mironov, I., Naor, M.: Our data, ourselves: privacy via distributed noise generation. In: Vaudenay, S. (ed.) EUROCRYPT 2006. LNCS, vol. 4004, pp. 486–503. Springer, Heidelberg (2006). https://doi.org/10.1007/11761679_29
11. Dwork, C., McSherry, F., Nissim, K., Smith, A.: Calibrating noise to sensitivity in private data analysis. In: Halevi, S., Rabin, T. (eds.) TCC 2006. LNCS, vol. 3876, pp. 265–284. Springer, Heidelberg (2006). https://doi.org/10.1007/11681878_14
12. Dwork, C., Rothblum, G.N., Vadhan, S.: Boosting and differential privacy. In: 51st Annual Symposium on Foundations of Computer Science, pp. 51–60. IEEE (2010)
13. Federal Trade Commission: FTC Policy Statement on Deception. 103 F.T.C. 110, 174 (1984). https://www.ftc.gov/public-statements/1983/10/ftc-policy-statement-deception
14. Federal Trade Commission: FTC Policy Statement on Unfairness. 104 F.T.C. 949, 1070 (1984). https://www.ftc.gov/public-statements/1980/12/ftc-policy-statement-unfairness
15. Feigenbaum, J., Weitzner, D.J.: On the incommensurability of laws and technical mechanisms: or, what cryptography can't do. In: Matyáš, V., Švenda, P., Stajano, F., Christianson, B., Anderson, J. (eds.) Security Protocols 2018. LNCS, vol. 11286, pp. 266–279. Springer, Cham (2018). https://doi.org/10.1007/978-3-030-03251-7_31
16. Gellman, R.: Fair information practices: a basic history. SSRN 2415020 (2017)
17. Hoofnagle, C.J.: Federal Trade Commission Privacy Law and Policy. Cambridge University Press, Cambridge (2016)
18. Hsu, J., et al.: Differential privacy: an economic method for choosing epsilon. In: 27th Computer Security Foundations Symposium, pp. 398–410. IEEE (2014)
19. Johnson, N., Near, J.P., Song, D.: Towards practical differential privacy for SQL queries. Proc. VLDB Endowment **11**(5), 526–539 (2018)
20. Kamarinou, D., Millard, C., Oldani, I.: Compliance as a service. Queen Mary School of Law Legal Studies Research Paper, No. 287/2018 (2018)
21. Kohli, N., Laskowski, P.: Epsilon voting: mechanism design for parameter selection in differential privacy. In: IEEE Symposium on Privacy-Aware Computing (PAC), pp. 19–30. IEEE (2018)
22. Kroll, J.A., et al.: Accountable algorithms. Univ. PA. Law Rev. **165**(3), 633–705 (2017)
23. Lee, J., Clifton, C.: How much is enough? Choosing ε for differential privacy. In: Lai, X., Zhou, J., Li, H. (eds.) ISC 2011. LNCS, vol. 7001, pp. 325–340. Springer, Heidelberg (2011). https://doi.org/10.1007/978-3-642-24861-0_22

24. Machanavajjhala, A., Gehrke, J., Kifer, D., Venkitasubramaniam, M.: L-Diversity: privacy beyond k-anonymity. In: 22nd International Conference on Data Engineering (ICDE 2006), pp. 24–24. IEEE (2006)
25. McSherry, F.D.: Privacy integrated queries: an extensible platform for privacy-preserving data analysis. In: Proceedings of the 2009 ACM SIGMOD International Conference on Management of Data, pp. 19–30. ACM (2009)
26. Mironov, I.: On significance of the least significant bits for differential privacy. In: Proceedings of the 2012 ACM Conference on Computer and Communications Security, pp. 650–661. ACM (2012)
27. Mulligan, D.K., Koopman, C., Doty, N.: Privacy is an essentially contested concept: a multi-dimensional analytic for mapping privacy. Philos. Trans. R. Soc. A 374(2083), 20160118 (2016)
28. Nabar, S.U., Kenthapadi, K., Mishra, N., Motwani, R.: A survey of query auditing techniques for data privacy. In: Aggarwal, C.C., Yu, P.S. (eds.) Privacy-Preserving Data Mining. Advances in Database Systems, vol. 34, pp. 415–431. Springer, Boston (2008). https://doi.org/10.1007/978-0-387-70992-5_17
29. Naldi, M., D'Acquisto, G.: Differential privacy: an estimation theory-based method for choosing epsilon. arXiv preprint arXiv:1510.00917 (2015)
30. Narayanan, A., Felten, E.W.: No silver bullet: de-identification still doesn't work. Manuscript (2014)
31. Narayanan, A., Huey, J., Felten, E.W.: A precautionary approach to big data privacy. In: Gutwirth, S., Leenes, R., De Hert, P. (eds.) Data Protection on the Move. LGTS, vol. 24, pp. 357–385. Springer, Dordrecht (2016). https://doi.org/10.1007/978-94-017-7376-8_13
32. Narayanan, A., Shmatikov, V.: Robust de-anonymization of large, sparse datasets. In: IEEE Security and Privacy (2008)
33. Narayanan, A., Shmatikov, V.: Myths and fallacies of personally identifiable information. Commun. ACM 53(6), 24–26 (2010)
34. Nissim, K., et al.: Bridging the gap between computer science and legal approaches to privacy. Harvard J. Law Technol. 31(2), 687–780 (2018)
35. Papernot, N., Abadi, M., Erlingsson, U., Goodfellow, I., Talwar, K.: Semi-supervised knowledge transfer for deep learning from private training data. arXiv preprint arXiv:1610.05755 (2016)
36. Selbst, A.D., Powles, J.: Meaningful information and the right to explanation. Int. Data Priv. Law 7(4), 233–242 (2017)
37. Sweeney, L.: k-anonymity: a model for protecting privacy. Int. J. Uncertainty Fuzziness Knowl. Based Syst. 10(05), 557–570 (2002)
38. Truex, S., Baracaldo, N., Anwar, A., Steinke, T., Ludwig, H., Zhang, R.: A hybrid approach to privacy-preserving federated learning. arXiv preprint arXiv:1812.03224 (2018)
39. United States Department of Health: Education, and Welfare: Secretary's Advisory Committee on Automated Personal Data Systems, Records, Computers, and the Rights of Citizens: Report. MIT Press (1973)
40. Wachter, S., Mittelstadt, B.: A right to reasonable inferences: re-thinking data protection law in the age of big data and AI. Columbia Bus. Law Rev. (2018)
41. Warren, S., Brandeis, L.: The right to privacy. Harvard Law Rev. 4, 193–220 (1890)
42. Wu, X., Li, F., Kumar, A., Chaudhuri, K., Jha, S., Naughton, J.: Bolt-on differential privacy for scalable stochastic gradient descent-based analytics. In: Proceedings of the 2017 ACM International Conference on Management of Data, pp. 1307–1322. ACM (2017)

Analyzing GDPR Compliance Through the Lens of Privacy Policy

Jayashree Mohan[1]($\boxtimes$), Melissa Wasserman[2], and Vijay Chidambaram[1,3]

[1] Department of Computer Science, University of Texas at Austin, Austin, USA
jaya@cs.utexas.edu
[2] School of Law, University of Texas at Austin, Austin, USA
[3] VMWare Research, Palo Alto, USA

Abstract. With the arrival of the European Union's General Data Protection Regulation (GDPR), several companies are making significant changes to their systems to achieve compliance. The changes range from modifying privacy policies to redesigning systems which process personal data. Privacy policy is the main medium of information dissemination between the data controller and the users. This work analyzes the privacy policies of large-scaled cloud services which seek to be GDPR compliant. We show that many services that claim compliance today do not have clear and concise privacy policies. We identify several points in the privacy policies which potentially indicate non-compliance; we term these *GDPR dark patterns*. We identify GDPR dark patterns in ten large-scale cloud services. Based on our analysis, we propose seven best practices for crafting GDPR privacy policies.

Keywords: GDPR · Privacy · Privacy policy · Storage

1 Introduction

Security, privacy, and protection of personal data have become complex and absolutely critical in the Internet era. Large scale cloud infrastructures like Facebook have focused on scalability as one of the primary goals (as of 2019, there are 2.37 billion monthly active users on facebook [12]), leaving security and privacy on the backseat. This is evident from the gravity of personal data breaches reported over the last decade. For instance, the number of significant data breaches at U.S. businesses, government agencies, and other organizations was over 1,300 in 2018, as compared to fewer than 500, ten years ago [4]. The magnitude of impact of such breaches is huge; for example, the Equifax breach [22] compromised the financial information of ~145 million consumers. In response to the alarming rise in the number of data breaches, the European Union (EU) adopted a comprehensive privacy regulation called the General Data Protection Regulation (GDPR) [29].

At the core of GDPR is a new set of rules and regulations, aimed at providing the citizens of the EU, more control over their personal data. Any company or organization operational in the EU and dealing with the personal data of EU citizens is legally bound by the laws laid by GDPR. GDPR-compliant services must ensure that personal data is collected legally for a specific purpose, and are

© Springer Nature Switzerland AG 2019
V. Gadepally et al. (Eds.): DMAH 2019/Poly 2019, LNCS 11721, pp. 82–95, 2019.
https://doi.org/10.1007/978-3-030-33752-0_6

obliged to protect it from misuse and exploitation; failure to do so, might result in hefty penalties for the company. As of Jan 2019, 91 reported fines have been imposed under the new GDPR regime [18]. The magnitude of fine imposed varies by the severity of non-compliance. For instance, in Germany, a €20,000 fine was imposed on a company whose failure to hash employee passwords resulted in a security breach. Whereas the French data protection authority, fined Google €50 million for not precisely disclosing how user data is collected across its services to present personalized advertisements. A series of lawsuits and fines have now forced companies to take a more *privacy-focused* future for their services [10].

While our prior work examined how GDPR affects the design and operation of Internet companies [31] and its impact on storage systems [30], this work focuses on a third dimension : privacy policies (PP). A privacy policy is a statement or a legal document (in privacy law) that states ways in which a party gathers, uses, discloses, and manages a customer or client's data [14]. The key to achieving transparency, one of the six fundamental data protection principles laid out by GDPR, is a clear and concise PP that informs the users how their data is collected, processed, and controlled. We analyze the privacy policies of ten large-scale cloud services that are operational in the EU and identify themselves as GDPR-compliant; we identify several *GDPR dark patterns*, points in the PP that could potentially lead to non-compliance with GDPR. Some of the patterns we identify are clear-cut non-compliance (e.g., not providing details about the Data Protection Officer), while others lie in grey areas and are up for interpretation. However, based on the prior history of fines levied on charges of GDPR non-compliance [18], we believe there is a strong chance that all identified dark patterns may lead to charges.

Our analysis reveals that most PP are not clear and concise, sometimes exploiting the vague technical specifications of GDPR to their benefit. For instance, Bloomberg, a software tech company states in its PP that *"Bloomberg may also disclose your personal information to unaffiliated third parties if we believe in good faith that such disclosure is necessary [...]"*, with no mention of who the third-parties are, and how to object to such disclosure and processing. Furthermore, we identify several dark patterns in the PP that indicate potential non-compliance with GDPR. First, many services exhibit all-or-none behaviors with respect to user controls over data, oftentimes requiring withdrawal from the service to enable deletion of any information. Second, most controllers bundle the purposes for data collection and processing amongst various entities. They collect multiple categories of user data, each on a different platform and state a bunch of purposes for which they, or their Affiliates could use this data. We believe this is in contradiction to GDPRs goals of attaching a purpose to every piece of collected personal information.

Based on our study, we propose seven policy recommendations that a GDPR-compliant company should address in their PP. The proposed policy considerations correspond to data collection, their purpose, the lawfulness of processing them, etc. We accompany each consideration with the GDPR article that necessitates it and where applicable, provide an example of violation of this policy by one of the systems under our study.

Our analysis is not without limitations. First, while we studied a wide category of cloud-services ranging from social media to education, our study is not exhaustive; we do not analyze categories like healthcare, entertainment, or government services. Second, we do not claim to identify all dark patterns in each PP we analyzed. Despite these limitations, our study contributes useful analyses of privacy policies and guidelines for crafting GDPR-compliant privacy policies.

2 GDPR and Privacy Policy

GDPR. The General Data Protection Regulation (GDPR) came into effect on May 25th 2018 as the legal framework that sets guidelines for the collection and processing of personal information of people in the European Union (EU) [29]. The primary goal of GDPR is to ensure protection of personal data by vesting the control over data in the users themselves. Therefore, the *data subject* (the person whose personal data is collected) has the power to demand companies to reveal what information they hold about the user, object to processing his data, or request to delete his data held by the company. GDPR puts forth several laws that a data collector and processor must abide by; such entities are classified either as *data controller*, the entity that collects and uses personal data, or as a *data processor*, the entity that processes personal data on behalf of a data controller, the regulations may vary for the two entities.

Key Policies of GDPR. The central focus of GDPR is to provide the data subjects extensive control over their personal data collected by the controllers. Companies that wish to stay GDPR-compliant must take careful measures to ensure protection of user data by implementing state-of-the-art techniques like pseudonymization and encryption. They should also provide the data subjects with ways to retrieve, delete, and raise objections to the use of any information pertaining to them. Additionally, the companies should appoint supervisory authorities like the Data Protection Officer (DPO) to oversee the company's data protection strategies and must notify data breaches within 72 h of first becoming aware of it.

Impact of GDPR. Several services shut down completely, while others blocked access to the users in the European Union(EU) in response to GDPR. For instance, the need for infrastructural changes led to the downfall of several multiplayer games in the EU, including Uber Entertainment's Super Monday Night Combat and Gravity Interactive's Ragnarok Online [16], whereas the changes around user consent for data processing resulted in the shut down of advertising companies like Drawbridge [8]. Failure to comply to GDPR can result in hefty fines; up to 4% of the annual global turnover of the company. 91 reported fines have been imposed under the new GDPR regime as of January 2019, with charges as high as €50 million [18].

GDPR and Privacy Policy. A privacy policy is a statement or a legal document (in privacy law) that discloses the ways a party gathers, uses, discloses, and manages a customer or client's data [14,28]. It is the primary grounds for transparent data processing requirements set forth by GDPR. GDPR article 12 sets the ground for transparency, one of the six fundamental principles of GDPR. It states that any information or communication to the users must be *concise, transparent, intelligible and in an easily accessible form, using clear and plain language.* The main objective of this article is to ensure that users are aware of how their data is collected, used, and processed. Therefore, the first step towards GDPR compliance at the controllers is updating the privacy policy, which is the primary information notice board between the controller and the customer.

3   Best Practices for GDPR Compliant Privacy Policies

GDPR has six general data protection principles (transparency; purpose limitation; data minimization; accuracy; storage limitation; and confidentiality) with data protection by design and default at the core. The first step to implementing these data-protection principles is to conceptualize an accurate privacy policy at the data controller.

Privacy policy documents issued by data controllers are oftentimes overlooked by customers either because they are too lengthy and boring, or contain too many technical jargons. For instance, Microsoft's privacy policy is 56 pages of text [26], Google's privacy policy spans 27 pages of textual content [19], and Facebook's data policy document is 7 pages long [11]. A Deloitte survey of 2,000 consumers in the U.S found that 91% of people consent to legal terms and service conditions without reading them [6].

Privacy policies of GDPR-compliant systems must be specific about the sharing and distribution of user data to third- parties, with fine-grained access control rights to users. On the contrary, Apple iCloud's privacy policy reads as follows [23] : *[...] You acknowledge and agree that Apple may, without liability to you, access, use, preserve and/or disclose your Account information and Content to law enforcement authorities, government officials, and/or a third party, as Apple believes is reasonably necessary or appropriate [...]* . While this contradicts the goals of GDPR, this information is mentioned on the 11th page of a 20 page long policy document, which most customers would tend to skip.

These observations put together, emphasizes the need for a standardized privacy-policy document for GDPR-compliant systems. We translate GDPR articles into precise questions that a user must find answer to, while reading any privacy policy. An ideal privacy policy for a GDPR-complaint system should at the least, answer all of the following questions prefixed with $\mathscr{P}$. The GDPR law that corresponds to the question is prefixed with $\mathscr{G}$.

($\mathscr{P}$1): **Processing Entities.** Who collects personal information and who uses the collected information ($\mathscr{G}$5(1)B, 6, 21).

The PP of a GDPR-compliant controller must precisely state the sources of data, and with whom the collected data is shared. While many controllers vaguely state that they *"may share the data with third-parties"*, GDPR requires specifying who the third parties are, and for what purpose they would use this data.

($\mathscr{P}$2): **Data Categories.** What personally identifiable data is collected ($\mathscr{G}$14, 20)

The controller must clearly state the attributes of personal data (name, email, phone number, IP etc) being collected or at the least, categories of these attributes. All the PP we studied fairly addresses this requirement.

($\mathscr{P}$3): **Retention.** When will the collected data expire and be deleted ($\mathscr{G}$5(1)E, 13, 17)

GDPR requires that the controller attach a retention period or a basis for determining this retention period to every category of personal data collected. Such retention periods or policies must be mentioned straight up in the PP. Apple's PP for instance, does not mention how long the collected data will reside in their servers [1]. It also provides no detail on whether user data will ever be deleted after its purpose of collection is served.

($\mathscr{P}$4): **Purpose.** Why is the data being collected ($\mathscr{G}$5(1)B)

Purpose of data collection is one of the main principles of data protection in GDPR. The PP must therefore clearly state the basis for collection of each category of personal data and the legal basis for processing it. The controller should also indicate if any data is obtained from third-parties and the legal basis for processing such data.

($\mathscr{P}$5): **User Controls.** How can the user request the following
  (a) All the personal data associated with the user along with its source, purpose, TTL, the list of third-parties to which it has been shared etc ($\mathscr{G}$15)
  (b) Raise objection to the use of any attribute of their personal data ($\mathscr{G}$21)
  (c) Personal data to be deleted without any undue delay ($\mathscr{G}$17)
  (d) Personal data to be transferred to a different controller ($\mathscr{G}$20)

Not all PP explicitly state the user's rights to access and control their personal data. For instance, Uber's PP has no option to request deletion of user travel history, without having to deactivate the account.

($\mathscr{P}$6): **Data Protection.** Does the controller take measures to ensure safety and protection of data
  (a) By implementing state-of-the-art techniques such as encryption or pseudonymization ($\mathscr{G}$25, 32)
  (b) By logging all activities pertaining to user data ($\mathscr{G}$30)
  (c) By ensuring safety measures when processing outside the EU ($\mathscr{G}$3)

GDPR puts the onus of data protection by design and default on the data controller. Additionally, whenever data is processed outside of the EU, the controller should clearly state the data protection guarantees in such case. The PP must also contain the contact details of the data protection officer (DPO) or appropriate channels to request, modify, or delete their information.

($\mathscr{P}$7): **Policy Updates.** Does the controller notify users appropriately when changes are made to the privacy policy ($\mathscr{G}$14)

The transparency principle of GDPR advocates that the users must be notified and be given the chance to review and accept the new terms, whenever changes are made to the policies. On the contrary, many services simply update the date of modification in the policy document rather than taking measures to reasonably notify the users (for e.g., using email notifications).

4   GDPR Dark Patterns: A Case Study

This section presents the case study of ten large-scale cloud services that are operational in the EU. We analyze various categories of applications and services ranging from social media applications like Whatsapp and Instagram to financial institutions like Metro bank. We study the privacy policies of each of these services and identify GDPR dark patterns that could lead to potential GDPR non-compliance. Table 1 categorizes companies in the descending order of GDPR dark patterns. The discussion below is grouped by the type of commonly observed patterns.

Table 1. GDPR dark patterns. The table shows GDPR dark patterns across 10 cloud services.

Cloud Service	$\mathscr{P}1$ Processing	$\mathscr{P}2$ Data	$\mathscr{P}3$ Retention	$\mathscr{P}4$ Purpose	$\mathscr{P}5$ Controls	$\mathscr{P}6$ Protection	$\mathscr{P}7$ Updates
Bloomberg	✗	✓	✗	✓	✗	✗	✗
Onavo	✗	✓	✗	✓	✗	✗	✓
Instagram	✗	✓	✗	✓	✓	✗	✓
Uber	✗	✓	✓	✓	✗	✗	✓
edX	✓	✓	✓	✓	✗	✗	✗
Snapchat	✓	✓	✓	✓	✓	✓	✗
iCloud	✗	✓	✓	✓	✓	✓	✓
Whatsapp	✓	✓	✓	✓	✓	✓	✓
FlyBe Airlines	✓	✓	✓	✓	✓	✓	✓
Metro bank	✓	✓	✓	✓	✓	✓	✓

Unclear Data Sharing and Processing Policies. Instagram, a photo and video-sharing social networking service owned by Facebook Inc discloses user information to all its Affiliates (the Facebook group of companies), who can use the information with no specific user consent [24]. The way in which Affiliates use this data is claimed to be *"under reasonable confidentiality terms"*, which is vague. For instance, it is unclear whether a mobile number that is marked private in the Instagram account, is shared with, and used by Affiliates. This can count towards violation of purpose as the mobile number was collected primarily for account creation and cannot be used for other purposes without explicit consent. Additionally, Instagram says nothing about the user's right to object to data processing by Affiliates or third-parties. It's PP says *"Our Service Providers will be given access to your information as is **reasonably necessary** to provide the Service under reasonable confidentiality terms"*. Uber on the other hand, may provide collected information to its vendors, consultants, marketing partners, research firms, and other service providers or business partners, but does not specify how the third parties would use this information [40]. On similar grounds, iCloud's PP vaguely states that information may be shared with third-parties, but does not specify who the third-parties are, and how to opt-out or object to such sharing [23]. Similarly, Bloomberg is vague about third-party sharing and says, *"Bloomberg may also disclose your personal information to unaffiliated third parties if we believe in good faith that such disclosure is necessary [...]"* [2].

Vague Data Retention Policies. Instagram does not guarantee that user data is completely deleted from its servers when a user requests for deletion of personal information. Data can remain viewable in cached and archived pages of the service. Furthermore Instagram claims to store the user data for a *"reasonable"* amount of time for *"backup"*, after account deletion, with no justification of why it is necessary, and whether they will continue to use the backup data for processing. Other companies including Bloomberg and Onavo do not specify a retention period, vaguely specifying that *personal information is retained for as long as is necessary for the purpose for which it is collected* [2,27].

Unreasonable Ways of Notifying Updates to Privacy Policy. Changes to PP should be notified to all users in a timely manner and users must be given the chance to review and accept the updated terms. However, edX, Bloomberg, and Snapchat would simply *"label the Privacy Policy as "Revised (date)[...]. By accessing the Site after any changes have been made, you accept the modified Privacy Policy and any changes contained therein"* [2,9,33]. This is un-reasonable as it is easy to miss such notifications, and a better way of notifying users is by sending an email to review the updated policy.

Weak Data Protection Policies. GDPR $\mathcal{G}$37 requires the controller to publish contact details of the data protection officer (DPO). The privacy policies of Instagram, Facebook, Bloomberg, and edX have no reference to who the DPO is, or how to contact them. Similarly, while most cloud services assure users that their data processing will abide by the terms in the PP irrespective of the location of processing, services like Onavo take a laidback approach. It simply states that it *"may process your information, including personally identifying information, in a jurisdiction with different data protection laws than your jurisdiction"*, with nothing said about the privacy guarantees in cases of such processing. Some other services like Uber, state nothing about data protection techniques employed or international transfer policies.

No Fine-Grained Control Over User Data. The edX infrastructure does not track and index user data at every place where the user volunteers information on the site. Therefore, they claim that, *"neither edX nor Members will be able to help you locate or manage all such instances."*. Similarly, deleting user information does not apply to *"historical activity logs or archives unless and until these logs and data naturally age-off the edX system"*. It is unclear if such data continues to be processed after a user has requested to delete his information. Similarly, Uber requires the user to deactivate their account to delete personal information from the system. Moreover, if a user objects to the usage of certain personal information, *"Uber may continue to process your information notwithstanding the objection to the extent permitted under GDPR"*. It is unclear to what extent, and on what grounds, Uber can ignore the objections raised by users. While most services provide a clear overview the rights user can exercise and the ways of doing so by logging into their service, Onavo simply states, *"For assistance with exercising rights, you can contact us at support@onavo.com"*. It does not specify what kind of objections can be raised, what part of the personal information can be deleted, etc.

4.1   A Good Privacy Policy

Flybe is a British airlines whose privacy policy was by far the most precise and clear document of all the services we analyzed [15], probably because it's based in the EU. Nonetheless, the effort put by Flybe into providing all necessary information pertaining to the collection and use of customer's personal data is an indicator of its commitment to GDPR-compliance. For instance, Flybe clearly categorizes types of user information collected, along with a purpose attached to each category. While most of the services we analyzed claim to simply share information with third-parties as necessary, Flybe enumerates each of its associated third-parties, the specifics of personal data shared with them, the purpose for sharing and a link to the third-parties privacy policy. In cases where it is necessary to process user data outside of EU, Flybe ensures a similar degree of protection as in the EU. We believe that a PP as clear as the one employed by Flybe, enables users to gain a fair understanding of their data and their rights over collected data. The level of transparency and accountability demonstrated by this PP is an indicator of right practice for GDPR-compliance.

4.2   Summary

The major GDPR dark patterns we identify in large-scale cloud services can be summarized as follows.

All or Nothing. Most companies have rolled out new policies and products to comply with GDPR, but those policies don't go far enough. In particular, the way companies obtain consent for the privacy policies is by asking users to check a box in order to access services. It is a widespread practice for online services, but it forces users into an all-or-nothing choice, a violation of the GDPR's provision around particularized consent and fine-grained control over data usage. There's a lawsuit against Google and Facebook for a similar charge [3].

This behavior extends to other types of user rights that GDPR advocates. For instance, GDPR vests in the users the right to object to the use of a part or all of their personal data, or delete it. Most controllers however, take the easy approach and enable these knobs only if they user un-registers for their service. This approach is not in the right spirit of GDPR.

Handwavy About Data Protection. GDPR requires controllers to adopt internal policies and implement measures which meet in particular, the principles of data protection by design and default. However, many cloud services seem to dodge the purpose by stating that in spite of the security measures taken by them (they do not specify what particular measures are taken), the user data may be accessed, disclosed, altered, or destroyed. Whether this is non-compliance is a debatable topic, however, the intent of GDPR $\mathscr{G}$24 and $\mathscr{G}$25 is to encourage controllers to implement state-of-the-art data protection techniques.

Purpose Bundling. Most controllers bundle the purposes for data collection and processing amongst various entities. They collect multiple categories of user data, each on a different platform and state a bunch of purposes for which they, or their Affiliates could use this data. Although this might not be explicit non-compliance, it kills GDPR's notion of a purpose attached to every unit of user data collected.

Unreasonable Privacy Policy Change Notifications. Privacy policy being the binding document based on which a user consents to using a service, any changes to the policy must be notified to the user in a timely and appropriate manner. This may include sending an email to all registered users, or in case of a website, placing a notification pop-up without reading and accepting which, the user cannot browse further. However, many services we analyzed have unreasonable update policies, where in they simply update the last modified date in the privacy policy and expect the user to check back frequently.

4.3   User Experiences with Exercising GDPR Rights in the Real World

Privacy policies provide an overview of techniques and strategies employed by the company to be GDPR-compliant, including the rights users can exercise over their data. While no lawsuit can be filed against a company unless there is a proof for violation of any of the GDPR laws claimed in the PP, this section is an account of some users' attempts to exercise the rights claimed in the PP.

A user of Pokemon Go raised an objection to processing her personal data, and to stop using her personal data for marketing and promotional purposes, both of which are listed under the user's rights and choices in Pokemon Go's PP. The response from the controller however, was instructions on how to delete the user account [37]. In another incident, Carl Miller, Research Director at the Centre for the Analysis of Social Media requested an unnamed company to return all personal data they hold about him (which is a basic right GDPR provides to a data subject). However, the company simply responded that they are not the controller for the data he was asking for [39]. Adding on to this, when a user requests for personal information, the company requires him to specify what data he needs [38]. This is not in the right spirit of GDPR because, a user does not know what data a controller might have. This violates the intent of GDPR because the main idea is to give users a better idea of what data is held about them.

These real experiences of common people show that GDPR has a long way to go, to achieve its goal of providing users with knowledge and control over all their personal information collected and processed by various entities.

5 Discussion

The negative responses received by users trying to exercise their GDPR rights, and the shut down of several services in the European Union(EU) in response to GDPR, motivated us to analyze the root cause of this behavior.

One of the notable examples of companies that temporarily shut down services in the EU in response to GDPR and is back in business now, is Instapaper, a read-it-later bookmarking service owned by Pinterest. It is unclear why Instapaper had to take a break; either because it did not have sufficient details on the type of user data its parent Pinterest was receiving from it, or it needed infrastructural support to comply to GDPR's data subject access request, which allows any EU resident to request all the data collected and stored about them. Interestingly, Instapaper split from Pinterest a month after the GDPR blackout, and soon after, made an independent comeback to the EU. The notable changes in the PP of Instapaper for its relaunch is the change of third-party tools involved in their service, and more detailed instructions on how users can exercise their rights [25].

These trends reveal two critical reasons for non-compliance to GDPR. First, some companies do not have well informed policies for sharing collected data across third-parties, or rely completely on information from third-parties for their data. Second, their infrastructure does not support identifying, locating, and packaging user data in response to user queries. While the former can be resolved by ensuring careful data sharing policies, the latter requires significant reworking of backend infrastructure. Primarily, the need for infrastructural changes led to the downfall of several multiplayer games in the EU, including Uber Entertainment's Super Monday Night Combat, Gravity Interactive's Ragnarok Online and Dragon Saga and Valve's entire gaming community [16]. In this context, we identify 4 primary infrastructural changes that a backend storage system must support in order to be GDPR-complaint [30] and suggest possible solutions in each case.

5.1 Timely Deletion

Under GDPR, no personal data can be retained for an indefinite period of time. Therefore, the storage system should support mechanisms to associate time-to-live (TTL) counters for personal data, and then automatically erase them from all internal subsystems in a timely manner. GDPR allows TTL to be either a static time or a policy criterion that can be objectively evaluated.

Challenges. With all personal data possessing an expiry timestamp, we need data structures to efficiently find and delete (possibly large amounts of) data in a timely manner. However, GDPR is vague in its interpretation of deletions: it neither advocates a specific timeline for completing the deletions nor mandates any specific techniques.

Possible Solutions. Sorting data by secondary index is a well-known technique in databases. One way to efficiently allow deletion is to maintain a secondary index on TTL (or expiration time of data) like timeseries databases [13]. Addressing the second challenge requires a common ground among data controllers to set an acceptable time limit for data deletion. This is an important clause of an ideal Privacy Policy document. Thus, it remains to be seen if efforts like Google cloud's guarantee [5] to not retain customer data after 180 days of delete requests be considered compliant behavior.

5.2 Indexing via Metadata

Several articles of GDPR require efficient access to groups of data based on certain attributes. For example, collating all the files of a particular *user* to be ported to a new controller.

Challenges. Storage systems must support interfaces that efficiently allow accessing data grouped by a certain attribute. While traditional databases natively offer this ability via secondary indices, not all storage systems have efficient or configurable support for this capability. For instance, inserting data into a MySQL database with multiple indexes is almost 4× slower when compared insertion in a table with no indexes [35].

Possible Solutions. Several research in the past have explored building efficient multi-index stores. The common technique used in multi-index stores is to utilize redundancy to partition each copy of the data by a different key [32,34]. Although this approach takes a hit on the recovery time, it results in better common-case performance when compared to naive systems supporting multiple secondary indexes.

5.3 Monitoring and Logging

GDPR allows the data subject to query the usage pattern of their data. Therefore, the storage system needs an audit trail of both its internal actions and external interactions. Thus, in a strict sense, all operations whether in the data path (say, read or write) or control path (say, changes to metadata or access control) needs to be logged.

Challenges. Enabling fine grained logging results in significant performance overheads (for instance, Redis incurs 20× overhead [30]), because every data and control path operation should be synchronously persisted.

Possible Solutions. One way to tackle this problem is to use fast non-volatile memory devices like 3D Xpoint to store logs. Efficient auditing may also be achieved through the use of eidetic systems. For example, Arnold [7] is able to remember past state with only 8% overhead. Finally, the amount of data logged may be optimized by tracking at the application level instead of the fine-grained low level audit trails. While this might be sufficient to satisfy most user queries, it does not guarantee strict compliance.

5.4   Access Control and Encryption

As GDPR aims to limit access to personal data to only permitted entities for established purposes and for a predefined duration of time, the storage system must support fine-grained and dynamic access control.

Challenges. Every piece of user data can have its own access control list (ACL). For instance, the user can provide Facebook access to his list of liked pages to be used by the recommendation engine, while deny access to his contact number to any application inside of Facebook. Additionally, users can modify ACLs at any point in time and GDPR is not specific if all previously accessed data for which access is revoked, must be immediately marked for deletion. Therefore, applications must validate access rights every time they access user data, because ACL might have changed between two accesses.

Possible Solutions. One way of providing fine grained access control is to deploy a trusted server that is queried for access rights before granting right to data [17]. The main downside is that, it allows easy security breaches by simply compromising this server. A more effective way is to break down user data and encrypt each attribute using a different public key. Applications that need to access a set of attributes of user data should posses the right private keys. This approach is termed Key-Policy Attribute-Based Encryption (KP-ABE) [20]. Whenever the ACL for a user data changes, the attributes pertaining to this data must be re-encrypted. Assuming that changes in access controls are infrequent, the cost of re-encryption will be minimal. While this approach addresses the issue of fine grained access control, more thought needs to go into reducing the overhead of data encryption and decryption during processing. One approach to reduce the cost of data decryption during processing is to explore techniques that allow processing queries directly over encrypted data, avoiding the need for decryption in the common case [21,36].

6   Conclusion

We analyze the privacy policies of ten large-scale cloud services, identifying dark patterns that could potentially result in GDPR non-compliance. While our study shows that many PP are far from clear, we also provide real world examples to show that exercising user rights claimed in PP is not an easy task. Additionally, we propose seven recommendations that a PP should address, to be close to GDPR-compliance.

With the growing relevance of privacy regulations around the world, we expect this paper to trigger interesting conversations around the need for clear and concrete GDPR-compliant privacy policies. We are keen to extend our effort to engage the storage community in addressing the research challenges in alleviating the identified GDPR dark patterns, by building better infrastructural support where necessary.

References

1. Apple privacy policy. www.apple.com/legal/privacy/en-ww/. Accessed May 2019
2. Bloomberg privacy policy. www.bloomberg.com/notices/privacy/. Accessed May 2019
3. Brandom, R.: Facebook and Google hit with $8.8 billion in lawsuits on day one of GDPR. The Verge, 25 May 2018
4. Data breaches. www.marketwatch.com/story/how-the-number-of-data-breaches-is-soaring-in-one-chart-2018-02-26. Accessed May 2019
5. Data Deletion on Google Cloud Platform. https://cloud.google.com/security/deletion/. Accessed May 2019
6. Deloitte privacy survey. www.businessinsider.com/deloitte-study-91-percent-agree-terms-of-service-without-reading-2017-11. Accessed May 2019
7. Devecsery, D., Chow, M., Dou, X., Flinn, J., Chen, P.M.: Eidetic systems. In: USENIX OSDI (2014)
8. Drawbridge shutdown. https://adexchanger.com/mobile/drawbridge-exits-media-business-europe-gdpr-storms-castle/. Accessed May 2019
9. edX privacy policy. www.edx.org/edx-privacy-policy. Accessed May 2019
10. Facebook privacy future. www.facebook.com/notes/mark-zuckerberg/a-privacy-focused-vision-for-social-networking/10156700570096634/. Accessed May 2019
11. Facebook data privacy policy. www.facebook.com/policy.php. Accessed May 2019
12. Facebook users. https://s21.q4cdn.com/399680738/files/doc_financials/2019/Q1/Q1-2019-Earnings-Presentation.pdf. Accessed May 2019
13. Faloutsos, C., Ranganathan, M., Manolopoulos, Y.: Fast subsequence matching in time-series databases, vol. 23. ACM (1994)
14. Flavián, C., Guinalíu, M.: Consumer trust, perceived security and privacy policy: three basic elements of loyalty to a web site. Ind. Manag. Data Syst. **106**(5), 601–620 (2006)
15. Flybe privacy policy. https://www.flybe.com/privacy-policy. Accessed May 2019
16. Gaming shutdown. https://www.judiciary.senate.gov/imo/media/doc/Layton%20Testimony1.pdf. Accessed May 2019
17. Gavriloaie, R., Nejdl, W., Olmedilla, D., Seamons, K.E., Winslett, M.: No registration needed: how to use declarative policies and negotiation to access sensitive resources on the semantic web. In: Bussler, C.J., Davies, J., Fensel, D., Studer, R. (eds.) ESWS 2004. LNCS, vol. 3053, pp. 342–356. Springer, Heidelberg (2004). https://doi.org/10.1007/978-3-540-25956-5_24
18. GDPR fines. https://www.dlapiper.com/en/uk/insights/publications/2019/01/gdpr-data-breach-survey/. Accessed May 2019
19. Google privacy policy. www.gstatic.com/policies/privacy/pdf/20190122/f3294e95/google_privacy_policy_en.pdf. Accessed May 2019
20. Goyal, V., Pandey, O., Sahai, A., Waters, B.: Attribute-based encryption for fine-grained access control of encrypted data. In: Proceedings of the 13th ACM conference on Computer and communications security, pp. 89–98. ACM (2006)
21. Hacigümüş, H., Iyer, B., Li, C., Mehrotra, S.: Executing SQL over encrypted data in the database-service-provider model. In: Proceedings of the 2002 ACM SIGMOD International Conference on Management of Data, pp. 216–227. ACM (2002)
22. Haselton, T.: Credit reporting firm Equifax says data breach could potentially affect 143 million US consumers. CNBC, 7 September 2017
23. iCloud privacy policy. https://www.apple.com/uk/legal/internet-services/icloud/en/terms.html. Accessed May 2019

24. Instagram privacy policy. https://help.instagram.com/402411646841720. Accessed May 2019
25. Instapaper privacy policy. https://github.com/Instapaper/privacy/commit/05db72422c65bb57b77351ee0a91916a8f266964. Accessed May 2019
26. Microsoft privacy policy. https://privacy.microsoft.com/en-us/privacystatement?PrintView=true. Accessed May 2019
27. Onavo privacy policy. https://www.onavo.com/privacy_policy. Accessed May 2019
28. Privacy policy. https://en.wikipedia.org/wiki/Privacy_policy. Accessed May 2019
29. General Data Protection Regulation: Regulation (EU) 2016/679 of the European Parliament and of the Council of 27 April 2016 on the protection of natural persons with regard to the processing of personal data and on the free movement of such data, and repealing Directive 95/46. Official Journal of the European Union, vol. 59, no. 1–88 (2016)
30. Shah, A., Banakar, V., Shastri, S., Wasserman, M., Chidambaram, V.: Analyzing the impact of GDPR on storage systems. In: 11th USENIX Workshop on Hot Topics in Storage and File Systems (HotStorage 2019), Renton, WA. USENIX Association (2019). http://usenix.org/conference/hotstorage19/presentation/banakar
31. Shastri, S., Wasserman, M., Chidambaram, V.: The Seven Sins of personal-data processing systems under GDPR. In: USENIX HotCloud (2019)
32. Sivathanu, M., et al.: INSTalytics: cluster filesystem co-design for big-data analytics. In: 17th USENIX Conference on File and Storage Technologies (FAST 2019), pp. 235–248 (2019)
33. Snapchat privacy policy. https://www.snap.com/en-US/privacy/privacy-policy/. Accessed May 2019
34. Tai, A., Wei, M., Freedman, M.J., Abraham, I., Malkhi, D.: Replex: a scalable, highly available multi-index data store. In: 2016 USENIX Annual Technical Conference (USENIX ATC 2016), pp. 337–350 (2016)
35. The Performance Impact of Adding MySQL Indexes. https://logicalread.com/impact-of-adding-mysql-indexes-mc12/#.XOMPrKZ7lPM. Accessed May 2019
36. Tu, S., Kaashoek, M.F., Madden, S., Zeldovich, N.: Processing analytical queries over encrypted data. Proc. VLDB Endowment **6**, 289–300 (2013)
37. Twitter - Pokemon GO information. https://twitter.com/swipp_it/status/1131410732292169728. Accessed May 2019
38. Twitter - requesting user information requires specification. https://twitter.com/carljackmiller/status/1117379517394432002. Accessed May 2019
39. Twitter - user information. https://twitter.com/carljackmiller/status/1127525870770577409. Accessed May 2019
40. Uber privacy policy. https://privacy.uber.com/policy/. Accessed May 2019

Privacy Changes Everything

Jennie Rogers[1(✉)], Johes Bater[1], Xi He[2], Ashwin Machanavajjhala[3],
Madhav Suresh[1], and Xiao Wang[1]

[1] Northwestern University, Evanston, USA
`jennie@northwestern.edu`
[2] University of Waterloo, Waterloo, Canada
[3] Duke University, Durham, USA

Abstract. We are storing and querying datasets with the private information of individuals at an unprecedented scale in settings ranging from IoT devices in smart homes to mining enormous collections of click trails for targeted advertising. Here, the *privacy* of the people described in these datasets is usually addressed as an afterthought, engineered on top of a DBMS optimized for performance. At best, these systems support *security* or managing access to sensitive data. This status quo has brought us a plethora of data breaches in the news. In response, governments are stepping in to enact privacy regulations such as the EU's GDPR. We posit that there is an urgent need for *trustworthy database system* that offer end-to-end privacy guarantees for their records with user interfaces that closely resemble that of a relational database. As we shall see, these guarantees inform everything in the database's design from how we store data to what query results we make available to untrusted clients.

In this position paper we first define trustworthy database systems and put their research challenges in the context of relevant tools and techniques from the security community. We then use this backdrop to walk through the "life of a query" in a trustworthy database system. We start with the query parsing and follow the query's path as the system plans, optimizes, and executes it. We highlight how we will need to rethink each step to make it efficient, robust, and usable for database clients.

1 Introduction

Now that storage is inexpensive, organizations collect data on practically all aspects of life, with much of it pertaining to individuals using their systems. They do so with little transparency regarding how they will analyze, share, or protect these records from prying eyes. Instead, their systems are optimized for performance. The way mainstream databases protect their contents today is haphazard at best. Beyond straightforward measures – like passwords, role-based access control, and encrypted storage – they offer scant protection for private data after the engine grants access to it and no commercial system takes into account the privacy of individuals in the database. As such, we see data

V. Gadepally et al. (Eds.): DMAH 2019/Poly 2019, LNCS 11721, pp. 96–111, 2019.
https://doi.org/10.1007/978-3-030-33752-0_7

breaches in the news with astounding regularity. We are already seeing governments step in to enact new laws in response to this, including the EU's GDPR and California's privacy act, the CCPA. The time has come for us to think more systematically about how to be good stewards of this growing resource. As database researchers and practitioners, we face a new challenge: how to keep the data entrusted to our systems private.

Trustworthy Database Systems offer end-to-end privacy guarantees with a user interface that closely resembles that of a relational database. They are designed to protect their contents as a first principle – informing how we store private data, run queries over it, and manage their outputs. In addition, they must be as easy to use as possible to make privacy-preserving techniques accessible to existing database administrators and clients. We need to reimagine these systems with privacy as a first-class citizen in their design. As we shall see, this calls for dramatic changes to almost every aspect of a DBMS's operations.

Privacy Changes Everything. We investigate this thesis by stepping through the life-cycle of a query with two use cases. First, we look at protecting the privacy of input data from an untrusted client who may view only approximate results from their queries. Second, we examine a scenario where private data owners outsource their operations – storage and querying – to an untrusted cloud service provider. Here, the data owners carefully choose what information, if any, about their secret records will be revealed to the service provider. The data owners may alone may view their query results.

In the private inputs setting, data owners run queries from untrusted clients. Here, the clients' query results must be sufficiently noisy such that they cannot reconstruct the data owner's private records even after repeatedly querying the engine. Differential privacy [16] addresses this by using a mechanism to introduce carefully controlled levels of noise into the query results. To date, most of the results in this space – with the exception of [28,29] – have been theoretical in nature. As we shall see integrating differential privacy into the query processing pipeline, rather than noising query results after evaluating them in a regular DBMS, may produce more precise results for the client [6,28,29].

In the cloud setting, an untrusted service provider offers storage and query processing of private data to its owner. Here, we need to ensure that data is encrypted at rest and that query processing is privacy-preserving and oblivious. A query execution is *oblivious* if its observable transcript – the movement of the program counter, accesses of the memory, network traffic – is independent of the query's inputs. *Secure computation* [57] supports these guarantees by constructing cryptographic protocols that simulate running the query on a hypothetical trusted third party by passing encrypted messages among the data owners. For settings where the database's schema as a security policy with public and private columns or tables, we may analyze these queries and create a hybrid execution plan that partitions a given query into subplans that may be executed in the clear or in secure computation [5,50,60]. Since secure computation has an overhead that is typically 1,000X or more slower than executing the same program in the clear, even incremental changes of this kind are a big performance win.

The security community has developed a myriad of techniques [13,23,31,53] for protecting private data in these settings and more. To date these solutions have been largely piece-wise, and they don't address the end-to-end workflow of a DBMS query execution. Moreover, the current offerings typically require multiple PhD-level specialists to deploy them and most of their applications are hard-coded, i.e., they support only a handful of "benchmark" queries and they do not accept ad-hoc queries written in SQL or any other well-known query language. There has been limited work on how to build end-to-end systems with provable privacy guarantees starting from how they store and query private records and concluding by perturbing their query outputs enough to prevent an attacker from revealing their secret inputs even with carefully targeted repeat querying. Offering these guarantees *while* providing a user experience that has the look and feel of a conventional DBMS will mean tackling many interesting research challenges in query processing, optimization, and more. Making trust-worthy database systems efficient, robust, and usable will require a more holistic view of how a database's internals work together. This is an opportunity for the database community since many of these technologies – including differential privacy and secure computation – are just now becoming robust and efficient enough for real-world deployment.

Building privacy-preserving data management systems is hard because of the inherent complexity of DBMSs. Until now, database researchers largely focused on providing high performance with semantic guarantees like referential integrity [8,55]. In contrast, trustworthy database systems need to optimize over a multi-objective decision space – trading off among performance, the data's long-term privacy, result accuracy, and the difficult-to-quantify value of additional guarantees such as cryptographically verifying the provenance of input data or the integrity of a query's execution. Moreover, composing these assurances is a non-monotonic cost model for query optimization – some are synergistic, antagonistic, or even mutually exclusive! Mere mortals cannot reason about composing these privacy-preserving techniques in a DBMS as they exist today.

At the same time, database researchers have a lot to offer to this emerging challenge of making privacy-preserving data analytics practical and usable. We have extensive research contributions in query optimization, parallelizing large-scale analytics, materialized view selection, and more. Generalizing these techniques to trustworthy database systems will be a non-trivial undertaking. For example, in the private-inputs setting a query plan may produce more accurate results when it runs over a differentially private view of a dataset [29] although querying the view has slower performance because it reads more data from disk. Many well-known query optimizations in the database community – such as using semi-joins for parallel databases, and splitting the execution of aggregates between local and distributed computation – generalize to the cloud setting to produce big performance gains [5]. Similarly, when we run oblivious queries in the cloud we will realize much greater performance if we build our secure computation protocols for each operator on the fly – such as compiling expressions into low-level circuits – and this will build from recent work on just-in-time query compilation [36,39,43].

The rest of this paper is organized as follows. We first define trustworthy database systems in detail with two illustrative reference architectures. We then describe privacy-preserving techniques that will lay the groundwork for query evaluation in these systems. After that, we walk through how we will need to rethink the query processing pipeline to support secure and trustworthy data management. We then conclude.

2 Background

We will now describe two motivating reference architectures for trustworthy database systems. We will then discuss two privacy-preserving techniques to support these systems: secure computation and differential privacy. As we shall see, they require integration throughout the entire query life-cycle, introducing substantial changes to most or all of the components in a DBMS.

2.1 Reference Architectures

Before delving into research challenges of trustworthy database systems, we look at two motivating scenarios for this work. To a first approximation, these systems have three roles: the data owner, the client, and the service provider. The data owner has private data that they wish to make available for querying. The client writes SQL queries against the trustworthy database system's schema and receives query results that may be precise or noisy. The service provider physically stores the private data and executes queries over it, returning the results to the client. A participant may support two of these roles. Trustworthy database systems address settings where there is at least one untrusted participant in a query over private data. Although the architectures below have a single data owner and one client, it is possible to extend these setting to multiple data owners and two or more independent clients.

It will be crucial for these systems to offer a user experience that is close to conventional engines to enable as many people as possible to benefit from privacy-preserving techniques. These systems will need to provide transparency about how they store and access data to the data owner and to the clients. They

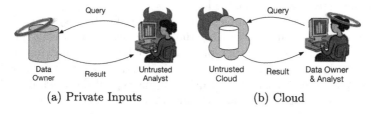

(a) Private Inputs   (b) Cloud

Fig. 1. Reference architectures for trustworthy database systems

will also need to automate compliance for companies by composing high-level declarative security policies and applying them to ad-hoc queries. Thus we frame the setup for these systems in terms of the whether the participants in each of these three roles are trusted or untrusted.

Figure 1 shows two reference architectures that we will use to motivate and illustrate this work. In each one, we denote a party as trusted with a halo. A trusted party is permitted to view the private input data we are querying. We can say that they sit within the privacy firewall. We show an untrusted party, who resides outside the privacy firewall, with horns.

In the *private inputs* architecture [26,28,35] a data owner acts as their own service provider by storing their private dataset locally and offering it for querying to an untrusted client. Hence, the client may only see noisy query results such that they cannot deduce the precise values in the data owner's tuples. From the client's perspective, this system behaves exactly like a standard DBMS. The engine will authorize the user, determine how much they are permitted to learn about the dataset, prepare and optimize a query plan that upholds the the system's privacy guarantees, execute it, and return a table of tuples to them.

When a data owner wishes to outsource their data storage and query processing to an untrusted service provider, we say that they are in the *cloud* setting [1,22,24]. Data owners encrypt their records before sending it to the service provider and issues queries over their private tuples remotely. Since the cloud provider cannot see the contents of the database, we will use advanced cryptographic techniques to protect this data, including fully homomorphic encryption [21] (to outsource the computation and storage), verifiable computation [41] (to outsource the storage), and zero-knowledge proofs [20,59] (to outsource the computation and storage). By systematically composing these techniques, a cloud service provider will execute the data owner's queries without learning anything about the private data it is storing even for ad-hoc workloads. Recall that a server's query evaluation is oblivious when it reveals no information about its secret inputs. For query evaluation, this means running in worst-case time and space to not leak information about its private inputs. Hence, a join of two relations of length n must do n^2 tuple comparisons, each of which emits a tuple that is either a dummy or a real one to mask the join's selectivity. Naturally this overhead cascades up the query tree creating an explosion in the query's intermediate cardinalities. In some cases, the outsourced server may run queries semi-obliviously, such as if they use computational differential privacy to make the query's program traces noisy [6] or if the system has a security policy where some columns are publicly readable [5,47].

The systems above are examples of trustworthy database systems. They are a small sample of the database settings that will benefit from privacy-preserving techniques. Others include privacy-preserving analytics for querying the union of the private data of multiple data owners [5,10,47,50], support for distributed "big data" platforms [3,18,60], and querying encrypted data [44,49]. The big data systems use trusted hardware to make their guarantees. Each of these settings substantially changes how we reason about and apply privacy-preserving techniques. In addition, we focus on two security guarantees in this work: privacy-preserving query processing and mechanisms for producing efficient and private query results. There are many other guarantees that are outside the scope of this work, and may be of interest in future research. They include running secret queries over publicly available data [51], running SQL over the secret inputs of multiple private data owners [5,50] and decentralized verifiable database tables a la blockchain [2,17,38].

2.2 Secure Computation

Secure computation refers to cryptographic protocols that run between a set of mutually distrustful parties. The security of these protocols allows all parties to perform computations as if there is a trusted third party who runs the program and reveals only its output. In the cloud setting, we run secure computation protocols by having two or more untrusted hosts work together to compute query results over secret data. This prevents any one host from being able to "unlock" the data on its own. The concept of secure computation was invented more than 30 years ago [58]; in the last decade, this technology has witnessed significant growth in its practicality. Numerous start-ups based on various secure computation technologies have been founded to use related cryptographic techniques to protect financial information [9], for anonymous reporting of sexual misconduct [45], private auctions [11], and more.

Secure computation has been used in the cloud and data federation settings for query evaluation over private data. In the cloud, data owners use secure computation to query their private records using an untrusted service provider [1,56]. In a data federation, oblivious query processing was researched in [5,6,47,50]. Almost all secure computation protocols follow the gate-by-gate paradigm with the following steps: (1) represent the computation as a circuit; (2) execute a secure subprotocol that securely encrypt the input data for evaluation in the circuit; (3) following the topological order of the circuit, evaluate all gates therein. Usually, the evaluation of each gate incurs some computational and communication cost, which becomes significant when the computation is complex. Many meaningful computations usually require billions of gates leading to a high computation and communication cost. Recent work studied optimizations of the cost of secure computation protocols and most practically efficient protocols right now are communication-bound owing to the need for data owners to pass messages amongst themselves to jointly evaluate each gate. In the past, secure computation was CPU-bound, but hardware optimizations, such as specialized instructions for cryptographic primitives, have shifted their bottleneck [7,25]. Presently, the only exceptions to this network-bound query evaluation are ones that heavily rely on public-key operations [27], where the computation returns to being the bottleneck. For example, secretly computing a single join with 1000 input tuples per relation incurs over 10 GB of network traffic with state of the art secure computation implementations.

Zero-knowledge proofs (ZKP) can be viewed as a special type of secure computation, where only one party (i.e., prover) has the input, and the other party (i.e., verifier) obtains one bit of output indicating if a certain public predicate is true on the prover's input. For our reference trustworthy database systems, they will be useful for the client to verify that their query was evaluated faithfully over the entirety of the relations it is querying. In the private inputs setting, the data owner may use ZKPs to prove to the client that the noisy results they are receiving are correct and complete. To do this, the data owner first publishes a digest of the database, which does not reveal any information about its contents but binds the database's contents. When the data owner receives a query, they will return the result to the client with a proof of its correctness that the client verifies by combining it with the initial digest. This was studied in VSQL [59]. Cloud-based systems may offer the same assurances with the service provider generating the digest and proofs for the data owner.

2.3 Differential Privacy

Secure computation maintains the confidentiality of the input dataset during query execution, but it offers no guarantees on whether sensitive values in the dataset can be inferred or "reconstructed" from the output of a query. The classic Dinur-Nissim result [15] (aka the fundamental law of information reconstruction) states that answering $n \log^2 n$ aggregate queries (with sufficient accuracy) on a database with n rows is sufficient to accurately reconstruct an entire database. This result has practical implications: recently, the US Census Bureau ran a reconstruction attack using only the aggregate statistics released under the 2010 Decennial Census, and was able to correctly reconstruct records of address, age, gender, race and ethnicity of about 46% of the US population.

Differential privacy is the only suite of techniques that ensure safety against reconstruction attacks [16]. An algorithm is said to satisfy differential privacy if its outputs do not change significantly due to adding/removing or updating a row in the input database. Differential privacy is currently considered the gold standard for ensuring privacy in most data sharing scenarios and has been adopted by several organizations, including the US Census Bureau (for their upcoming 2020 Decennial Census), and tech companies like Google, Apple, Microsoft and Uber.

Differential privacy injects carefully controlled levels of noise into a query's results. A private dataset begins with a privacy budget defining how much information about the data may be revealed in noisy query results. Each query receives some quantity of the privacy budget. We calibrate the noise with which we perturb our query results as a function of the query's privacy allocation and the sensitivity of the its operators. Speaking imprecisely, a query's sensitivity reflects how its output will change if we add, remove or modify an arbitrary row in the database.

An important property of differentially private algorithms is their composition also satisfies differential privacy. This is useful for proving the privacy guarantees of complex queries and it addresses the impossibility result by Dinur and Nissim. Moreover, querying a differentially private data release of a database does not incur any privacy cost other than that of initially noising the data release. This is useful for workloads with many queries over a single dataset.

Computational relaxations of standard differential privacy, known as computational differential privacy [37], aim to protect against computationally-bounded adversaries by protecting data in flight in the cloud. This serves as an alternative to full-oblivious query processing with its worst-case runtime. Instead computational differential privacy ensures that each party's view of the protocol is differentially private with respect to its secret inputs. For example, consider query evaluation with secure computation on two non-colluding cloud providers. Without the computationally bounded assumption on each party, any differentially private protocols for computing the Hamming distance between two n-bit vectors incur an additive error of $\Omega(\sqrt{n})$ [34]. On the other hand, by assuming each party is computationally bounded, this error can be reduced to $O(1)$.

3   The Life of a Privacy-Preserving Query

We now step through the workflow of a relational database query covering from when the client submits a query until they receive their results. We will examine how the major steps in the query processing pipeline will need to be redesigned in this emerging setting using our reference architectures from Sect. 2.1.

3.1   Query Parsing and Authorization

When a database engine receives a SQL statement, it first verifies that the query is free of syntax errors and resolves all names and references in it. It then converts the statement into one or more directed acyclic graphs (DAGs) of database operators. Lastly, it verifies that the user is authorized to run the query under the system's security policy.

When the parser initially verifies a SQL statement, a trustworthy database system may offer an extended syntax for queries. Although standard SQL queries are supported, the user may optionally give the system information about the how to run the query and manage its use of privacy, such that if a user is given a limited privacy budget they may split it as they see fit over their query workload giving more privacy for high-priority queries to increase the utility of their results. The parser may accept directives such as declaring a cardinality bound for a given database operator and annotations specifying the privacy budget that the query will use on the data it is accessing. Alternatively, the client may specify bounds on the accuracy of a query's results that he or she deems acceptable – ensuring that the utility of the data is not destroyed by over-noising the query results – and preventing the client from eroding the privacy budget for results that will not be useful to them.

When the planner converts the query into a DAG, it also needs to analyze the data it is querying and operations the user wishes to run to check that they are permitted by the data owner's security policy. Before we can optimize a query, we need to run information flow analysis over SQL to determine what type(s) of query processing will be necessary to uphold a given security policy. For example, if a database in the cloud has a mix of public and private columns, we will use differential privacy and secure computation only when we compute on private data. The engine will also need to solve for the sensitivity of a given operator in order to determine the noise it will need to inject for differentially private query results.

For checking query authorization, prior work has largely revolved around the user's privileges. A trustworthy database must consider many more factors such as the consent of the individuals in the dataset and the remaining privacy budget available for the data. It may also contend with how to compose many disparate privacy policies. For example, we are presently preparing to deploy a prototype of a trustworthy database system for analytics over electronic health records. Our colleagues in medicine compiled a memo listing all of the known state-level regulations pertaining to health data in the US. It is nearly 550 pages long. Research on how to compose privacy policies such as these will make it possible for trustworthy database systems to operate in complex regulatory environments.

3.2   Query Rewriting

The standard query rewriter takes the query tree from the parser and canonicalizes it for the optimizer. Here, the query planner coalesces SELECT blocks, expands any views, simplifies predicates, and more. This enables the query optimizer to produce efficient query plans and to make them consistent, i.e., where two semantically equivalent SQL statements yield identical query execution plans.

For queries running in the cloud, it is essential to have query rewrite rules that minimize the use of secure computation. Oblivious query processing typically runs at least three orders of magnitude slower than doing the same work in the clear. The query rewriter automatically applies any annotations from the query for bounding its intermediate cardinalities. It can also leverage information from the schema, such as integrity constraints and primary keys, to reduce the output size of the operators. Since the operators themselves must still run in worst-case time, the rewriter may inject "shrinkwrap" operators after an operator with a bounded cardinality to obliviously reduce its tuple count before passing them up to its parent. This technique was further developed to reduce the query's intermediate cardinalities using computational differential privacy to reveal padded versions of the true cardinality [6]. Despite a measurable privacy loss from the data owners observing intermediate results that are not exhaustively padded, clients receive precise query answers with a fast speed. Placing shrinkwrap operators in cloud query plan offers a new tuning knob in our query optimization space.

For the private inputs setting, we need to consider the level of noise added to a query's result. First we need to ensure that the sensitivity computation for the given query tree is correctly analyzed with regard to private tables for adding sufficient amount of noise. Prior work [19, 26, 28, 35] has focused on the linear aggregates at the end of the query tree, such as COUNT and SUM, and they add noise directly to the final aggregate. However, non-linear aggregates like AVG and STD call for more complicated perturbation algorithms that add noise to the intermediate results. For example, to release the average value of a column, we first compute the noisy sum of that column and the noisy count of that column, and then take their ratio. Whether to rewrite these aggregate into multiple operators (sub-queries) to facilitate noise addition and sensitivity analysis is an important extension. Next, for more accurate query results, we may rewrite a query in a form that is more DP-friendly and use inference to work back to the original SQL statement. In this approach, the rewritten query is no longer semantically equivalent to the initial SQL statement, but the noise added to the new query answer is much reduced. For instance, in the PrivateSQL system [29], *truncation* operators are added into the query tree to limit the maximum multiplicity of joins or range of an attribute's values so that query answers (or intermediate join cardinalities as in the case of Shrinkwrap) can be released with low noise. Where to insert the new operators in the query tree and how to set the truncation threshold remains challenging in practice. In addition, PrivateSQL is able to offer flexible privacy policies to the data owner, and the sensitivity of a query depends on the privacy policy. For example, a policy that protects entire households would generally have higher sensitivity than a policy that protects individuals. PrivateSQL rewrites queries to enable automatically calculation of the appropriate sensitivity for a class of foreign key based privacy policy. Generalizing this query rewriting approach for more rich set of class policies is an open question.

3.3   Query Optimization

A conventional query optimizer takes in a query tree from the rewriter and transforms it into an efficient query execution plan by selecting the order of commutative operators, the algorithms with which each one will execute, and the access paths for its inputs. The optimizer typically uses a cost model to compare plans to pick one that will run efficiently and enumerates plans using dynamic programming.

When we optimize a trustworthy database system query, we almost always do so in a multi-objective decision space. Depending on the setting, the optimizer may negotiate trade-offs among performance, information leakage, results accuracy, and storage size (if we use materialized views). For example, a cloud deployment using computational differential privacy to reduce the size of a query's intermediate results will have to decide how to split the privacy budget over its shrinkwrap operators to get the biggest performance boost. The more privacy an operator uses, the less padding its intermediate results will need. We will need to generalize multi-objective query optimization [4, 48] to tackle this challenge of creating query plans that satisfy these goals.

Moreover, optimizing information leakage gets more challenging when we consider database design. In the private inputs setting, we may create differentially-private views of the data for repeated querying so that we do not have to use our privacy budget for every query we run. We need to take a holistic view of how the major components in the DBMS work together in order to decide the best way to selectively leak information about private data so that we do not compromise information on individuals in a dataset yet still offer efficient query runtimes.

For the private inputs setting, the optimizer will need to balance competing goals of finding an efficient execution plan and one that produces private results with minimal noise. This two-dimensional optimization space will not be amenable to standard dynamic programming-style search algorithms. We suspect that the optimizer will use machine learning to find a plan that satisfies these competing goals. This will build on research in autonomic query optimization [14,33,42] and recent advances in using deep learning for the same [30,32,40,52]. The optimizer needs models for the sensitivity of a query plan and the expected noisiness of its results. It will select an access path from the initial relation, an index on it, or a differentially private view. The engine will need to automatically determine how using a noisy view of the data will impact the accuracy of a query's results and the speed of its execution. It would model its selectivity estimation using standard techniques since this information is only visible to the data owner. Unlike most prior query optimization research that is performance-focused, an engine with differentially private query results will need to work with the data owner or client to make explainable trade-offs between accuracy, privacy utilization, and runtime – perhaps by accepting bounds for one or more of these dimensions in an extended SQL syntax as described in Sect. 3.1.

For full-oblivious query processing in the cloud, our optimizer's decision space is limited. Since we exhaustively pad the output of each operator, reordering joins and filters does not matter. Shrinkwrapping expands our decision space by using computational differential privacy to reduce the size of intermediate cardinalities. On the other hand, the optimizer now faces the added challenge of splitting the privacy budget over the result sizes each intermediate operator in the query tree.

Even with privately padded intermediate results, the optimizer must make decisions that are data-independent. Without incorporating privacy into system catalog's statistics collection, it cannot use any statistics to order query operators, pick access paths, or to select operator algorithms. Instead the optimizer will use heuristics to estimate the size of intermediate cardinalities, like the $\frac{1}{10}$ selectivity rule [46]. Using these statistics, it will plug in a cost model for the query's secure computation.

For the optimizer's cost model, rather than estimating the number of I/Os or the CPU time a query will use, it will reason about a query's performance in terms of the number of secure computation operations – usually garbled circuit gates or arithmetic ops – it will run. This is because the cost of running the gates is predominantly network-bound, followed by being CPU bound when the network is exceptionally fast. Also, not all gates have the same CPU and network overhead. For example, XOR gates are "free" where as AND/OR gates are extremely costly. Thus finding the cheapest *circuit* representation for oblivious query operators will likely require low-level algorithm design. Optimizing at the level of a circuit will be quite different from working one operator at a time. In particular we will need new tactics to parallelize them circuits to maximize their throughput. In addition, there will be interesting research challenges in selecting the right secure computation protocol for a given query. This will require reasoning about the performance of each one and the guarantees it offers.

3.4   Plan Execution

After the query optimizer, we will have a secure and executable query plan. Right now, SQL queries usually run on a single machine or a cluster of machines that trust each other, where there is no privacy guarantee between the hosts. When privacy comes into the picture, we need to incorporate the aforementioned techniques to ensure that no (or limited information) can be revealed.

If we are operating in the cloud, for example, we can translate the optimized database operators into secure computation protocols. These programs are almost always fine-grained. Their unit of computation is the CPU instruction, usually a logical operation (AND/OR/NOT) or an arithmetic one (ADD/MULT). This means that secure computation Turing complete, but the cost of each operation is extremely high. Using secure computation, the engine now has a secure and executable physical query plan. Secure computation provides a strong security guarantee on the plan-execution computation. Recall that the query's execution must be oblivious – run such that its observable behavior is data-independent – and preserve the confidentiality of its input data. Ordinarily, we achieve the former using oblivious RAM. In SMCQL, they also tried to optimize the execution such that the non-secure portion of the program does not need to be executed in secure computation and thus improving the running time significantly. Differential privacy is an important tool to ensure the privacy of the secret input records by injecting a carefully controlled level of noise into the output of a query. A baseline approach to creating outputs is to do standard query processing and perturb the output of the query according to the cumulative sensitivity (i.e., how much an individual record can alter a query's outcome) of its operators [35]. Integrating differential privacy into our query executor will yield much better performance and query results with higher utility [12, 29].

Prior works are mostly focused on two-party secure computation protocols sometimes combined with oblivious RAM. Oblivious RAM is a general purpose platform to mask and disguise memory access patterns. Other tools can potentially be helpful in this context too. For example, a multi-party computation protocol can support more than two parties where a subset of them can be corrupted. However, new analysis is required to study how to generalize the techniques in the two-party setting to the multi-party setting. Oblivious data structures are another example, that can accelerate the execution by orders of magnitude [54, 60]. Existing oblivious data structures are general-purpose, and it is an important problem to design specialized oblivious data structures for query execution.

4   Conclusions

As organizations collect more and more sensitive data on their users, the need to build privacy-preserving techniques into database systems has never been greater. Ensuring the privacy of datasets as well as that of individuals within a database will require redesigns of numerous core database components. Guaranteeing that all of these components work together efficiently and correctly (in terms of composing their privacy guarantees) so that database users who are not privacy specialists may use them presents many novel research challenges. It will take deep collaborations between database researchers and members of the security community to make trustworthy database systems robust, usable, and scalable.

References

1. Aggarwal, G., et al.: Two can keep a secret: a distributed architecture for secure database services. In: CIDR (2005)
2. Allen, L., et al.: Veritas: shared verifiable databases and tables in the cloud. In: 9th Biennial Conference on Innovative Data Systems Research (CIDR) (2019)
3. Arasu, A., et al.: Secure database-as-a-service with cipherbase. In: Proceedings of the 2013 ACM SIGMOD International Conference on Management of Data, pp. 1033–1036. ACM (2013)
4. Balke, W.T., Güntzer, U.: Multi-objective query processing for database systems. In: Proceedings of the Thirtieth International Conference on Very Large Databases, vol. 30, pp. 936–947. VLDB Endowment (2004)
5. Bater, J., Elliott, G., Eggen, C., Goel, S., Kho, A., Rogers, J.: SMCQL: secure querying for federated databases. Proc. VLDB Endow. **10**(6), 673–684 (2017)
6. Bater, J., He, X., Ehrich, W., Machanavajjhala, A., Rogers, J.: Shrinkwrap: differentially-private query processing in private data federations. Proc. VLDB Endow. **12**(3), 307–320 (2019)
7. Bellare, M., Hoang, V.T., Keelveedhi, S., Rogaway, P.: Efficient garbling from a fixed-key blockcipher. In: 2013 IEEE Symposium on Security and Privacy, pp. 478–492. IEEE Computer Society Press, Berkeley, CA, USA, 19–22 May 2013
8. Benedikt, M., Leblay, J., Tsamoura, E.: Querying with access patterns and integrity constraints. Proc. VLDB Endow. **8**(6), 690–701 (2015)
9. Bogdanov, D., Kamm, L., Kubo, B., Rebane, R., Sokk, V., Talviste, R.: Students and taxes: a privacy-preserving social study using secure computation. In: Privacy Enhancing Technologies Symposium (PETS) (2016)
10. Bogdanov, D., Laur, S., Willemson, J.: Sharemind: a framework for fast privacy-preserving computations. In: Jajodia, S., Lopez, J. (eds.) ESORICS 2008. LNCS, vol. 5283, pp. 192–206. Springer, Heidelberg (2008). https://doi.org/10.1007/978-3-540-88313-5_13
11. Bogetoft, P., et al.: Secure multiparty computation goes live. In: Dingledine, R., Golle, P. (eds.) FC 2009. LNCS, vol. 5628, pp. 325–343. Springer, Heidelberg (2009). https://doi.org/10.1007/978-3-642-03549-4_20
12. Chowdhury, A.R., Wang, C., He, X., Machanavajjhala, A., Jha, S.: Outis: crypto-assisted differential privacy on untrusted servers. arXiv preprint arXiv:1902.07756, pp. 1–30 (2019)

13. Crockett, E., Peikert, C., Sharp, C.: Alchemy: a language and compiler for homomorphic encryption made easy. In: CCS (2018)
14. Deshpande, A., Ives, Z.G., Raman, V.: Adaptive query processing. Found. Trends Databases **1**(1), 1–140 (2007)
15. Dinur, I., Nissim, K.: Revealing information while preserving privacy. In: Proceedings of the Twenty-Second ACM SIGMOD-SIGACT-SIGART Symposium on Principles of Database Systems, PODS 2003, pp. 202–210. ACM, New York, NY, USA (2003)
16. Dwork, C.: Differential privacy. In: Bugliesi, M., Preneel, B., Sassone, V., Wegener, I. (eds.) ICALP 2006. LNCS, vol. 4052, pp. 1–12. Springer, Heidelberg (2006). https://doi.org/10.1007/11787006_1
17. El-Hindi, M., Heyden, M., Binnig, C., Ramamurthy, R., Arasu, A., Kossmann, D.: BlockchainDB-towards a shared database on blockchains. In: Proceedings of the 2019 International Conference on Management of Data, pp. 1905–1908. ACM (2019)
18. Eskandarian, S., Zaharia, M.: An oblivious general-purpose SQL database for the cloud. arXiv preprint 1710.00458 (2017)
19. Ge, C., He, X., Ilyas, I.F., Machanavajjhala, A.: APEx: accuracy-aware differentially private data exploration. In: Proceedings of the 2019 International Conference on Management of Data, SIGMOD 2019, pp. 177–194. ACM, New York, NY, USA (2019). https://doi.org/10.1145/3299869.3300092
20. Gennaro, R., Gentry, C., Parno, B., Raykova, M.: Quadratic span programs and succinct NIZKs without PCPs. In: Johansson, T., Nguyen, P.Q. (eds.) EUROCRYPT 2013. LNCS, vol. 7881, pp. 626–645. Springer, Heidelberg (2013). https://doi.org/10.1007/978-3-642-38348-9_37
21. Gentry, C.: Fully homomorphic eneryption using ideal lattices. In: Proceedings of the 41st Annual ACM Symposium on Theory of Computing, pp. 169–178. ACM (2009)
22. Gentry, C., Halevi, S., Raykova, M., Wichs, D.: Outsourcing private RAM computation. In: 2014 IEEE 55th Annual Symposium on Foundations of Computer Science, pp. 404–413. IEEE (2014)
23. Gupta, D., Mood, B., Feigenbaum, J., Butler, K., Traynor, P.: Using intel software guard extensions for efficient two-party secure function evaluation. In: Clark, J., Meiklejohn, S., Ryan, P.Y.A., Wallach, D., Brenner, M., Rohloff, K. (eds.) FC 2016. LNCS, vol. 9604, pp. 302–318. Springer, Heidelberg (2016). https://doi.org/10.1007/978-3-662-53357-4_20
24. He, Z., et al.: SDB: a secure query processing system with data interoperability. VLDB **8**(12), 1876–1879 (2015). 2150-8097/15/08
25. Ishai, Y., Kilian, J., Nissim, K., Petrank, E.: Extending oblivious transfers efficiently. In: Boneh, D. (ed.) CRYPTO 2003. LNCS, vol. 2729, pp. 145–161. Springer, Heidelberg (2003). https://doi.org/10.1007/978-3-540-45146-4_9
26. Johnson, N., Near, J.P., Song, D.: Towards practical differential privacy for SQL queries. Proc. VLDB Endow. **11**(5), 526–539 (2018). https://doi.org/10.1145/3187009.3177733
27. Keller, M., Pastro, V., Rotaru, D.: Overdrive: making SPDZ great again. In: Nielsen, J.B., Rijmen, V. (eds.) EUROCRYPT 2018. LNCS, vol. 10822, pp. 158–189. Springer, Cham (2018). https://doi.org/10.1007/978-3-319-78372-7_6
28. Kotsogiannis, I., Tao, Y., Machanavajjhala, A., Miklau, G., Hay, M.: Architecting a differentially private SQL engine. In: CIDR (2019)
29. Kotsogiannis, I., et al.: PrivateSQL: a differentially private SQL engine. Proc. VLDB Endow. **12**(12), 1371–1384 (2019)

30. Krishnan, S., Yang, Z., Goldberg, K., Hellerstein, J., Stoica, I.: Learning to optimize join queries with deep reinforcement learning. arXiv preprint arXiv:1808.03196 (2018)
31. Liu, C., Wang, X.S., Nayak, K., Huang, Y., Shi, E.: ObliVM : a programming framework for secure computation, Oakland, pp. 359–376 (2015). https://doi.org/10.1109/SP.2015.29
32. Marcus, R., Papaemmanouil, O.: Deep reinforcement learning for join order enumeration. In: Proceedings of the First International Workshop on Exploiting Artificial Intelligence Techniques for Data Management, p. 3. ACM (2018)
33. Markl, V., Lohman, G.M., Raman, V.: LEO: an autonomic query optimizer for DB2. IBM Syst. J. **42**(1), 98–106 (2003)
34. McGregor, A., Mironov, I., Pitassi, T., Reingold, O., Talwar, K., Vadhan, S.: The limits of two-party differential privacy. In: Proceedings of the 2010 IEEE 51st Annual Symposium on Foundations of Computer Science, FOCS 2010, pp. 81–90. IEEE Computer Society, Washington, DC, USA (2010). https://doi.org/10.1109/FOCS.2010.14
35. McSherry, F.D.: Privacy integrated queries: an extensible platform for privacy-preserving data analysis. In: Proceedings of the 2009 ACM SIGMOD International Conference on Management of Data, SIGMOD 2009, pp. 19–30. ACM, New York, NY, USA (2009). https://doi.org/10.1145/1559845.1559850
36. Menon, P., Mowry, T.C., Pavlo, A.: Relaxed operator fusion for in-memory databases: making compilation, vectorization, and prefetching work together at last. Proc. VLDB Endow. **11**(1), 1–13 (2017)
37. Mironov, I., Pandey, O., Reingold, O., Vadhan, S.: Computational differential privacy. In: Halevi, S. (ed.) CRYPTO 2009. LNCS, vol. 5677, pp. 126–142. Springer, Heidelberg (2009). https://doi.org/10.1007/978-3-642-03356-8_8
38. Nathan, S., Govindarajan, C., Saraf, A., Sethi, M., Jayachandran, P.: Blockchain meets database: design and implementation of a blockchain relational database (2019)
39. Neumann, T., Leis, V.: Compiling database queries into machine code. IEEE Data Eng. Bull. **37**(1), 3–11 (2014)
40. Ortiz, J., Balazinska, M., Gehrke, J., Keerthi, S.S.: Learning state representations for query optimization with deep reinforcement learning. arXiv preprint arXiv:1803.08604 (2018)
41. Parno, B., Howell, J., Gentry, C., Raykova, M.: Pinocchio: nearly practical verifiable computation. In: 2013 IEEE Symposium on Security and Privacy, pp. 238–252. IEEE (2013)
42. Pavlo, A., et al.: Self-driving database management systems. In: CIDR, vol. 4, p. 1 (2017)
43. Pirk, H., et al.: CPU and cache efficient management of memory-resident databases. In: 2013 IEEE 29th International Conference on Data Engineering (ICDE), pp. 14–25. IEEE (2013)
44. Popa, R., Redfield, C.: CryptDB: protecting confidentiality with encrypted query processing. In: SOSP, pp. 85–100 (2011). https://doi.org/10.1145/2043556.2043566
45. Rajan, A., Qin, L., Archer, D.W., Boneh, D., Lepoint, T., Varia, M.: Callisto: a cryptographic approach to detecting serial perpetrators of sexual misconduct. In: Proceedings of the 1st ACM SIGCAS Conference on Computing and Sustainable Societies, p. 49. ACM (2018)
46. Selinger, P.G., Astrahan, M.M., Chamberlin, D.D., Lorie, R.A., Price, T.G.: Access path selection in a relational database management system. In: SIGMOD, pp. 23–34 (1979). https://doi.org/10.1145/582095.582099

47. Suresh, M., She, Z., Wallace, W., Lahlou, A., Rogers, J.: KloakDB: a platform for analyzing sensitive data with k-anonymous query processing. CoRR abs/1904.00411 (2019). http://arxiv.org/abs/1904.00411
48. Trummer, I., Koch, C.: Multi-objective parametric query optimization. Proc. VLDB Endow. **8**(3), 221–232 (2014)
49. Tu, S., Kaashoek, M.F., Madden, S., Zeldovich, N.: Processing analytical queries over encrypted data. Proc. VLDB Endow. **6**(5), 289–300 (2013). https://doi.org/10.14778/2535573.2488336
50. Volgushev, N., Schwarzkopf, M., Getchell, B., Varia, M., Lapets, A., Bestavros, A.: Conclave: secure multi-party computation on big data. In: European Conference on Computer Systems (2019)
51. Wang, F., Yun, C., Goldwasser, S., Vaikuntanathan, V., Zaharia, M.: Splinter: practical private queries on public data. In: NSDI, pp. 299–313 (2017)
52. Wang, W., Zhang, M., Chen, G., Jagadish, H.V., Ooi, B.C., Tan, K.L.: Database meets deep learning: challenges and opportunities. ACM SIGMOD Record **45**(2), 17–22 (2016)
53. Wang, X., Ranellucci, S., Katz, J.: Authenticated garbling and efficient maliciously secure two-party computation. In: CCS (2017)
54. Wang, X.S., et al.: Oblivious data structures. In: Proceedings of the 2014 ACM SIGSAC Conference on Computer and Communications Security - CCS 2014, pp. 215–226 (2014). https://doi.org/10.1145/2660267.2660314
55. Wei, Z., Leck, U., Link, S.: Entity integrity, referential integrity, and query optimization with embedded uniqueness constraints. In: ICDE (2019)
56. Wong, W.K., Kao, B., Cheung, D.W.L., Li, R., Yiu, S.M.: Secure query processing with data interoperability in a cloud database environment. In: SIGMOD, pp. 1395–1406. ACM (2014)
57. Yao, A.C.: Protocols for secure computations. In: FOCS, pp. 160–164. IEEE (1982)
58. Yao, A.C.C.: How to generate and exchange secrets (extended abstract). In: 27th FOCS, pp. 162–167. IEEE Computer Society Press, Toronto, Ontario, Canada, 27–29 October 1986
59. Zhang, Y., Genkin, D., Katz, J., Papadopoulos, D., Papamanthou, C.: vSQL: verifying arbitrary SQL queries over dynamic outsourced databases. In: 2017 IEEE Symposium on Security and Privacy (SP), pp. 863–880. IEEE (2017)
60. Zheng, W., Dave, A., Beekman, J.G., Popa, R.A., Gonzalez, J.E., Stoica, I.: Opaque: an Oblivious and Encrypted Distributed Analytics Platform. In: NSDI, pp. 283–298 (2017)

POLY 2019: Building Polystore Systems

Learning How to Optimize Data Access in Polystores

Antonio Maccioni[1(✉)] and Riccardo Torlone[2]

[1] Collective[i], New York City, USA
amaccioni@collectivei.com
[2] Roma Tre University, Rome, Italy
riccardo.torlone@uniroma3.it

Abstract. Polystores provide a loosely coupled integration of heterogeneous data sources based on the direct access, with the local language, to each storage engine for exploiting its distinctive features. In this framework, given the absence of a global schema, a common set of operators, and a unified data profile repository, it is hard to design efficient query optimizers. Recently, we have proposed QUEPA, a polystore system supporting *query augmentation*, a data access operator based on the automatic enrichment of the answer to a local query with related data in the rest of the polystore. This operator provides a lightweight mechanism for data integration and allows the use of the original query languages avoiding any query translation. However, since in a polystore we usually do not have access to the parameters used by query optimizers of the underlying datastores, the definition of an optimal query execution plan is a hard task, as traditional cost-based methods for query optimization cannot be used. For this reason, in the effort of building QUEPA, we have adopted a machine learning technique to optimize the way in which query augmentation is implemented at run-time. In this paper, after recalling the main features of QUEPA and of its architecture, we describe our approach to query optimization and highlight its effectiveness.

1 Introduction

The concept of polyglot persistence, which consists of using different database technologies to handle different data storage needs [15], is spreading within enterprises. Recent research has shown that, on average, each enterprise application relies on at least two or three different types of database engines [17].

Example 1. Let us consider, as a practical example, the databases of a company called *Polyphony* selling music online. As shown in Fig. 1, each department uses a storage system that best fits its specific business objectives: (i) the sales department guarantees ACID properties for its transactions database with a relational system, (ii) a warehouse department supports search operations with a document store catalogue, where each item is represented by a JSON document, and (iii) a marketing department uses a graph database of similar-items supporting

© Springer Nature Switzerland AG 2019
V. Gadepally et al. (Eds.): DMAH 2019/Poly 2019, LNCS 11721, pp. 115–127, 2019.
https://doi.org/10.1007/978-3-030-33752-0_8

recommendations. In addition, there exists a key-value store containing discounts on products, which is shared among the three departments above.

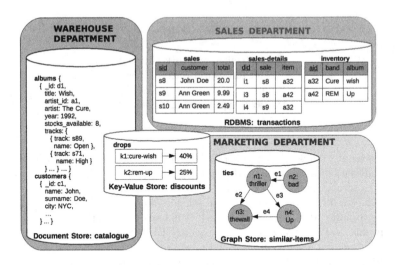

Fig. 1. A polyglot environment.

In this framework, it is of strategic importance to provide easy-to-use mechanisms for searching through all the available data [4]. The traditional approach to address this issue is based on a middleware layer involving a unified language, a common interface, or a universal data model [2,11]. However, this solution adds computational overhead at runtime and, more importantly, hides the specific features that these systems were adopted for. In addition, it is hard to maintain, having an inherent complexity that increases significantly as new systems take part to the environment.

Polystore systems (or simply, polystores) have been proposed recently as an alternative solution for this scenario [16]. The basic idea is to provide a loosely coupled integration of data sources and allow the direct access, with the local language, to each specific storage engine to exploit its distinctive features. This approach meets the "one size does not fit all" philosophy as well as the need to support business cases where heterogeneous databases have to co-exist. In polystores, it is common that a user is only aware of a single (or a few) available database but does not know anything about other databases (neither the content, nor the way to query them and, sometimes, not even their existence). This clearly poses new challenges for accessing and integrating data in an effective way. To recall a relevant discussion about this approach, the issue is that *"if I knew what query to ask, I would ask it, but I don't"* [16].

With the aim of providing a contribution to this problem, we have recently proposed (*data*) *augmentation* [9], a new construct for data manipulation in polystores that, given an object *o* taken from a database of a polystore, allows the automatic retrieval of a set of objects that: (i) are stored elsewhere in the polystore and (ii) are somehow related with o, according to a simple notion of probabilistic relationship between objects in different datastores.

The implementation of this operator does not require the addition of an abstraction layer involving query translation and therefore has a minimal impact on the applications running on top of the data layer. The goal is to provide a soft mechanism for data integration in polystores that complements other approaches, such as those based on cross-db joins [1,3,5,11].

The augmentation construct was implemented in QUEPA [8], a system that provides an effective method to access the polystore called *augmented search*. Augmented search consists of the automatic expansion of the result of a query over a local database with data that is relevant to the query but which is stored elsewhere in the polystore. This is very useful in common scenarios where information is shared across the organization and the various databases complement or overlap each other.

Assume for instance that Lucy, an employee of Polyphony working in the sales department who only knows SQL, needs all the information available on the album "Wish". Then, she submits in *augmented* mode the following query to the relational database transactions in Fig. 1.

```
SELECT *
FROM inventory
WHERE name like '%wish%'
```

By exploiting augmentation, the result of this query is the augmented object reported below, revealing details about the product that are not in the database of the sales department, including the fact that it is currently on a 40% discount.

$$< a32, Cure, Wish > \quad \Rightarrow \quad (catalogue:\{ title: Wish,$$
$$\Downarrow \qquad\qquad artist\_id: a1,$$
$$(discounts: 40\%) \qquad artist: The Cure,$$
$$year: 1992,$$
$$... \})$$

In an augmented search, each retrieved element e is associated with the probability that e is related to an element of the original result. Such probability is derived off-line from mining techniques and integrity constraints. Colors (as in the example above) and rankings can be used in practice to represent probability in a more intuitive way.

As it happens in traditional query optimization, the best performances of query answering in QUEPA are achieved by properly tuning a series of parameters. Some of these parameters depends of the polystore setting and can be configured by the system administrator once, when she has enough knowledge on the underlying databases. Other parameters depends on the specific query workload (e.g., the selectivity of queries) that are more difficult to tune. In general, traditional cost-based optimizers are hard to implement in a polystore because we might not have enough knowledge about the parameters affecting the optimization of each database system in play.

We saw this limitation as the opportunity to experiment different optimization approaches. To this aim, we equipped the system with a rule-based optimizer to dynamically predict the best configuration according to the query and the polystore characteristics. It relies on machine learning algorithms that learn from previous query executions what is the best execution plan given an input query. The idea of using machine learning within query optimization was then also explored by Krishnan et al. [7] and Marcus et al. [10]. They adopt deep reinforcement learning for optimizing joins. Other relevant work also use machine learning to improve the indexing of data [6].

In our approach, we train a series of decision trees with the statistics gathered from previous queries. These trees are then used at query time to determine the values of the configuration parameters to be used by the query orchestrator. In this way, neither the user nor the sysadmin need to do any tuning manually. The experiments have confirmed the effectiveness of the approach.

In the rest of the paper, after a brief overview of our approach and of the system we have developed (Sect. 2), we illustrate the way in which we have implemented query augmentation, the main operator of QUEPA, and the adaptive technique we have devised for predicting the best query plan for a query involving augmentation (Sect. 3). We also illustrate some experimental results supporting the effectiveness of the optimization technique (Sect. 4) and sketch future directions of research (Sect. 5).

2   Augmented Access to Polystores

2.1   A Data Model for Polystores

We model a polystore as a set of databases stored in a variety of data management systems (relational, key-value, graph, etc.). A database consists of a set of *data collections* each of which is made of a set of *(data) objects*. An object is just a key-value pair. A tuple and a JSON document are examples of data objects in a relational database and in a document store, respectively. We assume that a data object in the polystore can be uniquely identified by means of a *global key* made of: its key, the data collection C it belongs to, and the database including C. Basically, this simple model captures any database system satisfying the minimum requirement that every stored data object can be identified and accessed by means of a key.

We also assume that data objects of possibly different databases of a polystore can be correlated by means of *p-relations* (for relations in a polystore). A p-relation on two objects o_1 and o_2, denoted by $o_1 R_p o_2$, represents the existence of a relation R between o_1 and o_2 with probability p ($0 < p \leq 1$), where R can be one of the following types:

- the *identity*, denoted by $\sim$: an equivalence relation representing the fact that o_1 and o_2 refer to the same real-world entity;
- the *matching*, denoted by $\rightleftharpoons$: a reflexive and symmetric relation (not necessarily transitive), representing the fact that o_1 and o_2 share some common information.

Example 2. Consider the polystore in Fig. 1. By denoting the objects with their global keys we have for instance that:

- catalogue.albums.d1 $\sim_{0.8}$ discount.drop.k1:cure:wish,
- catalogue.albums.d1 $\sim_{0.9}$ transactions.inventory.a32,
- transactions.inventory.a42 $\sim_{0.6}$ similarItems.ties.n4,
- transactions.inventory.a32$\rightleftharpoons_1$transactions.sales-details.i4.

Basically, while the identity relation serves to represent multiple occurrences of the same entity in the polystore, the matching relation models general relationships between data different from the identity (e.g., those typically captured by foreign keys in relational databases or by links in graph databases). On the practical side, p-relations are derived from the metadata associated with databases in the polystore (e.g., from integrity constraints) or are discovered using probabilistic mining techniques. For the latter task, we rely on the state-of-the-art techniques for probabilistic record linkage [12], that is, algorithms able to score the likelihood that a pair of objects in different databases match.

2.2 Augmented Search

The augmentation construct takes as input an object o of a polystore and returns the augmented set $\alpha^n(o)$, which iteratively returns data objects in the polystore that are related to o with a certain probability. This probability is computed by combining the probabilities of the relationships that connect o with the retrieved objects.

Formally, the augmentation α^n of level $n \geq 0$ of a set of objects in a polystore $\mathcal{P}$ is a set $\mathbf{o}'$ of objects o^p, where $o \in \mathcal{P}$ and p is the probability of membership of o to $\mathbf{o}'$, defined as follows $(m > 0)$:

- $\alpha^0(\mathbf{o}) = \mathbf{o} \cup \{o^p \mid o \sim_p o' \wedge o' \in \mathbf{o}\}$
- $\alpha^m(\mathbf{o}) = \alpha^{m-1}(\mathbf{o}) \cup \{o^{\hat{p}} \mid o \rightleftharpoons_{p'} o' \wedge o'^p \in \mathbf{o} \wedge \hat{p} = p \cdot p'\}$

Example 3. Let o be the object in the polystore in Fig. 1 with global-key catalogue.albums.d1. Then, according to the p-relations in Example 2 we have $\alpha^0(\{o\}) = \{o, o_1^{0.8}, o_2^{0.9}\}$ where o_1 and o_2 are the objects with global-key discount.drop.k1:cure:wish and transactions.inventory.a32 respectively.

An augmented search consists of the expansion of the result of a query over a local database with data that are relevant to the query but are stored elsewhere in the polystore. Formally, the *augmentation of level* $n \geq 0$ of a query Q over a database $\mathcal{D}$ of a polystore (expressed in the query language of the storage system used for $\mathcal{D}$), denoted by $Q(n)(\mathcal{D})$, consists in the augmentation of level $n \geq 0$ of the result of Q over $\mathcal{D}$ ordered according to the probability of its elements.

Example 4. Let Q be an SQL query over the relational database **transactions** in Fig. 1 that returns the object o with global-key catalogue.albums.d1. Then we have $Q(0)(\mathbf{transactions}) = (o, o_2^{0.9}, o_1^{0.8})$, where o_1 and o_2 are the objects with global-key discount.drop.k1:cure:wish and transactions.inventory.a32, and $Q(1)(\mathbf{transactions}) = (o, o_2^{0.9}, o_3^{0.9}, o_4^{0.9}, o_1^{0.8})$, where o_3 and o_4 are the objects with global-key transactions.sales−details.i1 and transactions.sales−details.i4.

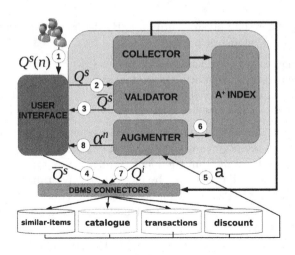

Fig. 2. Architecture of QUEPA.

2.3 Implementation

We have implemented our approach in a system called QUEPA. Its architecture is reported in Fig. 2 and includes the following main components:

- *Augmenter:* implements the augmentation operator and orchestrates augmented query answering.
- *A$^+$index:* stores the p-relations between data objects in the polystore.
- *Collector:* this component is in charge of discovering, gathering and storing p-relations in the A$^+$index.
- *Connectors:* they allow the communication with a specific database system by sending queries in the local language and returning the result.
- *Validator:* is used to assess whether a query can be augmented or not. The validator can also rewrite queries by adding all identifiers of data objects that are not explicitly mentioned in the query.
- *User Interface:* receives inputs and shows the results using a Rest interface.

Since QUEPA does not store any data, it is easy to deploy multiple instances of the system that can answer independent queries in parallel. In this case, each instance has its own A$^+$index replica and its own augmenter. Now we show the interactions among the components of QUEPA for answering a query Q in augmented mode with level n (step ① in Fig. 2).

The *validator* first checks if the query is correct (step ②) and possibly rewrites it into $\overline{Q}$ (step ③) before its execution over the target database (step ④). The local answer **a** is returned to the *augmenter* which is now ready to compute the augmentation (step ⑤). It gets from the A$^+$index the global keys of data objects reachable from **a** with n applications of the augmentation primitive (step ⑥). These global keys are used to retrieve data objects from the polystore with local queries Q^i (step ⑦). Finally, the augmented answer is returned to the user (step ⑧).

3   Efficient Implementation of Augmented Search

3.1   Augmenters

The augmentation operator is inherently distributed because it retrieves data from independent databases. We leverage that and other characteristics of this operator to make the augmentation more efficient.

Figure 3(a) illustrates the augmentation process done in a sequential fashion: circles stand for data objects and each database is represented by a different color. The original answer contains four results, i.e. the green circles. Each result is connected, by means of arrows, to the objects to include in the augmented answer. The augmentation iterates over the four results and retrieves 11 additional objects with 11 direct-access queries.

Network-Efficient Augmenter. Polystores are often deployed in a distributed environment, where network traffic has a significant impact on the overall performance of query answering. Augmentation, in particular, generates a non-negligible traffic by executing many local queries over the polystore, each one requesting a single data object. We implemented a BATCH augmenter that groups global keys by target database and submits them in one query. Next, BATCH arranges returned data objects to produce the answer. This batching mechanism tends to minimize the number of queries over the polystore, and so it also limits the burden of communication roundtrip on the overall execution. BATCH uses the parameter BATCH_SIZE that holds the maximum number of global keys per query. In Fig. 3(b) we show the process of the BATCH augmenter in a graphical fashion on the same augmented query answering represented in Fig. 3(a). Global keys are grouped by store, as represented by the dotted internal boxes, and are retrieved with one query once the corresponding group reaches the BATCH_SIZE limit or when the process terminates. In the example, we set BATCH_SIZE = 4 and only one query per database is submitted, resulting in six queries less than the sequential augmentation (i.e. 5 instead of 11).

CPU-Efficient Augmenter. Augmented answers include data objects coming from different databases and so local queries can be submitted in parallel. We have designed a few strategies that leverage the multi-core nature of modern CPUs by assigning independent queries to parallel threads. These strategies are implemented in different augmenters, all parameterized with THREADS_SIZE, the maximum number of simultaneous running threads.

Inner Concurrency. This strategy exploits the observation that objects sharing an identity relation can be retrieved in parallel. In Fig. 3(c) we show this augmentation with THREADS_SIZE = 2 on the example in Fig. 3(a). The main process iterates over the result of the local query and, for each object in the result, two threads compute the augmentation. This augmenter is very efficient for augmented exploration, in which a single result at a time needs to be augmented.

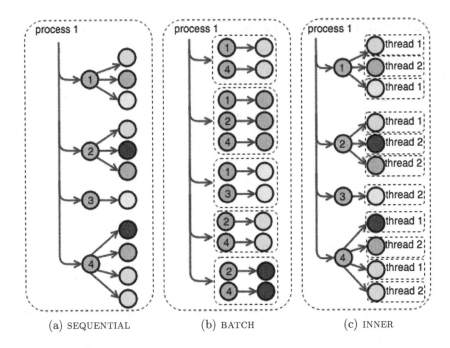

(a) SEQUENTIAL   (b) BATCH   (c) INNER

Fig. 3. Augmenters.

Outer Concurrency. Differently from the previous strategy, the OUTER augmenter parallelizes the computation over the result of the local query. As shown in Fig. 4(a), the main process of OUTER iterates over the results in the result launching a thread for each of them without waiting for their completion. Then, each thread retrieves all objects related to the result in a sequential way.

Outer-Batch Concurrency. The OUTER-BATCH augmenter combines multithreading with batching. Differently from BATCH, the groups of global keys are processed by several threads. The main advantage here is that the main process can continue filling these groups while threads are taking care of query execution. This augmenter is parameterized with both THREADS_SIZE and BATCH_SIZE. In Fig. 4(b) we show the augmented process of the OUTER-BATCH with BATCH_SIZE = 4 and THREADS_SIZE = 2.

Outer-Inner Concurrency. The OUTER-INNER augmenter tries to benefit from both "inner" and "outer" concurrency. The number of available threads, i.e. THREADS_SIZE, are used for the two levels of parallelism. It follows that $\frac{THREADS\_SIZE}{2}$ threads process the results of the original answer in parallel, and further $\frac{THREADS\_SIZE}{2}$ threads perform the augmentation for each result. Of course, this strategy tends to create many threads because of many simultaneous inner parallelizations. In Fig. 4(c) we show the augmentation process in OUTER-INNER with THREADS_SIZE = 4.

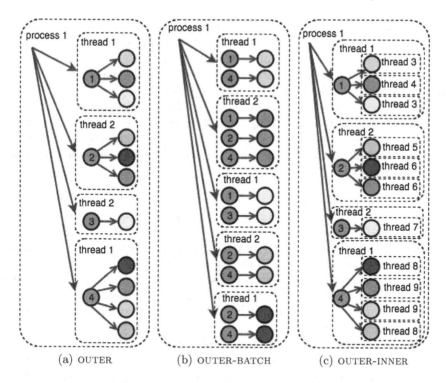

Fig. 4. Outer concurrency based augmenters.

Memory-Efficient Strategies. All augmenters rely on a caching mechanism with a LRU policy that allows the fast access to the last accessed data objects by means of their global-key. The cache is implemented using Ehcache[1] with a suitable choice of CACHE_SIZE, the maximum number of objects in the cache. At runtime, we check whether the data object is already in the cache before asking for it to the polystore. Caching is potentially useful in two cases: (i) with augmented exploration, where the user accesses objects that were likely retrieved in previous queries, and (ii) with queries having level > 0, where augmented results of the same answer can overlap. The level represents the hops of distance in A^+ index between the objects of the original result set and the objects in the augmented result.

3.2 Adaptive Augmentation: Learning the Access Plans

QUEPA can run with different configurations. A configuration is a combination of the augmenter in use, CACHE_SIZE and, if needed, BATCH_SIZE and THREADS_SIZE. As the experiments in Sect. 4 of [9] point out, none of the various configurations of QUEPA outperform the others in all possible scenarios.

---

[1] http://www.ehcache.org/.

For example, some configuration excels on huge queries only, while others excel in a distributed environment. It follows that an optimizer is needed to choose the right augmenter and its parameterization in any possible situation.

As we have observed in the Introduction, traditional cost-based optimizers are difficult to implement in a polystore because we might not have enough knowledge about each database system in play. Therefore, we designed an ADAPTIVE, rule-based optimizer to dynamically predict the best configuration according to the query and the polystore characteristics. It relies on a machine learning technique that generates rules able to select a well-performing configuration for the augmentation. The full process is as follows.

- *Phase 1: Logs collection.* We keep the logs of the completed augmentation runs. They include QUEPA parameters such as BATCH_SIZE or THREADS_SIZE, the overall execution time and the characteristics of the query (i.e. target database, number of original data objects in the result, number of augmented data objects). All these historical logs form our *training set*. In general, the larger is the training set, the higher is the accuracy of the trained models. When the training set is too small, we run, in background, previously executed queries with different configurations or we execute random queries against the polystore.
- *Phase 2: Training.* We train the following models:

  T_1: a decision tree to decide the augmenter to use among those available (e.g., OUTER, INNER, BATCH, etc.). The tree is trained with the C4.5 algorithm [14];

  T_2: a regression tree to decide BATCH_SIZE whenever T_1 selects OUTER-BATCH or BATCH. As we use Weka[2], this tree is trained with the REPTree algorithm [13];

  T_3: a regression tree to decide THREADS_SIZE whenever a concurrent augmenter is selected by T_1. This is also trained with the REPTree algorithm;

  T_4: a regression tree to decide CACHE_SIZE. This is trained with the REPTree algorithm.

  The training of the models can be done periodically when a fixed number of run logs are added to the training set.
- *Phase 3: Prediction.* Given a query, we use our models to predict the parameters of QUEPA on how to augment the query. First, we determine with T_1 which augmenter we have to use. Then, according to the result, we use T_2 and T_3 for BATCH_SIZE and THREADS_SIZE. Finally, T_4 is used to decide the CACHE_SIZE. Since the benefits of the cache are spread over all future queries to run and not only on the next one, it has not much sense to change continuously the CACHE_SIZE. For example, increasing a lot CACHE_SIZE would just insert many empty cache slots. Rather, we want to determine slight variations of CACHE_SIZE that adapt to the queries currently being issued by the user. The variation is calculated in the following way. We consider the

---

[2] http://www.cs.waikato.ac.nz/ml/weka/.

CURRENT_CACHE_SIZE and the PREDICTED_CACHE_SIZE determined by T_4. Then, we use the formula

$$\frac{\left(\text{PREDICTED\_CACHE\_SIZE} - \text{CURRENT\_CACHE\_SIZE}\right)}{10}$$

where 10 is an arbitrary value set by us experimentally.

Figure 5 shows an example of the decision tree T_1. When a new query has to be executed, we navigate the tree from the root to a leaf according to the characteristics of our setting. The leaves indicate the final decision, i.e. the augmenters to choose.

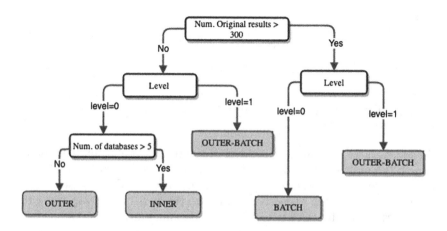

Fig. 5. An example of decision tree T_1.

4   Summary of Experiments

In this section we show the effectiveness of our learning mechanism only. The full report of the results is shown in [9].

The ADAPTIVE augmented has been trained with the logs of almost 2 million runs. We compare ADAPTIVE against a HUMAN optimizer and a RANDOM optimizer. The campaign was planned as follows. We have generated 25 queries of a different kind that were not present in the training set. Each query is run on a polystore with a different number of databases (4, 7, 10 and 13).

For the HUMAN optimizer, we defined the configuration for each run that could, in our opinion, result to be the most performing. A configuration consists of THREAD_SIZE, BATCH_SIZE and CACHE_SIZE. Each configuration is executed for each of the six available augmenters. In addition, we defined a random configuration for each run in order to emulate a RANDOM optimizer. Finally, we have another run whose configuration is determined by ADAPTIVE. Note that the use of CACHE_SIZE in this campaign of experiments work in the same way it is described in Sect. 3.2. For this reason, we first run all the HUMAN runs, followed by RANDOM and then ADAPTIVE.

For each configuration, we need to select the best performing run out of the 13 (i.e. 1 for ADAPTIVE and 6 for both HUMAN and RANDOM).

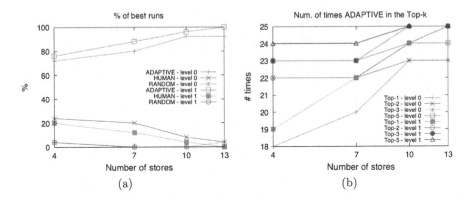

Fig. 6. Accuracy of the ADAPTIVE augmenter optimization.

In Fig. 6(a) we compare the number of times that an optimizer is the best. Although the number of candidates for ADAPTIVE was six times lower than the other optimizers, it was the best in most of the cases. In Fig. 6(b) we show the number of times that the ADAPTIVE run was in the top-1, top-2, top-3 and top-5 runs. ADAPTIVE is always able to find a good configuration for the query. The accuracy of ADAPTIVE increases as the number of databases increases because the differences of execution times between configurations increase, thus making it easier for the decision trees to split the domain of the parameters.

5   Conclusion and Future Work

In this paper we have shown that machine learning can be used to optimize the access to data in a polystore. Indeed, as the database systems in a polystores are black boxes, a mechanisms that learns automatically the best way to exploit them with no knowledge of their internals can be very effective. In particular, we adopted this solution to optimize the query augmentation mechanism offered by our polystore system, QUEPA. Augmentation provides an effective tool for information discovery in heterogenous environments that, according to the polystore philosophy, does not require any query translation. A number of experiments have confirmed feasibility and accuracy of the optimization technique.

As a direction of future work, we would like to extend the optimization algorithms with more evolved techniques of machine learning such as deep learning.

References

1. Apache MetaModel. http://metamodel.apache.org/. Accessed Sept 2017
2. Atzeni, P., Bugiotti, F., Rossi, L.: Uniform access to NoSQL systems. Inf. Syst. **43**, 117–133 (2014)
3. Duggan, J., et al.: The BigDAWG polystore system. SIGMOD Record **44**(2), 11–16 (2015)
4. Haas, L.M.: The power behind the throne: information integration in the age of data-driven discovery. In: SIGMOD, p. 661 (2015)
5. Kolev, B., Bondiombouy, C., Valduriez, P., Jiménez-Peris, R., Pau, R., Pereira, J.: The CloudMdsQL Multistore System. In: SIGMOD, pp. 2113–2116 (2016)
6. Kraska, T., Beutel, A., Chi, E.H., Dean, J., Polyzotis, N.: The case for learned index structures. In: SIGMOD, pp. 489–504 (2018)
7. Krishnan, S., Yang, Z., Goldberg, K., Hellerstein, J.M., Stoica, I.: Learning to optimize join queries with deep reinforcement learning. CoRR, abs/1808.03196 (2018)
8. Maccioni, A., Basili, E., Torlone, R.: QUEPA: QUerying and exploring a polystore by augmentation. In: SIGMOD, pp. 2133–2136 (2016)
9. Maccioni, A., Torlone, R.: Augmented access for querying and exploring a polystore. In: ICDE, pp. 77–88 (2018)
10. Marcus, R., Papaemmanouil, O.: Deep reinforcement learning for join order enumeration. In: aiDM@SIGMOD 2018 (2018)
11. Ong, K.W., Papakonstantinou, Y., Vernoux, R.: The SQL++ semi-structured data model and query language: a capabilities survey of SQL-on-Hadoop, NoSQL and NEWSQL databases. CoRR, abs/1405.3631 (2014)
12. Fellegi, I.P., Sunter, A.B.: A theory for record linkage. J. Am. Stat. Assoc. **64**, 1183–1210 (1969)
13. Quinlan, J.R.: Simplifying decision trees. Int. J. Man-Mach. Stud. **27**(3), 221–234 (1987)
14. Quinlan, J.R.: C4.5: Programs for Machine Learning. Morgan Kaufmann, San Francisco (1993)
15. Sadalage, P.J., Fowler, M.: NoSQL Distilled: A Brief Guide to the Emerging World of Polyglot Persistence, 1st edn. Addison-Wesley Professional, Boston (2012)
16. Stonebraker, M.: The case for polystores, July 2015. http://wp.sigmod.org/?p=1629
17. The DZone Guide To Data Persistence. https://dzone.com/guides/data-persistence-2. Accessed Sept 2017

Midas: Towards an Interactive Data Catalog

Patrick Holl[(✉)] and Kevin Gossling

Technical University of Munich, 85748 Garching b. Muenchen, Germany
{patrick.holl,kevin.gossling}@tum.de

Abstract. This paper presents the ongoing work on the Midas poly-store system. The system combines data cataloging features with ad-hoc query capabilities and is specifically tailored to support agile data science teams that have to handle large datasets in a heterogeneous data landscape. Midas consists of a distributed SQL-based query engine and a web application for managing and virtualizing datasets. It differs from prior systems in its ability to provide attribute level lineage using graph-based virtualization, sophisticated metadata management, and query offloading on virtualized datasets.

Keywords: Polystore · Data catalog · Metadata management

1 Introduction

To provide data consumers, e.g., analysts and data scientists, with the data they need, enterprises create comprehensive data catalogs. These systems crawl data sources for metadata, manage access rights and provide search functionality. Such catalogs are the starting point for almost every analytical task. Once a data scientist has found a potentially interesting dataset in the catalog, he/she has to move to another tool in order to prepare it for analysis. This is because data catalogs often cannot interact with their referenced data sources directly. Instead, engineers have to build ETL pipelines to move and shape data in a way that it is ready for analysis. This process is time consuming, costly, unscalable, and can even lead to the insight that the dataset is unsuitable for the intended task because it is hard to asses the data quality based on raw metadata. Even highly sophisticated systems like Goods from Google require such processes [6]. Another challenge for data catalogs is tracking the provenance of derived datasets, specifically when the schema and the location is different from the origin data. In such cases, the datasets need to be registered manually back to the catalog.

In this paper, we present the ongoing work on the polystore system Midas that tackles the stated problems by providing a large scale data virtualization environment that combines ad-hoc analytical query access with sophisticated metadata management features. Midas is an interactive data catalog designed for data science teams working in heterogeneous data landscapes. In this context, we define interactive as the ability for a data scientist to run large scale ad-hoc queries within the same application that manages the metadata of connected

V. Gadepally et al. (Eds.): DMAH 2019/Poly 2019, LNCS 11721, pp. 128–138, 2019.
https://doi.org/10.1007/978-3-030-33752-0_9

data stores. This approach enables data science teams to share schema details, comments, and other important information in the same place where they access, prepare and analyze the data.

Midas builds upon the concepts of Google's Dremel and other in-situ polystore systems like Apache Drill and Presto [7,12]. It uses a SQL-based query engine as the backbone to provide uniform ad-hoc access to a heterogeneous data landscape and implements a novel approach to represent and virtualize datasets. We are working on graph-based views enriched with arbitrary meta information to represent virtual datasets. This approach allows global lineage tracking down to the attribute level. To achieve interactive performance on large scale datasets and to provide query offloading, we implement an adaptive, columnar-oriented cache that partitions entity attributes based on their occurrence in virtual datasets. Additionally, Midas offers an intuitive web-based user interface to allow for easy data preparation, curation, and sharing among data science teams.

The core concepts of Midas are: Virtualized and sharable datasets, sophisticated metadata management, comprehensible data lineage, interactive performance through adaptive columnar-oriented caches, and ease-of-use.

2   Differentiation to Existing Systems

In the following, we compare Midas to similar systems we have identified. First, we compare it with polystore query engines. Second, we compare it to related data catalog systems.

The publication of the Dremel concept led to several open source implementations of SQL-based query engines that provide ad-hoc access to large, distributed datasets for OLAP use cases [10]. Apache Drill and Presto are the most known open source implementations [7,12]. Both query engines focus on ad-hoc analytical tasks without providing sophisticated user interfaces or metadata management features.

Data catalog systems like Goods from Google [6] or the dataspace concept by Franklin et al. [5] are very close to the goal of Midas. However, Midas is provisioning datasets in a way that a user can directly interact with it and query the actual data without being limited on certain metadata.

The closest system to Midas is Dremio [2]. Dremio is a data management platform based on Apache Drill and Apache Arrow. Similar to Midas, Dremio implements cataloging and lineage features. However, compared to Midas, Dremio does not allow global lineage tracing on attribute level. Furthermore, Dremio does not allow the attachment of arbitrary metadata to attributes.

Extensive research on data lineage has already been done [3,4,13]. Most approaches use annotations to keep track of data transformations and schema changes. Midas does not annotate data but maintains an attribute graph for tracking the lineage.

3   System Design

We are making design decisions specifically tailored to the requirements of agile data science teams. The most important metric is fast access to data in a processable format. Additionally, it must work together with already established workflows and tools like Spark, Jupyter Notebooks, and Tableau. The main components of the Midas system are a query engine that enables users to create virtualizations even on massive scale datasets and the user interface as an interactive data catalog. Figure 1 depicts the overall architecture of the Midas system.

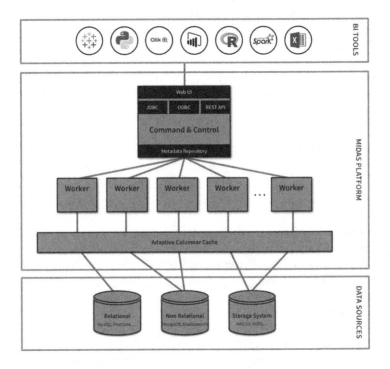

Fig. 1. Midas system architecture

3.1   Query Engine

The primary component of Midas is an extensible, distributed, SQL-based query engine written in Java that follows a similar architecture as Dremel, Presto, and Apache Drill [7,10,12]. The *Command & Control* node takes incoming queries and creates a logical execution plan which is then distributed to the worker nodes that materialize the data.

All three systems are practically proven and show that they can handle analytical queries even on multiple terabyte large datasets [7,10,12]. Internally, Midas uses a columnar-oriented data representation based on Apache Arrow that supports complex data models [1]. The query engine materializes data through an extensible set of connectors, currently, it supports: MySQL, MongoDB, HBase, Hive, Amazon S3, MapR-DB, JSON - File, CSV and Parquet.

All of the listed sources can be virtualized, joined, and queried via SQL.

The main reason for choosing SQL as the main language for interacting with the system is that almost any data scientist knows it and can work with it. Additionally, with open standards like ODBC, almost any tool and framework can directly use it.

3.2 Graph-Based Data Virtualization

Managing metadata and tracking data lineage on attribute level is challenging for polystore systems. Especially when data from multiple stores is combined. Even sophisticated metadata management systems like Goods from Google track provenance on a dataset-basis, i.e., upstream and downstream datasets are tracked as a whole [6]. Combining data from multiple sources makes it complex to reconstruct the origin of a specific attribute. Another challenge for data catalogs is the inheritance of metadata like schema information to derived datasets, especially when attributes are renamed.

To tackle the stated problems, we are working on a novel approach to represent and virtualize datasets. In Midas, a virtual dataset is a view on one or multiple datasets defined by a SQL statement. Technically, Midas implements a rooted graph-based approach to represent these views.

Each dataset D consists of a name N, a list of arbitrary metadata objects $META$ and a set of attribute graphs SAG:

$$D := (N, META, SAG)$$

The name N is an arbitrary string which is usually a reference to the name of a table, a file, or a collection. $META$ is a JSON document that contains arbitrary metadata for a dataset like a description or access rights.

The attribute graph $AG \in SAG$ represents the provenance and metadata of a particular attribute $a \in D$ and denotes as follows:

$$AG := (V, E)$$

The vertex V consists of a name N_a and a list of arbitrary metadata objects $META_a$:

$$V := (N_a, META_a)$$

The edges E denote operations on an attribute.

Example: A data scientist defines a virtual dataset *VD* by creating a view that joins the two dataset D_1 with the attributes a_{1_1} and a_{1_2}, and D_2 with the attributes a_{2_1}, a_{2_2}, and a_{2_3} together. D_1 and D_2 are combined based on their common join key a_{1_1} and a_{2_1}, respectively. The SQL statement looks like the following:

```
1  CREATE VIEW VD AS (SELECT (a_1_1+a_1_2) as `sum`, a_1_2, a_2_2,
2  a_2_3 FROM D1, D2 WHERE D1.a_1_1 = D2.a_2_1)
```

Midas takes the incoming query and creates the attribute graphs for *VD*. Figure 2 depicts the set of attribute graphs for *VD*.

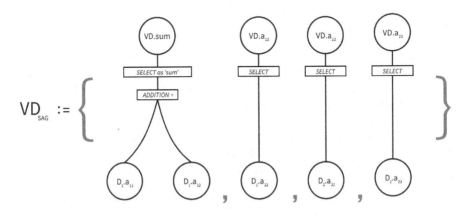

Fig. 2. The set of attribute graphs (SAG) for the virtual dataset VD

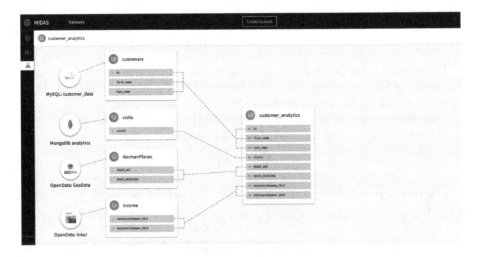

Fig. 3. Full lineage graph of a virtual dataset. The red icons on the left to the dataset names indicate a physical dataset and the blue icon on *customer_analytics* a virtual one. (Color figure online)

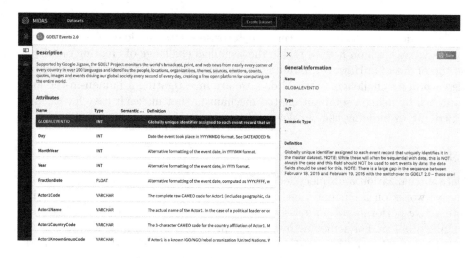

Fig. 4. Interface for editing metadata

By traversing the attribute graph using a depth-first search (DFS) algorithm, we can now visualize the full provenance of an attribute. Additionally, it is possible to add weights to edges for each operation done on an attribute. Having a weighted graph could potentially be used to do cost-based query optimization. However, the determination of the actual costs is tricky since the underlying data sources could be running on different systems in different locations, which makes it hard to do proper cost estimations. Figure 3 shows the full lineage graph of a virtualized dataset in the Midas application.

3.3 Initial Graph Creation and Metadata Management

Midas triggers a discovery process and creates a new graph-based representation of a dataset whenever a user queries it for the first time. During this discovery process, the attribute graphs are created based on the dataset's schema information. For self-describing data stores like Parquet or MySQL, the schema is taken directly from the store. For non-self-describing formats like CSV, the user has to define where to find the schema manually, e.g., on the first row. The actual implementation of the discovery method depends on the individual data store and is defined in the corresponding adapter. For future versions, we are working on the implementation of a crawler-based approach like Goods from Google to facilitate the discovery process on massive heterogeneous data landscapes.

The metadata for datasets and attributes is added separately by other applications via API or manually by users through the Midas catalog interface. Figure 4 shows this catalog interface for data owners and scientists. Currently, the Midas interface supports arbitrary descriptions and the attachment of a semantic type which is a reference to a class or an attribute in an ontology. Creating these links is either done manually by the data owner or automatically by making a lookup in a pre-defined ontology. For now, this lookup is a simple string match on the DBpedia ontology. The long term goal is to enable data scientists to do semantic queries over an enterprise's data ontology. There has been extensive research on how to tackle the technical challenge of creating ontologys on top of data [9]. However, building these ontologies is not only a technical but also a process challenge. With Midas, we are investigating a human-in-the-loop approach by using a semi-automated mechanism that makes it easy for users to contribute in building the ontology.

3.4   Adaptive Caching Layer

Data virtualization and query federation comes with the advantage that a user always works on a current view of the actual source data. However, achieving interactive performance on massive datasets in such a federated setup is a challenging problem. For achieving interactive query performance, Midas implements an adaptive columnar-oriented cache similar to column caches in Apache Spark.

The implementation is straightforward and the algorithm is as follows:

1. Scan the referenced columns in the logical execution plan.
2. Store the selected columns in a columnar format (Parquet) and add a freshness indicator.
3. For all upcoming queries, do not query the actual source but use the Parquet reference files if the freshness is above a certain threshold.

The cache files are not linked to a certain query but rather adapt to selected columns, i.e., other queries referencing the same columns can use the same cache reference.

For improving the caching behavior, we are currently working on a more sophisticated approach based on query predictions. Recent research in information retrieval shows how search intents and queries can potentially be predicted by using pre-search context and user behavior like past search queries [8]. Querying a dataset using SQL is very similar to querying a search engine, both will lead to a result set of data based on some input parameters. We believe that a similar approach can potentially lead to better caching behavior by pre-calculating result sets based on predicted queries. Current observations in our prototype usage indicate, that more than 75% of all queries contain some aggregate function on one or more attributes. Specifically, we are working on a query prediction model based on past queries of a user, queries of the data science team as a whole, and queries on a certain dataset. The goal of this model is to pre-generate caches for dataset columns that are most likely to be accessed in a query. This approach could potentially lead to more responsive queries but also to offload production systems from analytical workloads in critical times.

3.5   User Experience

The web client is the primary interface for building, managing, and querying datasets. Figure 5 depicts the workspace of a logged-in user where all virtual and physical datasets he/she has access to are listed.

Fig. 5. Workspace containing 10 virtual datasets, 5 physical data stores, and access to third party data hub

Studies show that in the majority of data science teams there is no established process for sharing data [11]. The lack of a clearly defined process often leads to datasets send via email and shadow analytics environments. Midas tackles this problem by providing data science teams a shared workspace for discovering and sharing already integrated data in an analytics-ready format.

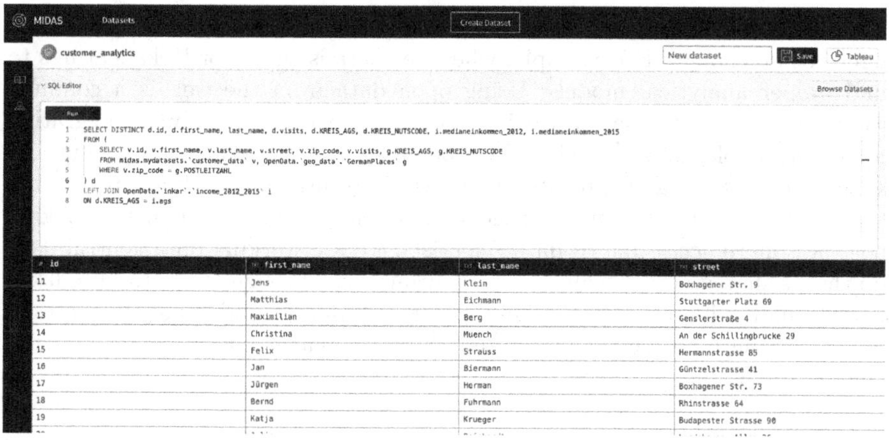

Fig. 6. Interface for running ad-hoc queries and creating new virtual datasets

The main interface for creating a new virtual dataset is shown in Fig. 6. Datasets are created by defining SQL statements which can be saved as a virtual dataset.

Data Discovery. An efficient process to find and explore data is crucial to enable data science teams to fulfill their job. In Midas, we are implementing several approaches to tackle the discovery problem:

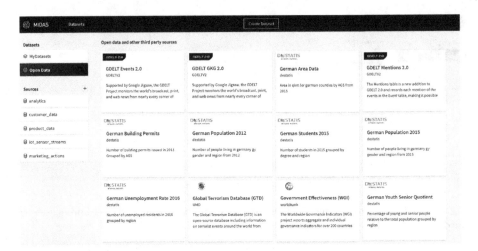

Fig. 7. Interface for the centrally shared open data hub in Midas

1. Providing a search interface for the dataset and attribute metadata.
2. Mapping ontologies to datasets, which potentially allows semantic queries.
3. Implementing a centrally shared hub for open data as shown in Fig. 7.

For modern data science workloads, solely focusing on internal enterprise data might not be enough. For example, whenever data is sparse or lacks features to build proper analytical models. Using open data from the web is a common practice to enrich internal data with additional features. However, integrating publicly available datasets using ETL pipelines is costly, time-consuming and usually requires a search process on the web. Additionally, column names are often cryptic and hard to understand without further information. For making open data more accessible to data scientists, we are working on a central data hub that is shared across teams and organizations. Through the data hub, users can formulate ad-hoc queries on any integrated dataset and collaboratively fill missing attribute descriptions. Figure 7 shows the current user interface of the open data hub.

4   Lessons and Challenges

In this section, we discuss challenges that are occurring while developing Midas and highlight areas that require future work. One of the biggest challenges that we are facing in developing Midas is providing interactive query performance on virtual datasets that are compound of complex queries and span across multiple and different source systems. Limited and sub-optimal query push-downs to the source systems lead to expensive materializations and overhead of used computational resources. Currently available open source implementations of the Dremel concept like Apache Drill and Presto suffer from the same problem. Even though data virtualization is not the primary use case for those systems, it is similarly essential for ad-hoc analytical queries. Using an efficient and optimized caching structure can help in achieving interactive query performance even on massive virtualized datasets by simultaneously offloading the underlying sources. Query predictions may lead to a significantly better cache hit ratio and therefore to a better overall performance. However, we are currently in the beginning of building and evaluating such algorithms and propose to explore this area further in future research. In addition to that, for reaching the next level in data virtualization, we see it as important to build query federation layers that can leverage the core abilities of a high variety of data store technologies and formats. A potential research direction could be the investigation of learned system components for pushdowns.

Midas focuses on analytical use cases and does, therefore not support write federation to the underlying data stores. It follows the "one size does not fit all" principle, and the expressive power of SQL limits its capability. However, for future work, the system has the potential to support more languages like a limited, read-only subset of SPARQL.

5   Conclusion

In this paper, we outlined the current status of the Midas polystore system tailored to analytical use cases and some challenges for future work. We are currently evaluating the system together with data science teams in three large enterprises (>300.000 combined employees). A video demonstrating the current version of Midas is available at https://demo.midas.science/poly19.

References

1. Apache arrow homepage. https://arrow.apache.org/. Accessed 15 Mar 2019
2. Dremio is the data-as-a-service platform. - dremio. https://www.dremio.com/. Accessed 15 Dec 2018
3. Aggarwal, C.C.: Trio a system for data uncertainty and lineage. In: Aggarwal, C. (ed.) Managing and Mining Uncertain Data, vol. 35, pp. 1–35. Springer, Boston (2009). https://doi.org/10.1007/978-0-387-09690-2_5
4. Cui, Y., Widom, J.: Lineage tracing for general data warehouse transformations. VLDB J. Int. J. Very Large Data Bases 12(1), 41–58 (2003)
5. Franklin, M., Halevy, A., Maier, D.: From databases to dataspaces: a new abstraction for information management. ACM SIGMOD Rec. 34(4), 27–33 (2005)
6. Halevy, A., et al.: Goods: organizing Google's datasets. In: Proceedings of the 2016 International Conference on Management of Data, pp. 795–806. ACM (2016)
7. Hausenblas, M., Nadeau, J.: Apache drill: interactive ad-hoc analysis at scale. Big Data 1(2), 100–104 (2013)
8. Kong, W., Li, R., Luo, J., Zhang, A., Chang, Y., Allan, J.: Predicting search intent based on pre-search context. In: Proceedings of the 38th International ACM SIGIR Conference on Research and Development in Information Retrieval, pp. 503–512. ACM (2015)

9. Lenzerini, M.: Ontology-based data management. In: Proceedings of the 20th ACM International Conference on Information and Knowledge Management, pp. 5–6. ACM (2011)
10. Melnik, S., et al.: Dremel: interactive analysis of web-scale datasets. Proc. VLDB Endow. **3**(1–2), 330–339 (2010)
11. Tenopir, C., et al.: Data sharing by scientists: practices and perceptions. PLoS ONE **6**(6), e21101 (2011)
12. Traverso, M.: Presto: Interacting with petabytes of data at facebook (2013). Accessed 4 Feb 2014
13. Woodruff, A., Stonebraker, M.: Supporting fine-grained data lineage in a database visualization environment. In: Proceedings 13th International Conference on Data Engineering, pp. 91–102. IEEE (1997)

Evolution Management
of Multi-model Data
(Position Paper)

Irena Holubová[1(✉)], Meike Klettke[2], and Uta Störl[3]

[1] Charles University, Prague, Czech Republic
holubova@ksi.mff.cuni.cz
[2] University of Rostock, Rostock, Germany
meike.klettke@uni-rostock.de
[3] University of Applied Sciences, Darmstadt, Germany
uta.stoerl@h-da.de

Abstract. The variety of data is one of the most challenging issues for the research and practice in data management. The so-called *multi-model data* are naturally organized in different, but mutually linked formats and models, including structured, semi-structured, and unstructured. In this position paper we discuss the so far neglected, but from the point of view of real-world applications important aspect of evolution management of multi-model data. We provide a motivation scenario and we discuss key related challenges, such as multi-model data modelling, intra vs. inter model changes, global and local evolution operations, eager vs. lazy migration, and schema inference.

Keywords: Multi-model data · Evolution management · Eager and lazy migration · Inter-model changes · Multi-model schema inference

1 Introduction

In recent years, the Big Data movement has broken down borders of many technologies and approaches that have so far been widely acknowledged as mature and robust. One of the most challenging issues is the *variety* of data. It means that data may be present in multiple types and formats – structured, semi-structured, and unstructured – and independently produced by different sources. Hence, data natively conform to various models.

Example 1. Let us consider an example of a multi-model scenario as shown in Fig. 1, backing an enterprise management information system. Social network of customers is captured by graph *G*. Relational table *Customer* records basic information about customers, such as their name and credit limit. *Orders* submitted by customers are stored as JSON documents, with a key/value mapping *ShoppingCart* maintaining their current shopping carts. By storing each record

© Springer Nature Switzerland AG 2019
V. Gadepally et al. (Eds.): DMAH 2019/Poly 2019, LNCS 11721, pp. 139–153, 2019.
https://doi.org/10.1007/978-3-030-33752-0_10

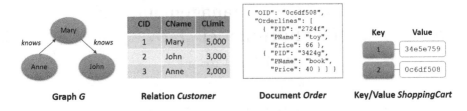

Fig. 1. A multi-model scenario [37]

in the best fitting model, we avoid impedance mismatch. A query over the multi-model data instance might return all products ordered by a friend of a customer whose credit limit is greater than 3,000 USD.

Although traditional relational databases have been the systems of the first choice for decades, with the arrival of Big Data their capabilities have become insufficient in many aspects and so new types of systems, such as NoSQL or NewSQL, have appeared. As indicated by Example 1, the variety of so-called *multi-model data* brings another dimension of complexity since multiple models must be efficiently supported at a time.

Currently, there exist more than 20 representatives of so-called *multi-model databases* [35], involving well-known tools, both traditional relational and novel NoSQL (such as Oracle DB, IBM DB2, Cassandra, or MongoDB), having distinct features and, hence, being classified according to various criteria [36]. The core difference is the strategy used to extend the original model to other models or to combine multiple models. The new models can be supported via adoption of an entirely new storage strategy, extension of the original storage strategy, creation of a new interface, or even no change in the original storage strategy (which is used for trivial cases).

On the other hand, the recent idea of polystores does not assume a single store capable of supporting various data models, but multiple dedicated ones under the "hood" of a single integrated platform. The integration can be either loose or tight, depending on the level of autonomy of particular subsystems. Especially *tightly-integrated polystores* [1,8,10,11,18,24,33,47] bear important similarities with multi-model databases [37], as they represent a single point of access for all related data (as well as administration tasks). They can be seen as a particular kind of federated databases, which trade autonomy of the subsystems for efficiency and usability in enterprise scenarios. This can be seen as their main common trait to multi-model databases, leading in many aspects to similar ideas and challenges.

In the rest of this position paper we will deal with the problem of multi-model data management. We will not focus on technical details of a particular multi-model database or polystore, but we will discuss our ideas at a more abstract level which enables to cover a wider set of multi-model data management systems.

As in all databases that are in productive use for a long time, multi-model databases and also polystores have to consider evolutions. Intra-model evolutions (e.g., adding, deleting, changing, and reorganizing data) have to be realized.

Having multiple models, extensions and changes of the data in one model can cause changes in other data models, too. A formalism for evolving multi-model data and preserving all integrity constraints (e.g., validity of data and link structures) is needed for such systems. It has to guarantee intra-model changes and also inter-model changes, especially in case of inter-model links, data entries which are duplicated, and data which are stored redundantly in different models.

In short, in this paper we discuss the need of a solution for realizing "alter database" operations for multi-model data. The main contributions can be summed up as follows:

1. We introduce the area of evolution management of multi-model data and related key challenges.
2. We outline possible solutions to the challenges together with a wide set of state-of-the-art related work which might serve as good starting points.
3. Our overview makes this paper useful for researchers looking for new research opportunities in the field.
4. For practitioners, we provide an enumeration of subtasks and questions that they should consider, namely a checklist for executing evolution in multi-model data management systems.

The rest of the paper is structured as follows: In Sect. 2 we provide a motivation example introducing a multi-model scenario and its possible evolution. In Sect. 3 we discuss the key challenges of multi-model data management. In Sect. 4 we give a short conclusion.

2   Motivation Example

In our simple multi-model motivation example (partially borrowed from [27]) we first show how the sample data from Fig. 1 can be stored in a particular multi-model database, namely OrientDB (version 3.0.22). Next, we show selected examples of evolution of the application and their consequences motivating a general discussion of challenges of multi-model data management in Sect. 3.

We start out with customer data in the relational format. We could store the relational tuples as flat documents and declare the schema for managing customers as an OrientDB class:

```
CREATE CLASS Customer;
CREATE PROPERTY Customer.CID    INTEGER (MANDATORY TRUE, NOTNULL TRUE);
CREATE PROPERTY Customer.CName  STRING  (MANDATORY TRUE);
CREATE PROPERTY Customer.CLimit INTEGER (MANDATORY TRUE);
CREATE INDEX Customer.CID UNIQUE;

INSERT INTO Customer (CID, CName, CLimit)
  VALUES (1, 'Mary', 5000), (2, 'John', 3000), (3, 'Anne', 2000);
```

Next, we add the graph data. In OrientDB, we register all customers as vertices in the generic class of vertices V (by declaring the customer class a subclass of V). Then, we create a new edge class *knows* (inheriting from the generic edge class E), and add the instances.

```
ALTER CLASS Customer SUPERCLASS V;
CREATE CLASS knows EXTENDS E;

CREATE EDGE knows
  FROM (SELECT FROM Customer WHERE CID = 3) TO (SELECT FROM Customer WHERE CID = 1);
CREATE EDGE knows
  FROM (SELECT FROM Customer WHERE CID = 1) TO (SELECT FROM Customer WHERE CID = 2);
```

Third, we integrate data on the customers' shopping carts and orders. In OrientDB, order documents are straightforward to integrate as nested OrientDB classes:

```
CREATE CLASS Orderline;
CREATE PROPERTY Orderline.PID    STRING  (MANDATORY TRUE, NOTNULL TRUE);
CREATE PROPERTY Orderline.PName STRING  (MANDATORY TRUE);
CREATE PROPERTY Orderline.Price INTEGER (MANDATORY TRUE);

CREATE CLASS Order;
CREATE PROPERTY Order.OID         STRING (MANDATORY TRUE, NOTNULL TRUE);
CREATE PROPERTY Order.Orderlines EMBEDDEDLIST Orderline;

INSERT INTO Order SET
  OID = "0c6df508",
  Orderlines = [
    { "@type":"d", "@class":"Orderline", "PID": "2724f", "PName": "toy",  "Price": 66 },
    { "@type":"d", "@class":"Orderline", "PID": "3424g", "PName": "book", "Price": 40,
      "QTY": 2} ];
```

Finally, we implement the key/value mappings from the shopping cart using OrientDB links:

```
CREATE CLASS ShoppingCart;
CREATE PROPERTY ShoppingCart.key    LINK Customer (MANDATORY TRUE, NOTNULL TRUE);
CREATE PROPERTY ShoppingCart.value LINK Order     (MANDATORY TRUE, NOTNULL TRUE);

INSERT INTO ShoppingCart SET
  key   = (SELECT @rid FROM Customer WHERE CName = "John"),
  value = (SELECT @rid FROM Order    WHERE OID  = "0c6df508");
```

The query from Example 1 returning "all products ordered by a friend of a customer whose credit limit is greater than 3,000 USD" could be now expressed as follows:

```
SELECT value.Orderlines.PName FROM ShoppingCart
WHERE key.CID IN
  (SELECT both("knows").CID FROM Customer WHERE CLimit > 3000);
```

As user requirements change, we may need to add a new property to one of the models (e.g., a shipping address to the orders). Such *intra-model* change is restricted to a single (document) model:

```
CREATE PROPERTY Orderline.Address STRING;
```

Now, let us assume that we perform an *inter-model* schema change to merge the *ShoppingCart* key/value mappings with *Customer*[1]:

```
CREATE PROPERTY Customer.ShoppingCart LINK Order;

UPDATE Customer SET ShoppingCart = (SELECT @rid FROM Order WHERE OID = "0c6df508")
  WHERE CName = "John";

DROP CLASS ShoppingCart;
```

---

[1] Note that the UPDATE command should be done for all the key/value records.

Apparently, such change in the structure of the data requires also a respective modification of the cross-model query:

```
SELECT both("knows").ShoppingCart.Orderlines.PName FROM Customer WHERE CLimit > 3000;
```

Last but not least, a classical optimization strategy, typical for read-mostly Big Data applications, is *data redundancy*. Due to the amounts of data, non existing or expensive joins (e.g., when retrieving data from multiple subsystems of a polystore), it might be more efficient to pre-compute results of a query or simply store the same information several times. Also in our motivation example we can encounter the same situation. For example, there might be a requirement for storing an address also for particular customers to be used, e.g., as a default shipping address of orders:

```
CREATE PROPERTY Customer.Address STRING;
```

A change in the structure of the address (e.g., a requirement to divide the string to particular fields street, city, and zip code) then influences all occurrences of each instance (from a higher level of perspective once occurring in the relational model and once occurring in the document model). In addition, we might need to distinguish whether the change should affect all types of addresses, or just their subset (e.g., those specified for the customer, those used in orders as shipping addresses, etc.).

Another requirement might be to pre-compute a materialized view of the frequency of orders of particular combinations of products:

```
SELECT Orderlines.PName, count(*) FROM Order GROUP BY Orderlines.PName;
```

A change of the structure of orders (e.g., extracting information about products, i.e., names and prices, to a separate document collection of products) also triggers a necessary change of the structure of this query. In addition, since we assume that the result of this query is pre-computed for optimization purposes, its immediate (*eager*) re-computation might not be required and kind of a *lazy* approach should be used instead.

3   Challenges of Evolution Management

Following the motivation example, in this section we discuss in detail five key challenges related to successful evolution management of multi-mode data, together with possible solutions and related work.

3.1   Modeling of Multi-model Data

First, we clarify our core terminology to avoid confusion brought by different, related, or even synonymous terms used within distinct models:

- *Record* is a representation of a single data entity. This would be, for example, a tuple in the relational model, a single JSON document in a document model, a vertex in a graph database, or one object in a key/value store.

- *Kind* is an abstract type, label, or class allowing to group related and similar records and organize them in logical collections, such as tables in the relational model, collections in ArangoDB, classes in OrientDB, etc.
- *Property* is a record characteristic, attribute, or feature, e.g., an attribute of a relational tuple, a field in a JSON document, or a vertex/edge property.

Most of the existing multi-model databases are based on the assumption that records of a given kind all reside in the same model. However, this assumption is not so obvious and even natural from the general point of view. Multi-model databases, when classified according to the original model extended towards other models, appear among both relational and NoSQL systems. Representatives of polystores also combine, e.g., relational and NoSQL subsystems. While in the relational world there is a strong formalism of normal forms representing the necessity to avoid redundancy, in the NoSQL world a repeated storage of the same piece of information is a usual optimization strategy. Thus not only the multi-model systems have to face this contradiction, but we can even assume that there might be records of the same kind stored in different models, i.e., a *cross-model redundancy*.

Another important aspect to mention are the *links* between separate data items. In single-model systems the links have different semantics and representation, involving, e.g., foreign keys in the relational model, pointers in the object model, or embedding and references in document models. And even within a single data model we can find different approaches, such as, e.g., datatypes ID and IDREF/IDREFS in DTD and elements unique, key, and keyref in XML Schema. For multi-model data we need to consider *cross-model links*, whose semantics and features can differ depending on the types of interlinked models.

When working with several logical models at a time, these often mutually share a couple of the same principles on the one hand, while can also have certain specifics on the other. At least two basic approaches are currently distinguished: *aggregate-oriented* (key/value, document, wide column) and *aggregate-ignorant* (relational, graph). When data across distinct models are to be processed together, their schemas inferred, or query expressions evaluated, kind of a unified data abstraction has to be found first. For this purpose, widely used conceptual modeling languages ER [13] and UML [41] could be utilized and in a *top-down* way adjusted to the needs of individual logical models. (This idea is already used, e.g., for NoSQL graph databases [2] or aggregate-oriented NoSQL systems [14].) While the former language exists in several notations yet provides more complex constructs better grasping the real-world relationships among entities, the latter one is standardized but unfortunately only too data-oriented and concealing important details (e.g., weak entity types and their identification and existential dependencies or unclear meaning of minimal multiplicities in ternary associations [22]). On the contrary, *bottom-up* approaches could find an inspiration in the proposal of the NoSQL AbstractModel [12], a system-independent model for aggregate-oriented databases.

Regardless of the adopted strategy, the theory of categories [34], associative arrays [30], or description logics [4] could be utilized to internally model the data in a formal, abstract, and rigorous way. Complex non-relational systems often involve a variety of heterogeneous and interrelated models – models that are, unfortunately, expressed using several modeling languages (the already mentioned ER or UML as well as BPMN [39], ORM2 [25], etc.). While these languages share certain aspects and still being widely considered as distinct, it is no doubt challenging to propose a common unifying interface that would respect all or at least a majority of their features [3,9,28]. If there are only a few solutions targeting conceptual modeling of NoSQL databases in general, modeling of graph databases is even more non-trivial [16,17,40]. Nonetheless, unified processing of data also involves corresponding cross-model data transformations, for example, using a transformation language NotaQL [44].

3.2   Intra vs. Inter-model Operations

Despite the number of models used in a particular system, sooner or later user requirements change and so has to change also the respective application. There is the need for an *evolution management*. From the point of view of data management the key aspect are changes in data structures, i.e., evolution operations that modify the data structures respectively. In multi-model databases, we distinguish *intra-model* and *inter-model* evolution operations. While intra-model operations only affect the records in a single model, inter-model operations change records in more than one model. In multi-model databases or polystores inter-model operations occur in the following cases:

1. Evolution of properties which serve as links between different models, or
2. Evolution of records or properties of records which are stored redundantly in different data models (see Sect. 3.1).

Hence, we need an evolution language which has to serve as a unified language interface for defining all schema changes of all models – the *lingua franca* for defining evolutions in all models (see a proposal in Fig. 2). This language also has to contain complex operations like *split* and *merge* or *move* and *copy* between different models. Inter-model changes entail three new challenges:

1. Schema changes between different models have to be discovered and propagated.
2. For execution of the evolution operations, the consistency of the multi-model database has to be guaranteed. For that, global schema information (organized in a data dictionary) is needed for finding links and cross-model redundancies and evolving them at the same time.
3. The specified evolution operations have to be translated into the intra-model evolution operations of each model.

In [43] we introduced a schema evolution language for NoSQL databases. This schema evolution language is implemented in *Darwin* [46], a dedicated middleware for managing schema evolutions. In Fig. 2 we extended this language for schema evolution within multi-model systems using **mname** as the identifier for the specific model and adding **split** and **merge** operations.[2]

```
evolutionop = typeop | propertyop;

typeop     = createtype | droptype | renametype | split | merge;
createtype = "create type" kind;
droptype   = "drop type" kind;
renametype = "rename type" kind "to" kind;
split      = "split" kind "into" kind ":" pnames and kind ":" pnames;
merge      = "merge" kind ":" pnames "and" kind ":" pnames complexcond "into" kind;

propertyop = add | delete | rename | move | copy;
add        = "add" [datatype] property [defaultValue];
delete     = "delete" property;
rename     = "rename" property "to" pname;
move       = "move" property "to" ( kind | property ) complexcond;
copy       = "copy" property "to" ( kind | property ) complexcond;

complexcond = "where" joinconds ["and" conds];
joinconds  = joincond {"and" joincond};
joincond   = property "=" property;
conds      = cond {"and" cond};
cond       = property "=" value;

pnames     = pname ["as" pname] {"," pname ["as" pname]};
property = kind "." pname;
kind       = [mname "."] kname;
kname      = identifier;
mname      = identifier;
pname      = identifier;

defaultvalue = value;
```

Fig. 2. EBNF syntax of Multi-Model Schema Evolution Language

To illustrate the advantages of the language we use our running example from Sect. 2. There we have given examples of intra- and inter-model changes. The adding of a shipping address to the orders (intra-model change) would be expressed as follows:

```
add STRING Orderline.Address;
```

For the inter-model changes we consider two variants. The *ShoppingCart* key/value mapping may be additionally stored in the *Customer* table.

```
copy ShoppingCart.value to Customer.CShoppingCart where ShoppingCart.key = Customer.CID;
```

Or we merge (as in Sect. 2) the *ShoppingCart* key/value mapping into the *Customer* table. This operation can be expressed in two different ways – with **move** and **drop** or with the **merge** operation:

```
move ShoppingCart.value to Customer.CShoppingCart where ShoppingCart.key = Customer.CID;
drop type ShoppingCart;
```

or

```
merge ShoppingCart:value as CShoppingCart and Customer:CID, CName, CLimit
    where ShoppingCart.key = Customer.CID into Customer;
```

---

[2] For a concrete implementation, the definitions of **identifier** and **value** must still be specified.

3.3   Global vs. Local Evolution Operations

In a multi-model system, *global schema evolution operations* can be defined for an abstract schema model and have to be propagated and translated into the local models. Starting with these global evolution operations entails the following requirements: It is necessary to define and maintain an abstract model consisting of all local models in a unified presentation. All global evolution operations have to be translated into evolution operations in the languages of the local models.

In each multi-model system *local schema changes* can be executed. Here, the operations affect only a single model and can be executed locally. Inter-model operations have to propagate their changes first into the global model and second from there into other local models. For example, when the customer identifier CID in the relational model is replaced by another identifier, this evolution has to be propagated to the abstract model and from it also into the key/value model which stores the same information and uses it as links between records in different models.

In [31] we developed a method for discovering schema changes with a reverse engineering process. From a NoSQL dataset, we derive a series of schema versions over time and evolution operations that transform each schema version into its successors schema version. This process can be performed not only initially, but also incrementally for newly added or changed records and thus can find new schema versions and evolution changes [31]. With this approach, datasources are monitored and local schema changes, represented as evolution operations, are detected. These evolution operations are handled in the same way. Inter-model operations propagate the evolutions to the global model for ensuring consistency of the whole multi-model database.

3.4   Eager vs. Lazy Migration

In databases which host Big Data, an *eager* data migration that immediately updates all records causes high update costs and a long system down-time. Applying *lazy* data migration instead is the solution used in many systems [32,42]. Databases are only migrated on demand, i.e., records which shall be accessed are migrated into the newest version only before their reading or updating.

In Fig. 2, we have already stated, that the evolution language consists of *single-type operations* (like *add*, *delete*, or *rename*) and *multi-type operations* (like *copy*, *move*, or *merge*). For multi-type operations, we have to guarantee that source and target records are in the same version so that the operation can be executed without information loss. In multi-model systems, these multi-type operations can be defined on datasets in different models and accordingly different database systems. For realizing such multi-type operations, there is a need for a schema version management between different models. In general, there are two different solutions for this:

1. A *version number* can be added to each record (e.g., as an attribute in a relational database, an element or attribute in an XML document, a property in

a JSON document, etc.). It is possible to use local or global version numbers: Local version numbers are valid within each model. Global version numbers have to be managed for the whole multi-model system.

2. *Timestamps* which store the last write operation of a record can be applied for distinguishing different versions. In this case we need an additional information which schema version is valid in which time interval. This information has to be maintained in the metadata of the multi-model system.

Queries over a multi-model database assume that all records have the latest schema version [15]. Considering lazy migration, a *query rewriting* approach has to be applied that distributes all queries over all models and within each model over all structural versions [26]. We do not know if all datasets which form the result of a certain query are already available in the latest version, so the query rewriting approach also has to query records in previous versions and has to migrate these records on demand. For this, the query rewriting approach has to apply the inverse operations of the schema evolution operations [15].

3.5   Inference of Multi-model Schema

With multi-model data, we may distinguish several levels of schema support:

- *Schema-full*: The description of a schema for records of a given kind is expected to be provided explicitly, properties of a given kind are declared as required or optional. All records of this kind are then validated against this schema.
- *Schema-less*: The schema is neither provided nor required; although in principle two records of the same kind do not need to have exactly the same structure, a similar structure is usually expected.
- *Schema-mixed* (or *schema-hybrid*): Certain properties are declared as required by a schema (and therefore validated), while additional properties may be added without validation.

In reality, however, even in schema-less systems, there typically exists an implicit schema, i.e., kind of an agreed structure of the data expected by the application. Hence, the idea of schemalessness is often rather characterized as *schema-on-demand*. This observation motivates the necessity of research in the area of multi-model schema inference. Unfortunately, since there exists no generally accepted or standard definition of such a schema, there is also a lack of the respective inference approaches.

On the other hand, there exists a number of techniques for single-model schema inference. As a consequence of Gold's theorem [23], e.g., XML schema languages are not identifiable from positive examples only (i.e., sample data to be valid against the inferred schema). Hence, either an *identifiable* subclass of such a language has to be inferred, or various heuristics must be utilized. Despite these limitations, probably the largest of inference approaches, both heuristic [38] and grammar-inferring [6,7,21], can be found for XML data, probably thanks to the

Table 1. Summary of challenges of evolution management of multi-model data

Challenge	State of the art	Multi-model open issues
Modelling	– General conceptual modeling languages (UML, ER, ...), eventually utilized for specifics of graph or aggregate-oriented systems – General formal apparatuses (e.g., theory of categories, associative arrays, description logic, ...)	– Formal definition of intra-/inter-model links – Multi-model conceptual modeling language – Multi-model schema definition language – Support for inter-model links, cross-model redundancy, ...
Intra-/Inter-Model Operations	– Intra-model operations are currently supported in some, but not all models	– Implementation of intra-model operations in all models/systems – Implementation of inter-model evolution operations
Global/Local Operations	– Local single-type evolution operations are available in most systems – Multi-type operations (like split, merge, copy or move) are only available in research prototypes	– Implementation of the detection and propagation of local operations – Implementation of the propagation of global operations
Eager/Lazy Migration	– Eager/lazy migration is supported by some systems for single-type operations – Eager/lazy migration for multi-type operations is currently only supported in research prototypes	– Realizing lazy migration over different models/systems in case of inter-model operations – Synchronizing eager migration over different models/systems
Schema Inference	– Single-model inference approaches (XML, JSON, RDF hierarchies, ...)	– Multi-model (i.e., target) schema definition – Multi-model inference approaches (heuristic/grammar-inferring) – Mutual enrichment of single-model subschemas (using, e.g., inter-model links, redundancy, ...)

existence of standard schema definition languages DTD and XML Schema with precisely defined syntax and semantics. With the dawn of NoSQL databases and the related popularity of the JSON format, there appeared approaches inferring (big) JSON data [5,19] or general approaches for aggregate-oriented databases [14,45]. And there are even related methods which identify schemas or aggregation hierarchies in RDF data [20,29].

In the case of multi-model schema inference we can primarily focus on heuristic approaches. On the other hand, the research on possibilities and limitations of inference of an identifiable subclass of the multi-model schema language is another challenging aspect. Apart from multi-model extensions of existing verified single-model approaches, mutual links between records across the models can bring another piece of important information. Inference approaches may thus benefit from information extracted from related data in distinct models. Similarly, if we assume that redundancy is allowed in multi-model data, the inference process can again benefit from this fact, where information from one model (e.g., having a more complex structure) can enrich another one.

3.6   Summary

Most of the mentioned research areas were extensively studied in traditional single-model data management systems. However, interconnection of multiple models does not usually mean only a straightforward combination of these approaches. We sum up both the state-of-the-art solutions and the main challenges and open issues of evolution management of multi-model data in Table 1.

4   Conclusion

As the current trends indicate, both multi-model databases and polystores represent a dignified and promising successor of the traditional approaches for the newly emerging and challenging use cases. Yet they first need to gain solid foundations and reach the same level of both applied and theoretical maturity in order to become a robust alternative to the relational databases. One of the important aspects discussed in this paper is evolution management of multi-model data. We believe that this paper points an important and interesting research direction for the scientific community, as well as practical issues to be considered by practitioners.

Acknowledgements. This work was partly supported by the German Research Foundation *(Deutsche Forschungsgemeinschaft (DFG))*, grant number 385808805 (M. Klettke, U. Störl) and the Charles University project PROGRES Q48 (I. Holubová). We want to thank Stefanie Scherzinger and Mark Lukas Möller for numerous interesting and helpful discussions and several comments on this work.

References

1. Abouzeid, A., Bajda-Pawlikowski, K., Abadi, D., Silberschatz, A., Rasin, A.: HadoopDB: an architectural hybrid of MapReduce and DBMS technologies for analytical workloads. Proc. VLDB Endow. **2**(1), 922–933 (2009)
2. Akoka, J., Comyn-Wattiau, I., Prat, N.: A four V's design approach of NoSQL graph databases. In: de Cesare, S., Frank, U. (eds.) ER 2017. LNCS, vol. 10651, pp. 58–68. Springer, Cham (2017). https://doi.org/10.1007/978-3-319-70625-2_6

3. Atzeni, P., Bugiotti, F., Rossi, L.: Uniform access to NoSQL systems. Inf. Syst. **43**, 117–133 (2014)
4. Baader, F., Calvanese, D., McGuinness, D., Patel-Schneider, P., Nardi, D.: The Description Logic Handbook: Theory, Implementation and Applications. Cambridge University Press (2003)
5. Baazizi, M.-A., Colazzo, D., Ghelli, G., Sartiani, C.: Parametric schema inference for massive JSON datasets. VLDB J. **28**(4), 497–521 (2019)
6. Bex, G.J., Gelade, W., Neven, F., Vansummeren, S.: Learning deterministic regular expressions for the inference of schemas from XML data. ACM Trans. Web **4**(4), 14:1–14:32 (2010)
7. Bex, G.J., Neven, F., Schwentick, T., Vansummeren, S.: Inference of concise regular expressions and DTDs. ACM Trans. Database Syst. **35**(2), 11:1–11:47 (2010)
8. Bonaque, R., et al.: Mixed-instance querying: a lightweight integration architecture for data journalism. PVLDB **9**(13), 1513–1516 (2016)
9. Bruneliere, H., Perez, J.G., Wimmer, M., Cabot, J.: EMF views: a view mechanism for integrating heterogeneous models. In: Johannesson, P., Lee, M.L., Liddle, S.W., Opdahl, A.L., López, Ó.P. (eds.) ER 2015. LNCS, vol. 9381, pp. 317–325. Springer, Cham (2015). https://doi.org/10.1007/978-3-319-25264-3_23
10. Bugiotti, F., Bursztyn, D., Deutsch, A., Ileana, I., Manolescu, I.: Invisible glue: scalable self-tuning multi-stores. In: CIDR 2015, Seventh Biennial Conference on Innovative Data Systems Research, Asilomar, CA, USA, 4–7 January 2015, Online Proceedings (2015). www.cidrdb.org
11. Bugiotti, F., Bursztyn, D., Deutsch, A., Manolescu, I., Zampetakis, S.: Flexible hybrid stores: constraint-based rewriting to the rescue. In: 32nd IEEE International Conference on Data Engineering, ICDE 2016, Helsinki, Finland, 16–20 May 2016, pp. 1394–1397 (2016)
12. Bugiotti, F., Cabibbo, L., Atzeni, P., Torlone, R.: Database design for NoSQL systems. In: Yu, E., Dobbie, G., Jarke, M., Purao, S. (eds.) ER 2014. LNCS, vol. 8824, pp. 223–231. Springer, Cham (2014). https://doi.org/10.1007/978-3-319-12206-9_18
13. Chen, P.: The entity-relationship model - toward a unified view of data. ACM Trans. Database Syst. **1**(1), 9–36 (1976)
14. Chillón, A.H., Morales, S.F., Sevilla, D., Molina, J.G.: Exploring the visualization of schemas for aggregate-oriented NoSQL databases. In: Proceedings of the ER Forum 2017 and the ER 2017 Demo Track co-located with the 36th International Conference on Conceptual Modelling (ER 2017), Valencia, Spain, 6–9 November 2017, CEUR Workshop Proceedings, vol. 1979, pp. 72–85. CEUR-WS.org (2017)
15. Curino, C., Moon, H.J., Tanca, L., Zaniolo, C.: Schema evolution in wikipedia - toward a web information system benchmark. In: ICEIS 2008 - Proceedings of the Tenth International Conference on Enterprise Information Systems, Volume DISI, Barcelona, Spain, 12–16 June 2008, pp. 323–332 (2008)
16. Daniel, G., Sunyé, G., Cabot, J.: UMLtoGraphDB: mapping conceptual schemas to graph databases. In: Comyn-Wattiau, I., Tanaka, K., Song, I.-Y., Yamamoto, S., Saeki, M. (eds.) ER 2016. LNCS, vol. 9974, pp. 430–444. Springer, Cham (2016). https://doi.org/10.1007/978-3-319-46397-1_33
17. De Virgilio, R., Maccioni, A., Torlone, R.: Model-driven design of graph databases. In: Yu, E., Dobbie, G., Jarke, M., Purao, S. (eds.) ER 2014. LNCS, vol. 8824, pp. 172–185. Springer, Cham (2014). https://doi.org/10.1007/978-3-319-12206-9_14
18. DeWitt, D.J., et al.: Split query processing in polybase. In: Proceedings of the ACM SIGMOD International Conference on Management of Data, SIGMOD 2013, New York, NY, USA, 22–27 June 2013, pp. 1255–1266. ACM (2013)

19. Gallinucci, E., Golfarelli, M., Rizzi, S.: Schema profiling of document-oriented databases. Inf. Syst. **75**, 13–25 (2018)
20. Gallinucci, E., Golfarelli, M., Rizzi, S., Abelló, A., Romero, O.: Interactive multi-dimensional modeling of linked data for exploratory OLAP. Inf. Syst. **77**, 86–104 (2018)
21. Garofalakis, M., Gionis, A., Rastogi, R., Seshadri, S., Shim, K.: XTRACT: a system for extracting document type descriptors from XML documents. SIGMOD Rec. **29**(2), 165–176 (2000)
22. Génova, G., Llorens, J., Martínez, P.: Semantics of the minimum multiplicity in ternary associations in UML. In: Gogolla, M., Kobryn, C. (eds.) UML 2001. LNCS, vol. 2185, pp. 329–341. Springer, Heidelberg (2001). https://doi.org/10.1007/3-540-45441-1_25
23. Gold, E.M.: Language identification in the limit. Inf. Control **10**(5), 447–474 (1967)
24. Hacigümüs, H., Sankaranarayanan, J., Tatemura, J., LeFevre, J., Polyzotis, N.: Odyssey: a multi-store system for evolutionary analytics. PVLDB **6**(11), 1180–1181 (2013)
25. Halpin, T.: Object-Role Modeling Workbook: Data Modeling Exercises Using ORM and NORMA, 1st edn. Technics Publications, LLC, USA (2015)
26. Herrmann, K., Voigt, H., Rausch, J., Behrend, A., Lehner, W.: Robust and simple database evolution. Inf. Syst. Front. **20**(1), 45–61 (2018)
27. Holubová, I., Scherzinger, S.: Unlocking the potential of nextgen multi-model databases for semantic big data projects. In: Proceedings of the International Workshop on Semantic Big Data, SBD 2019, New York, NY, USA, pp. 6:1–6:6. ACM (2019)
28. Keet, C.M., Fillottrani, P.R.: Toward an ontology-driven unifying metamodel for UML class diagrams, EER, and ORM2. In: Ng, W., Storey, V.C., Trujillo, J.C. (eds.) ER 2013. LNCS, vol. 8217, pp. 313–326. Springer, Heidelberg (2013). https://doi.org/10.1007/978-3-642-41924-9_26
29. Kellou-Menouer, K., Kedad, Z.: Schema discovery in RDF data sources. In: Johannesson, P., Lee, M.L., Liddle, S.W., Opdahl, A.L., López, Ó.P. (eds.) ER 2015. LNCS, vol. 9381, pp. 481–495. Springer, Cham (2015). https://doi.org/10.1007/978-3-319-25264-3_36
30. Kepner, J., et al.: Associative array model of SQL, NoSQL, and NewSQL databases. In: HPEC 2016: Proceedings of the High Performance Extreme Computing Conference, pp. 1–9. IEEE (2016)
31. Klettke, M., Awolin, H., Störl, U., Müller, D., Scherzinger, S.: Uncovering the evolution history of data lakes. In: 2017 IEEE International Conference on Big Data, BigData 2017, Boston, MA, USA, 11–14 December 2017, pp. 2462–2471. IEEE Computer Society (2017)
32. Klettke, M., Störl, U., Shenavai, M., Scherzinger, S.: NoSQL schema evolution and big data migration at scale. In: 2016 IEEE International Conference on Big Data, BigData 2016, Washington DC, USA, 5–8 December 2016, pp. 2764–2774. IEEE Computer Society (2016)
33. LeFevre, J., Sankaranarayanan, J., Hacigumus, H., Tatemura, J., Polyzotis, N., Carey, M.J.: MISO: souping up big data query processing with a multistore system. In: Proceedings of the 2014 ACM SIGMOD International Conference on Management of Data, New York, NY, USA, pp. 1591–1602. ACM (2014)

34. Liu, Z.H., Lu, J., Gawlick, D., Helskyaho, H., Pogossiants, G., Wu, Z.: Multi-model database management systems - a look forward. In: Gadepally, V., Mattson, T., Stonebraker, M., Wang, F., Luo, G., Teodoro, G. (eds.) DMAH/Poly -2018. LNCS, vol. 11470, pp. 16–29. Springer, Cham (2019). https://doi.org/10.1007/978-3-030-14177-6_2
35. Lu, J., Holubová, I.: Multi-model data management: what's new and what's next? In: EDBT 2017: Proceedings of the 20th International Conference on Extending Database Technology, pp. 602–605 (2017)
36. Lu, J., Holubová, I.: Multi-model databases: a new journey to handle the variety of data. ACM Comput. Surv. **52**(3), 55:1–55:38 (2019)
37. Lu, J., Holubová, I., Cautis, B.: Multi-model databases and tightly integrated polystores: current practices, comparisons, and open challenges. In: CIKM 2018: Proceedings of the 27th ACM International Conference on Information and Knowledge Management, pp. 2301–2302 (2018)
38. Mlýnková, I., Nečaský, M.: Heuristic methods for inference of XML schemas: lessons learned and open issues. Informatica Lith. Acad. Sci. **24**(4), 577–602 (2013)
39. OMG.: Business Process Model and Notation (BPMN), Version 2.0. OMG Standard, Object Management Group, January 2011
40. Pokorný, J.: Conceptual and database modelling of graph databases. In: IDEAS 2016: Proceedings of the 20th International Database Engineering & Applications Symposium, New York, NY, USA, pp. 370–377. ACM (2016)
41. Rumbaugh, J., Jacobson, I., Booch, G.: Unified Modeling Language Reference Manual. Pearson Higher Education (2004)
42. Saur, K., Dumitras, T., Hicks, M.W.: Evolving NoSQL Databases Without Downtime. CoRR, abs/1506.08800 (2015)
43. Scherzinger, S., Klettke, M., Störl, U.: Managing schema evolution in NoSQL data stores. In Proceedings of DBPL 2013: Proceedings of the 14th International Symposium on Database Programming Languages (2013)
44. Schildgen, J., Lottermann, T., Deßloch, S.: Cross-system NoSQL data transformations with NotaQL. In: Proceedings of the 3rd ACM SIGMOD Workshop on Algorithms and Systems for MapReduce and Beyond, BeyondMR 2016, New York, NY, USA, pp. 5:1–5:10. ACM (2016)
45. Sevilla Ruiz, D., Morales, S.F., García Molina, J.: Inferring versioned schemas from NoSQL databases and its applications. In: Johannesson, P., Lee, M.L., Liddle, S.W., Opdahl, A.L., López, Ó.P. (eds.) ER 2015. LNCS, vol. 9381, pp. 467–480. Springer, Cham (2015). https://doi.org/10.1007/978-3-319-25264-3_35
46. Störl, U., Müller, D., Tekleab, A., Tolale, S., Stenzel, J., Klettke, M., Scherzinger, S.: Curating variational data in application development. Proc. ICDE **2018**, 1605–1608 (2018)
47. Tian, Y., Zou, T., Ozcan, F., Goncalves, R., Pirahesh, H.: Joins for hybrid warehouses: exploiting massive parallelism in hadoop and enterprise data warehouses. In: Proceedings of the 18th International Conference on Extending Database Technology, EDBT 2015, Brussels, Belgium, 23–27 March 2015, pp. 373–384. OpenProceedings.org (2015)

WIP - SKOD: A Framework for Situational Knowledge on Demand

Servio Palacios[1(✉)], K. M. A. Solaiman[1(✉)], Pelin Angin[2], Alina Nesen[1],
Bharat Bhargava[1], Zachary Collins[3], Aaron Sipser[3], Michael Stonebraker[3],
and James Macdonald[4]

[1] Purdue University, West Lafayette, IN 47906, USA
{spalacio,ksolaima,anesen,bbshail}@purdue.edu
[2] METU, Ankara, Turkey
pangin@ceng.metu.edu.tr
[3] MIT CSAIL, Cambridge, MA 02139, USA
{zcollins,asipser,stonebraker}@csail.mit.edu
[4] Northrop Grumman Corporation, Falls Church, USA
jim.macdonald@ngc.com

Abstract. Extracting relevant patterns from heterogeneous data streams poses significant computational and analytical challenges. Further, identifying such patterns and pushing analogous content to interested parties according to mission needs in real-time is a difficult problem. This paper presents the design of SKOD, a novel Situational Knowledge Query Engine that continuously builds a multi-modal relational knowledge base using SQL queries; SKOD pushes dynamic content to relevant users through triggers based on modeling of users' interests. SKOD is a scalable, real-time, on-demand situational knowledge extraction and dissemination framework that processes streams of multi-modal data utilizing publish/subscribe stream engines. The initial prototype of SKOD uses deep neural networks and natural language processing techniques to extract and model relevant objects from video streams and topics, entities and events from unstructured text resources such as Twitter and news articles. Through its extensible architecture, SKOD aims to provide a high-performance, generic framework for situational knowledge on demand, supporting effective information retrieval for evolving missions.

Keywords: Query engine · Multi-modal information retrieval ·
Knowledge base · Stream processing · Targeted information
dissemination

1 Introduction

The past decade has witnessed an unprecedented *volume* of data being generated by a *variety* of sources at very high *velocity*, resulting in the rise of the *big*

This research is supported by Northrop Grumman Mission Systems' University Research Program.
S. Palacios and K.M.A. Solaiman contributed equally and are considered to be co-first authors.

© Springer Nature Switzerland AG 2019
V. Gadepally et al. (Eds.): DMAH 2019/Poly 2019, LNCS 11721, pp. 154–166, 2019.
https://doi.org/10.1007/978-3-030-33752-0_11

data paradigm. Specifically, the developments in social networks and Internet of Things (IoT) have created a plethora of multi-modal data sources that generate billions of data records every second, only a small fraction of which readily translates into useful information. While the availability of such vast amounts of data has made it possible to build large knowledge bases, on-demand extraction of highly relevant situational knowledge for specific missions from those heterogeneous data clouds remains a difficult task for the following reasons: (1) Accurate correlation of data from different resources for billions of data items is a daunting task; (2) A knowledge base built upon a specific ontology may not cater to the needs of a mission when additional mission requirements/user interests are defined later; (3) The storage of the most relevant data in the knowledge base is essential to avoid performance degradation with growing data; (4) Generalization of knowledge bases irrespective of mission needs is a challenge.

Many critical missions will require real-time targeted dissemination of information to interested parties as information becomes available. Achieving high-performance, accurate information extraction and propagation requires (1) accurate modeling of the different users' interests; (2) application of intelligent filters on streaming data to capture and correlate the most relevant aspects; (3) triggers for communicating the gathered information to the interested parties.

In this paper, we propose SKOD, a framework for situational knowledge on demand, which provides high-performance real-time analysis of streaming data of multiple modalities from different sources to dynamically and continuously build mission-specific knowledge bases. In order to capture data most relevant to user needs, SKOD uses past user query patterns to construct the knowledge base.

Our approach provides a scalable solution for modeling different user interests over vast amounts of data while allowing flexibility for future incoming data. Additional interests can immediately be integrated by defining new queries on the knowledge base. SKOD currently handles pattern extraction from streaming video and text data, but the extensible architecture allows facile integration of additional data modalities such as audio, sensor data, signals, and others.

2 Model

2.1 Example Application Scenario

In order to clearly illustrate the objectives and operation of SKOD, we describe an example application scenario of the system in this section. Let us consider a city information system, which provides access to multiple agents (e.g., police, public works department, citizens, emergency personnel, homeland security) with varying missions, hence varying information needs. In such a system, while the police would be interested in patterns such as unsafe lane changes, locations visited by a suspicious person, to name a few; the public works department would be interested in patterns such as potholes and occluded street signs. An example query to be submitted to this system by a police officer is:

Q1: *List cars parked next to fire hydrants illegally today.*

To answer Q1, we will require detecting cars and fire hydrants in video frames and tweets, given the available data sources are city surveillance cameras and Twitter. The query response will provide information that the policeman will always be interested in, therefore as new data streams in, patterns matching the query should be communicated to the policeman and other police officers as well, due to the similarity of their profiles to the user submitting the query. A different user of the system (a firefighter) can later submit **Q2:** *Get locations of leaking fire hydrants.* While this query will be able to utilize the knowledge base created in response to Q1, it will build upon it to find patterns of the act *leak* in both data sources as they stream additional data to the system.

2.2 SKOD System Architecture

The SKOD architecture consists of three large modules - (1) streaming platform to handle the vast amount of heterogeneous incoming data, (2) multi-modal query engine to model the user interest based on their previous queries and (3) the front end with the indexing layer. The query engine also accommodates the unit for feature-analysis of heterogeneous data for identifying personalized events. SKOD includes fixed queries on data streams from multiple sources, both separate and combined. The queries are then stored to build the knowledge base, which in return models the user interests. SKOD can provide users with information similar to their previous queries as well as missing information on their existing information. This information is delivered to the user using trigger events in the relational database. Similar queries and repeated accesses to similar data are cached to provide better throughput. The front-end queries an indexing layer based on Lucene indexes to improve throughput. In Fig. 1, we show an overview of SKOD's architecture. We describe the three modules below.

Streaming Broker. Due to the latency-sensitive set of applications that SKOD aims to tackle to consume data from heterogeneous sources, this work relies on Apache Kafka to expose a real-time stream processing pipeline. Apache Kafka is a scalable and fault-tolerant publish-subscribe messaging system. Kafka achieves the capability to store and process data from multiple applications (producers) through a topic abstraction system. As an output, multiple applications can consume the inserted data from all the producers asynchronously and without any loss. The producers/consumers abstraction allows SKOD architecture to provide real-time analysis and recommendation capability. Apache Kafka features allow to store the raw incoming data in Postgres and consume the same data by text and video processing applications simultaneously.

Currently SKOD architecture consumes both RESTful, and streaming data from Twitter and video feeds through Kafka. SKOD is capable of integrating data from other real-time applications (i.e., sensor, audio, files, JDBC) through Kafka Clients or Kafka Connect. Kafka Clients allow to pass and retrieve messages directly to and from Kafka as long as the message can be converted to bytes.

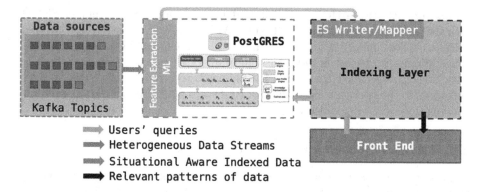

Fig. 1. SKOD architecture. Kafka topics partition layout diagram.

We show a detailed view of SKOD data streaming pipeline in Fig. 3 for different types of Twitter data.

Multi-modal Query Engine. The multi-modal query engine consists of several sub-modules. The first sub-module consumes the streams of data provided by the *streaming broker* and stores them directly in the relational database (Postgres). The second sub-module extracts features from each mode of data with a separate processing unit. For our current implementation, we focus on processing video and unstructured text to extract features relevant to most domains. We explain these processes in Sects. 2.3 and 2.4. In the final module of the multi-modal query engine, SKOD utilizes users' SQL queries to build the knowledge base on top of a relational database and pushes relevant content to users without user intervention. We explain this module in detail in Sect. 2.5. In Figs. 1 and 2 we observe the overall architecture.

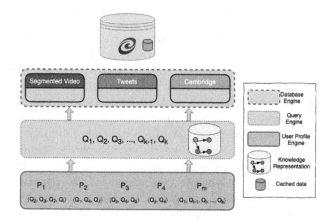

Fig. 2. Multimodal query engine representation utilizing situational knowledge.

Indexing. Elasticsearch is a distributed indexing and search engine. SKOD queries Elasticsearch through a RESTful API. Moreover, Elasticsearch utilizes Lucene indexes under the hood. Naturally, Elasticsearch achieves fast response times because it queries an index instead of querying text or video directly. The basic structure is called *Document*. Elasticsearch returns a ranked set of results according to the relevance of the query. SKOD uses Elasticsearch to rank relevant content to push to the end user.

2.3   Feature Extraction from Video Streams

Video data represents a separate and unique modality in the SKOD multi-modal system for storing and extracting knowledge on demand. Video data comes in large amounts, unstructured, and raw video is unlabeled, frequently in need of processing, cleaning, and preparing for the next stage in the data flow.

Video can be viewed as a sequence of frames, where each frame is characterized by its bitmap that can later be transformed into a multidimensional array or a tensor. The need to work with extensive digital representations requires specific ways of storing and operating with the video data, which are different from those of text and structured data. When the knowledge must be extracted efficiently on demand from the heterogeneous multi-modal database, there are several challenges to be resolved: (1) Entities from each frame have to be accessible for user queries, user-defined stored procedures, and event triggers; (2) For connecting with other modalities in a poly-store environment, these entities must be stored in a way that they can be matched with the text data and text metadata as well as data from other modalities for further analysis; (3) There must be a way to obtain entities in an ad-hoc manner to extract knowledge from streams of video. We resolve these challenges utilizing two off-the-shelf solutions: Apache Kafka for streaming video in a scalable, fault-tolerant manner and the YOLOv3 real-time object detection system [18].

2.4   Feature Extraction from Unstructured Text

Data Collection and Initial Processing. For unstructured text, currently SKOD processes tweets. There are two types of tweet data available for scraping - RESTful data (historic data) and streaming data. SKOD uses Twitter search API to collect RESTful data and Twitter streaming API for collecting real-time tweet streams. It creates independent docker containers for the producers, which can take tags and timelines as environment variables and run simultaneously. Since there can be overlap of tweet data from multiple producers, SKOD uses the Kafka streaming platform to handle the asynchronous, scalable and fault tolerant flow of tweets using the same topic abstraction for all. After the data is in Kafka, SKOD uses two separate consumers - (1) to parse and populate Postgres with the tweet and associated metadata, and (2) to pass the raw tweets to a feature extraction engine. Figure 3 shows an overview of the architecture.

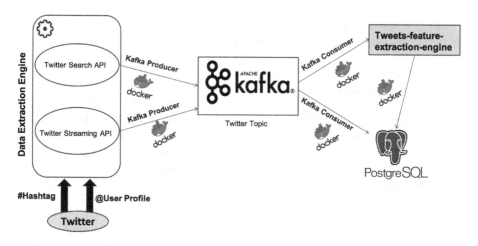

Fig. 3. Data streaming pipeline from restful and streaming tweets to applications.

Feature Extraction. Understanding unstructured texts has always been a daunting task. Even with the recent rise of language models it is hard to parse unstructured social texts into domain-independent features.

We first preprocess the text using Stanford CoreNLP [13], extract named entities and co-reference chains. Then we create a separate table in Postgres to save each tweet with its associated named entities i.e., LOCATION, ORGANI-ZATION, PERSON, saving them as text arrays and associated topic with the tweet. Further, we create another column `objects`, which are any words in the tweet except stop words and the ones identified in named entities.

2.5   Knowledge Representation

Unified knowledge representation for all streamed data is required for the query engine to extract useful knowledge and disseminate information to relevant parties efficiently. In SKOD, we represent knowledge using relational data and SQL queries on the data, which persist for the lifetime of the knowledge base and grow with additional user interests. Representation of textual data such as tweets and online news is more straightforward through the extraction of topics and keywords, which can directly be entered into the corresponding columns in the RDBMS tables. Multimedia data such as video and audio are represented both with the binary data and the text data extracted as a result of the processing performed on the binary data. The stored data also includes available metadata for all modalities, such as timestamp, geolocation, and some others. The metadata is especially useful when correlating multiple forms of data for the same events.

The schemas of the PostgreSQL tables storing the extracted features from the tweet text and video frames are as follows:

```
TWEETS(tweet_id INT,
    locations VARCHAR(100)[],
    objects VARCHAR(100)[],
    organizations VARCHAR(100)[],
    persons VARCHAR(100)[],
    dates VARCHAR(100)[],
    times VARCHAR(100)[],
    topic VARCHAR(100)[]
    created_at DATE)

VIDEO_FRAMES(video_id INT,
    frame_id INT,
    locations VARCHAR(100),
    objects VARCHAR(100)[],
    people VARCHAR(100)[],
    timestamp DATE,
    image BYTEA)
```

Here locations, organizations, and persons are different classes of named entities and other classes can be defined as necessary. Typical attributes are used to facilitate joins between the tables for data correlation. Attributes in different tables may have different names, but have commonalities, i.e., timestamp and created_at, or people and persons. Given the initial knowledge base is built upon **Q1** mentioned in Sect. 2.1, new streams of video data will result in running the object detector for cars and fire hydrants, and the extracted data will be inserted into the database. Similarly for streaming Twitter data, tweets that have the objects car and fire hydrant will be inserted into the relevant table.

Q1 for a system with these two data sources will translate into multiple SQL queries for the situational knowledge query engine:

```
SELECT video_id, frame_id
FROM VIDEO_FRAMES
WHERE 'car' = ANY(objects)
AND 'fire hydrant'= ANY(objects)

SELECT tweet_id
FROM TWEETS
WHERE 'car' = ANY(objects)
AND 'fire hydrant'= ANY(objects)
```

```
SELECT t.tweet_id, v.video_id, v.frame_id
FROM TWEETS t, VIDEO_FRAMES v
WHERE 'car' = ANY(t.objects) AND 'fire hydrant' = ANY(t.objects)
AND 'car' = ANY(v.objects) AND 'fire hydrant' = ANY(v.objects)
AND v.location = ANY(t.locations)
```

As data from either resource is streaming in, patterns matching these queries will create triggers for relevant data to be communicated to interested users. Note that the complete system requires translation of natural language questions into SQL queries through entity recognition, and constructs for creating all related queries given the tables for different data sources and their common attributes. Although this initial design is limited to recognition of objects, a richer knowledge base will require incorporation of activity recognition in videos and tweets.

3   Implementation

3.1   Twitter Data Collection and Feature Extraction

Since the city of Cambridge was the point-of-focus for the data used in this work, the target was to collect a million tweets that discuss events and entities in Cambridge, MA along with all the metadata from Twitter. Twitter data can be collected by hashtags, user timelines, geo-data, and general queries. In SKOD, we chose to search by hashtags and user timelines. For that purpose, about 15 hashtags and 15 user timelines were manually selected after going through profiles in timelines and descriptions for hashtags. For example, @CambridgePolice warns about any possible crimes or street law changes, while @bostonfire talks about fire-related incidents in Boston. At a much broader scale, hashtags like #CambMA include all tweets by many Cambridge, MA departments.

For the implementation of twitter APIs, SKOD uses tweepy.api[1]. There is a class method API() which allows to search by both hashtags and timelines by providing a wrapper for twitter APIs. The Twitter streaming API is used to download twitter messages in real time. In Tweepy, an instance of tweepy.Stream establishes a streaming session and routes messages to StreamListener instance by allowing a connection to twitter streaming API.

Currently, we have around 80K tweets in Postgres. More are being accumulated as the module keeps running. The consumers inherit twitter data as JSON messages. The JSON message is parsed to extract relevant metadata. Different types of tweets are identified, i.e., original, retweet, and quoted tweets. The tweet text with all the parsed metadata along with the original JSON message is saved in Postgres. With the tweet text, we obtain a social network connected by retweets and follows.

The feature extraction process from the tweet text is explained in Sect. 2.4. We ran the pretrained 7 class NER CRFs from Stanford toolkit [13] to identify the entities. For topic extraction, SKOD uses the Latent Dirichlet Allocation (LDA) method [4]. We show the schema of the PostgreSQL table storing the extracted features from the Tweet text in Sect. 2.5. SKOD wraps the producers and consumers in docker containers. The producers and consumers take the Kafka hostname and port number as input, along with the tags and timelines in files.

3.2   Feature Extraction from Video

Real-time video broadcasting in a massively scaled and distributed system requires architectural solutions that are resilient to node failures and supportive for automatic recovery. The video data may come with metadata such as geolocation, the movement speed and IP address of the camera, and timestamp; therefore, the message broker needs to scale horizontally as well. In SKOD, Apache Kafka utilizes different topics that represent categories for different modalities of the data.

---

[1] http://docs.tweepy.org/en/v3.5.0/api.html.

Similarly, producers transform the videos into a stream of frames and metadata with OpenCV. Then, the consumers read messages from topics and forward the data for computation and knowledge extraction. In the prototype implementation, SKOD uses a universal pre-trained neural network as a tool for object extraction and recognition in the video data. SKOD's video processing

Fig. 4. Result of applying the pre-trained neural network to the Cambridge dataset.

feature differentiates between 150 object classes. SKOD identifies the objects in the video on a frame-by-frame basis. Each frame is divided into several regions that are classified by the neural network to assign the most probable class along with a confidence score; this helps to establish the exact boundaries of the objects in the frame. The non-maximum suppression algorithm dismisses all the proposed bounding boxes where the confidence score is not the maximum one. Thus, the approach allows assigning classes and boundaries at the same time in one run. The result obtained for a particular video frame in the collected Cambridge dataset using the proposed neural network architecture is shown in Fig. 4. For each processed frame, the recognized data and metadata are stored in the RDBMS and can be used for queries that involve the video data modality.

3.3   Front End and Indexing Layer

The front-end utilizes React[2], which is a JavaScript library for building user interfaces. Also, we manage states and side effects using the Cerebral[3] library. We leverage interactive maps via the Leaflet[4] library integrated with React and Cerebral. SKOD caches the most frequent queries to provide faster response times. SKOD's architecture comprises a set of Node.js and python microservices, i.e., Docker containers. In Fig. 5, we demonstrate the integration of multimodality combining the extracted Twitter data with the front-end (we utilize GPS coordinates in the Twitter data in GeoJSON format to render the Twitter data in the Leaflet map). The Tweets come through the Apache Kafka broker. Then the data is stored in the backend (Postgres). Finally, the Web application queries the indexing layer and it also watches for new changes utilizing WebSockets[5]. SKOD provides an additional layer of cache storing content in the browser using

---

[2] https://reactjs.org/.

[3] https://github.com/cerebral/cerebral.

[4] https://leafletjs.com/.

[5] The Web application was developed utilizing ideas from the OATS Center at Purdue. In particular, the OADA framework https://github.com/OADA.

PouchDB[6] similar to the OADA cache library[7]. SKOD future releases include the creation of an elastic cache-layer building a rich set of network topologies on the edge of the network utilizing Web Browsers with Real-Time Communication (WebRTC[8]) [16].

Fig. 5. Situational knowledge on demand proof-of-concept. Incoming streams of data shown in a Leaflet map.

4   Related Work

The rise of the big data paradigm in the past decade has resulted in a variety of approaches for processing and fusion of data of multiple modalities to extract useful knowledge. Poria et al. proposed an approach for fusing audio, visual and textual data for sentiment analysis [17]. Foresti et al. introduced a socio-mobile and sensor data fusion approach for emergency response to disasters [8]. Meditskos et al. developed a system for multi-modal fusion of data including language analysis results, and gestures captured from multimedia data streams to provide situational awareness in healthcare [14]. Adjali et al. proposed an approach for multi-modal fusion of data from sensors to provide ambient intelligence for robots [2]. While successful for the specific domains considered, these approaches may not generalize to other domains.

One application of multi-modal data fusion that has gained increasing interest is visual question answering. Zhu et al. [21] tackle the visual question answering problem by building an external knowledge base via iterative querying of the

---

[6] https://pouchdb.com/.

[7] https://github.com/OADA/oada-cache.

[8] https://webrtc.org/.

external sources. Their system uses a neural approach where task-driven memories are actively obtained by iterative queries and produces the final answer based on these evidences. Although they take a query based approach for the QA task, their data source is just limited to images. Our approach aims to build a knowledge base integrating visual, textual, and structured data along with the relations among them.

Likewise, Wu et al. propose a method combining an internal representation of image content with information from an external knowledge base to answer complex image queries [20]. Video analytics represents a class of problems related to one of the dimensions of multi-modal systems exploration, namely efficient and fast video querying. In [10], the authors develop a declarative language for fast video analytics and enhance it with the engine that accepts, automatically optimizes and executes the queries in this language efficiently.

While many multi-modal knowledge bases are constructed using learning-based data fusion approaches on large static datasets, query-driven approaches construct knowledge bases through repeated querying of text and multimedia databases. Nguyen et al. [15] propose QKBfly, an approach for on-the-fly construction of knowledge bases from text data driven by queries. QKBfly utilizes a semantic-graph representation of sentences through which named-entity disambiguation, co-reference resolution and relation extraction are performed. Bienvenu et al. propose an approach for utilizing user queries and the associated user feedback to repair inconsistent DL-Lite knowledge bases [3]. The constructed knowledge bases will in most cases include inconsistencies and missing information. Probabilistic knowledge bases have been introduced to handle these inconsistencies by assigning belief scores to facts in the knowledge bases [5,7], followed by approaches to fuse data from multiple probabilistic bases [19].

Traditional knowledge bases are used for information extraction to answer user queries as they are submitted. On the other hand, dynamic detection of events on streaming data is important for many systems today, due to the need to make users aware of important events in real time. This has resulted in the development of complex event processing systems for purposes such as crisis management [9], to create triggers when streaming data matches pre-defined patterns [6]. Although these systems provide real-time event notification to interested parties, their rule base in most cases is fixed, not supporting evolving mission requirements and users with different interests.

5   Conclusions and Future Work

In this paper we proposed SKOD, a situational knowledge on demand engine that aims to provide a generic framework for dynamically building knowledge bases from multi-modal data to enable effective information extraction and targeted information dissemination for missions that might have evolving requirements. In order to provide the best run-time performance and accuracy, SKOD uses a query-driven approach to knowledge base construction. Being query-driven, it is expected to enable effective information retrieval and dissemination in a variety of fields including law enforcement, homeland defense, healthcare etc., all building knowledge upon the specific interests of the system users.

The development of SKOD is in progress with components for stream data processing, feature extraction from video and text data currently in place. Our future work will involve the development of components for query processing, user similarity modeling, and user relevance feedback to achieve highly accurate real-time targeted information propagation. The system will be evaluated with multiple rich multi-modal datasets such as Visual Genome [11], COCO [12], YouTube-8M [1], and collected tweets and video data set of our own for various missions and user types.

Funding Information. Distribution Statement A: Approved for Public Release; Distribution is Unlimited; #19-1107; Dated 07/18/19.

References

1. Abu-El-Haija, S., et al.: YouTube-8M: a large-scale video classification benchmark. CoRR abs/1609.08675 (2016). http://arxiv.org/abs/1609.08675
2. Adjali, O., Hina, M.D., Dourlens, S., Ramdane-Cherif, A.: Multimodal fusion, fission and virtual reality simulation for an ambient robotic intelligence. In: ANT/SEIT. Procedia Computer Science, vol. 52, pp. 218–225. Elsevier (2015)
3. Bienvenu, M., Bourgaux, C., Goasdoué, F.: Query-driven repairing of inconsistent DL-Lite knowledge bases. In: Proceedings of the Twenty-Fifth International Joint Conference on Artificial Intelligence, IJCAI 2016, New York, 9–15 July 2016, pp. 957–964 (2016). http://www.ijcai.org/Abstract/16/140
4. Blei, D.M., Ng, A.Y., Jordan, M.I.: Latent Dirichlet allocation. J. Mach. Learn. Res. **3**, 993–1022 (2003). http://dl.acm.org/citation.cfm?id=944919.944937
5. Chen, Y., Wang, D.Z.: Knowledge expansion over probabilistic knowledge bases. In: Proceedings of the 2014 ACM SIGMOD International Conference on Management of Data, SIGMOD 2014, pp. 649–660. ACM, New York (2014). https://doi.org/10.1145/2588555.2610516. http://doi.acm.org/10.1145/2588555.2610516
6. Cugola, G., Margara, A.: Processing flows of information: from data stream to complex event processing. ACM Comput. Surv. **44**(3), 15:1–15:62 (2012). https://doi.org/10.1145/2187671.2187677
7. Dong, X., et al.: Knowledge vault: a web-scale approach to probabilistic knowledge fusion. In: KDD, pp. 601–610. ACM (2014)
8. Foresti, G.L., Farinosi, M., Vernier, M.: Situational awareness in smart environments: socio-mobile and sensor data fusion for emergency response to disasters. J. Ambient Intell. Humanized Comput. **6**(2), 239–257 (2015)
9. Itria, M.L., Daidone, A., Ceccarelli, A.: A complex event processing approach for crisis-management systems. CoRR abs/1404.7551 (2014)
10. Kang, D., Bailis, P., Zaharia, M.: BlazeIt: fast exploratory video queries using neural networks. CoRR abs/1805.01046 (2018)
11. Krishna, R., et al.: Visual genome: connecting language and vision using crowd-sourced dense image annotations. CoRR abs/1602.07332 (2016). http://arxiv.org/abs/1602.07332
12. Lin, T.-Y., et al.: Microsoft COCO: common objects in context. In: Fleet, D., Pajdla, T., Schiele, B., Tuytelaars, T. (eds.) ECCV 2014. LNCS, vol. 8693, pp. 740–755. Springer, Cham (2014). https://doi.org/10.1007/978-3-319-10602-1_48

13. Manning, C., Surdeanu, M., Bauer, J., Finkel, J., Bethard, S., McClosky, D.: The Stanford CoreNLP natural language processing toolkit. In: Proceedings of 52nd Annual Meeting of the Association for Computational Linguistics: System Demonstrations, pp. 55–60. Association for Computational Linguistics, Baltimore, June 2014. https://doi.org/10.3115/v1/P14-5010. https://www.aclweb.org/anthology/P14-5010

14. Meditskos, G., Vrochidis, S., Kompatsiaris, I.: Description logics and rules for multimodal situational awareness in healthcare. In: Amsaleg, L., Guðmundsson, G., Gurrin, C., Jónsson, B., Satoh, S. (eds.) MMM 2017, Part I. LNCS, vol. 10132, pp. 714–725. Springer, Cham (2017). https://doi.org/10.1007/978-3-319-51811-4_58

15. Nguyen, D.B., Abujabal, A., Tran, N.K., Theobald, M., Weikum, G.: Query-driven on-the-fly knowledge base construction. Proc. VLDB Endow. **11**(1), 66–79 (2017). https://doi.org/10.14778/3151113.3151119

16. Palacios, S., Santos, V., Barsallo, E., Bhargava, B.: MioStream: a peer-to-peer distributed live media streaming on the edge. Multimedia Tools Appl. (2019). https://doi.org/10.1007/s11042-018-6940-2

17. Poria, S., Cambria, E., Howard, N., Huang, G.B., Hussain, A.: Fusing audio, visual and textual clues for sentiment analysis from multimodal content. Neurocomputing **174**(PA), 50–59 (2016). https://doi.org/10.1016/j.neucom.2015.01.095. http://dx.doi.org/10.1016/j.neucom.2015.01.095

18. Redmon, J., Divvala, S., Girshick, R., Farhadi, A.: You only look once: unified, real-time object detection. In: Proceedings of the IEEE conference on computer vision and pattern recognition, pp. 779–788 (2016)

19. Rodríguez, M.E., Goldberg, S., Wang, D.Z.: SigmaKB: multiple probabilistic knowledge base fusion. PVLDB **9**(13), 1577–1580 (2016)

20. Wu, Q., Wang, P., Shen, C., Dick, A.R., van den Hengel, A.: Ask me anything: free-form visual question answering based on knowledge from external sources. In: IEEE Conference on Computer Vision and Pattern Recognition, CVPR 2016, Las Vegas, 27–30 June 2016, pp. 4622–4630 (2016). https://doi.org/10.1109/CVPR.2016.500

21. Zhu, Y., Lim, J.J., Fei-Fei, L.: Knowledge acquisition for visual question answering via iterative querying. In: CVPR, pp. 6146–6155. IEEE Computer Society (2017)

Development of a Polystore Data Management System for an Evolving Big Scientific Data Archive

Manoj Poudel[✉], Rashmi P. Sarode, Shashank Shrestha,
Wanming Chu, and Subhash Bhalla

University of Aizu, Aizu-Wakamatsu, Fukushima, Japan
{m5212201, d8202102, d8201104, w-chu,
bhalla}@u-aizu.ac.jp

Abstract. Handling large datasets can be a big challenge in case of most astronomical data repositories. Many astronomical repositories manage images, text, key-values, and graphs that make up the enormous volume of data available in the astronomical domain. Palomar Transient Factory (PTF/iPTF) is one such project which has relational data, image data, lightcurve data sets, graphs, and text data. Organizing these data in a single data management system may have low performance and efficiency issue. Thus, we propose to demonstrate a prototype system to manage such heterogeneous data with multiple storage units using polystore based approaches. The prototype supports a set-theoretic query language for access to cloud-based data resources.

Keywords: Astronomical data · Multi data stores · Query management system · PTF/iPTF data · ZTF data

1 Introduction

Since the year 2009, a new era has begun in astronomy. The project on Palomar Transient Factory (PTF) is an astronomical survey [1]. One of the key goals of this survey is to monitor the northern night sky, observe the changes in astronomical bodies, and study optical transients and variable sources, i.e., star, supernovae, asteroids, comets, fast-moving solar system object, and other stellar explosions through different telescopes. PTF performs two types of data processing, stream processing in real-time and maintaining an up to date data with an image archive [2]. The data is processed in real-time for sky information updates. It is maintained as an archive for research studies, considering various domains in the sky. The grant agencies require all astronomy data to be made shareable by astronomers' worldwide. These archival data are publically available through the web-based system of Infrared Science Archive (IRSA/IPAC) [3, 4]. Infrared Processing and Analysis Center (IPAC) in collaboration with PTF has developed science operation (e.g. develop a high-quality photometry pipeline) and data management (e.g., searchable database), data archives (e.g., images archives), community supports for astronomy and planetary science missions (e.g., Graphical User Interface).

© Springer Nature Switzerland AG 2019
V. Gadepally et al. (Eds.): DMAH 2019/Poly 2019, LNCS 11721, pp. 167–182, 2019.
https://doi.org/10.1007/978-3-030-33752-0_12

Palomar Transient Factory has large amount of astronomical data. PTF presents a case example of data store that is shared resource for all astronomers. The data is huge in size and variety. The data type varies from images of the astronomical objects, unstructured texts, relations and key-value pairs. This project performs tasks for new discoveries of astronomical objects. So, data schemas may be changed and more data products can be added frequently.

The publicly archived data products were released between 2009–2017. There have been three data releases within this time, which include photometrically calibrated single exposure images for a selected region of the sky and source catalog file for the same images. The source catalog files have information about the imagery data. With the start of 2013, Intermediate Palomar Transient Factory (iPTF) project was built upon the legacy of the Caltech-led Palomar Transient Factory (PTF) [5]. iPTF improved software for the data reduction and source classification through the historical Palomar Transient Factory data and rapid follow-up studies of transient sources. In 2017, iPTF transitioned into the Zwicky Transient Factory (ZTF) using a reworked version of the same telescope as iPTF. ZTF uses a new camera to provide a new reference images catalogs, lightcurves and transient candidates [6]. ZTFs large data will act as a reference for the next project on Large Synoptic Survey Telescope (LSST). LSST will survey measurement of position, fluxes and shapes, lightcurve and calibrated images. The evolution of PTF project with details about the products are described in Table 1.

Optical time-domain astronomy is on the verge of major growth in data rate and volume. The data is expected to increase 300 times by 2022. To manage these data, highly efficient machine learning techniques will be required to classify source types. Major growth in number of detected sources will require efficient and well-designed databases.

Table 1. PTF data overview

Project name	Duration	Data download	No of FITS file	Product
PTF Level 0 Level 1	2009–2012	0.1 TB/night	$\sim$3 million	Epochal images Photometric catalogs
iPTF Level 2	2013–2017	0.3 TB/night	$\sim$5 million	Deep reference, lightcurves
ZTF Data release 1	2017–2020	1.4 TB/night	$\sim$50 million	New reference, lightcurves, transient candidates, catalog
LSST	2020–2023	30 TB/night	$\sim$500 million	Calibrated images, measure of position, flux and shapes, and lightcurve

The rest of the paper starts with description of PTF/iPTF data processing i.e., real time and archives in Sect. 2. Retrieving the catalog file from IRSA remote source is described in Sect. 3 where importing FITS header file to Local PostgresDB and data migration method are discussed. We then provide a brief system overview and query system with multiple databases via query formulation, query transformation, query execution and visualization in Sect. 4. In Sect. 5, we provide comparison with other polystore systems. Finally, we conclude our work and discuss future directions.

2 PTF/iPTF Data Processing Overview

The Palomar Observatory is a collection of telescopes located in San Diego, California, USA. The telescope takes high-resolution images of the night sky. These images are called raw images which are stored in Flexible Images Transport System (FITS) file format with multiple extensions [7]. Each image file is single camera exposure with header and data unit (HDU). Each data unit (DU) is accompanied by a header unit (HU) containing summary header information. There are different levels of data, i.e., Level-0, Level-1, and Level-2 [8]. It is divided according to the number of CCDs and exposure difference as shown in Table 2.

Table 2. Level of PTF data

Level of PTF data	Overview	Data access
Level-0	Received from the observatory as a multi-extension FITS file containing all 12 CCDs	Level 0 data is raw data which is not publicly available to download and use
Level-1	Processed data corresponding to the original single CCD exposures	Publicly available to download and use with its own images search query interface
Level-2	Products derived from combining the Level-1 data, such as deep sky co-added data and the catalogs derived from such data	Publicly available to download and use with its own catalog query interface

2.1 Real-Time Data Processing

The raw multi-extension FITS files flow from Palomar via a microwave link to IPAC for processing through different pipelines, creating a variety of science products [9]. Science products are constructed using the following four pipelines.

Real-time Pipeline is primarily an image-subtraction pipeline. The raw data goes through an initial calibration using pre-existing calibration files from a previous night for data aggregation and comparison. Any changes in the images get indexed in their archives or else is rejected [10]. After image subtraction, a refined photometric calibration, transient candidates and solar system objects are derived.

Photometric Pipeline starts up at the "end of the night" indicating that no further data is expected. The data from the entire night is used to produce calibrated images, optimal co-addition, object extraction, and standard photometric products. In this pipeline matching, bit-masks are created by reduced images which provides information such as radiation hits, CCD bleeds, saturation and filtering ghosts. Sources catalogs are also generated with aperture photometry and Point-Spread Function Fitting (PSF) Photometry [9, 11]. Aperture photometry is the measurement of light which fall inside a particular aperture. All point sources imaged by the atmosphere-telescope-detector are represented by a point-spread function.

Reference Image Pipeline produces deep images of the sky. The inputs of this pipeline are the images produced by the photometric pipeline. Through that input highest quality data gets co-added and a new photometric and astrometric calibration is derived. Also, the final pipeline layer uses both aperture photometry and Point-Spread Function Fitting to produced deep reference catalogs [10, 12].

Light Curve Pipeline is also known as relative photometry which uses sources catalogs from the photometry to produce high accuracy light curves. An analysis is performed by the combination of each tile, CCD, and filter to find the object within the field with the lowest variances [10]. A lightcurve database for a subset of fields and epochs are publically available with separate user interfaces.

2.2   IRSA Archives

IRSA provides an interface for the archive of PTF data through Image Server Program Interface named IBE [13]. IBE is a cloud API that uses HTTP syntax, providing low-level, program friendly methods for querying astronomical images, metadata tables, including support for the International Virtual Observatory Alliance (IVOA), Simple Image Access Protocol, Simple Spectral Access Protocol, and Table Access Protocol. User has an option to search imagery products provided by IRSA using these different protocols. These protocols help users query to retrieve metadata columns, row or list of image URLs. IRSAs images and spectra are stored in browsable web directories.

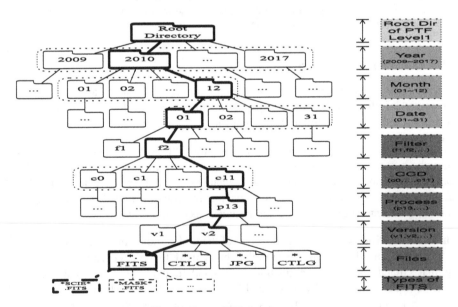

Fig. 1. B-tree PTF data structure

In web directory IRSA maintain the PTF FITS file in B-tree data structure as shown in Fig. 1 [14]. The top node is called the root node and the bottom nodes in the index are called the leaf nodes. The leaf nodes contain the PTF FITS images data. All insertions or update starts at a leaf node.

This directory has image URL links which are indexed to support approximate 3 million PTF FITS files. Each record is captured in a simplified form, as shown in Table 3. These record level addressing with API supports for visualization of images. This makes it easy to embed to the archive directly in user's software.

The ith record contains an absolute identity as, x_i to identify the base record. The components with x_i consist of year, month, date, filter, CCD, processes, version, files as shown in Fig. 1. There are approximately 3 million record in PTF archive. Each record has up to sixty thousand (60000) fields data units, that are identified as y_{ij} ($y_{i,1}$ .... $y_{i,60000}$) where (i,j) indicate the record identity (x_i) and position of the field (y_{ij}) in the individual record.

Table 3. PTF FITS file index in browsable web directory with absolute and relative addressing

Header	Data	
x_i, y_{ij}, Size and index for the data (1, ..., 60000)	y_{ij}	
	Name, size, data	Data type
	–	–

2.3 IRSA Web Based System

The IRSA provides easy access to PTF/iPTF data, including Images services, catalog services, and Time Series tools [15]. IRSA provides both raw and processed data, including full FITS frames, image cutouts, and, supermosaics. IRSA provides two graphical program interfaces to search for astronomical objects.

From the images service, users can query through GUI to view and download PTF images. The astronomical objects can be searched by position, PTF field ID, and, solar system object/orbit. The IRSA image services provide low-level, a method for searching astronomical images of metadata tables. IRSA images search services have a single object search and multi-object search function. For the single object search, the system allows the user to search for astronomical bodies by name or position of the object. The result is displayed in a multi-column table in the web browser. When the user selects specific data from the column, the corresponding processed images are displayed. For the multi-object search, the user has to generate complex query manually and upload a file in the infrared science archive workplaces to get images information. Analyzing this scenario, previous work (Datawnt0 PDSPTF) supports multi-object search where users from astronomical domain do not have to write complex query manually [16]. Range of the queries that can be performed in our past work (Datawnt0 PDSPTF) is higher because of multi-object search support.

From the catalog services, the user can query through a catalog query engine to view and download lightcurve images information. The source and lightcurve database have three tables i.e. PTF Objects, PTF Sources Catalog, and PTF Lightcurve Table. Each of these tables can be queried independently. The astronomical object can be searched by Single Object Search, Polygon Search, Multi-Object Search, and All-Sky Search. For the Single Object Search, user can search by a single position and either a search radius or a box size centered on this position. Based on user input, all objects and their lightcurves result will be displayed in a multi-column table on a web browser after clicking "Run Query". This multi-column table can be saved in ASCII (IPAC-table) format.

For the Polygon search, the user can query a large search region e.g. specific PTF field or CCD images. Polygon Search result format and functionality is the same as single object search. From polygon search, more object lightcurves are returned. For the multi-object search, the user has to generate complex SQL Query manually and upload a file in the system. The system allows loading a file from local disk or infrared science archive workplaces.

The purpose of All-sky search is to get counts from the entire database table either in ASCII (IPAC-table) format or in HTML or XML. The All-sky search option does not return the lightcurves [17].

3   Access to PTF/iPTF Data

PTF/iPTF image data products (Level-0, Level-1, and Level-2) are released at different time with different features. Level-0 data is raw data. This is derived from the observatory as a multi-extension FITS file containing all 12 CCDs. This Level-0 data is not available publically for download and use. The Level-1 data is processed data corresponding to the original single CCDs exposures. Images of Level-1 data can be searched through IRSA web interface. Level-1 data have its own images search query interface [18]. These data can be downloaded through their interactive Graphical User Interface (GUI) or API named IBE. IBE uses HTTP syntax for downloading data. The download process for the Level-1 data is described in the earlier research [16]. The Level-2 data products are derived from combining the Level-1 data. Level-2 data are deep co-added data and the catalogs derived from this data. Level-2 data also have its own catalog query engine (Lightcurve database) for viewing and downloading catalog images information [17]. Level-2 data is also called the light curve data. A light curve is a graph of light intensity of a celestial object over a period of time. The study of celestial object which change their brightness over the time can help astronomers to achieve wide range of science goals. For example, lightcurve helps to identify an object. The downloading process for Level-2 data is same as the process for Level-1 data. The information for the lightcurve data, the process of data migration and data modeling for the downloaded data are described in the following sub-sections.

3.1 Retrieving the Catalog File from IRSA Remote Resource

Lightcurves are derived by using the IPAC source-matching and relative-photometry pipeline. In the next phase, the sources and lightcurves databases are new deliverables to access and query the lightcurve images data. All the images data are released in FITS format with epochal images and photometric catalogs. Epochal images are one image per CCD exposure, astrometrically, and photometrically calibrated [19]. Each exposure has a mask file where bit encoded information about specific pixels are described. The sources are extracted from a subset of epochal images and co-added (reference) images from Mar 1, 2009 to Jan 28, 2015. The photometric catalog includes each individual exposure images information by a catalog file. The catalog file contains all detected objects in that exposure with information about key-value pairs and header information of the images as discussed in Sect. 2.2.

For the purpose of study, we create a local repository which consists of downloaded imagery information provided by the IRSA cloud service. The downloaded raw data are restructured in a relation form (Fig. 2). The attributes of the relations (key-value) are defined and stored in a local repository. These tables are PTF Objects, PTF Sources Catalog, and PTF Lightcurve Table [20].

PTF Objects – In the PTF Object table, reference image objects provide target position to seed source matching across multiple epochs. The matched epochal define as transient detection and flagged i.e. transient_flag = 0, and transient_flag = 1. The transient flag = 0 tied to a reference image detection whereas transient_flag = 1 not tied to a reference images detection.

PTF Source Catalogs – In the PTF Sources Catalogs table, sources detection is performed using the sources extractor (SExtractor) package. Table containing epoch based source photometry and metadata are extracted from the epochal (single exposure) images. These source detection matching is performing by co-adding exposures to construct reference image and catalog.

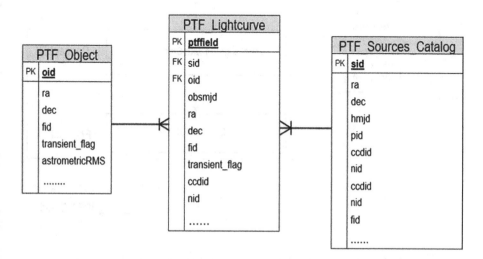

Fig. 2. ER model for Level-2 data

PTF Lightcurve Table – The lightcurves are constructed using the IPAC source-matching/relative photometry pipeline. This table contains the individual lightcurves, i.e. detection of that object in the source catalog. The lightcurves table combines all columns and metadata from both the objects and sources catalog tables.

3.2 Data Migration

In a database management system, the catalogs record discussed in Sect. 2.2 may constitute the local database. However, the FITS file contents may change and minor changes to design are expected to occur frequently. Besides, the future projects (ZTF, LSST) will produce high volume of data that cannot fit into a local store. Therefore, the indexed data is required to be kept at IRSA web server. The data is accessible through web services, wizard, API, URL and other possibilities to facilitate the usage.

For the purpose of creating an Information Requirements Elicitation (IRE) style query interface for PTF/iPTF data, the data is accessed using a three-level architecture in ANSI dictionary in relational form (Fig. 3) [21]. The conceptual level includes the local catalogs with stored index. The catalogs are stored in local RDBMS (Postgres). Furthermore, the current three-level architecture is connected to remote cloud service at IRSA server to download and migrate data through the use of different APIs (Astropy and DS9) [22, 23]. Any changes in the remote data store can be reflected in the local architecture because of the similarity in schema design. More external views can be added supporting more user workflows. The conceptual schema can also be extended by adding more indexes in the local catalogs if required. The system maintains a

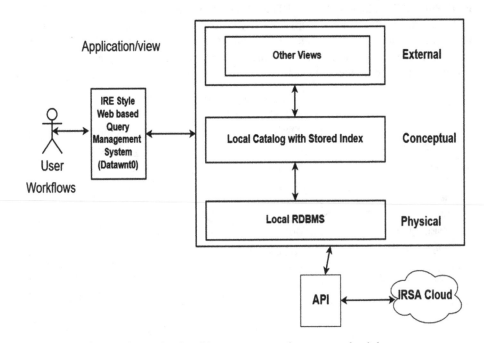

Fig. 3. Local three-level architecture connected to remote cloud data source

web-based GUI named Datawnt0 with an image visualizer where simple and complex queries can be executed [24]. It supports complex query manipulation where SQL is generated dynamically as per user interaction with the GUI. The query generated is then transformed into predefined URL requests to get the images from the IPAC/IRSA web service.

4 System Overview

Like many other astronomical data repositories, PTF/iPTF contains different types of data, i.e. high-resolution images, Lightcurves, Graphs, Key-value, relations, and unstructured text file.

In view of its size, growth, changes, user needs and workflows, managing this data in a single database system is not a practical approach. Therefore, in this study, we propose a web based polystore system to manage the complex problem of such heterogeneous data for getting domain-specific search result across the multiple storage systems. We use open source PostgreSQL to store the header information and key and values in our local server. All the PTF data information and images are stored in the IRSA Cloud, which is designed, maintained, and operated at IPAC.

The proposed system improves integration for different data analysis and visualization of images for the astronomers to encourage the use of scientific data for further research and analysis of time-domain astronomy. Proposed system includes the extension of the past system (Datawnt0) for Level-1 data with Level-2 data. The system for Level-1 data was designed to provide online tools for data query. Moreover, the proposed system includes query support for Level-2 data, which provides a second workflow query system for the lightcurve services along with scattered plots and visualization of images.

The proposed architecture helps in migrating and transforming the data between the local RDBMS and the remote IRSA cloud to retrieve images (Fig. 4). The proposed Information Requirements Elicitation (IRE) style web based system uses workflow method for user convenience and supports easily accessible query language [25]. The IRE is used for query formulation. The downloaded entities and relations are defined as objects in the query management system. The query management system allows the users to formulate the queries where they can select the attributes from an object or multiple objects to download data and to view images. The method of selecting from multiple objects is possible through join operation where the user can select an object and relate with other objects as per the query requirement. The web application contains a visualizer which is an API named DS9 FITS viewer [23]. The DS9 image viewer API establishes a communication protocol between the local and the remote data stores. DS9 API helps in visualizing the queried images with scattered plots after migrating the data from IRSA cloud to the web application.

The web system has a built-in query processor to map the queries, transform and migrate the data from local to the remote data store. The query processor communicates with the web application and the underlying DBMS through SQL. The queries formulated by the user in the web application forms two SQL's, one for the local DBMS and one to connect the remote IRSA data source. The formulated queries are sent to local RDBMS. The image SQL is formed by joining the resulting SQL with PTF Lightcurve table, PTF Object table and PTF source catalog table which have information about the header files of images. The query processor then matches the Image SQL with the header files which contains the URL links of the images in the IRSA data cloud. Finally, the Image SQL generates server requests to retrieve the images from IRSA data cloud and display it in the web application's visualizer.

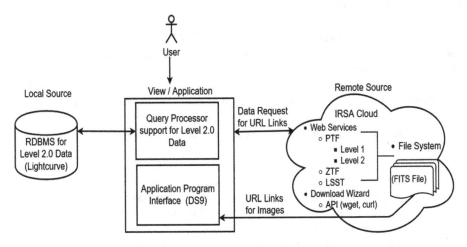

Fig. 4. Proposed web based polystore system architecture

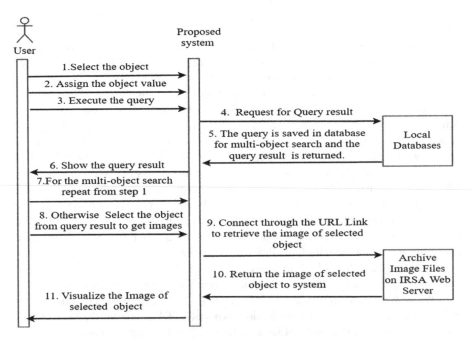

Fig. 5. Workflow across the multiple data store

The proposed system allows user to query Level-2 data and get information of astronomical objects lightcurves with images and scattered plots using API named DS9. The users according to their search criteria can select the object and add values in the input box. The user can select and add an object and its attributes, which are predefined in the system. The query language interface provides set-theoretic query language that can relate the object of interest. It is built over the relational database containing the catalog in the local database. The workflow query system for lightcurve services as shown in Fig. 5.

Use Case Example 1: Let us consider a single object query where a user wants to find an image and lightcurve (scattered plots) of a certain astronomical body from a certain object value (OID).

Process: First the user selects the Object Table. Enters object value "OID" in the query system, then clicks on the search button and gets the results.

Use Case Example 2: Now lets us consider that the user wants to find out the images and scattered plots of certain Object and sources of that object.

Process: First the user selects the Object table. Enters OID values in the query system. then, the user clicks on the search button and then related button and relate to the source table. The user can now enter source value "SID" in the system, then click on the search button and get the results.

4.1   Future Generation and Utilization of Data (ZTF Project 2017–2020)

The Zwicky Transient Facility (ZTF) is a next-generation optical time-domain survey currently in operation. The ZTF is designed to detect near-Earth asteroids, rare and fast-evolving flux transient and all classes of Galactic variable sources. ZTF observations use a new camera that consists of 16 CCDs, each of which is partitioned into 4 readout quadrants. Therefore, 64 CCD-quadrant images are generated per ZTF exposure [6]. A CCD-quadrant is the basic image-unit for pipeline processing and from which all science data products are derived as shown in Table 4.

Table 4. ZTF public data release overview

ZTF public data release	Release date	Product
Data release 1	May 8th 2019	~3.4 million single-exposure images ~102 thousand co-added images ~63 billion sources detected from source catalog files ~2 billion lightcurves constructed from the single-exposure extractions

ZTF data product are available through the IRSA browserable directory including, ZTF Science Exposure Metadata, calibration metadata, raw metadata, and reference image metadata [26]. The web directory at IRSA maintains the PTF, iPTF, ZTF FITS files using B-tree data structures with images (URL links) which are indexed with API supports for visualization of images. There are two methods to access the ZTF images and catalog products from the ZTF archive. The first access method is via GUI and the second method is via an API called IRSA Image Server Program Interface (IBE). The downloading process for ZTF data is same as the process for PTF Level-1 data.

For the purpose of study, we aim to create a local repository which consists of downloaded imagery header information provided by the IRSA cloud services. The downloaded raw header data are restructured in a similar array Database. The Polystore architecture proposed earlier can incorporate other heterogeneous databases for the ZTF architecture. Other studies include integrating the heterogeneous databases with a different data model and providing a unified single query language. A mediator/wrapper model can be used to connect the query processor in the local view with the remote data stores. The local data store can be scaled up by integrating multiple databases which are distributed. Each query from the underlying databases can be transformed by the query processor into a uniform query language understandable by the web application as presented in the case of BigDAWG Polystores [27].

The proposed web based polystore architecture can be used for managing different data models across various scientific domains.

5   Comparison with Other Polystore Systems

Recently many scientific data organizations are facing the challenges of providing data management solution for large, heterogeneous data which have different types of data and models. Many solutions have been proposed to manage these challenges. Polystore system is one of the solutions which supports integration of disparate data and database management systems. Polystore systems are also called multistore system which provides integrated access to multiple heterogeneous cloud data store, NoSQL RDMS and so on. In study [28], authors have mentioned the taxonomy of polystore systems which are categorized as loosely coupled, tightly coupled and hybrid systems. A loosely coupled multistore system utilize the concept of mediator or wrapper. It has a familiar user interaction interface and ability to locally control the data store which is independent of the multistore. Similarly, a wrapper interacts with data store through API for query formulation, query transformation, and query execution and provides a result to the operator engine. Finally, the tightly coupled multistore system allows local user interaction interface for better performance by shared workload with multiple systems. It also allows the joining of data from distinct data stores. The hybrid system is a combination of loosely coupled multistore system and tightly coupled system. It allows optimization by the use of native subqueries and operator ordering to query multiple data store sources in the cloud [28].

Over the past few decades, data archives have been dealing with different data models and storage engines in their native formats. Data sets have been used without converting them to a common data model. Recent developments in polystore system follow a bottom-up approach where information processing is based on incoming data from the source environment. The main difference is that the bottom-up approach to make a polystore considers language translation as the main task as shown in Fig. 6.

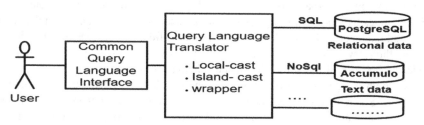

Fig. 6. Bottom-up design polystore system

5.1 Existing Bottom-Up Design Polystore Systems

The BigDAWG (Data Analysis Working Group) demonstrates the MIMIC II (Multi-parameter Intelligent Monitoring in Intensive Care) application from a tightly coupled polystore system [27]. In the application for MIMIC II dataset, authors demonstrate varieties of data as in standard SQL analytics (e.g. how many patients were given a particular drug), Complex analytics (e.g., patients waveform data and then compared to normal patient), text search (e.g., find patient who responded well to particular drug or treatment) and real-time monitoring (e.g., detect abnormal heart rhythms) with different storage systems i.e., Postgres, SciDB, S-stores, and Apache Accumulo. These database systems are connected through cast which allows query transformation from one engine or island to another. In an island, users interact with multiple programming and model choice. Each of the Islands are connected by shim which allows translation of one model to another through the API or adapter.

CloudMdsQL presents a scalable SQL query engine with extended capabilities for seamless querying of heterogeneous non-relational database engines [29]. The system uses a query language which is SQL based with embedded functional sub-queries written in the native query languages of the underlying database engines. The system employs transparent wrappers on the query interface of each database engine, as well as a table based common data model for storing intermediate results and exchanging data.

5.2 Top-Down Design for Web Polystore Systems

The concept of polystore system can be implemented using different technologies. In this study, we present a set-theoretic query language over web based polystores containing PTF/iPTF data sets. We have adopted a Top-down approach for designing the system. The existing top-down design for web polystore systems is shown in Fig. 7. Future designs for the top-down approach with all the component databases (RDBMS, noSQL, newSQL and other DB) may support API calls in the raw form of shared data. Thus for every header entry hk, there is an API response available at IRSA level API (hk), that provides the data. A list of shared data resources must be utilized to make a common 3-level ANSI data dictionary, on the lines of Datawnt0. Querying over the dictionary resources, a user can utilize the SQL and final calls to data which may be supported by component systems. A simple workflow support can be built on the top of the SQL query available for users not familiar with database programming.

The top-down approach used in this study can handle huge growth potential of IRSA archives as top-down design is robust against changes in data. Generally, more views and data stores can be added to accommodate frequent changes in data with the help of three-level ANSI dictionary. Any changes in the original source can be duplicated because of the simplicity of the schema design.

Top-down design focuses on organizing and developing systems through stepwise refinement. Stepwise refinement helps to break up tasks into subtasks and similarly refine data structure. A good design avoids errors in several ways, robust against frequent changes in size, no need for language translation and reduce cost of data integration. The PTF data is public and well-documented so it makes a good test platform for research on database algorithms and performance. The top down design used in the research highlights a modest step towards the goal of providing excellent data analysis and visualization tools for growing archives.

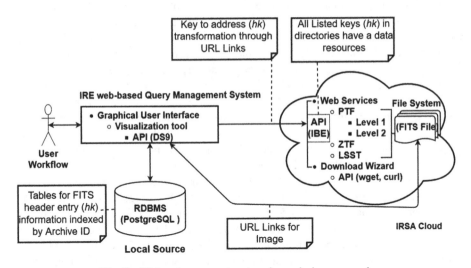

Fig. 7. Web polystore system top-down design approach

5.3   Challenges

There are many challenges while managing growing archives by using top-down database design. Top down design requires specific data analysis for conceptual and logical data modeling. This data modeling takes time and effort, and more so if dealing with big data. Another challenge arises when automating large scale data from the web.

The large amount and variety of data available in the astronomical domain pose a major challenge in managing it. Analysis and modeling of new variety data viz. lightcurves must consider user and system requirements as well as focus on providing a query language which will federate the information, transform and effectively migrate data within the underlying data stores. The solution should additionally maintain data integrity when compared to the original source of PTF data.

6 Summary and Conclusions

The proposed system supports multiple storage systems for domain-specific query language for managing astronomical data with visualization interfaces. The system interacts with multiple databases via query formulation in GUI, query transformation via URL link, query execution by connecting with multiple data stores through API and visualization with FITS images viewer DS9 API with scattered plots.

To handle PTF/iPTF data, we present query by cloud workflow system across the multiple storage engines using web based polystore in our proposed system. The system is fully automated and requires minimal human effort in operation. Proposed system can query astronomical data provided by PTF/iPTF repository to gain domain-specific information.

In the future work, we consider scalability of the system by adding new databases for Zwicky Transient Factory data. The challenges faced by adding a new database to existing polystore architecture can be addressed.

References

1. Law, N.M., et al.: The Palomar Transient Factory: system overview, performance, and first results. Publ. Astron. Soc. Pac. **121**(886), 1395 (2009)
2. Grillmair, C.J., et al.: An overview of the Palomar Transient Factory pipeline and archive at the infrared processing and analysis center. In: Astronomical Data Analysis Software and Systems XIX, vol. 434 (2010)
3. About IRSA. https://irsa.ipac.caltech.edu/frontpage/
4. About IPAC. https://www.ipac.caltech.edu/
5. About Intermediate Palomar Transient Factory. https://www.ptf.caltech.edu/page/about
6. Smith, R.M., et al.: The Zwicky transient facility observing system. In: Ground-Based and Airborne Instrumentation for Astronomy V, vol. 9147. International Society for Optics and Photonics (2014)
7. Pence, W.D., et al.: Definition of the flexible image transport system (fits), version 3.0. Astron. Astrophys. **524**, A42 (2010)
8. About Level of data. https://irsa.ipac.caltech.edu/onlinehelp/ptf/overview.html
9. Surace, J., et al.: The Palomar Transient Factory: high quality realtime data processing in a cost-constrained environment. arXiv preprint arXiv:1501.06007 (2015)
10. Rusu, F., Nugent, P., Wu, K.: Implementing the Palomar Transient Factory real-time detection pipeline in GLADE: results and observations. In: Madaan, A., Kikuchi, S., Bhalla, S. (eds.) DNIS 2014. LNCS, vol. 8381, pp. 53–66. Springer, Cham (2014). https://doi.org/10.1007/978-3-319-05693-7_4

11. Ofek, E.O., et al.: The Palomar Transient Factory photometric calibration. Publ. Astron. Soc. Pac. **124**(911), 62 (2012)
12. Laher, R.R., et al.: IPAC image processing and data archiving for the Palomar Transient Factory. Publ. Astron. Soc. Pac. **126**(941), 674 (2014)
13. Information about IBE, June 2019. https://irsa.ipac.caltech.edu/ibe/
14. Koruga, P., Bača, M.: Analysis of B-tree data structure and its usage in computer forensics. In: Central European Conference on Information and Intelligent Systems (2010)
15. About PTF Mission. https://irsa.ipac.caltech.edu/Missions/ptf.html
16. Shrestha, S., et al.: PDSPTF: polystore database system for scalability and access to PTF time-domain astronomy data archives. In: Gadepally, V., Mattson, T., Stonebraker, M., Wang, F., Luo, G., Teodoro, G. (eds.) DMAH/Poly 2018. LNCS, vol. 11470, pp. 78–92. Springer, Cham (2019). https://doi.org/10.1007/978-3-030-14177-6_7
17. Level-2 data catalog query engine, June 2019. https://irsa.ipac.caltech.edu/cgi-bin/Gator/nph-scan?mission=irsa&submit=Select&projshort=PTF
18. Level-1 data images search query interface, June 2019. https://irsa.ipac.caltech.edu/applications/ptf/
19. About Data product, June 2019. https://www.ptf.caltech.edu/page/first_data_release
20. About Lightcurve and source Database, June 2019. https://www.ptf.caltech.edu/page/lcgui
21. Samos, J., Saltor, F., Sistac, J., Bardés, A.: Database architecture for data warehousing: an evolutionary approach. In: Quirchmayr, G., Schweighofer, E., Bench-Capon, T.J.M. (eds.) DEXA 1998. LNCS, vol. 1460, pp. 746–756. Springer, Heidelberg (1998). https://doi.org/10.1007/BFb0054530
22. Robitaille, T.P., et al.: Astropy: a community Python package for astronomy. Astron. Astrophys. **558**, A33 (2013)
23. About Images Visualizer API DS9, June 2019. http://ds9.si.edu/site/Home.html
24. About Datawnt0 workflow based query system, June 2019. http://datawnt0.u-aizu.ac.jp/demo/dbv4-20180320/astrodemo-newdbv4/
25. Sun, J.: Information requirement elicitation in mobile commerce. Commun. ACM **46**(12), 45–47 (2003)
26. About Zwicky Transient Facility data products, June 2019. https://www.ztf.caltech.edu/page/dr1
27. Gadepally, V., et al.: Version 0.1 of the BigDAWG polystore system. arXiv preprint arXiv:1707.00721 (2017)
28. About Polystore System, June 2019. https://slideplayer.com/slide/13365730/#.W03B0ytPNl4.gmail
29. Kolev, B., et al.: CloudMdsQL: querying heterogeneous cloud data stores with a common language. Distrib. Parallel Databases **34**(4), 463–503 (2016)

DMAH 2019: Database Enabled Biomedical Research

Patient Centric Data Integration for Improved Diagnosis and Risk Prediction

Hanie Samimi[(⊠)], Jelena Tešić, and Anne Hee Hiong Ngu

Department of Computer Science, Texas State University,
San Marcos, TX 78666, USA
h_s163@txstate.edu

Abstract. A typical biological study includes analysis of heterogeneous biological databases, e.g., genomics, proteomics, metabolomics, and microarray gene expression. These datasets correlate at the patient-level, e.g., decrease in the workload of a group of genes in body cells increases the work of other group and raises the number of their products. Joint analysis of correlated patient-level data sources improves the final diagnosis. State-of-art biological methods, such as differential expression analysis, do not support heterogeneous data source integration and analysis. Recently, scientists in different computational fields have made significant improvements in classical algorithms for data integration to enable investigation of different data types at the same level. Applying these methods on biological data gives more insight into associating diseases with heterogeneous groups of patients. In this paper, we improve upon our previous study and propose the use of a combination of a data reduction technique and similarity network analysis (SNF) as a scalable mechanism for integrating new biological data types. We demonstrated our approach by analyzing the risk factors of Acute Myeloid Leukemia (AML) patients when multiple data sources are presented and uncover new correlations between patients and patient survival time.

1 Introduction

Computational biology has made significant advances in the last decade as more heterogeneous data is collected and analyzed, and new genes associated with the diseases are uncovered. The current state of the art for biological studies tends to focus on one dataset and or to study one specific correlation between gene and disease. The ultimate goal in computational biology is to be able to include and analyze all relevant biological datasets within a given biological study.

In the past decade, scientists were able to gain a detailed view of cellular processes and to advance the modeling of supramolecular assemblies. These advances led to insights into genome regulation processes and motivated the collection and analysis of genomics, proteomics, metabolomics, and microarray gene expression data [21]. All these datasets are related to the patient level, e.g., a decrease in the workload of a group of genes in body cells increases the work of other group and raises the number of their products [7]. Due to the

© Springer Nature Switzerland AG 2019
V. Gadepally et al. (Eds.): DMAH 2019/Poly 2019, LNCS 11721, pp. 185–195, 2019.
https://doi.org/10.1007/978-3-030-33752-0_13

complex nature of biological systems, any model trained on a single dataset can only offer a one-dimensional projection view of the complex relationship between genomic, clinical, and diagnosis data. No single biological data type can capture the complexity of all the factors relevant to understanding a phenomenon such as a disease or patient-level biological processes [27].

Our work expands on the recently proposed integration method for biological data to analyze DNA methylation and gene expression data [19]. Genes are clustered into correlated groups using hierarchical clustering, and these gene groups are found to have their expression values or methylation levels highly correlate with the survival time of patients. Authors used Acute Myeloid Leukemia (AML) gene expression, DNA methylation, and survival time patients dataset. The method performed superbly in terms of predicting the risk level of patients that had an unknown risk level based on their clinical information. The average accuracy of the method in terms of newly identified patients is greater than 90%, as evaluated on different datasets. However, the proposed method only managed to re-classify a small percentage of the population with unknown risk level based on the ground truth provided by the clinical information. The number of patients whose predicted risk level is undetermined remains high, so the overall effectiveness of the proposed method is hard to evaluate for the broader patient population as the recall is low. The proposed approach does not scale to other datasets such as the messenger RNA (mRNA) and micro RNA (miRNA) datasets provided in the same study due to the expensive prohibitory computation required for integrating multiple datasets.

In patient-centric similarity networks, patients are clustered or classified based on their similarities in genomic and clinical profiles. This precision medicine paradigm has shown to have a high intractability and accuracy, and it helps advance the diagnosis and treatment [17]. The main downside of this state of the art method is their scalability for contemporary genetic cohorts, and the ability to incorporate a wide range of genomics and clinical data. In this paper, we propose to expand and scale multi-source data analysis at patient-level by (a) parallelizing single source dataset processing step that allows for scaling and multi-source integration; (b) adapting graph-based approach for data integration at patient level; and (c) introducing new exploratory result analysis methods that correlate genomics and clinical data. The proposed data analysis pipeline (see Fig. 1) is demonstrated with AML cancer patient dataset. The rest of the paper is organized as follows: related work in Sect. 2, our proposed approach is described in Sect. 3, Results, and Discussion are in Sect. 4, and directions of ongoing work are presented in Sect. 5.

2   Related Work

No single biological data type can capture the complexity of all the factors relevant to understanding a phenomenon such as a disease. Integration aims to harness heterogeneous data across several dimensions of biological variation without losing important information. The main challenge in biological data integration is how to optimally combine and interpret data from multiple sources, which are heterogeneous, high dimensions, noisy, dynamics, bias, and incomplete. In general, biological data integration approaches can be grouped based on when in the processing pipeline, the data is integrated, early, intermediate, or late integration [22].

Early data integration approach concatenates individual dataset points prior to analysis. Each data set is individually processed and normalized, and data points are concatenated into a broader feature set for the data analysis step. Multi-array Analysis approach [9] is an example of early concatenation, where sample's CEL files are normalized to different Affymetrix platforms. Early integration proved to be useful for homogeneous data types, even as it increases the dimensionality of the data. Concatenation assumes pseudo-orthogonality of the space, and lots of contextual information is lost using this simple merging technique. The approach does not support data integration for biological data sets of a different abstraction. *Late* data integration focuses on individual data set analysis, as if no other related data sets are available. Differential expression analysis for data sets of different levels is an example of late data integration [18] where findings are combined and merged at the end. Late data integration does not take advantage of the underlying correlation and or complementary information datasets provide. *Intermediate* data integration supports the pre-processing step for each data set first and focuses on finding the correlation between the object of the study and all data sets at the same level before data analysis. Multi-view analysis, dimensionality reduction, and graph integration are examples of intermediate data integration [22]. Each of the proposed methods is unique to a fixed set of data types, and the main challenge for intermediate data integration is its generalizability to different types of biological studies, and its extension to different types of data sets within the same study [19].

Biological data is inherently heterogeneous and noisy, as the signal is collected using multiple sampling techniques on a very small subspace of the population for a particular phenotype. The high-dimensionality and sparsity of the datasets make it extremely challenging to make meaningful insights, even when the number of subjects is high. The genetic correlations can be viewed as inconclusive due to population stratification [6,10]. There has been a large number of omics data integration approaches, including biochemical pathway-, ontology-, network-, and empirical-correlation-based methods [26]. They all suffer from the same downsides, as an extension of the analysis is hindered by the system's inability to extend to multiple data types and lack of generalization due to noisy nature of collected samples, and inherent high dimensionality curse in data analysis [1,15].

Lately, the biological data analysis turned to machine learning tools as a way to address these pressing issues: sophisticated dimensionality reduction methods and ensemble classification methods show some improvements over baseline integration techniques but do not generalize well [27]. Big data approaches from social network analysis and computer vision show more promise: incoherent, missing, noisy, small sample high-dimensional data has been extensively studied in those areas [14]. Network-based integration of multi-omics data approach showed promising results in correlating genes and diagnosis [17]. Graph diffusion-based method for prioritizing cancer genes by integrating diverse molecular data types on a directed functional interaction network is proposed in [4]. The network prioritizes genes by their mediator effect individually and integrates them using the rank aggregation approach.

Similarity Network Fusion (SNF) that integrates mRNA expression data, DNA methylation data, and microRNA expression data for five cancer data sets was proposed in [24]. Integration of these similarity networks follows the construction of a similarity network for patients for each single data type into a single fused similarity network using a nonlinear combination method that iteratively updates each network making it more similar to each other. Machine learning approaches for genomics and clinical data integration bridge the gap between big data processing and interpreting the data [27]. In this paper, we focus on how to scale the integrative data analysis and correlate the genomic and clinical datasets.

3   Approach

Patient-similarity networks offer ease of interpretability and ease of discovery of the underlying correlations between patients genomics and clinical data in precision medicine. Here, we propose an approach to scale the network-based algorithm in terms of various heterogeneous datasets and processing. We demonstrate the scalability and improved analysis capability of the proposed approach when applied to AML genome and clinical patient-level analysis. The processing pipeline included the data preparation, dimensionality reduction, similarity network fusion, and unsupervised/supervised data classification for interpretability analysis, as illustrated in Fig. 1(left). To better comprehend the proposed approach, we compare it to previous work pipeline Fig. 1(right) as outlined in [19].

3.1   Data Preparation and Dimensionality Reduction

Setup: The Genome Cancer Atlas (TCGA) data portal provides different types of genomic and clinical data related to a type of cancer in the form of a project [8], and this is the dataset of choice for this work. All scripts for the experiments were written in R and running on a machine with Ubuntu 16.04 operating system, 32 GB of RAM and 500 GB of the hard disk.

Data Preparation: Some of the gene expression or DNA methylation values are not available for more than 50% of patients analyzed. We normalize the dataset to accommodate missing values. DNA methylation data is cleaned and normalized using RnBeads R packages [2]. Next, we omit the DNA methylation level of those loci that had low Spearman correlation with the survival time of death patients. After that, we group remaining genes based on their similar biological features and behavior. For this step, we analyze datasets separately, and construct two different Pearson similarity matrices, one for gene expression and

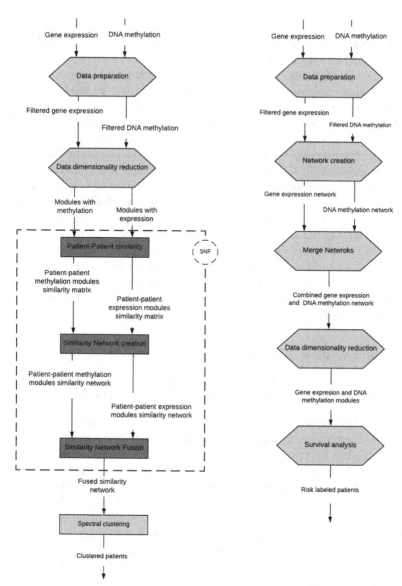

Fig. 1. Flowchart of proposed methods. The left one is related to the newly proposed method while the right one shows the steps that have been taken in the previously proposed method.

one for DNA methylation data, and construct one network per each of the data types. The nodes in both networks are genes, and edges are the Pearson correlation between every two genes.

Data Dimensionality Reduction: Clustering genes using these two networks results in groups of genes which are highly correlated with each other based on either their methylation levels or gene expression values. We have used the *Blockwisemodule* function from the WGCNA R package. This function performs hierarchical clustering using average linkage. The output from the hierarchical clustering is correlated clusters of genes which are called gene modules. For each of the modules, we computed a weighted average value using Principal Component Analysis (PCA). PCA is a data reduction method that summarizes the information of a high dimensional dataset into a few vectors in the direction with the highest variance [12]. The first principal component is the direction that the projected data has the most significant variance. We used the coefficients of the first principal components to compute a weighted average for the gene expression and DNA methylation modules separately. As an output of the data preparation step, each of the similar gene groups is represented by a single feature vector per dataset level (gene expression values or DNA methylation levels). Note that this approach scales to different types of input dataset, as each dataset is prepared independently using the proposed method. The output of data preparation and dimensionality reduction is two gene modules: module with DNA methylation and module with gene expression.

3.2   Patient-Centric Network Fusion and Analysis

To integrate two gene modules produced in Sect. 3.1, we apply network fusion paradigm at the patient level, that consists of four generic steps:

1. *C*ompute The similarity between patients for each data type: similarity metric is constructed for each datatype using pairwise correlation of gene module, as described in Sect. 3.1 between two patients.
2. *C*onstruct A patient network per data type: a graph where patients are nodes and edges represent patients' pairwise similarities calculated for that dataset.
3. *M*erge Two constructed patient similarity networks using Similarity Network Fusion approach [24]. Nodes of both networks are the same (patients), and edges' weights are iteratively updated to converge to a joint network.
4. Produce A final single patient-centric fused network where nodes are the patients and edges define the similarity value between the patients based on integrated data types.

*C*ompute and *C*onstruct steps in the approach are per dataset. For multiple datasets, patient-centric network constructions can be executed concurrently, scaling data preparation and dimensionality reduction phase of the pipeline. *M*erge and *P*roduce steps can use any network fusion and metric normalization method. Network-based fusion approaches can capture local and general similarity of multiple datasets provided in a study [4]. As the proof-of-concept, we employ Similarity Network Fusion analysis from [24].

Spectral Clustering step is a data analysis approach of the patient-centric fused network output [23]. Most stable clustering is given by the value of K that maximizes the eigen-gap (difference between consecutive eigenvalues), and we use this method to find the optimal high value of K for spectral clustering, as proposed in [13]. We have experimented with clustering results and visualize them for data analysis purpose, as shown in Sect. 4.

In our previous work, network was created from two datasets using early integration and it does not scale to new data types, see *Network Creation* module on the left in Fig. 1(right), [19]. This proposed work proceeds with data preparation and data dimensionality reduction for each data type separately, see *Data dimensionality reduction* in Fig. 1. Previous work merged the network based on the linear combination of similarity scores, and then applied dimensionality reduction approach to obtain relevant gene modules per patient for survival analysis, see *Merge Networks, Data dimensionality reduction*, and *Survival analysis* modules in Fig. 1(right), [19]. Proposed approach is more generic as it supports similarity network fusion of any number of data type modules, see SNF group in Fig. 1(left).

4   Results for the AML Study

Acute myeloid leukemia (AML) is a type of blood and bone marrow cancer in which the bone marrow makes abnormal myeloblasts (a type of white blood cell), red blood cells, or platelets. This type of cancer usually gets worse quickly if it is not treated, and accounts for 1.2% of cancer deaths in the United States [11]. Acute myeloid leukemia is a category of diseases with a common aggressive clinical presentation but with prognosis and management that is dependent upon the underlying genetic characteristics of the neoplasm. AML treatments have consistently improved, yet the treatment remains unchanged for the past three decades with the majority of patients eventually relapsing and dying of the disease [20]. Cytogenetics and mutation testing remain a critical prognostic tool for post-induction treatment as it identifies a subgroup of AML patients characterized by poor response to induction chemotherapy and poor long-term survival after

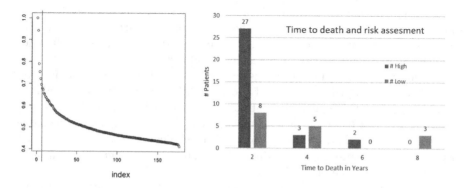

Fig. 2. AML Study Data Analysis: Eigenvalues of fused similarity matrix (left) and correlation of risk assessment and time of survival (right)

treatment with consolidation chemotherapy. There are effective high-precision predictors for high risk and low risk patients that aid the course of treatment for AML [20]. Current methods for labeling risk level in AML patients leave out most of the diagnosed population, as most of the people with AML diagnosis do not fall into high or low risk group [19]. Treatment for such patients is unknown and risky. Here, we focus on the patient-level analysis of the people with AML diagnosis to improve the patient's risk level classification.

Experiments are run using the TCGA-LAML project's data that has several biological data types of 200 AML patients [8]. Each type of data in TCGA-LAML project is collected using several types of platforms. The clinical data of patients contain several different information such as their vital status, gender, days to death, days to last follow-up, race, etc. We used days to the death of dead patients and days to the last follow-up of alive patients as their survival values. The risk levels assessment of patient are based on their mutation and cytogenetic abnormalities and broadly grouped as low, medium, and high.

In the data preparation step, we have used Gene Expression Quantification values of the HTSeq-FPKM workflow. Each gene is mapped from at most 4 loci with a probability of 95% resulting in 19911 genes. Loci that had low correlation (<0.1) with the survival time of the dead AML patients are excluded, bringing down the number of genes to 6637. Next, applying the Dimensionality reduction step resulted in 39 groups of genes. The second dataset was DNA methylation Beta values collected using Illumina Human Methylation 450 platform. Dimensionality reduction grouped DNA methylation data into 37 groups of genes. Two patients-patients similarity networks for 176 patients were created using the average value of the gene expression modules and DNA methylation modules. For unknown values in networks, we used the K Nearest Neighbour (KNN) [3] method for 10 iterations. Similarity Network Fusion approach was used for merging these two networks. The result is a single fused network where the nodes are patients, and the edges are the combined similarity value based on both gene expression and DNA methylation values.

Spectral clustering step for data analysis results is shown in Fig. 2. As shown in the left of Fig. 2, values of eigenvalues accelerate up to $K = 7$. Thus, we limit our experimentation on optimal K values with the limit of 7 to evaluate the difference in the performance. Using the fused similarity network, we classified the patients into sub-classes $K \in [2, 7]$ using the spectral clustering function from the SNF R package [25]. The results are illustrated in Fig. 3.

The most interesting finding in this data analysis is that a group of 14 patients is consistently grouped regardless of the value of K, circled in Fig. 3. What is interesting about this cluster is that 11 out of 14 patients in this cluster are labeled as low risk based on their mutations, and the rest of them are labeled as high risk in clinical data. When we analyzed the clinical data, this specific group of patients had a similar survival time, even though their assigned risk measure and predicted the time of survival was different.

This type of patient-centric analysis shows that risk assignment needs to take more data into account, as these patients strongly correlate according to multiple

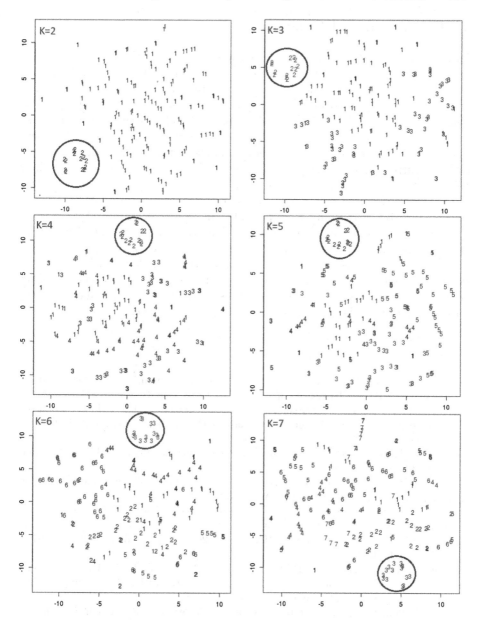

Fig. 3. Clustering visualization for various number K of clusters.

datasets. Figure 2(right) shows the study correlation of survival time (in years) with the assigned risk factor. It shows that the labeling based on cytogenetic mutations only is not reliable, and more patient-centric studies like ours need to be incorporated in assigning the risk factor [16].

5 Discussion and Conclusion

Patient-centric analysis has emerged as the most effective paradigm to offer an interpretable diagnosis for precision medicine [17]. This strategy can be viewed as a standard medical diagnosis for big data era, has excellent performance, is interpretable, and can preserve patient privacy. In this paper, we have proposed a path forward to scalable patient-centric genomic and clinic data analysis, as illustrated in Fig. 1. We have demonstrated the usability of our approach, and new correlation discovery using patient-centric datasets from TCGA-LAML project [8]. Our current work includes the testing of the proposed pipeline by adding additional data types such as mRNA and miRNA as well as investigating the use of a recently published labeling method, ELN 2017 to examine how much the classification of risks in cancer patients can be further improved.

Our goal is to advance patient-centric data analysis by exploiting links between genomic and clinical data. Clustering, as a data analysis tool, suffers from sensitivity to noisy examples, and classification techniques such as Support Vector Machine can do a better job in capturing complex data correlations. Our next step is to incorporate network fused distance matrix as a distance measure for classification method and assess its practical implications [5].

References

1. Alyass, A., Turcotte, M., Meyre, D.: From big data analysis to personalized medicine for all: challenges and opportunities. BMC Med. Genomics **8**(1), 33 (2015)
2. Assenov, Y., Müller, F., Lutsik, P., Walter, J., Lengauer, T., Bock, C.: Comprehensive analysis of DNA methylation data with RnBeads. Nat. Methods **11**(11), 1138 (2014)
3. Cunningham, P., Delany, S.J.: k-nearest neighbour classifiers. Multiple Classifier Syst. **34**(8), 1–17 (2007)
4. Dimitrakopoulos, C., et al.: Network-based integration of multi-omics data for prioritizing cancer genes. Bioinformatics **34**, 2441–2448 (2018)
5. Haasdonk, B., Bahlmann, C.: Learning with distance substitution kernels. In: Rasmussen, C.E., Bülthoff, H.H., Schölkopf, B., Giese, M.A. (eds.) DAGM 2004. LNCS, vol. 3175, pp. 220–227. Springer, Heidelberg (2004). https://doi.org/10.1007/978-3-540-28649-3_27
6. Hu, Y., Shmygelska, A., Tran, D., Eriksson, N., Tung, J.Y., Hinds, D.A.: GWAS of 89,283 individuals identifies genetic variants associated with self-reporting of being a morning person. Nat. Commun. **7**, 10448 (2016)
7. Huynh-Thu, V.A., Sanguinetti, G.: Gene regulatory network inference: an introductory survey. In: Sanguinetti, G., Huynh-Thu, V.A. (eds.) Gene Regulatory Networks. MMB, vol. 1883, pp. 1–23. Springer, New York (2019). https://doi.org/10.1007/978-1-4939-8882-2_1
8. National Cancer Institute: TCGA-LAML. https://portal.gdc.cancer.gov/projects/TCGA-LAML. Accessed 30 May 2019
9. Irizarry, R.A., Bolstad, B.M., Collin, F., Cope, L.M., Hobbs, B., Speed, T.P.: Summaries of affymetrix genechip probe level data. Nucleic Acids Res. **31**(4), e15 (2003)
10. Jansen, P.R., et al.: Genome-wide analysis of insomnia in 1,331,010 individuals identifies new risk loci and functional pathways. Nat. Genet. **51**, 394–403 (2019)

11. Jemal, A., Thomas, A., Murray, T., Thun, M., et al.: Cancer statistics, 2002. Ca-A Cancer J. Clin. **52**(1), 23–47 (2002)
12. Jolliffe, I.: Principal Component Analysis. Springer, New York (2011)
13. Kodinariya, T.M., Makwana, P.R.: Review on determining number of cluster in k-means clustering. Int. J. **1**(6), 90–95 (2013)
14. Marx, V.: Machine learning, practically speaking. Nat. Methods **16**, 463–467 (2019)
15. Meng, C., Zeleznik, O.A., Thallinger, G.G., Kuster, B., Gholami, A.M., Culhane, A.C.: Dimension reduction techniques for the integrative analysis of multi-omics data. Briefings Bioinform. **17**(4), 628–641 (2016)
16. Moarii, M., Papaemmanuil, E.: Classification and risk assessment in AML: integrating cytogenetics and molecular profiling. Hematol. Am. Soc. Hematol. Educ. Program **2017**(1), 37–44 (2017)
17. Pai, S., Bader, G.D.: Patient similarity networks for precision medicine. J. Mol. Biol. **430**(18, Part A), 2924–2938 (2018). Theory and Application of Network Biology Toward Precision Medicine
18. Robinson, M.D., McCarthy, D.J., Smyth, G.K.: edgeR: a bioconductor package for differential expression analysis of digital gene expression data. Bioinformatics **26**(1), 139–140 (2010)
19. Samimi, H.: Identification of gene sets that predict acute myeloid leukemia prognosis using integrative gene network analysis. Master's thesis, Texas State University, August 2018. txi:b4789711
20. Saultz, J.N., Garzon, R.: Acute myeloid leukemia: a concise review. J. Clin. Med. **5**(3), 33 (2016)
21. Schadt, E.E., Linderman, M.D., Sorenson, J., Lee, L., Nolan, G.P.: Computational solutions to large-scale data management and analysis. Nat. Rev. Genet. **11**(9), 647 (2010)
22. Serra, A., Fratello, M., Greco, D., Tagliaferri, R.: Data integration in genomics and systems biology. In: 2016 IEEE Congress on Evolutionary Computation (CEC), pp. 1272–1279. IEEE (2016)
23. Von Luxburg, U.: A tutorial on spectral clustering. Stat. Comput. **17**(4), 395–416 (2007)
24. Wang, B., et al.: Similarity network fusion for aggregating data types on a genomic scale. Nat. Methods **11**(3), 333 (2014)
25. Wanga, B., et al.: SNFtool: similarity network fusion, Published 24 April 2018. https://CRAN.R-project.org/package=SNFtool
26. Wanichthanarak, K., Fahrmann, J.F., Grapov, D.: Genomic, proteomic, and metabolomic data integration strategies. Biomark. Insights **10s4** (2015)
27. Zitnik, M., Nguyen, F., Wang, B., Leskovec, J., Goldenberg, A., Hoffman, M.M.: Machine learning for integrating data in biology and medicine: principles, practice, and opportunities. Inf. Fusion **50**, 71–91 (2019)

An Architecture to Support Real-World Studies that Investigate the Autonomic Nervous System

Danielle Groat[1]($\boxtimes$), Ramkiran Gouripeddi[1,2], Randy Madsen[2],
Yu Kuei Lin[3], and Julio C. Facelli[1,2]

[1] Department of Biomedical Informatics, University of Utah,
Salt Lake City, UT 84108, USA
danielle.groat@utah.edu
[2] Center for Clinical and Translational Science, University of Utah,
Salt Lake City, UT 84108, USA
[3] Department of Endocrinology, University of Utah,
Salt Lake City, UT 84108, USA

Abstract. Diabetes is a chronic disease with complications related to the autonomic nervous system (ANS) that can affect quality of life and lead to mortality. Clinicians and researchers currently rely on subjective and/or invasive means that don't necessarily translate to real-world setting when assessing severity of certain diabetes complications. We elicited use-cases of studies aimed at understanding ANS in the context of diabetes to gather system requirements for designing an architecture to support sensor-based studies. Real-world studies would need to be capable of gathering contextual data as well as proxies for ANS symptoms from digital markers from an evolving sensor landscape, while also supporting the data needs of researchers before, during, and after data acquisition. The proposed architecture makes use of open source and commercially available mobile health technologies, and informatics platforms to meet the design criteria. Building and testing a prototype of the proposed architecture is planned to confirm the system performs as expected.

Keywords: Real-world studies · Diabetes complications · Autonomic nervous system · Software architecture · Sensors · Digital biomarkers

1 Introduction

Diabetes is a chronic disease that effects 30.3 million in the US; about 5% have type 1 diabetes (T1D) [1]. When diabetes is treated with insulin, patients are at risk for developing hypoglycemic associated autonomic failure (HAAF) and impaired awareness of hypoglycemia (IAH) [2], which can lead to life-threatening acute episodes of hypoglycemia. Hyperglycemia can lead to diabetic neuropathy (DN) and associated pain (DN-P). DN-P is often treated with opioids, which is concerning due to current epidemic [3]. Clinicians and researchers in both these areas of complications rely on validated surveys or invasive methods that pose risks to patients to properly diagnose [4–6]. Improved understanding of the autonomic nervous system (ANS) as well as its

© Springer Nature Switzerland AG 2019
V. Gadepally et al. (Eds.): DMAH 2019/Poly 2019, LNCS 11721, pp. 196–203, 2019.
https://doi.org/10.1007/978-3-030-33752-0_14

measurement in real-world scenarios using sensors could provide insightful data and information for biomedical researchers and lead to new therapies, treatments, and minimally-invasive methods for diagnosing diabetes related complications.

While many Internet-of-Things (IoT) and mobile health (mHealth) systems have been proposed to support patients with self-management of diseases that allow their health care providers to have real-time access to data [7], these systems do not provide all the necessary components to support investigators who desire to conduct research in real-world settings, nor do they provide sufficient security to guarantee privacy and accuracy. The objective of this study was to gather requirements for conducting real-world studies of the ANS and propose an informatics architecture to support the studies.

2 Methods

We elicited use-cases of studies focused on ANS and diabetes from researchers with whom we have ongoing collaborations [8]. Using the general model for software architecture design, which encompasses the process of translating system requirements into real world solutions in terms of software code, frameworks, and components; we gathered the requirements necessary to conduct studies related to IAH/HAAF and DN/DN-P. We selected existing technologies and informatics methods that could support the studies. We pinpointed where current technologies would need to interface and additional component development needed, resulting in a prototype architecture.

3 Results

3.1 Use Case Descriptions

Crossover Clinical Trial of a Pharmacological Intervention for IAH. Patients with T1D and history of IAH would be randomized to receive a pharmaceutical intervention or placebo for several weeks, then crossover after a washout period. The following ANS symptoms and other clinically relevant information would be measured: shaking, trembling, skin surface temperature, palpitation, perspiration, blood flow, blood glucose, physical activity, and injected insulin. Other symptoms, such as anxiety, nervousness, irritability, dry mouth, and hunger, would be self-reported by the participants. Time-series analysis would be conducted to assess the efficacy of the intervention in improving IAH and to validate a non-invasive methodology to diagnose IAH [9].

Case-Control Observational Study of DN and DN-P. Patients with T2D diagnosed with DN/DN-P would be matched with controls. The following ANS symptoms would be gathered: skin surface temperature, palpitation, perspiration, blood flow, muscle contractions, physical activity, and urine output. Participants would self-report on tingling, numbness, burning, pain, digestive and sexual irregularities, dizziness, and healing of cuts. Data analyses would develop a model that uses ANS symptoms collected by sensors to classify DN/DN-P.

3.2   Requirements for Conducting Real-World ANS Studies

Surrogates for measuring ANS symptoms and an understanding of their uncertainty would be necessary. Data sources for ANS symptoms and clinically relevant information, which are primarily generated by non-invasive sensors or self-report, have been identified, Table 1 [8]. The assimilation of sensor data streams along with their contextual information would be required for analyses and event detection.

Preferably sensor data streams would be acquired centrally in real-time fashion. This would allow for participants to be solicited for contextual information by sending a message that can be triggered by an event-detection algorithm, a method know as ecological momentary assessment (EMA). The frequency at which participants are sent messages would need monitoring, and the event-detection algorithms would need mid-study calibration to ensure sufficient capture of contextual information while also preventing alert-fatigue in patients. Flexibility for sending EMA messages would also be important. Sending messages at regular intervals (e.g. daily, weekly) would need to be supported, as well as triggering messages peripherally (i.e. participant's devices) and centrally. Both studies would also need to conduct data analyses on assimilated data that would generate hypotheses for future bench or bedside studies.

Table 1. Measurement data sources of ANS symptoms and clinically relevant information.

ANS symptom	Measurement data source	ANS symptom	Measurement data source
Anxiety	Self-report	Muscle Contractions	EEG
Blood Flow	Thermal Actuator	Nervousness	Self-report
Blood Glucose	CGMS	Numbness	Self-report
Burning	Self-report	Palpitation	ECG
Digestive Patterns	Self-report	Perspiration	Galvanic Skin Response
Dizziness	Self-report	Physical Activity	Activity Tracker
Dry Mouth	Self-report	Shaking	Accelerometer
Healing of cuts	Self-report	Sexual Patterns	Self-report
Hunger	Self-report	Skin Temperature	Thermometer
Insulin	Insulin pump/pen	Trembling	Self-report
Irritability	Self-report	Urine Output	Strain Gage

After reviewing IAH/HAAF and DN/DN-P studies, we identified the following requirements that would inform the architecture for conducting real-world studies: (1) ability to discover, evaluate, and develop new digital biomarkers, (2) capture contextual information related to sensor measurements, (3) support multiple means for gathering real-time status of participants, e.g. EMA at regular intervals and at the time of specific events, as well as digital journals, (4) mid-study calibration of EMA triggering algorithms, (5) integration and assimilation of big data that can support analyses required to identify correlations and associations of ANS symptoms and contextual information with the status of diabetes complications, and (6) provisioning of integrated data in different data models to varied analysis including temporal reasoning, machine learning, and traditional statistics.

3.3 An Existing Informatics Platform that Supports Real-World Studies

The Exposure Health Informatics Ecosystem (EHIE), is a scalable informatics structure that has been developed by informatics researchers at the University of Utah [10–12]. EHIE has been designed to address challenges faced when conducting sensor-based exposomic research. The infrastructure is a standards-based and open-source informatics platform that employs an event-driven architecture and graph and document store technologies. This allows the system to provide semantically consistent, metadata-driven, and event-based management of exposomic study related data. EHIE currently consists of the following components, Fig. 1:

Data Acquisition Pipeline. Consists of hardware, software, and networking protocols to support sensor deployment and sensor data collection. EpiFi was developed to observe devices and notify the study team of their status and to prevent data loss [13].

Participant Facing Tools. Allows participants to collect and annotate data and provides feedback to them. REDCap [14], an open-source study data management tool, has been extended to support the sending and receiving of text message based EMAs.

Researcher Facing Platforms. Provides tools and processes for researchers conducting exposomic research or for clinical care. Tools provide assistance with study design, collecting data, study monitoring, and data analysis.

Computational Modeling Platform. Resources are provided to quantify the uncertainty that might be present in the data, which can be used to augment data analysis and interpretation of results.

Big Data Federation And Integration. Integrates measured and computationally generated data with biomedical data along with characterizing uncertainties associated with the data. EHIE leverages and extends the OpenFurther (OF) platform, which was developed for data integration and federation [15–17]. OF provides syntactic and semantic interoperability for dynamically federating data and information. OF contains a Sensor Common Metadata Specification (SCMS), which includes all types of sensors including nanosensors, satellites, wearables, and monitoring stations. The Event Document Store (EDS) is a primitive storage format that allows linkage across different root objects and transformation of events into higher analytical models to support diverse translational archetypes. Data is stored in the EDS on a study by study basis.

Many of the functionalities and services provided by EHIE that support exposomic research are also necessary for conducting real-world studies of ANS and diabetes complications, particularly the flexibility in data acquisition and integration. Where EHIE does not meet the needs for real-world ANS studies lies in the assimilation of data on the fly to facilitate real-time event detection of sensor data streams to trigger interventions or further automated data collections. Supporting these ANS studies would require augmenting EHIE with decision support for researchers to design and monitor studies in real-time, as well as the computational modeling platforms with data assimilation capabilities to create event-detection algorithms.

3.4   Diabetes Technology Informatics Capabilities

Digital diabetes medical devices have capabilities that vary across vendors. For example, many CGMS have Bluetooth connectivity between the transmitter and the device manufacturer's proprietary FDA approved smartphone application (app) (e.g. Dexcom) for real-time viewing by the patient. In some cases, CGMS data sent to an app can be shared with health data frameworks, e.g. GoogleFit for Android or HealthKit for iOS. The CGMS data can then be shared within an ecosystem of mHealth apps. Also, CGMS data can be transmitted directly to an insulin pump, and the assimilated data from the CGMS and insulin pump can be uploaded to manufacturer specific web portals (e.g. CareLink) and data can be retrieved in raw flat files or static reports.

3.5   Next Generation ANS Research Informatics Platform

We propose an architecture to support real-life ANS studies, Fig. 1. It uses open-source informatics infrastructure (EHIE), messaging standards (Open mHealth, FHIR, SensorML), and commercial products (GoogleFit, HealthKit, Dexcom). Many of the components exist, but researcher and participant tools would need to be developed.

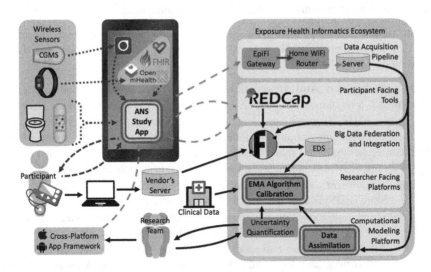

Fig. 1. Green lines represent real-time streaming of data, orange lines represent data transfers that prevent data loss, and black lines represent user- or client-initiated requests for data. Double purple outlined objects do not currently exist and would need to be developed and tested. (Color figure online)

4   Discussion

Depending on the study design, our proposed architecture supports various deployment designs. Wireless sensors and IoT devices transmit data in real-time through participants' smartphones and home networks. Having participants bring their own smart device to the study would exclude few individuals from participating since most Americans own a smartphone [18]. The smartphone provides a participant facing platform for study specific apps. These study apps would have data assimilation and storage capabilities arising from various sensor data streams and self-tracked data. Storing data on the smartphone provides two functionalities important to real-world studies, it helps to prevent data loss if mobile networks, gateway, or WiFi connections are unavailable and in conjunction with storing EMA logic within the study app, it allows peripheral EMAs and participant initiated self-tracking to proceed even when the smartphone is offline.

As the architecture builds on the meta-data centric EHIE, it is capable of accommodating different health data frameworks (e.g. GoogleFit or HealthKit), and messaging standards (e.g. Open mHealth, Fast Healthcare Interoperability Resources (FHIR), SensorML). Participant facing tools, which could be a smartphone app, software deployed on any other form factor, text messaging, email, or a patient portal, would be capable of EMAs by sending structured messages to the participant at regular intervals (e.g. nightly, weekly, etc.) or when triggered by an algorithm that considers the assimilated data stream. These tools would also support participant-initiated self-tracking. Participant's access to a gateway or home WiFi router would allow for secure transmission of data stored on sensors or a mobile device (e.g. smartphone) to a dedicated study server.

The EHIE computational platform currently supports post-study analysis of study data. The computational module, along with researcher facing tools, would need to be expanded to allow for the research team to calibrate EMA algorithms before the study begins by using pilot or simulated data, and potentially during the study on currently acquired study data. The EMA calibration would be capable of supporting all aspects of artificial intelligence: rule-based, Bayesian/statistics, and neural networks. Researchers could benefit from decision support during the study design process, data collection stage, and when conducting data analysis. The data analysis stage could be supported by a process workflow module that would facilitate reproducibility by documenting data assimilation and analyses pipelines [19, 20].

Future work includes building and testing a prototype of the proposed architecture to ensure the design requirements are met and to conduct testing with a performance modeling framework to guarantee the system performs and scales as expected [21]. Comparing the system's capabilities against requirements for real-world studies of other chronic diseases would indicate the generalizability of the system.

5   Conclusion

We identified requirements for conducting next-generation ANS studies and designed an architecture that would support the informatics aspects of such studies. These real-world studies would be capable of gathering contextual data from participants engaged in real-time self-tracking and objectively measured ANS responses from streaming wireless sensors, while also supporting the data needs of researchers before, during, and after data acquisition. The architecture makes use of commercially available and open source mHealth technologies and informatics platforms to support virtual clinical trials. There plans to build the and test a prototype of the proposed architecture.

Acknowledgements. This research is supported by NIH/NIDDK Ruth L. Kirschstein National Research Service Award, Diabetes & Metabolism Research Center at the University of Utah, the England Family Foundation, the Ardene Bullard "Of Love" Tennis Tournament, Jacobsen Construction, NIH/NCATS UL1TR002538, and NIH/NIBIB U54EB021973. Computational resources were provided by the Utah Center for High Performance Computing, which is partially funded by the NIH Shared Instrumentation.

Computational resources were provided by the Utah Center for High Performance Computing, which is partially funded by the NIH Shared Instrumentation Grant 1S10OD021644-01A1.

References

1. National Center for Chronic Disease Prevention and Health Promotion. National Diabetes Statistics Report, 2017, Estimate of Diabetes and Its Burden on the United States [Internet] (2017). https://www.cdc.gov/diabetes/pdfs/data/statistics/national-diabetes-statistics-report.pdf
2. Garg, S.K., Rewers, A.H., Akturk, H.K.: Ever-Increasing Insulin-Requiring Patients Globally. Diab. Technol. Ther. **20**(S2), S2–1 (2018)
3. Patil, P.R., Wolfe, J., Said, Q., Thomas, J., Martin, B.C.: Opioid use in the management of diabetic peripheral neuropathy (DPN) in a large commercially insured population. Clin. J. Pain **31**(5), 414 (2015)
4. Geddes, J., Wright, R.J., Zammitt, N.N., Deary, I.J., Frier, B.M.: An evaluation of methods of assessing impaired awareness of hypoglycemia in type 1 diabetes. Diabetes Care **30**(7), 1868–1870 (2007)
5. Bennett, M.: The LANSS pain scale: the leeds assessment of neuropathic symptoms and signs. Pain **92**(1), 147–157 (2001)
6. Myers, M.I., Peltier, A.C.: Uses of skin biopsy for sensory and autonomic nerve assessment. Curr. Neurol. Neurosci. Rep. **13**(1), 323 (2013)
7. Deshkar, S., Thanseeh, R., Menon, V.G.: A review on IoT based m-Health systems for diabetes. Int. J. Comput. Sci. Telecommun. **8**(1), 13–18 (2017)
8. Groat, D., Lin, Y.K., Gouripeddi, R., Facelli, J.: Measuring the autonomic nervous system for translational research: identification of non-invasive methods. Translational Science, Washington, D.C., March 2019
9. Mehta, M., Groat, D., Lin, Y.K., Gouripeddi, R., Facelli, J.: Classifying Impaired Awareness of Hypoglycemia with Convolutional Neural Networks. In: Institute of Electrical and Electronics Engineers Engineering in Medicine and Biology Society International Conference on Biomedical & Health Informatics, Chicago, IL, May 2019

10. Gouripeddi, R., Collingwood, S., Wong, B., Cummins, M., Facelli, J., Sward, K.: The Utah PRISMS Informatics Ecosystem: An Infrastructure for Generating and Utilizing Exposomes for Translational Research. Total Exposure Health Conference 2018, Bethesda, MD, 7 Sep 2018

11. Sward, K., Facelli, J.: Pediatric Research Using Integrated Sensor Monitoring Systems (PRISMS) – Utah Informatics Center Federated Integration Architecture. In: International Society of Exposure Science Annual Meeting, Utrecht, Netherlands, October 2016

12. Sward, K., Patwari, N., Gouripeddi, R., Facelli, J.: An Infrastructure for Generating Exposomes: Initial Lessons from the Utah PRISMS Platform. In Research Triangle Park, NC (2017)

13. Lundrigan, P., et al.: EpiFi: An in-home IoT Architecture for Epidemiological Deployments. In: IEEE, pp. 30–37 (2018)

14. Harris, P.A., Taylor, R., Thielke, R., Payne, J., Gonzalez, N., Conde, J.G.: Research electronic data capture (REDCap)—a metadata-driven methodology and workflow process for providing translational research informatics support. J. Biomed. Inform. 42(2), 377–381 (2009)

15. Bradshaw, R.L., Matney, S., Livne, O.E., Bray, B.E., Mitchell, J.A., Narus, S.P.: Architecture of a federated query engine for heterogeneous resources. In American Medical Informatics Association, p. 70 (2009)

16. Livne, O.E., Schultz, N.D., Narus, S.P.: Federated querying architecture with clinical & translational health IT application. J. Med. Syst. 35(5), 1211–1224 (2011)

17. OpenFurther. http://openfurther.org/. Accessed 10 Nov 2017

18. Pew Research Center. Demographics of Mobile Device Ownership and Adoption in the United States. Mobile Fact Sheet. https://www.pewinternet.org/fact-sheet/mobile/. Accessed 13 May 2019

19. Groat, D., et al.: Identification of High-Level Formalisms that Support Translational Research Reproducibility. In: Research Reproducibility Conference, Salt Lake City, Utah, June 2018

20. Groat, D., Gouripeddi, R., Dere, W., Facelli, J.: Development of a Framework for Scalable On-Demand Data Integration for Complex Diseases. In: American Medical Informatics Association Clinical Informatics Conference, Scottsdale, Arizona, May 2018

21. Gribaudo, M., Iacono, M., Kiran, M.: A performance modeling framework for lambda architecture-based applications. Future Gener. Comput. Syst. 1(86), 1032–1041 (2018)

Comparison of Approaches for Querying Chemical Compounds

Vojtěch Šípek, Irena Holubová, and Martin Svoboda(✉)

Faculty of Mathematics and Physics, Charles University, Prague, Czech Republic
sipekvojtech@gmail.com, {holubova,svoboda}@ksi.mff.cuni.cz

Abstract. Chemical compounds form a database with specific features that can be utilized for more efficient query processing. Currently, there exists no comparison of performance and memory usage of the respective and most efficient approaches on the same data set. In this paper, we address this lack of information and we create an unbiased benchmark of the most popular index building methods for subgraph querying of chemical databases. In addition, we compare the results with the performance of an SQL and a graph database for which there exist various unconfirmed hypotheses on their efficiency.

Keywords: Chemical database · Subgraph querying · Graph database · Subgraph isomorphism

1 Introduction

Querying is an essential utility of each database, and the same applies to chemical databases. Nowadays, the largest publicly accessible chemical databases contain around 100 million compounds. The chemical compounds can be naturally represented as graphs where atoms are represented as vertices and bonds as edges. A typical chemical compound is a connected sparse graph with labeled edges and vertices, where the size of the labeling alphabet for edges is less than 10, and the size of the labeling alphabet for vertices is in the order of low hundreds. On the other hand, the size of chemical compounds is variable. The vertex count varies typically from very small compounds with less than 10 vertices to huge compounds with hundreds of vertices. These sizes multiplied by the size of the database implies that querying over such databases is a challenging task.

The most common queries over chemical databases are exact match queries, the shortest path search, similarity search, and substructure search, which are all usually supported in graph databases. The latter one, probably the most common, is also the main point of interest in this paper. The goal of subgraph querying is to obtain a list of graphs from the database which contain the queried graph as its subgraph. The result of this process has a wide range of utilization, e.g., in chemoinformatics or bioinformatics, and, therefore, in the pharmaceutic industry.

This work was partially supported by the Charles University project PROGRES Q48.

V. Gadepally et al. (Eds.): DMAH 2019/Poly 2019, LNCS 11721, pp. 204–221, 2019.
https://doi.org/10.1007/978-3-030-33752-0_15

Several indexing techniques have been proposed to minimize the number of subgraph isomorphism tests since it is a well-known NP-complete problem. There also currently exist several benchmarks of the respective indexing techniques. Unfortunately, all of them were created by the authors of one of the indexing techniques, and therefore the intention of the benchmark is to show that a particular index is more efficient than the others. In other words, there is a lack of independent benchmarks which would compare the best performing indices on the same data and the same hardware.

The main contributions of this paper can be summed up as follows:

1. Contrary to all the existing benchmarks, we compare the best performing indexing techniques using the same environment. Our aim is to provide an unbiased comparison.
2. We compare the indexing techniques also with the usage of a traditional relational database and a modern graph database. We want to (dis)prove common hypotheses related to these systems.
3. We believe that this analysis shows new research directions in the area of efficient querying of databases of chemical compounds, as well as similar datasets with highly specific features.

Structure. In Sect. 2, we provide a general overview of approaches for querying databases of chemical compounds. In Sect. 3, we describe the process of the experimental analysis, while in Sect. 4 we overview and comment on the most interesting findings. Finally, we conclude in Sect. 5.

2   Related Work

First, we summarize and compare the algorithms which were developed for subgraph isomorphism matching. Next, we describe indices which might be used for obtaining the candidate set, and algorithms which are used for their construction. We then focus on approaches which utilize query mechanisms of particular relational and graph databases. And, finally, we provide a summary of popular commercially used solutions.

2.1   Subgraph Isomorphism Algorithms

Almost all papers related to subgraph query methods refer two algorithms: *Ullmann* [26] and *VF2* [10]. These two algorithms are compared in detail in [12], where *VF2* outperforms *Ullmann*.

In paper [19], there is a comparison of four algorithms derived from Ullmann's algorithm. These are *VF2*, *QuickSI* [25], *GraphQL* [15], *GADDI* [33], and *SPath* [34]. They were compared using three real-world data sets. Although all three comparisons have a different winner, it seems that the most efficient algorithm is *QuickSI* in an average use case.

2.2   Index Building Methods

The introduced methods for building index structures on top of chemical compound databases, i.e., the main target of this paper, involve *GraphGrep* [11], *GIndex* [31], *GString* [17], *GraphGrepSX* [9], *GIRAS* [7], *C-tree* [14], and *GDIndex* [29]. They form just a selection from a much bigger set of applicable methods and they were chosen for different reasons: (1) The method is mentioned in a majority of relevant articles. (2) The method uses an original algorithm or data structure. (3) The method has excellent results in existing benchmarks.

GraphGrep is a simple and intuitive indexing technique which can be used in any graph database with labeled graphs. The presumption is that every vertex has a unique ID. For each graph in the database, there is an index represented as a hash table where the key is a hashed value of a *label-path* (a concatenation of the vertex/edge labels on the path) and the value is a number of unique *id-paths* (a concatenation of the vertex IDs on the path) which represent a particular *label-path* in the graph. In the hash table there are all *label-paths* which are present in the graph up to length l, where l is a parameter. This hash table is called a *graph fingerprint*.

The query q itself is also a graph and, therefore, the hash table can be created too. Then, in the candidate set creation part, each graph's fingerprint is compared to the query fingerprint of q.

GraphGrepSX is an improved version of *GraphGrep*. The core of the improvement lies in the data structure, where the index is stored. This method stores the paths in a suffix tree. Each node in this suffix tree represents a path (which is an extension of its parent) and contains a set of pairs $(graph, count)$, where *graph* is an ID of the database record and *count* is the number of occurrences of the represented path in the *graph*.

gIndex utilizes the concepts of *frequent subgraphs* and *discriminative fragments*, because the number of all subgraphs grows exponentially with the size of the graph. It also introduces an innovative data structure for storing the index.

Frequent subgraphs are all subgraphs which are contained in at least *minSup* (minimum support) graphs in the database. If the query graph q is frequent, we have the candidate set immediately. If not, we can get the candidate set as an intersection of matched graphs sets of all frequent subgraphs of q. In addition, the described method utilizes a *size-increasing support function*. It takes the graph size as an argument (defined as the number of edges) and returns the *minSup* for a given size. *Discriminative fragments* concept brings a new metric γ, which measures how much discriminative a frequent subgraph is in comparison with the set of its subgraphs in the index.

gIndex itself is a prefix tree data structure. Its nodes are of 2 types: *discriminative* and *redundant*. Each node's key is a text string which represents a subgraph. Discriminative nodes are both frequent (based on given *size-increasing support function*) and discriminative (based on γ) and they contain a list of IDs of all graphs in the database which contain the particular subgraph. Redundant nodes are present just to satisfy the structure of the *gIndex* tree.

GIRAS indexes rare and discriminative fragments. The idea is to get higher pruning power and shift the indexing focus to the graph features which are specific for a particular record in the database – ultimately, to have a unique index for each graph in the database. This leads to a much smaller index size.

For getting the rare fragments, it utilizes the modified version of algorithm *gSpan* [30]. Although the original *gSpan* is designed to get all subgraphs whose support in the database is *f or higher*, the modified version finds all the subgraphs whose support is equal to *f*. GIRAS uses the modified *gSpan* starting with support $f = 1$. After each call of modified *gSpan*, it checks which database records are represented by the result set of *gSpan*. If there are database records which are not indexed yet, the modified *gSpan* is called iteratively with $f + 1$. Once there are all database records indexed, the index is finished. The last f is called f_{min}, and it is the threshold defining the meaning of a rare substructure.

Although the paper [7] does not discuss what data structure it uses for index representation, we found out from the source code obtained from Dr. Azaouzi, the author of the described research, that it uses a data structure similar to *gIndex*, as well as the same technique for the querying process.

GString is an approach specific for the organic chemical databases (but can be internally modified to support graph databases with similar specific content). The main idea results from the knowledge of common structures of the graphs in the database. Naturally, chemical compounds consist of 3 types of semantic structures – paths, cycles, and stars (a central node with a fan-out). Each chemical compound can be converted into a graph whose nodes are not atoms but one of the mentioned structures and which is thus significantly smaller. Other optimization observations are that (1) we can omit the hydrogens since their number can be easily computed and (2) we can omit the labels of carbon atoms and single (saturated) bonds.

C-Tree, contrary to the previous methods, builds a tree structure where the nodes are *closures* of their children, so they contain the same substructures as their whole subtrees. It also introduces a term *pseudo sub-isomorphism*, which is similar (and weaker) to subgraph isomorphism but it can be verified in polynomial time.

GDIndex's approach is quite different from the previous ones. It tries to completely omit the verification step, and, therefore, any computationally hard usage of a subgraph isomorphism detection algorithm. It is achieved by indexing all subgraphs of all database records. In particular, it uses two structures in the index: (1) a directed acyclic graph (DAG) of all subgraphs and (2) a lookup hash table of subgraphs.

Both index building and querying are straightforward. To build the index, we just take each graph, add it to the DAG and by gradual removing of its vertices, we repeat the same procedure for all its subgraphs. In each step, we only need to check whether such node already exists in the DAG, which we can easily achieve using the lookup table. To reduce the number of subgraphs, a canonization technique is introduced, so that from all isomorphic subgraphs only one is used in the index. Querying is even simpler. All we need to do is to create a canonical representation of the query graph q and use the lookup table.

Benchmark Results. *GraphGrep*, *GIndex*, *GString*, and *C-Tree* were compared in [17]. As the testing data set, the AIDS Antiviral Screen Dataset [32] was used. It contains 43,000 molecules with an average number of 25 vertices. All measured metrics except for the speed of index creation had the same winner. The *GString* algorithm outperforms the others in the size of index, accuracy of the candidate data set, and the search time.

On the other hand, in [9], we can find the benchmark of *GraphGrepSX*, which looks like a more generic version of *GString*. While in [17] *GString* outperforms *CTree* just by few percents, in [9] *GraphGrepSX* outperforms *CTree* by two levels of magnitude despite larger candidate sets.

In [29], there is a comparison of *GDIndex* and *C-tree*, where *GDIndex* significantly outperforms *C-tree* in all measured metrics – the size of the index, its construction time, and the search time. What we may question is that how *GDIndex* would perform over a database with larger graphs such as the AIDS dataset, which was used in experimental parts of other methods.

In [7], we can find a benchmark of *GIRAS*, *C-tree*, *gIndex*, and a couple of other approaches. On the AIDS dataset, *GIRAS* outperforms *gIndex* and *C-tree* in all query sizes. In the dataset with bigger graphs, *GIRAS* outperforms the other two methods only in larger query sizes (12 vertices and more). What is not measured in [7], is the size of index and time needed for index construction.

2.3 DBMSs Utilization for Subgraph Querying

Surprisingly, there do not exist many papers dealing with substructure querying in DBMSs, when just their specific query language and native way how to structure data are considered.

The first approach [13] focuses on the utilization of relational database management system and SQL queries. The database contains 3 tables – molecules, atoms, and bonds. The bonds have an extended type column, which is a string identifier that identifies the bond type and types of both end atoms (e.g., there is a unique identifier of two carbons connected by a double bond). The bond table has three indices built on top of it – for bond type, for column ATOM1_ID (a reference to the atoms table), and for the unique identifier of records in bond table by atom pairs.

The second approach [16] refers about utilizing a graph DBMS, Neo4j [3], and its query language Cypher, and describes a case study of mining protein graphs. The authors found out that the query time is factorial with respect to the number of edges in the query. Beginning from size 15, the queries were impossible to execute in a reasonable time, and, therefore, they recommend the usage of Neo4j only for small subgraph queries. They have also tried to compare their results with results for an SQL database. However, the SQL results significantly outperform Neo4j.

2.4   Commercially Used Solutions

Last but not least, we introduce three most popular real-world solutions. The first one, project *AMBIT* [1], offers chemoinformatics functionality via REST web services. One of the functionalities is the substructure search. This project represents a standalone solution – the querying is not dependent on any DBMSs.

The second solution, the *JChem Cartridge* [27], is an example of an Oracle cartridge. It has the best results in the benchmark presentation in [20].

The third solution, the *ABCD Cartridge* [6], is a pure commercial one developed by the Johnson & Johnson company. Contrary to most of the other commercial solutions, its architecture is well described in [6], despite the fact that the software is not publicly available.

3   Experiments

During the analysis of the related work, many questions have arisen. The papers are usually very brief, and they miss a lot of implementation details. Sadly, even if we tried to contact the authors, we did not get the original source code for the described methods, nor for the described benchmarks. The only exception is *GIRAS*, where we were successful in contacting its author, and so we have the complete implementation.

All the benchmarks we mentioned in Sect. 2.2 were a part of the papers which describe a particular method. So, naturally, it outperformed the other selected methods. The question is whether we can get the same results on different data sets and when adding other approaches.

Another interesting question is how the winners of the various benchmarks would perform on the same data set. For example, when *GString* outperforms *C-tree* just by few percents in [17] and *GraphGrepSX* outperforms *C-tree* by two levels of magnitude, we cannot implicitly say that *GraphGrepSX* would outperform *GString*. There might be three reasons for this observation:

- *The lack of knowledge of the tested dataset:* In most of the papers, there is an information which dataset was used, but not which part. Moreover, the benchmarks use different datasets.
- *The lack of knowledge about the implementation of the verification step:* None of the mentioned papers provides an information about which algorithm was used for the final subgraph isomorphism testing.
- *The unknown level of optimization:* We do not even know how much time the authors spent on the optimization of the code itself, e.g., whether they optimized the code, which languages and compilers were used etc.

What we did not find at all is a comparison of the performance of the described indexing techniques and utilization of SQL or graph databases. It might be interesting to see how significant difference in performance we get when we use a very graph specific technique comparing to the very generic ones which the traditional databases offer.

In general, using the experiments, we want to (dis)prove the following hypotheses:

Issue 1: GString vs. GraphGrepSX. Both *GString* and *GraphGrepSX* use very similar data structures for indexing the database. The main difference is that *GraphGrepSX* uses all graph paths, whereas *GString* uses all paths in the condensed graph. Also, *GString* uses heuristics, which are very specific for organic chemical databases.

- *Hypothesis H1.1*: The index size of *GString* will be significantly smaller compared to *GraphGrepSX* due to the condensed graph usage.
- *Hypothesis H1.2*: Due to the specificity of *GString*, it will outperform *GraphGrepSX*, which can be used for any graph dataset.

Issue 2: GIRAS performance for large queries. As described in [7], for small queries (of size 4 and 8), the performance of *GIRAS* is about the same as *C-tree*. On the other hand, for larger queries, the performance is ten times better comparing to *C-tree* and there are even better results for the candidate set sizes. What we may question is how it will perform compared to *GString* and *GraphGrepSX*.

- *Hypothesis H2.1*: Based on the benchmark results, we expect that *GraphGrepSX* will outperform *GIRAS* despite the smaller candidate sets.
- *Hypothesis H2.2*: Time to build *GIRAS* index will be significantly larger compared to other methods, since the algorithm seems to be computationally more complicated.

Issue 3: How do the SQL and graph oriented databases perform in comparison with the domain specific solutions? We may question what performance we may get when we use an SQL or a graph database. In this case, we do not need to implement any special algorithm for index building, we just use the capabilities of the databases, i.e., to create a query which describes the subgraph and, in case of SQL databases, to build the indices to help the query process.

- *Hypothesis H3.1*: Domain specific indices will perform much better, i.e., methods where we build the index will perform better than an SQL or a graph database.
- *Hypothesis H3.2*: The graph database will perform better than the SQL database because it runs completely in memory and it is optimized for querying graph data.

3.1   Experimental Work

Based on the uttered hypotheses, we have implemented: (1) *GraphGrepSX* and *GString* algorithms, (2) an adapter for the *GIRAS* implementation obtained from Dr. Azaouzi, and (3) tools for inserting and querying an SQL and a graph database. The whole implementation was written in Java. Most of the work uses Java version 10, the graph database adapter uses Java version 8 due to technology dependencies. For the chemical database parsing, we use the *Chemistry Development Kit* [5] version 2.1.1, a Java library for working with chemical formats and data structures. In case of the verification step for *GraphGrepSX* and *GString*, we use the *SMARTSQueryTool* from the Chemistry Development Kit utilizing Ullmann's algorithm.

GraphGrepSX. Since the *GraphGrepSX* algorithm is simple, the implementation is straightforward, just with a small modification. The original description of the algorithm expects that the suffix tree represents the vertex-label paths. Since we need to represent also the edge labels, we changed the original suffix tree presumption so that the odd levels of the suffix tree represent the vertices and the even levels of the suffix tree represent the edges. It does not affect the maximum path length parameter l. For our experiments we set $l = 6$.

GString. The algorithm description involves a wide range of pieces which were not described at all. Most of the unknown parts are related to the original graph reduction process, where the graph representing the atoms and bonds is transformed into a graph consisting only of nodes (representing cycles, stars, and paths) and edges (representing the connections between these structures).

The first issue we faced was the process of extracting the cycles from the original graph. Cycles can share both vertices and edges, and in some cases, the vertices and edges can be shared even by several cycles. We have found out that the Chemistry Development Kit has a utility for retrieving *MCB – Minimum Cycle Basis* (also known as *SSSR – Smallest Set of Smallest Rings*) described in [8]. *Cycle basis* is defined as a set of cycles by which one can express any other cycle present in a particular graph as the result of a symmetric difference operation on the cycle basis. The *MCB* finder utility requires specification of the maximum cycle size parameter. This parameter defines a threshold above which the cycles are not considered as cycles. When we tried to set this threshold high enough not to omit any cycle in the testing database, we encountered big issues with performance. Thus we set the threshold to 10, which covers the vast majority of real-world cases. Bigger cycles are described as paths of length equal to the cycle size.

Another question which arose was how to set the threshold which defines the minimum degree of an atom to be considered as a star. The original idea was to set this threshold to 3. The reason was that if we set this threshold to a higher number, we get another problem to solve – how to handle path joins. However, during the testing, we found out that it is possible to use this threshold, but in practice, we would lose the majority of results, because, e.g., instead of a longer path having a branch, which is quite a common case, we get a star and a shorter path (or a set of paths) and connected to the star, thus, we cannot query the longer path. Hence, we implemented a DFS which finds all the paths, and all these paths are included in the *GString* graph.

SQL Database. We have based our implementation on the proposal in [13]. We have chosen the Oracle Database 12c. For the Java API, we used the Oracle Database JDBC driver 12.2.0.1. Based on the mentioned paper, we designed our table with 5 columns: `ATOM1_ID`, `ATOM2_ID`, `BOND_ID`, `BOND_TYPE`, and `COMPOUND_ID`. The implementation itself is quite straightforward and it consists of two parts. The first part is a routine for database creation. In this routine, we just iterate through the whole database and for each molecule, first, we iterate through all its atoms and assign a unique ID to each of them. Then, we iterate through all the bonds, and for each, we create one statement `INSERT`.

The second part of the implementation is the query building. As proposed in [13], first, we build the minimal spanning tree of the query graph. The edge value is based on the database statistics which we gather during the insert phase. In particular, for spanning tree construction, we implemented the Kruskal algorithm [18]. Then, in the spanning tree, we find the edge with the lowest value, from this edge, we start a BFS algorithm, and for each edge, we add the rule into the statement `SELECT`. We also need to mark all the neighbors by stating that an atom ID of one edge is equal to the atom ID of the neighbor edge. We have to do the same for non-neighbors. For each such a pair, we have to explicitly state that their atom IDs are not equal. We have to do the same for the bonds. We need all the bonds unique, so we have to state for each pair of bonds that their IDs are not equal.

As an example of SQL query building process, we may use the path of 4 carbons connected by single bonds. The statement `SELECT` is as follows:

```
SELECT DISTINCT b0.compound_id
```

As we use only the bonds table, we need to specify that we want to join three instances of bonds table, one per each bond in the query graph:

```
FROM BONDS b0, BONDS b1, BONDS b2
```

Next, we need to specify that all bonds are distinct:

```
WHERE b0.BOND_ID != b1.BOND_ID AND b0.BOND_ID != b2.BOND_ID AND b1.BOND_ID != b2.BOND_ID AND
```

Finally, we need to specify all the constraints for each bond. First, we define which atoms are shared with the previous bonds to mimic BFS. Next, we describe the type of the bond which should help a lot with pruning. In the last step, we have to specify that all the atoms which were not marked in the first part are distinct, i.e., that every pair of atom IDs has to be distinct:

```
/* first bond */
b0.BONDTYPE='C-C' AND
/* second bond */
b1.ATOM1_ID = b0.ATOM2_ID AND b1.BONDTYPE='C-C' AND
b1.ATOM2_ID != b0.ATOM1_ID AND b1.ATOM2_ID != b0.ATOM2_ID AND
/* third bond */
b2.ATOM1_ID = b1.ATOM2_ID AND b2.BONDTYPE='C-C' AND
b2.ATOM2_ID != b0.ATOM1_ID AND b2.ATOM2_ID != b0.ATOM2_ID AND b2.ATOM2_ID != b1.ATOM2_ID
```

Graph Database. As observations of paper [16] state that Neo4j is not performing well in subgraph querying, we have tried to look for alternative graph databases which can perform better. We found the graph analytic tool *PGX* [23], a toolkit for graph analysis, with an ability to load and store graphs from/to various data formats. It supports an SQL-like query language called *PGQL* [24] and it advertises a scalable solution with a focus on high performance. Also, Oracle performed a benchmark which compares the performance of subgraph matching in PGX and Neo4j. The results are available at presentation [22] on slide 31 and are quite convincing. Although there are huge differences of result times according to the query size, PGX outperforms Neo4j in all categories.

The first issue we had to solve was that, although Oracle offers Windows batch files for starting PGX, we were not successful to run the database. To make the results of the performance measuring as precise as possible, we did not want to use other hardware or a different operating system. As a viable compromise we have decided to use the Windows 10 Subsystem for Linux utility [21] and we have downloaded the Ubuntu system to be used in this way. On Ubuntu, there were no issues with the PGX database usage.

The client side was implemented in Windows environment using the PGX Java client library. The implementation is quite straightforward. Instead of creating the graph in PGX for every single molecule in the database, we create one huge graph for all 10,000 compounds, where each graph component represents one molecule. This helps the performance since we do not have to load and store a huge number of small files, we execute a query on several big graphs instead. For each vertex, we generate a unique ID, we use a label to mark the representing atom symbol, and we store a molecule ID as a vertex's property. For each edge, we use a label to mark the type of represented bond.

For the querying, we use the PGQL, which is supported by PGX. For each atom in the query graph, we generate a unique ID, and then for each bond in the query graph, we insert a rule into the query, where we define that the two atoms with particular IDs and of a particular type are connected by a bond of a particular type. Finally, we need to state for each pair of atom IDs that they represent a different vertex.

A demonstration of the simplicity of PGQL usage in our case might be a query representing the path of three carbons. We start the query with the following statement:

```
SELECT DISTINCT a1.moleculeId
```

The following part of a PGQL query describes the bonds in the query graph:

```
MATCH (a1:C)-[:S]-(a2:C), (a2:C)-[:S]-(a3:C)
```

As the last part, we need to state that all atoms a1, a2 and a3 are different. (Otherwise the query would match every pair of connected carbons since a1 and a3 could represent the same atom.)

```
WHERE a1 <> a2 AND a1 <> a3 AND a2 <> a3
```

GIRAS. As we were successful with the request of the original implementation of *GIRAS*, we use the original solution. We had to implement only an adapter which translates the chemical database we use for other methods to the format – vertex and edge lists – accepted by the *GIRAS* code.

However, during the testing, we have found out that the results do not match the results of other methods. After some investigation, we have realized that the problem is not in the implementation, but in the algorithm itself. The *GIRAS* method is trying to find the rare substructures with the condition that every graph in the database has to be represented by at least one rare subgraph. We have found out that when we create a query which has only several results, everything works fine. On the other hand, when we create a query which should match nearly the whole database, we do not get any results at all.

We did an explicit test which proves that the algorithm cannot work properly in all cases. We have created a database with 4 molecules, where each of them contains a path of 4 aromatic carbons, but in each of them, there is a unique substructure which does not contain this particular path. When we have executed a query of the mentioned path, we did not get any results. When we added a new molecule into the database which represents the query itself, i.e., a path of 4 aromatic carbons, the query matched all 5 graphs in the database. This observation invalidates the statement in [7] that the indexing is complete.

4   Results of Experiments

We have measured the results using a laptop Dell Inspiron 15 7000 with Intel(R) Core(TM) i7-6700HQ CPU processor with a frequency of 2.60 GHz and 16 GB of RAM with operating system Windows 10.

As a dataset, we have used the first 100,000 compounds of the *ChEMBL* database [2] release 24. We wanted to have a large enough dataset to have as precise results as possible. On the other hand, most of the experiments are computed just in memory, and, therefore, the dataset could not be larger. Since we did not find any order pattern in which the compounds are placed into the database, we assume that this order is random.

The particular characteristics of the used dataset are as follows:

– Number of vertices of the smallest compound: 1
– Number of vertices of the largest compound: 548
– Average number of vertices: 28
– Average number of edges: 30
– Number of vertex labels: 18
– Number of edge labels: 4

For query testing, we created four sets of queries with sizes of 4, 8, 16, and 24 vertices respectively. Each set contains 10 different queries defined in the SMILES language [4]. The list of queries and all measured values can be found in [28].

4.1   Index Building Time

We define the index building time as the time difference between the time when the chemical database is loaded into the memory and the time the index/database is ready to execute queries.

In case of *GraphGrepSX*, *GString* and *GIRAS*, it means the index building itself, in case of SQL and graph database, it means the set of API calls to upload the data into the database. The complete results are provided in Fig. 1. For a better graph scale, we also present results with omitted SQL database results in Fig. 2.

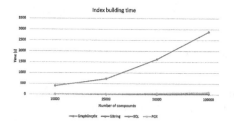
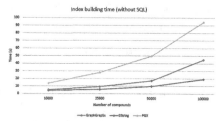

Fig. 1. Index building time   **Fig. 2.** Index building time (without the SQL database)

As expected, we can see that it is significantly slower to build the whole database from scratch than to create just an index, as it is in case of *Graph-GrepSX* and *GString*. The results of database methods are also quite convincing – SQL database creation time is 50 times slower compared to PGX. This is quite an expected result since PGX works only in memory contrary to the SQL database which stores all the data to the disk.

In the other two cases, the difference is not so significant. *GraphGrepSX* is two times slower than *GString*. There might be two reasons for this observation. The first one is that for *GString* we have used smaller parameter l compared to *GraphGrepSX*. The other explanation might be that it is worth to spend some time for the condensation process, because it significantly reduces the number of distinct paths in the graph, and, therefore, it makes the index building process faster.

Unfortunately, we cannot present the results for *GIRAS*. The reason is that we were not able to get the results in a reasonable time. Even for 10,000 compounds, we did not get the built index even after two days of computation. The reason is that the dataset contains small structures which are substructures of many others, and, thus, there are no rare subgraphs. After two days of computation for 10,000 compounds, we stopped at the moment where we were missing indexing of 39 compounds, and the currently searched support level was 600. In other words, these 39 compounds do not contain any subgraph (of the maximal size of 8 vertices) which is rare enough to be a part of less than or equal to 600 compounds in the dataset. Just for verification, we tested *GIRAS* on small datasets (hundreds of compounds) and the computation has finished in a reasonable time (several hours) and with expected results. Since we were not able to build the *GIRAS* index for our dataset, we do not present the results of other metrics for this method, because we had no way to measure them.

4.2   Index and Data Size

Since it is tricky to measure just the index size (and in a graph database this term does not even make sense), we have decided to measure the size of memory needed for a particular method. In case of *GraphGrepSX* and *GString*, it is the memory used by the running process after the index is built and garbage collection being triggered. In case of the SQL database, we query the size of the index structure and table BONDS. The query is as follows:

```
SELECT sum(bytes)/1024/1024 as "SIZE in MB" FROM dba_segments
            WHERE segment_name='BONDS/INDEX_NAME'
```

Last but not least, in case of the graph database, we use method *getMemoryMb*, which is offered by the Java API of PGX graph representation.

The results are provided in Fig. 3. What we found as an interesting observation is the size of the *GString* index. We found out that the premise that using the condensed graph to reduce the number of different paths is not valid. The built index on the tested database contains more than a half million nodes in the *GString* index tree. The root node itself has almost 150 children, i.e., there are almost 150 different node types. This is a huge number compared to *GraphGrepSX*, which contains only 21 vertex node types.

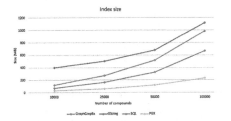

Fig. 3. Index size

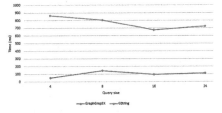

Fig. 4. Candidate set creation time

Other results are quite expected. The reason why PGX data representation is significantly smaller compared to the SQL database is that PGX does not build any indices. The amount of memory consumed by SQL table representation (without the indices) is about the same as for PGX.

4.3   Candidate Set Creation Time

By candidate set creation, we mean the time difference between the time when a query is executed and the time when we finish the index utilization for the particular query. As we have mentioned, this metric is meaningful only for *Graph-GrepSX* and *GString*. The results are provided in Fig. 4. We can see that *GString* is significantly slower compared to *GraphGrepSX*. This is most probably because of the significantly bigger index size.

The other interesting fact for *GString* is that due to the "stars versus paths" issue described in Sect. 2.2, it is almost impossible to get meaningful results for large queries, and so the candidate sets are cut down to almost empty sets.

4.4   Verification Time

Verification time has two different meanings in this context. For methods where we create the candidate set, we understand verification time as the time needed to verify the candidate set. In case of SQL and graph databases, where we do not work with the candidate set concept, we understand verification time as the time needed for executing the query, since we need to verify every single record in the database.

The results are provided in Fig. 5, where we can observe several interesting outcomes. At first, we can be surprised by very low numbers for verification time in case of *GString*. This is caused by a significantly smaller candidate set compared to *GraphGrepSX*. On the other hand, the candidate set is not smaller due to a better pruning ability of *GString* index, but because of the fact that *GString* invalidates even the results which are valid for other methods. This was described in detail in Sect. 2.2.

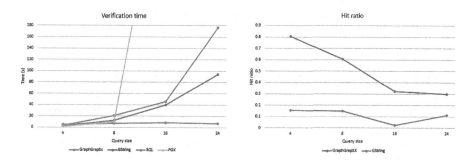

Fig. 5. Verification time   **Fig. 6.** Candidate set hit ratio

The other interesting observation represents the values for PGX. Although the values for queries of sizes 4 and 8 are very good (even better than for *Graph-GrepSX* which is indexed), we have found out that for queries with the size bigger than 14, it is barely usable. We have tried to test it even on a database with 1 graph having 2 vertices and 1 edge between them. We would expect that any query will be executed quickly because there is not much to compute. However, we have found that even on this small graph, big queries are very slow, and the complexity grows exponentially: While a query with 12 vertices took 46 s, a query with 14 vertices took 50 min. Even after 3 h of computation, we were not able to get results for a query with 16 vertices.

It seems that PGX spends a lot of time on PGQL query parsing and creation of the execution plan. We have investigated this surprising finding and found out that this problem probably occurs only in the single-node in-memory engine mode of PGX 19.1.0 we used for experiments. An interested reader can compare this finding with results described in [22], where very promising numbers even for large queries are presented.

4.5 Hit Ratio of Candidate Set

The metric is defined as a ratio between the candidate set size and the result set size. It measures the quality of the index, i.e., the higher the ratio is, the better results are obtained from the index. It is again only applicable for methods which create the candidate set.

As we can see in Fig. 6, for *GraphGrepSX*, the efficiency of its index decreases with the query size. This is natural since the *GraphGrepSX*'s index describes only paths of length up to 6. Therefore, it is expectable that with the growing size of the query, the accuracy will decrease, because the indexed paths cover a smaller portion of the query.

On the other hand, even queries of size 24 are not big enough to overflow the capacity of *GString*. The condensed graph does not contain paths longer than 5 in these cases, and, therefore, we would expect more or less constant hit ratio for all query sizes which matches the actual results. However, we can see that the hit ratio is significantly smaller compared to *GraphGrepSX*.

4.6 Query Execution Time

The whole query process can be defined as the sum of the candidate set creation time and verification time. Note that in the case of SQL and graph databases, this is equal to the verification time. However, for the end user, this is probably the most crucial metric.

The results are provided in Fig. 7. The first aspect we can observe is that this graph is not much different from the one in Fig. 5. In other words, the time for obtaining a candidate set plays only very minor role in the total query time.

The very good performance of *GString* is the result of the fact that the result set is smaller compared to the other methods. This might be confusing and a user of such a method has to be aware of its limitations. On the other hand, if the user knows what the *GString* restrictions are, it may be a very efficient way of querying.

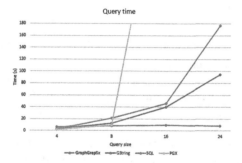

Fig. 7. Query time

In case of small queries, the best choice seems to be PGX. The implementation is very straightforward and most of the work is very intuitive. Also, the implementation of PGX handler is very easily improvable to work with even much bigger datasets which cannot fit into the memory.

In the case of the SQL database, we can be quite surprised that, contrary to usual expectations, it is a viable solution. The difference in performance times from the other methods is not that significant as we would expect. Besides, the SQL solution is the only one which does not have to fit into memory as it is.

Although all the other methods have their own benefits, *GraphGrepSX* seems to be an overall winner. It is quite simple to implement, it has the best overall performance and reasonable index size, as well as its built time.

Finally, we summarize the results of the original hypotheses in Table 1.

Table 1. Hypotheses results

Hypothesis	Result	Comments
H1.1	False	Index of *GString* is significantly larger. The number of distinct nodes in case of *GString* is much bigger compared to *GraphGrapSX* on a real-world dataset
H1.2	Uncertain	The performance of *GString* is indeed better compared to *GraphGrepSX*. On the other hand, the main reason is a smaller result set, because the rules for candidate set creation are too restrictive in some cases
H2.1	Unknown	We were not able to build the *GIRAS* index in a reasonable time
H2.2	True	We were not able to build the *GIRAS* index in a reasonable time even for the one tenth of the tested dataset size
H3.1	True	In general, both *GraphGrepSX* and *GString* perform better than SQL and PGX approaches. On the other hand, for small queries, the PGX is slightly faster. Moreover, in the case of the SQL database, we expected much worse results
H3.2	Uncertain	The hypothesis is definitely valid for small queries, in which case the performance difference is enormous. On the other hand, for larger queries PGX starts to be barely usable due to the issues with PGQL query parsing, but this is probably a problem only in the particular version we used

5   Conclusion

The aim of this paper was "to fill a market niche" of objective benchmarks of approaches for efficient querying over databases of chemical compounds. Among the existing approaches, we have selected three indexing algorithms (*Graph-GrepSX*, *GString* and *GIRAS*), and compared them both mutually and also with a classical relational database (Oracle) and a graph analytics tool (PGX). In all five cases, we targeted the most efficient representatives of their kind. We have created a benchmark which uses a data set of 100,000 chemical compounds, and we primarily measured the index size and its creation time, efficiency of the index, and the total time needed for queries of various sizes.

As expected, we have confirmed some of the common hypotheses. But, on the other hand, we have found many of the results of related papers not completely valid, and we have also disproved some of the common assumptions. In general, our aim was to provide an unbiased comparison and show the current potential as well as shortcomings of the existing approaches used for querying chemical compounds.

References

1. AMBIT, 19 May 2017. http://ambit.sourceforge.net/
2. ChEMBL, 2 May 2019. https://www.ebi.ac.uk/chembl/
3. Neo4j database, 19 May 2017. https://neo4j.com/
4. SMILES, 2 May 2019. http://www.daylight.com/dayhtml/doc/theory/theory. smiles.html
5. The Chemistry Development Kit, 19 May 2017. https://github.com/cdk/
6. Agrafiotis, D.K., et al.: Efficient substructure searching of large chemical libraries: the ABCD chemical cartridge. J. Chem. Inf. Model. **51**(12), 3113–3130 (2011)
7. Azaouzi, M., Ben Romdhane, L.: A minimal rare substructures-based model for graph database indexing. In: Madureira, A.M., Abraham, A., Gamboa, D., Novais, P. (eds.) ISDA 2016. AISC, vol. 557, pp. 250–259. Springer, Cham (2017). https:// doi.org/10.1007/978-3-319-53480-0_25
8. Bauer, U.: Minimum cycle basis algorithms for the chemistry development toolkit (2004)
9. Bonnici, V., Ferro, A., Giugno, R., Pulvirenti, A., Shasha, D.: Enhancing graph database indexing by suffix tree structure. In: Dijkstra, T.M.H., Tsivtsivadze, E., Marchiori, E., Heskes, T. (eds.) PRIB 2010. LNCS, vol. 6282, pp. 195–203. Springer, Heidelberg (2010). https://doi.org/10.1007/978-3-642-16001-1_17
10. Cordella, L.P., Foggia, P., Sansone, C., Vento, M.: A (sub)graph isomorphism algorithm for matching large graphs. IEEE Trans. Pattern Anal. Mach. Intell. **26**(10), 1367–1372 (2004)
11. Dongoran, E.S.S., Saleh, W.K.R., Gozali, A.A.: Analysis and implementation of graph indexing for graph database using GraphGrep algorithm. In: ICoICT 2015, pp. 59–64 (2015)
12. Ehrlich, H.-C., Rarey, M.: Systematic benchmark of substructure search in molecular graphs - from Ullmann to VF2. J. Cheminform. **4**(1), 13 (2012)
13. Golovin, A., Henrick, K.: Chemical substructure search in SQL. J. Chem. Inf. Model. **49**(1), 22–27 (2009)

14. He, H., Singh, A.K.: Closure-tree: an index structure for graph queries. In: ICDE 2006, p. 38 (2006)
15. He, H., Singh, A.K.: Graphs-at-a-time: query language and access methods for graph databases. In: 2008 ACM SIGMOD, pp. 405–418. ACM, New York (2008)
16. Hoksza, D., Jelínek, J.: Using Neo4j for mining protein graphs: a case study. In: DEXA 2015, pp. 230–234, September 2015
17. Jiang, H., Wang, H., Yu, P.S., Zhou, S.: GString: a novel approach for efficient search in graph databases. In: ICDE 2007, pp. 566–575 (2007)
18. Kruskal, J.B.: On the shortest spanning subtree of a graph and the traveling salesman problem. Am. Math. Soc. **7**(1), 48–50 (1956)
19. Lee, J., Han, W.-S., Kasperovics, R., Lee, J.-H.: An in-depth comparison of subgraph isomorphism algorithms in graph databases. VLDB Endow. **6**(2), 133–144 (2012)
20. May, J.: Substructure search face-off: are the slowest queries the same between tools? NextMove Software (2015), 19 May 2017
21. Microsoft: Windows Subsystem for Linux Documentation, 25 April 2019. https://docs.microsoft.com/en-us/windows/wsl/about
22. Oracle: An Introduction to Graph: Database, Analytics, and Cloud Services, 25 April 2019. https://www.slideshare.net/JeanIhm/an-introduction-to-graph-database-analytics-and-cloud-services
23. Oracle: Parallel Graph AnalytiX (PGX), 25 April 2019
24. Oracle: PGQL - Property Graph Query Language, 25 April 2019
25. Shang, H., Zhang, Y., Lin, X., Yu, J.X.: Taming verification hardness: an efficient algorithm for testing subgraph isomorphism. VLDB Endow. **1**(1), 364–375 (2008)
26. Ullmann, J.R.: An algorithm for subgraph isomorphism. J. ACM **23**(1), 31–42 (1976)
27. Vajda, K.: JChem Cartridge for Oracle. ChemAxon Ltd. (2015), 19 May 2017
28. Šípek, V.: Comparison of approaches for querying of chemical compounds. Master thesis, Charles University, Prague, Czech Republic (2019). http://www.ksi.mff.cuni.cz/~holubova/dp/Sipek.pdf
29. Williams, D.W., Huan, J., Wang, W.: Graph database indexing using structured graph decomposition. In: ICDE 2007, pp. 976–985 (2007)
30. Yan, X., Han, J.: gSpan: graph-based substructure pattern mining. In: ICDM 2002, pp. 721–724 (2002)
31. Yan, X., Yu, P.S., Han, J.: Graph indexing: a frequent structure-based approach. In: 2004 ACM SIGMOD, pp. 335–346. ACM, New York (2004)
32. Zaharevitz, D.: AIDS Antiviral Screen Data. NIH/NCI (2015), 19 May 2017
33. Zhang, S., Li, S., Yang, J.: GADDI: distance index based subgraph matching in biological networks. In: EDBT 2009, pp. 192–203. ACM, New York (2009)
34. Zhao, P., Han, J.: On graph query optimization in large networks. VLDB Endow. **3**(1–2), 340–351 (2010)

DMAH 2019: AI for Healthcare

Differential Diagnosis of Heart Disease in Emergency Departments Using Decision Tree and Medical Knowledge

Diyang Xue[1(✉)], Adam Frisch[2], and Daqing He[1]

[1] University of Pittsburgh, Pittsburgh, PA 15260, USA
{dix2,dah44}@pitt.edu
[2] University of Pittsburgh Medical Center, Pittsburgh, PA 15213, USA
frischan@upmc.edu

Abstract. Generating differential diagnosis has been a subjective process primarily relying on a physician's experience. However, the increased availability of electronic health records (EHRs) means that this process has the potential to benefit from machine learning-based decision support technology. No differential diagnosis models are currently available for heart disease, particularly for physicians in emergency departments (EDs). In this paper, we applied the decision tree method to automatically build a heart disease differential diagnosis model from structured and unstructured ED data. Our results show that the automatically learned model can achieve a classification accuracy of 89%. Our study demonstrates that data-driven differential diagnosis rules can be automatically learned from analyzing EHR data and that this learning can be clinically meaningful when merged with external medical knowledge.

Keywords: Heart disease · Differential diagnosis · Decision tree · Electronic health records

1 Introduction

Differential diagnosis provides a list of possible diseases that might explain a patient's presenting clinical signs and symptoms [21]. Clinicians use historical information, physical exam findings, and diagnostic studies to narrow this list. Often level of differential diagnosis capability relies on physician's experience, and it can be further impacted when physicians work in high demand environments such as EDs. Physicians in the EDs must make correct diagnoses in a short time, with only partial information.

A diagnosis error emerges when a diagnosis is missed, inappropriately delayed or is wrong [17]. The overall rate of diagnostic error has been estimated at 10–15% [3], and diagnostic error is the number one reason for malpractice lawsuits arising from events originating in EDs [6]. Unfortunately, reducing diagnostic error is difficult. Suggested approaches include improving clinicians' diagnostic

© Springer Nature Switzerland AG 2019
V. Gadepally et al. (Eds.): DMAH 2019/Poly 2019, LNCS 11721, pp. 225–236, 2019.
https://doi.org/10.1007/978-3-030-33752-0_16

abilities and the use of diagnostic aid systems to augment doctors' diagnostic abilities. However, there are currently no available tools which use real-world data to automatically aid differential diagnosis generation for ED clinicians.

In this paper, we proposed a method of building a differential diagnosis aid system automatically from EHR data and medical knowledge using a decision tree algorithm. To build this system, we first used the natural language processing (NLP) method to extract useful clinical findings and symptoms from discharge reports, then built models using patients' demographic information, clinical findings and symptom information along with external medical knowledge.

We applied the proposed method to actual EHR data obtained from the University of Pittsburgh Medical Center (UPMC). The results indicated that our approach is effective in finding clinically meaningful differential diagnosis rules.

The remainder of this paper is organized as follows. Related work is reviewed in Sect. 2. Our proposed method is described in Sect. 3. Experiments are described in Sect. 4. The conclusion is in Sect. 5.

2   Related Work

Differential diagnosis generators were first developed in the 1960s [10,16]. These earliest systems, for example, INTERNIST-1 [15], MYCIN [20] and DXplain [1], used structured knowledge or a manually constructed knowledge base to do predictions.

In the 1990s, Iliad [24] was developed. It used more probability reasoning methods. Each disease in this system was assigned a prior probability and a list of findings, along with the sensitivity (the fraction of patients who have the disease and at the same time have the finding), and 1-specificity (the fraction of patients who do not have the disease but have the finding).

In 2000, NLP techniques began to be applied in diagnosis systems. For example, ISABEL [19] uses automatic information retrieval techniques and a database of medical documents to retrieve appropriate findings and diagnoses.

However, current differential diagnosis generators [4] are designed to give a potential disease list, rather than providing physicians suggestions for the next physical exams, lab tests or treatments.

3   Method

The goal of this study is to find a way that effective differential diagnosis rules can be created through mining of EHR data and medical knowledge. EHRs are widely used in hospitals and medical practices nationwide now, and this high volume facilitates data-drive clinical research to enhance patient care [7].

We decided to adopt the decision tree algorithm to perform data-driven differential diagnosis. The reasons for this decision are two-fold. Like machine learning algorithms such as deep neural networks [12], random forest [13], and support vector machines [22], the decision tree algorithm is commonly used, and it has comparable effectiveness in decision making. However, the decision tree has the advantage over the other types because its building process is consistent with what physicians think of as differential diagnosis, and it is easy for physicians to check the inside of the model. This makes it easier for physicians when deciding whether to trust a prediction made by a decision tree or not.

Because inferences made by machine learning algorithms are often limited by the patterns in the data, extra domain or background knowledge are often integrated to resolve this limitation. For example, domain knowledge has been used to improve machine learning algorithm performance in clinical notes de-identification [8], intensive care monitoring [14], and medical risk factors identification [23].

Word embeddings are a type of popular word representation for high-dimensional data in NLP. They capture the similarity or correlation between different words. Andrew Beam et al. [2] published a set of medical concept embeddings learned from an extremely large collection of medical data. We used this dataset to calculate the correlation between cardiac disease and symptoms and incorporate this relationship as external medical knowledge. We added in this medical knowledge to improve the differential diagnosis performance of the decision tree algorithm.

Below we describe how we extracted useful information from EHR data, how we applied the decision tree algorithm, how we enabled calculation of the relationship between disease and symptoms, and finally, how we combined the two types of information obtained to enable differential diagnosis.

3.1   Feature Extraction Using NLP

In addition to retrieving basic structured demographic information from the cohort population, including gender, race, age, and insurance, we also collected unstructured ED discharge summaries.

From the ED discharge summaries, we extracted medical findings using MedLEE [9], a well-known NLP tool. For each report, MedLEE returned a set of Unified Medical Language System Concept Unique Identifiers (UMLS CUIs), each of which represents a clinical concept. Each concept was associated with a certainty level, e.g., "no," "negative," "rule out," "unable," etc. For each clinical concept CUI, we assigned the value "True" or "False" based on its corresponding certainty level. For example, the NLP output from processing the sentence, "The patient denied chest pain" would be C0008031 (CUI code representing chest pain) with a value of "False." When a CUI did not appear in one report, we treated it as "False."

In UMLS, each concept's CUI code is associated with a semantic type code such as finding (T033), sign or symptom (T184), etc. To avoid the extraction of final diagnosis from a report, we limited our concepts to two types, namely finding and symptom or sign. We extracted 8,464 distinct UMLS CUI codes overall.

3.2   Decision Tree Algorithm

Decision tree learning is a commonly used predictive modeling technique. A decision tree model starts from the root node and partitions data recursively into subgroups. One classic decision tree learning algorithm, the ID3 algorithm, was designed by Quinlan [5]. At each node, the ID3 selects the attribute that has the highest information gain among all candidate attributes, splits the data set, and grows the branches on values of the attribute.

1. Entropy $H(T)$ is a measure of uncertainty of one set T.

$$H(T) = \sum_{x \in X} -p(x)\log_2 p(x)$$

   – $H(T)$: the entropy of set T
   – T: the set for which entropy is calculated
   – X: classes in set T
   – $p(x)$: the probability of each class in set T
2. Information gain $IG(T, F)$ is the entropy difference before and after set T is split by feature F.

$$IG(T, F) = H(T) - \sum_{y \in Y} p(y)H(y)$$

   – $H(T)$: the entropy of set T
   – Y: the subsets after T is split by feature F
   – $p(y)$: the proportion of the number of elements in y to the number of elements in set T
   – $H(y)$: entropy of subset y

3.3   Medical Knowledge Learned from Word Embedding

Cosine similarity is a measure of similarity between two vectors by calculating the cosine of the angle between them. Two identical vectors have a cosine similarity value of 1. The larger the cosine similarity value is, the more similar the two vectors are.

$$Cosine\ Similarity = cos(\theta) = \frac{X \times Y}{\|X\| \times \|Y\|} = \frac{\sum_{i=1}^{n} X_i \times Y_i}{\sqrt{\sum_{i=1}^{n} X_i^2} \sqrt{\sum_{i=1}^{n} Y_i^2}}$$

where X_i and Y_i are components of vectors X and Y.

Andrew Beam, et al. [2], at Harvard Medical School, created the most comprehensive clinical embeddings to date using extremely large medical data and literature. Each clinical concept (e.g., disease, symptom) is represented by a numeric vector. We used Beam's numeric representations of UMLS CUIs.

Because we do not have enough samples to do differential diagnosis for each ICD code, we merged 238 heart disease ICD-9-CM codes into six categories (see datasets description in Sect. 4.1). Each category has multiple vectors, so we used the centroid of these vectors to represent the category.

For each feature, we calculated the similarity of its cosine with the vector centroid of each category and got six values. We used the Softmax method to transform these six similarity values to probabilities and calculated the entropy of these six probability values. Finally, we used this entropy value to represent this feature's clinical differential diagnosis capability.

3.4 Combining Decision Tree and Medical Knowledge

The ID3 decision tree algorithm chooses splitting nodes based on the information gain of each feature. We combined the information gain and clinical information entropy values to generate a new score for decision tree development.

$$New\ Criterion = (1 - \alpha) \times InformationGain$$
$$+ \alpha \times DifferentialDiagnosisScore$$

4 Experiment

4.1 Experiment Setup

Datasets. We retrieved data from all heart disease visits to 15 EDs at UPMC between January 1, 2008 and December 31, 2014. The University of Pittsburgh Institutional Review Board approved this study (Study No. 18100069). We identified a cardiac disease visit if its primary ED diagnosis included one of the 238 ICD-9-CM codes for cardiac disease. We then used Clinical Classification Software (CCS) 7.2 to merge all of the ICD-9-CM codes into six clinically meaningful categories. CCS is a widely used diagnosis and procedure categorization scheme [11].

Although CCS has 11 categories (CCS 7.2.1 - CCS 7.2.11) for heart disease, we did not include CCS 7.2.5 because it refers to nonspecific chest pain, which is not a clear indication of cardiac disease. We combined conduction disorders (CCS 7.2.8) and cardiac dysrhythmias (CCS 7.2.9) as category 7.2.89 because they are treated similarly in acute settings. We combined heart valve disorders (CCS 7.2.1), pulmonary heart disease (CCS 7.2.6), other and ill-defined heart disease (CCS 7.2.7), and cardiac arrest and ventricular fibrillation (CCS 7.2.10) into a category we called "OTHER" due to their small number of visits and clinical unimportance. Detailed information about the six categories is shown in Table 1. Each of these six CCS groups has sufficient training and test data to evaluate our new scoring methods to combine EHR data and medical knowledge.

We removed visits whose primary diagnosis and secondary diagnosis belonged to more than one heart disease CCS categories. We made this decision because we found that there were more than 500 distinct CCS category combinations in our research data. We did not have enough samples to conduct differential diagnosis for all these combinations. Moreover, when there was more than one CCS category, it was unclear which heart disease caused which clinical abnormality.

Table 1. Sample size of training and test datasets.

CCS level	Description	Training, 2008–2013	Test, 2014
7.2.2	Peri-; endo-; and myocarditis; cardiomyopathy (except that caused by TB and STD)	84	20
7.2.3	Acute myocardial infarction	121	53
7.2.4	Coronary atherosclerosis and other heart disease	294	88
7.2.89	Conduction disorders Cardiac dysrhythmias	8418	2552
7.2.11	Congestive heart failure; nonhypertensive	402	108
OTHER	Heart valve disorders Pulmonary heart disease Other and ill-defined heart disease Cardiac arrest and ventricular fibrillation	1379	374

We used data from 2008 to 2013 as training data and data from 2014 as test data. Overall, the training data and test data had comparable demographic distributions. Table 2 lists the demographic information of the training and test data. We defined age categories as follows: Child: 0–17; Adult: 18–64; Old: 65 and older. We estimated income level in units of a thousand, based on home zip code and census data, and divided income into three categories: Lower_income: less than 40,000; Middle_income: 40,000–120,000; High_income: greater than 120,000.

Implementation Details. To evaluate performance of the decision tree algorithm, we varied two input parameters for the decision tree model learned from EHR data (DT_EHR): maximum tree depth $(3, 4, 5, 6, 7, 8)$ and minimal leaf sample size $(60, 80, 100, 120)$; we varied three parameters for the decision tree model learned from both EHR and medical knowledge (DT_EHRMK): maximum tree depth $(3, 4, 5, 6, 7, 8)$, minimal leaf sample size $(60, 80, 100, 120)$ and parameter α (0.01 to 1 per 0.01). We used a ten-fold cross validation technique to find the best hyperparameters on the training data, then used those parameters to fit the decision tree model to the whole training data set. The best hyperparameters for DT_EHR were: best tree depth = 8, and best minimal leaf sample size = 60. The best hyperparameters for DT_EHRMK were: best tree depth = 8, best minimal leaf sample size = 60, and best $\alpha = 0.81$.

4.2   Results and Discussion

Classification Performance. The test data classification accuracy of DT_EHR was 0.8908. Its confusion matrix is reported in Table 3. The test data classification accuracy of DT_EHRMK was 0.8814, and its confusion matrix is reported in Table 4.

Table 2. Statistical summary of demographic information.

Characteristic	Training data (n = 10698)	Test data (n = 3195)
Gender	Female: 6087(57%)	Female: 1784(56%)
	Male: 4611(43%)	Male: 1411(44%)
Race	Black: 1899(18%)	Black: 458(14%)
	White: 8413(79%)	White: 2646(83%)
	Other: 386(3%)	Other: 91(3%)
Age	Child: 530(5%)	Child: 201(6%)
	Adult: 7349(69%)	Adult: 2133(67%)
	Old: 2819(26%)	Old: 861(27%)
Income	Lower_income: 6799(64%)	Lower_income: 2003(63%)
	Middle_income: 3884(36%)	Middle_income: 1189(37%)
	High_income: 15(0.1%)	High_income: 3(0.09%)
Insurance	Commercial: 1109(10%)	Commercial: 321(10%)
	Medicare: 1031(10%)	Medicare: 336(11%)
	Other: 8558(80%)	Other: 2538(79%)

Table 3. Confusion matrix for DT_EHR.

	Predicted						
Actual	CCS7.2.2	CCS7.2.3	CCS7.2.4	CCS7.2.89	CCS7.2.11	OTHER	SUM
CCS7.2.2	0(0%)	0(0%)	0(0%)	15(75%)	5(25%)	0(0%)	20(100%)
CCS7.2.3	0(0%)	0(0%)	2(4%)	44(83%)	5(9%)	2(4%)	53(100%)
CCS7.2.4	0(0%)	0(0%)	19(21%)	57(65%)	12(14%)	0(0%)	88(100%)
CCS7.2.89	0(0%)	0(0%)	1(0%)	2528(99%)	19(1%)	4(0%)	2552(100%)
CCS7.2.11	0(0%)	0(0%)	2(2%)	45(42%)	60(55%)	1(1%)	108(100%)
OTHER	0(0%)	0(0%)	0(0%)	120(32%)	15(4%)	239(64%)	374(100%)

The classification performance of DT_EHR and DT_EHRMK was very similar. The difference in accuracy was less than 0.01. Neither of them made CCS7.2.2 and CCS7.2.3 predictions.

Because the sample size for CCS7.2.89 was very large, most of the prediction errors occurred because visits in other categories were mistakenly predicted to be CCS7.2.89.

Decision Tree Model. The DT_EHR model is shown in Fig. 1 and the DT_EHRMK model is shown in Fig. 2. While the two decision trees have many similarities, the second decision tree found more clinically meaningful nodes. There are some slight differences in the distal nodes. Clinically, these seemingly small differences often have immense importance in differentiating between acute coronary and non-coronary related diagnoses. In the acute emergency

Table 4. Confusion matrix for DT_EHRMK.

Actual	Predicted						
	CCS7.2.2	CCS7.2.3	CCS7.2.4	CCS7.2.89	CCS7.2.11	OTHER	SUM
CCS7.2.2	0(0%)	0(0%)	0(0%)	19(95%)	1(5%)	0(0%)	20(100%)
CCS7.2.3	0(0%)	0(0%)	1(1%)	48(91%)	2(4%)	2(4%)	53(100%)
CCS7.2.4	0(0%)	0(0%)	10(11%)	77(88%)	1(1%)	0(0%)	88(100%)
CCS7.2.89	0(0%)	0(0%)	3(0%)	2544(100%)	1(0%)	4(0%)	2552(100%)
CCS7.2.11	0(0%)	0(0%)	1(1%)	87(81%)	19(17%)	1(1%)	108(100%)
OTHER	0(0%)	0(0%)	0(0%)	130(35%)	1(0%)	243(65%)	374(100%)

department setting, these differences can have a real time impact on the need for urgent/emergent coronary intervention. Delays in coronary intervention have been associated with worse clinical outcomes in vulnerable populations. For example, in the second decision tree, the terminal nodes of pain and angina pectoris are used to differentiate between categories 2 and 3. Category 2 represents diagnoses that involve structural abnormalities of the heart, whereas category 3 often describes electrical abnormalities. These two categories are often treated differently, and often treated by two different types of cardiologists. The independent variable combinations used in the second decision tree are the same ones used by clinicians to differentiate patients while working in the emergency department.

Assigning Missing Status as False Status. Commonly, a free-text medical report will not mention all clinical findings, and missing usually indicates absences of clinical findings. For example, a medical report of a trauma patient in the emergency department may not mention whether the patient has pneumonia or not (and usually the patient does not). Strategies of handling missing include (1) treating missing as "False"; (2) treating missing as a third category: "missing"; (3) not assigning any value for missing data by assuming missing happened completely at random; (4) using imputation methods to estimate values when they are missing. Pineda et al. [18] compared strategies 1–3 for influenza detection using NLP-extracted clinical findings. Their experiment results showed that missing as "False" performed similarly as missing as "Missing," and these two strategies performed better than missing at random strategy. Thus, we used the missing as "False" strategy, because the binary value of clinical findings (true or false) will lead to a larger sample size in subgroups than three value (true, false, or missing). We plan to compare different strategies of handling missing in the future work.

Studying the Impact of Class Imbalance. Since the vast majority number of samples belongs to 7.2.89, the resulting class imbalance in real-world data may have an impact on the machine learning. Because our method (DT-EHRMK)

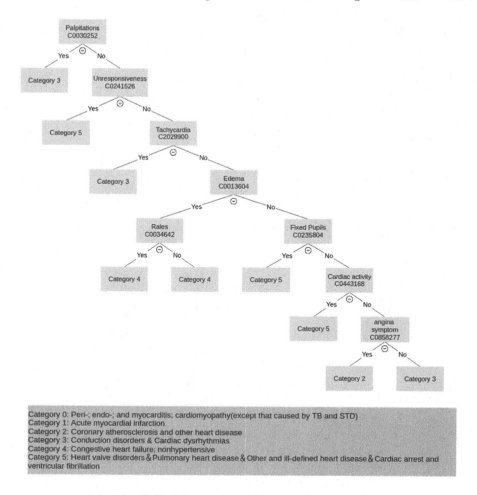

Category 0: Peri-; endo-; and myocarditis; cardiomyopathy(except that caused by TB and STD)
Category 1: Acute myocardial infarction
Category 2: Coronary atherosclerosis and other heart disease
Category 3: Conduction disorders & Cardiac dysrhythmias
Category 4: Congestive heart failure; nonhypertensive
Category 5: Heart valve disorders & Pulmonary heart disease & Other and ill-defined heart disease & Cardiac arrest and ventricular fibrillation

Fig. 1. Decision tree model learned from EHR.

does not take into account class imbalance issue, to study the impact of class imbalance, we conducted additional experiments using a downsampling method. In the downsampling experiments, we reduced the sample size of 7.2.89 to 404, we reduced the sample size of the OTHER category to 402 by randomly dropping samples. The training samples of the remaining categories remained the same. We conducted five random downsamplings to obtain five training samples. Using these five training samples, we used our DT_EHRMK method to generate five trees and tested their accuracies using the original test dataset that had been used to evaluate other models. These five trees had much lower accuracies than the trees that were generated without downsampling (accuracy: 0.8041, 0.7202, 0.7396, 0.7202, 0.7202). Although downsampling can create a more balanced training dataset, the downsampling method did not generate more accurate trees

Category 0: Peri-; endo-; and myocarditis; cardiomyopathy(except that caused by TB and STD)
Category 1: Acute myocardial infarction
Category 2: Coronary atherosclerosis and other heart disease
Category 3: Conduction disorders & Cardiac dysrhythmias
Category 4: Congestive heart failure; nonhypertensive
Category 5: Heart valve disorders & Pulmonary heart disease & Other and ill-defined heart disease & Cardiac arrest and ventricular fibrillation

Fig. 2. Decision tree model learned from EHR and medical knowledge.

in our experiments. The reason may be that the clinical data heterogeneity was very large, so we simply could not use the downsampling method.

Comparison with Other Machine Learning Methods. We chose a decision tree framework instead of other machine learning methods because we hope to discover diagnosis pathways that are clinically meaningful and actionable. A decision tree framework can produce these pathways for classification tasks. In a preliminary experiment, we developed two other classification models and their performance was similar with decision tree methods: SVM (default parameters in the sklearn package, overall accuracy; 0.8942), random forest (default parameters in the sklearn package except number of estimators: 1000, overall accuracy: 0.9061).

Innovation of This Study. To the best of our knowledge, this is the first study to combine medical embedding with use of decision trees for diagnosis pathway modeling. The medical embeddings were developed using insurance claims (60 million members), clinical notes (20 million), and full text biomedical journal articles (1.7 million). These embeddings are reliable representations of medical knowledge with different levels of semantic correlations among clinical concepts. Although the embedding technique has been successfully used in many natural language processing tasks, there are very few studies that have used medical embeddings for machine learning of electronic medical records.

5   Conclusion

While we do not believe that this current decision tree is ready for clinical use, these techniques and ideas could generate future decision support machines for clinical decision-making. The results also show that combining domain knowledge and the decision tree algorithm can lead to more clinically meaningful models.

With increased accuracy, and expanded diagnostic categories, decision trees like this one could be used in educational or clinical situations. Trees could teach medical students key points in history-taking for generating a differential diagnosis. Trees could allow clinicians to narrow the differential diagnosis, support clinical impressions, suggest important alternative diagnoses, and guide more cost effective testing.

Acknowledgement. We thank Dr. Fuchiang Tsui at the Children's Hospital of Philadelphia for helpful discussions.

References

1. Barnett, G.O., Cimino, J.J., Hupp, J.A., Hoffer, E.P.: DXplain: an evolving diagnostic decision-support system. JAMA **258**(1), 67–74 (1987)
2. Beam, A.L., et al.: Clinical concept embeddings learned from massive sources of multimodal medical data. arXiv preprint arXiv:1804.01486 (2018)
3. Berner, E.S., Graber, M.L.: Overconfidence as a cause of diagnostic error in medicine. Am. J. Med. **121**(5), S2–S23 (2008)
4. Bond, W.F., Schwartz, L.M., Weaver, K.R., Levick, D., Giuliano, M., Graber, M.L.: Differential diagnosis generators: an evaluation of currently available computer programs. J. Gen. Intern. Med. **27**(2), 213–219 (2012)
5. Breiman, L.: Classification and Regression Trees. Routledge, Abingdon (2017)
6. Brown, T.W., McCarthy, M.L., Kelen, G.D., Levy, F.: An epidemiologic study of closed emergency department malpractice claims in a national database of physician malpractice insurers. Acad. Emerg. Med. **17**(5), 553–560 (2010)
7. Cowie, M.R., et al.: Electronic health records to facilitate clinical research. Clin. Res. Cardiol. **106**(1), 1–9 (2017)
8. Dehghan, A., Kovacevic, A., Karystianis, G., Keane, J.A., Nenadic, G.: Combining knowledge-and data-driven methods for de-identification of clinical narratives. J. Biomed. Inform. **58**, S53–S59 (2015)

9. Friedman, C., Alderson, P.O., Austin, J.H., Cimino, J.J., Johnson, S.B.: A general natural-language text processor for clinical radiology. J. Am. Med. Inform. Assoc. **1**(2), 161–174 (1994)
10. Gorry, G.A., Barnett, G.O.: Experience with a model of sequential diagnosis. Comput. Biomed. Res. **1**(5), 490–507 (1968)
11. Agency for Healthcare Research and Quality: Clinical classifications software (CCS) for ICD-9-CM (2015)
12. LeCun, Y., Bengio, Y., Hinton, G.: Deep learning. Nature **521**(7553), 436 (2015)
13. Liaw, A., Wiener, M., et al.: Classification and regression by randomforest. R News **2**(3), 18–22 (2002)
14. Morik, K., Brockhausen, P., Joachims, T.: Combining statistical learning with a knowledge-based approach: a case study in intensive care monitoring. Technical report, SFB 475: Komplexitätsreduktion in Multivariaten ... (1999)
15. Myers, J.D.: The background of INTERNIST I and QMR. In: Proceedings of ACM Conference on History of Medical Informatics, pp. 195–197. ACM (1987)
16. Neurath, P.W., Enslein, K., Mitchell Jr., G.W.: Design of a computer system to assist in differential preoperative diagnosis for pelvic surgery. N. Engl. J. Med. **280**(14), 745–749 (1969)
17. World Health Organization: Diagnostic errors: technical series on safer primary care (2016)
18. Pineda, A.L., Ye, Y., Visweswaran, S., Cooper, G.F., Wagner, M.M., Tsui, F.R.: Comparison of machine learning classifiers for influenza detection from emergency department free-text reports. J. Biomed. Inform. **58**, 60–69 (2015)
19. Ramnarayan, P., Tomlinson, A., Rao, A., Coren, M., Winrow, A., Britto, J.: ISABEL: a web-based differential diagnostic aid for paediatrics: results from an initial performance evaluation. Arch. Dis. Child. **88**(5), 408–413 (2003)
20. Shortliffe, E.H., Buchanan, B.G.: Rule-Based Expert Systems: The MYCIN Experiments of the Stanford Heuristic Programming Project. Addison-Wesley Publishing Company, Boston (1985)
21. Sox, H.C., Blatt, M.A., Higgins, M.C., Marton, K.I.: Medical Decision Making. ACP Press, Sydney (2007)
22. Steinwart, I., Christmann, A.: Support Vector Machines. Information Science and Statistics. Springer, New York (2008). https://doi.org/10.1007/978-0-387-77242-4
23. Sun, J., et al.: Combining knowledge and data driven insights for identifying risk factors using electronic health records. In: AMIA Annual Symposium Proceedings, vol. 2012, p. 901. American Medical Informatics Association (2012)
24. Warner, H.R., et al.: Iliad as an expert consultant to teach differential diagnosis. In: Proceedings of the Annual Symposium on Computer Application in Medical Care, p. 371. American Medical Informatics Association (1988)

Deep Autoencoder Based Neural Networks for Coronary Heart Disease Risk Prediction

Tsatsral Amarbayasgalan[1] , Jong Yun Lee[1] , Kwang Rok Kim[2] ,
and Keun Ho Ryu[3,4(✉)]

[1] Database Laboratory, School of Electrical and Computer Engineering,
Chungbuk National University, Cheongju 28644, Korea
tsatsral@dblab.chungbuk.ac.kr, jongyun@chungbuk.ac.kr
[2] School of Law, Chungbuk National University, Cheongju 28644, Korea
laws@cbnu.ac.kr
[3] Faculty of Information Technology, Ton Duc Thang University,
Ho Chi Minh City 700000, Vietnam
khryu@tdtu.edu.vn
[4] Department of Computer Science, College of Electrical and Computer
Engineering, Chungbuk National University, Cheongju 28644, Korea
khryu@chungbuk.ac.kr

Abstract. The World Health Organization (WHO) reported that coronary heart disease (CHD) is one of the top causes of global mortality, and it is also highly ranked in Korea. The wrong lifestyle such as alcohol, tobacco, and high fatty food is directly involved in the main risk factors for CHD. In the early stage, it is possible to prevent suffering from CHD by an appropriate drug and healthy lifestyle which lead to effective treatment. In this paper, we propose a deep autoencoder based neural networks (DAE-NNs) to predict CHD risk. First, a dataset is divided into two groups by their divergence using a deep autoencoder model. Then, deep neural network (NN) classifiers are trained on each group of dataset separately. As a result, the performance measurements including accuracy, F-measure and AUC score reached 83.53%, 84.36%, and 84.02%, respectively in the Korean population. These results show that our proposed DAE-NNs approach outperformed typical data mining based classifiers for CHD risk prediction.

Keywords: Coronary heart disease · Data mining · Deep autoencoder · Reconstruction error · Neural network

1 Introduction

CHD is the type cardiovascular disease (CVD), and according to the report by the WHO, CVDs are the number one cause of death globally with regard to 2017, an estimated 17.9 million people die of CVDs every year, 85% (15.2 million) of these deaths are due to CHD and stroke [1].

CHD is caused by unhealthy blood cholesterol level, high blood pressure (HBP), smoking, bad eating habits, lack of physical activity and obesity [2–4]. If suffering from CHD, a waxy substance called plaque will be built up inside the coronary arteries that deliver oxygen and nutrients to the heart muscle. This plaque narrows the arteries

V. Gadepally et al. (Eds.): DMAH 2019/Poly 2019, LNCS 11721, pp. 237–248, 2019.
https://doi.org/10.1007/978-3-030-33752-0_17

and the flow of oxygen-rich blood to the heart muscle is limited [5]. Over time, the arteries are more narrowed and blocks the blood flow. Then, heart attack or death can be occurred because of the blockage [6]. If CHD reaches a serious situation, it will require advanced treatments such as heart transplant, stent surgery that helps keep coronary arteries open and reduce the chance of a heart attack, and coronary artery bypass grafting that improves blood flow to the heart [7]. In the early stage, it is possible to prevent suffering from CHD by a healthy diet, active exercises, and convenient medication. However, most patients are diagnosed in the middle or late stage because CHD does not have any symptoms at the early stage. Also, making a precise diagnosis is difficult, a doctor will diagnose it based on many clinical tests such as electrocardiogram, echocardiography, chest X-Ray, and blood tests and so on [8].

There is a need for accurate CHD detection tool the early stage to increase the chance of successful treatment. Data mining discovers useful knowledge hidden in a dataset and a lot of research studies have been suggesting data mining supervised learning algorithms for a disease prediction [9–11]. Supervised learning is used when a class labels for a disease are available. It trains a model on the labeled dataset, then predicts the class label from given unknown data based on previously obtained knowledge. Artificial Neural Network (ANN), Decision Tree (DT), Random Forest (RS), Naïve Bayes (NB), K-Nearest Neighbors (KNN) and Support Vector Machine (SVM) are generally used supervised learning algorithms for purpose of CHD risk prediction. Another way of CHD risk identification is to calculate the Framingham Risk Score (FRS); it is a gender-specific multivariable statistical model to estimate CHD risk of an individual. Age, sex, smoking status, systolic blood pressure (SBP), diastolic blood pressure (DBP), total cholesterol, high-density lipoprotein (HDL) cholesterol, and diabetes status are features used in this model [12]. However, FRS cannot well estimate risk in populations other than the US population [13, 14] because it was developed based on residents of the city of Framingham, Massachusetts.

Abdullah et al. proposed the RF algorithm with 10 number of trees for CHD prediction on Cleveland benchmark dataset and showed 63.33% accuracy [15]. Srinivas et al. and Nahar et al. suggested NB algorithm for heart disease prediction [16, 17]. Chaurasia et al. presented the comparison between CART, ID3 and Decision table algorithms on the Cleveland dataset and CART algorithm gave the highest accuracy 83.49% [18]. Das et al. suggested neural networks ensembles that consist of 3 NN models with one hidden layer. The accuracy was 89.01% on the Cleveland dataset [19].

According to the Korea National Health and Nutrition Examination Survey (KNHANES) dataset, Kim et al. proposed fuzzy logic and decision tree based CHD risk prediction model [10]. Their suggested model was based on age, sex, total cholesterol, low-density lipoprotein (LDL), HDL, SBP, DBP, smoking status, and diabetes. Result proves that the proposed method provides more accuracy (69%) over NN, SVM, and DT algorithms. A Neural network with feature correlation analysis (NN-FCA) approach has been presented by Kim et al. [11]. They have performed feature selection using statistical analysis for KNHANES-VI dataset. Total 9 number of selected features including age, body mass index (BMI), total cholesterol, HDL, SBP, DBP, triglyceride, smoking status, and diabetes were given into the input of NN model. Compared to the results of the FRS and linear regression model in the Korean population, their proposed model has shown high accuracy and AUC score of 82.51% and 74%, respectively.

Most of the previous literature suggested a single classification model or an ensemble classification model on particular dataset. However, we proposed 2 NN classifiers that are trained on different groups of the dataset. First, the dataset is partitioned into two groups by their divergence using deep autoencoder model (DAE). Autoencoder is one kind of neural network that tries to learn to represent its input to output as close as possible. First, it compresses its input into a low dimensional representation and then reconstructs the input to the output from the compressed representation. Reconstruction error is a difference between input and its reconstructed output. We used reconstruction error measurement from the DAE model to partition the whole dataset into the 2 groups, and each group consists of a subset labeled the high-risk and low-risk. Then, deep neural network (DNN) classifiers are trained on each group separately using CHD risk factors according to the FRS. Each NN classifiers are the same structure and class labels including high-risk and low-risk. The main difference is that they trained on a different group of dataset. First, it checks whether the data belongs to group 1 or 2 when predicting unseen data. Depends on selected group, only appropriate classification model predicts the CHD risk. In other words, both of the trained classifiers can predict CHD risk is high or low, but only a corresponding classifier is used for prediction based on a related group with unseen data. We have compared our proposed approach with FRS and data mining based classification models including NB, KNN, SVM, DT, and RF in the Korean population.

2   Materials and Methods

An architecture of our proposed method for CHD risk prediction is represented on Fig. 1.

Before the first step, we integrated the fifth and sixth KNHANES datasets, and removed rows with missing values and unrelated features for CHD prediction; we used the Framingham risk factors for our proposed method. First, the DAE model learns from the whole training dataset, and reconstruction errors of the training dataset are calculated through the difference between input and output of the DAE model. Based on reconstruction errors, an upper threshold value is estimated by interquartile range. After that, the training dataset is divided into 2 groups depending on whether their reconstruction error is higher or lower than the upper threshold, and NN based classifiers are trained on each group. For test data, it is given as an input of the trained DAE model to receive reconstruction error. Depending on the received value, the appropriate classifier is used to predict CHD risk label. The entire process is described in the following subsections.

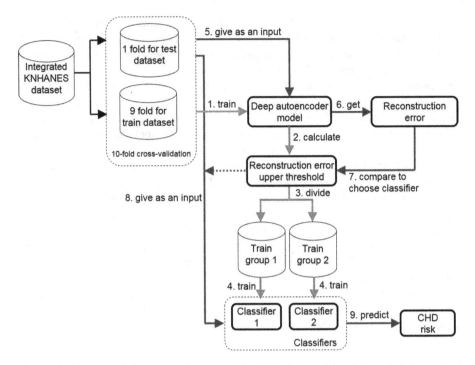

Fig. 1. Architecture of the proposed approach for CHD risk prediction. Steps 1–4 (green line) are for model training and steps 5–9 (blue line) for model evaluation. (Color figure online)

2.1 Data Integration

We used the fifth and sixth KNHANES datasets over 2010–2015 years; it includes 48,492 records of Korean population. KNHANES is the Nationwide Program to evaluate Koreans' health and nutritional status. The survey consists of 3 parts: Health examination, health interview and nutrition survey. This dataset is available on Korea National Health & Nutrition Examination Survey website [20].

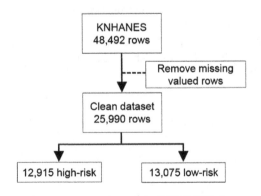

Fig. 2. Data integration of the KHNANES datasets

Our experimental dataset consists of 25,990 records including 12,915 records are high risky people who have probability to suffer from CHD and 13,075 records are low-risky people as shown in Fig. 2. Hypertension, dyslipidemia, stroke, myocardial infarction, angina, and hyperlipidemia were used to identify high-risk or low-risk labeling. If one of these 6 disorders is identified, the individual will be considered to have high-risky of CHD.

2.2 Compared Data Mining Algorithms

Data mining techniques are deployed to scour large databases to find novel and useful patterns that might otherwise remain unknown [21]. We have compared the proposed approach to the following algorithms.

FRS. FRS is a gender-specific multivariable statistical model to estimate CHD risk of an individual. We used the Wilson et al.'s proposed Framingham equation [22] for CHD risk identification.

NB. NB classifier estimates the conditional probability for each class label by assuming the attributes are conditionally independent and chooses the class label that has the highest probability.

KNN. KNN classifier calculates the distances between the test set and all the training set. Then, it sorts the distances and determines k nearest neighbors with minimum distance. Finally, it counts each class label in nearest neighbors and, the most majority voted class label considered as prediction value.

SVM. SVM performs classification by finding a separator line called the hyper-plane that differentiate the classes very well. First it finds the points closest to the hyper-plane from each classes. These points called support vector. SVM learns maximize the margin, which is distance between the hyper-plane and the support vectors. The hyperplane with the maximum margin is the optimal hyper-plane.

DT. DT is a flowchart like structure, where each internal node denotes a test on an attribute, each branch represents the outcome of the test, and each leaf node holds a class label. It is useful that a decision tree has few nodes and solves the problems very effectively.

RF. RF is one kind of ensemble algorithms, and the DT algorithm is used as a learning algorithm. Each tree in the forest is trained from the different dataset by random sampling with replacement. It combines predictions that made by multiple DT classifiers and majority voted class label will be final output.

2.3 Evaluation Methods

The confusion matrix is used to evaluate the performance of a classification model. It is a summary of prediction results including the number of correct and incorrect predictions. We built a total of 8 classifiers and evaluated them on test dataset using accuracy, precision, recall, F-measure, and area under curve (AUC). The accuracy of a classifier can be obtained by the following Eq. (1).

$$\text{Accuracy} = \frac{\text{number of correct predictions}}{\text{total number of elements}} \qquad (1)$$

The precision shows the positive predictive rate, and the recall shows the true positive rate. They can be defined as:

$$\text{Precision} = \frac{\text{number of true positive prediction}}{\text{total number of positive prediction}} \qquad (2)$$

$$\text{Recall} = \frac{\text{number of true positive prediction}}{\text{total number of actual positive elements}} \qquad (3)$$

F-measure combines precision and recall and gives the harmonic mean of them; it can be defined as:

$$\text{F-measure} = \frac{2 \times \text{Precision} \times \text{Recall}}{\text{Precision} + \text{Recall}} \qquad (4)$$

The AUC represents how much model is capable of distinguishing between classes, and high AUC indicates the good result.

2.4 Proposed Approach

In this section, we described the proposed DAE-NNs approach which is developed by combining the deep autoencoder with 2 neural network classifiers. The approach consists of 3 basic parts such as deep autoencoder for dataset partitioning, NN classifiers, and CHD risk prediction. Each of these parts is explained in the following subsections.

Deep Autoencoder for Data Partitioning. In practically, a dataset can include a subset which is higher variance than the most dataset and those highly biased dataset degrades a result of classification techniques. Therefore, we isolated highly biased dataset and normally distributed dataset using the deep autoencoder model (DAE) for CHD risk prediction model. The dataset with high variance can be modeled independently for improving the performance of prediction.

Autoencoder is one kind of ANN, which is the unsupervised algorithm for learning to copy its own input $(x_1 \ldots x_n)$ to its output $(y_1 \ldots y_n)$ as close $(x_i = y_i)$ as possible by reducing the gap between inputs and outputs [23]. Generally, it is used for dimensionality reduction or data denoising purpose. The structure is the same as NN; it consists of input layer, hidden layers and output layer. First, its input is compressed into a small dimension, and then the compressed data is reconstructed back to the output; the difference between input data and reconstructed data is calculated for changing weights assigned to reduce that difference. Some data that is different from most data have higher reconstruction error than normal data. Therefore, we trained deep autoencoder model on the whole training dataset for calculating reconstruction errors of all data.

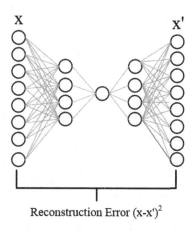

Reconstruction Error $(x-x')^2$

Fig. 3. Structure of the autoencoder neural network

As shown in Fig. 3, the proposed DAE model has input layer with 8 neurons, 3 hidden layers with 4, 1, and 4 neurons, respectively, and output layer with 8 neurons. The *ReLu* activation function was used to the first 2 hidden layers, and the *tanh* activation function was used to the last two layers (one hidden layer and the output layer).

The reconstruction errors of training dataset are calculated by squared difference between input and output of the trained DAE model. The upper threshold of reconstruction error is estimated by the interquartile range, it can be described as:

$$\text{threshold} = (q3 - q1) * 1.5 + q3 \qquad (5)$$

Where q3 is the third quartile and q1 is the first quartile of the sorted reconstruction errors.

After that, the training dataset is partitioned into 2 parts; the first part contains dataset with higher reconstruction error than the threshold, and the second part includes the rest of dataset.

NN Classifiers. Neural network is an interconnected group of nodes, and each node represents an artificial neuron. The output of one artificial neuron connected to the input of all other neurons. Each connection between nodes has a weight that adjusts as learning proceeds. The proposed NN has 5 hidden layers with 17, 9, 5, 3, and 2 nodes, respectively. The *ReLu* activation function is applied to each hidden layers and the *Sigmoid* activation function is applied to the output layer. Also, Adam optimizer which is a stochastic gradient based optimizer is used for weight optimization. As shown in Fig. 1, there are 2 independent NN classifiers are learned from previously partitioned training subsets.

CHD Risk Prediction. In the CHD risk prediction process, test data is first given as an input to the trained DAE model, and reconstruction error is calculated. If that value is higher than the previously estimated threshold classifier 1 is used otherwise classifier 2 is used for prediction.

3   Evaluation and Discussion

This section provides a detailed overview of our experiments for CHD risk prediction.

3.1   Data Pre-processing

KNHANES is an ongoing surveillance system in Korea that monitors trends in health behavior, dietary intake and the prevalence of major chronic diseases such as obesity, hypertension, diabetes, dyslipidemia, and oral disease and provides data to researchers. However, missing data is a common problem in survey datasets, and the resulting datasets tend to contain many missing values. We used real dataset KNHANES collected from 2010–2015, and it consists of 48,492 records. After removing missing values, there were 25,990 records remained. The Framingham risk factors such as age, sex, total cholesterol, HDL, SBP, DBP, smoking status and diabetes status were used as risk factors of CHD prediction model. Finally, we scaled our dataset by standardization method that calculates mean value and standard deviation for each attribute of a dataset. Then each value is subtracted by mean, and the subtracted result is then divided by the standard deviation.

3.2   Performance Evaluation

We compared the proposed method with FRS and data mining based classifiers named NB, KNN, SVM, DT, and RF, using the selected features. We applied k-fold cross validation approach for evaluation of the each prediction models. It splits the whole dataset into k distinct equally sized subsets. Then k rounds of cross-validation are performed using these partitions, and validation results are averaged over the rounds. One round of cross-validation involves training process on $k - 1$ subsets and validation process on remained one subset. In other words, if the first partition is used for testing, the remained partitions will be used to train a model. Then next round, the second partition is used for testing, and others are used for training. In our experiment, k was configured equal to 10, and all partitions were saved in random access memory (RAM) in the experiment. We used the scikit-learn that is open-source machine learning library in Python.

According to compared algorithms, we have adjusted input parameters by changing their values until decrease the performance and chose optimal values. For each parameter configuration, we have performed the 10-fold cross-validation. In NB classifier, it is possible to set a threshold value to determine a class label instead of choosing a class label that has the highest probability [24–26]. Table 1 shows the configuration of input parameters.

In the proposed method, the training dataset was divided into 2 groups by the DAE model, and each group was modeled by NN independently. According to our experiment, the first group was 6% of the total dataset, it contained data with high reconstruction error, and 75% was labeled high-risk. In this group, a total length of age, SBP, DBP, total cholesterol, and HDL were averaged 58 ± 15.68, 127.89 ± 25.66, 74.92 ± 16.47, 195.27 ± 58.35, 52.56 ± 19.74, respectively. However, a variance of the second group was lower than the first group, and 48% was labeled by high-risk.

Table 1. Input parameters of compared algorithms

Algorithm	Parameter configuration	Optimal values
NB	**threshold:** Probability threshold for determining class label. Threshold is configured between 0.1 and 0.9 for each class label. Also, we tried without a threshold value	Threshold on label 1 = 0.4 (If the probability of label 1 is higher than 0.4, prediction label will be 1.)
KNN	**n_neighbors:** Number of neighbors. n_neighbors parameter is configured between 2 and 25	n_neighbors = 21
DT	**criterion:** 'gini' for the Gini impurity and 'entropy' for the information gain measurements of the criterion of a split were used to identify the best decision tree splitting candidate	criterion = 'entropy'
RF	**n_estimators:** The number of trees in the forest. It was configured between 10 and 200 and increased by 10 **criterion:** "gini" and "entropy" were used for splitting criteria	n_estimators = 150 criterion = 'entropy'
SVM	**kernel:** it specifies the kernel type to be used in the algorithm. It must be one of 'linear', 'poly', 'rbf', 'sigmoid'	kernel = 'rbf'
NN	**neurons of hidden layers:** (2), (3, 2), (5, 3, 2), (8, 5, 3, 2), (17, 9, 5, 3, 2)	5 hidden layers with 17, 9, 5, 3, and 2 neurons, respectively

The total length of age, SBP, total cholesterol, and HDL were averaged 48 ± 18.13, 118.09 ± 16.19, 74.98 ± 10.08, 187.09 ± 34.40, 50.25 ± 11.32, respectively. The proportion of individuals in each group who were recorded as smokers was 40% in the first group, and 17% in the second group. Also, 61% of dataset had diabetes in the first group, but only 4% of the dataset had diabetes in the second group.

Also, we tested the proposed NN classifier on the whole testing dataset without the DAE model. As a result, the recall of the proposed DAE-NNs decreased by 7.76% from the one NN based approach, but the precision increased by 9.61%. The recall is a fraction of the true positive predictions over the total amount of positively labeled dataset, while the precision is a fraction of the true positive predictions among the all positive predictions. Therefore, the recall measures what proportion of actual positives was identified correctly, and the precision evaluates the effectiveness of true positive predictions. However, as recall gives a high score, the number of false true prediction can be increased relatively. If the false true prediction increases, the precision will be decreased. That is, improving recall typically reduces recall and vice versa. In this case, it is difficult to compare models with low precision and high recall or high precision and low recall. Thus, F-measure is used to measure recall and precision at the same time, where the highest F-measure indicates a good result. Table 2 presents the measurements of performance such as accuracy, precision, recall, F-measure and AUC of compared algorithms and best results are highlighted in bold. In Table 2, data mining based prediction models showed higher performance than the FRS. Moreover, the proposed DAE-NNs outperformed the other classifiers to predict CHD risk prediction.

Table 2. Evaluation results of all classifiers (%).

Classifier	Accuracy	Precision	Recall	F-measure	AUC
FRS	52.33	51.88	72.34	60.42	52.20
NB	73.06	69.57	82.56	75.51	73.00
NB with threshold	74.44	72.98	78.11	75.46	74.42
KNN (n_neighbors = 21)	79.59	78.10	82.60	80.29	79.58
DT (criterion = 'entropy')	75.13	75.62	74.61	75.11	75.13
RF (n_estimators = 150, criterion = 'entropy')	81.24	78.38	86.59	82.28	81.20
SVM (kernel = 'rbf')	80.45	79.60	82.21	80.88	80.44
NN with 5 hidden layers	82.67	79.95	**87.50**	83.55	82.64
DAE-NNs	**83.53**	**89.56**	79.74	**84.36**	**84.02**

4   Conclusion

In this work, we proposed the DAE-NNs approach to predict CHD risk and evaluated it in the Korean population. Our proposed method combined the deep autoencoder model and neural network models successfully. Based on reconstruction error of the deep autoencoder model, the whole training dataset was partitioned into 2 different subsets. Then, 2 independent NN classifiers were trained on each group. In the prediction process, we checked the reconstruction error of each testing data and chose an appropriate classifier from these 2 learned NN classifiers depends on the previously determined threshold value. By using 2 NN classifiers, we improved the performance of only one NN classifier on the whole dataset. Experimental results showed that the proposed DAE-NNs outperformed all the compared classifiers with accuracy, precision, F-measure and AUC score of 83.53%, 89.56%, 84.36%, and 84.02%, respectively. The proposed DEA-NNs can be applied to the hospital for predicting CHD risk on clinical data. However, the limitation of the proposed method is that it does not allow missing value. In a real case, it is rare to obtain complete medical records and relevant information when analyzing chronic diseases. Therefore, our future work will be focused to handle missing values.

Acknowledgement. This research was supported by Basic Science Research Program through the National Research Foundation of Korea (NRF) funded by the Ministry of Science, ICT & Future Planning (No. 2017R1A2B4010826), by NRF funded by the Ministry of Education (No. 2017R1D1A1A02018718), by Business for Cooperative R&D between Industry, Academy, and Research Institute funded Korea Small and Medium Business Administration in 2017 (Grants No. C0541451), and by the Private Intelligence Information Service Expansion (No. C0511-18-1001) funded by the NIPA (National IT Industry Promotion Agency).

References

1. World Health Organization (WHO). https://www.who.int/news-room/fact-sheets/detail/cardiovascular-diseases-(cvds). Accessed 01 Mar 2019
2. American Heart Association. https://www.ncbi.nlm.nih.gov/pmc/articles/PMC5408160/pdf/nihms852024.pdf. Accessed 01 Mar 2019
3. Park, H.W., Li, D., Piao, Y., Ryu, K.H.: A hybrid feature selection method to classification and its application in hypertension diagnosis. In: Bursa, M., Holzinger, A., Renda, M.E., Khuri, S. (eds.) ITBAM 2017. LNCS, vol. 10443, pp. 11–19. Springer, Cham (2017). https://doi.org/10.1007/978-3-319-64265-9_2
4. Park, H.W., Batbaatar, E., Li, D., Ryu, K.H.: Risk factors rule mining in hypertension: Korean National Health and Nutrient Examinations Survey 2007–2014. In: 2016 IEEE Conference on Computational Intelligence in Bioinformatics and Computational Biology, pp. 1–4. IEEE (2016)
5. National Heart, Lung, and Blood Institute. https://www.nhlbi.nih.gov/health-topics/coronary-heart-disease. Accessed 01 Mar 2019
6. Nucleus Medical Media. http://www.nucleushealth.com/. Accessed 01 Mar 2019
7. Hausmann, H., Topp, H., Siniawski, H., Holz, S., Hetzer, R.: Decision-making in end-stage coronary artery disease: revascularization or heart transplantation. Ann. Thorac. Surg. 64(5), 1296–1302 (1997)
8. Diamond, G.A., Forrester, J.S.: Analysis of probability as an aid in the clinical diagnosis of coronary-artery disease. N. Engl. J. Med. 300(24), 1350–1358 (1979)
9. Kim, H., Ishag, M.I.M., Piao, M., Kwon, T., Ryu, K.H.: A data mining approach for cardiovascular disease diagnosis using heart rate variability and images of carotid arteries. Symmetry 8(6), 47 (2016)
10. Kim, J., Lee, J., Lee, Y.: Data-mining-based coronary heart disease risk prediction model using fuzzy logic and decision tree. Healthcare Inform. Res. 21(3), 167–174 (2015)
11. Kim, J.K., Kang, S.: Neural network-based coronary heart disease risk prediction using feature correlation analysis. J. Healthcare Eng. (2017)
12. Greenland, P., LaBree, L., Azen, S.P., Doherty, T.M., Detrano, R.C.: Coronary artery calcium score combined with Framingham score for risk prediction in asymptomatic individuals. JAMA 291(2), 210–215 (2004)
13. Brindle, P., et al.: Predictive accuracy of the Framingham coronary risk score in British men: prospective cohort study. BMJ 327(7426), 1267 (2003)
14. Sacco, R.L., et al.: Improving global vascular risk prediction with behavioral and anthropometric factors: the multiethnic Northern Manhattan Cohort Study. J. Am. Coll. Cardiol. 54(24), 2303–2311 (2009)
15. Abdullah, A.S., Rajalaxmi, R.: A data mining model for predicting the coronary heart disease using random forest classifier. In: International Conference in Recent Trends in Computational Methods, Communication and Controls, pp. 22–25 (2012). International Journal of Computer Applications
16. Srinivas, K., Rani, B.K., Govrdhan, A.: Applications of data mining techniques in healthcare and prediction of heart attacks. Int. J. Comput. Sci. Eng. (IJCSE) 2(02), 250–255 (2010)
17. Nahar, J., Imam, T., Tickle, K.S., Chen, Y.P.P.: Computational intelligence for heart disease diagnosis: A medical knowledge driven approach. Expert Syst. Appl. 40(1), 96–104 (2013)
18. Chaurasia, V., Pal, S.: Early prediction of heart diseases using data mining techniques. Carib. J. Sci. Technol. 1, 208–217 (2013)
19. Das, R., Turkoglu, I., Sengur, A.: Effective diagnosis of heart disease through neural networks ensembles. Expert Syst. Appl. 36(4), 7675–7680 (2009)

20. KNHANES. https://knhanes.cdc.go.kr/knhanes/eng/index.do. Accessed 01 Mar 2019
21. Tan, P.N., Steinbach, M., Kumar, V.: Introduction to Data Mining, 1st edn. Pearson Education, Boston (2006)
22. Wilson, P.W., D'Agostino, R.B., Levy, D., Belanger, A.M., Silbershatz, H., Kannel, W.B.: Prediction of coronary heart disease using risk factor categories. Circulation **97**(18), 1837–1847 (1998)
23. Amarbayasgalan, T., Jargalsaikhan, B., Ryu, K.: Unsupervised novelty detection using deep autoencoders with density based clustering. Appl. Sci. **8**(9), 1468 (2018)
24. Ezawa, K.J., Norton, S.W.: Constructing Bayesian networks to predict uncollectible telecommunications accounts. IEEE Expert **11**(5), 45–51 (1996)
25. Rennie, J.D., Shih, L., Teevan, J., Karger, D.R.: Tackling the poor assumptions of Naive Bayes text classifiers. In: Proceedings of the 20th International Conference on Machine Learning, (ICML-03), pp. 616–623 (2003)
26. Gao, D., Madden, M., Chambers, D., Lyons, G.: Bayesian ANN classifier for ECG arrhythmia diagnostic system: a comparison study. In: Proceedings of the IEEE International Joint Conference on Neural Networks, vol. 4, pp. 2383–2388 (2005)

Towards Automated Hypothesis Testing
in Neuroscience

Daniel Garijo[1], Shobeir Fakhraei[1(✉)], Varun Ratnakar[1], Qifan Yang[3],
Hanna Endrias[2], Yibo Ma[1], Regina Wang[1], Michael Bornstein[3],
Joanna Bright[3], Yolanda Gil[1,2], and Neda Jahanshad[3]

[1] Information Sciences Institute, University of Southern California, Los Angeles, USA
{dgarijo,shobeir,varunr,yiboma,gil}@isi.edu
[2] Department of Computer Science, University of Southern California,
Los Angeles, USA
endrias@usc.edu
[3] Imaging Genetics Center, Stevens Neuroimaging and Informatics Institute,
Keck School of Medicine of USC, Los Angeles, USA
{qifan.yang,mbornste,joannabr,neda.jahanshad}@usc.edu

Abstract. Scientific data generation in the world is continuous. However, scientific studies once published do not take advantage of new data. In order to leverage this incoming flow of data, we present Neuro-DISK, an end-to-end framework to continuously process neuroscience data and update the assessment of a given hypothesis as new data become available. Our scope is within the ENIGMA consortium, a large international collaboration for neuro-imaging and genetics whose goal is to understand brain structure and function. Neuro-DISK includes an ontology and framework to organize datasets, cohorts, researchers, tools, working groups and organizations participating in multi-site studies, such as those of ENIGMA, and an automated discovery framework to continuously test hypotheses through the execution of scientific workflows. We illustrate the usefulness of our approach with an implemented example.

Keywords: Hypothesis evaluation · Scientific workflow · Ontology ·
Automated discovery · Neuroscience

1 Introduction

Scientific discoveries are based on hypothesis testing and rigorous data analysis. Such analyses are often time consuming and include steps that are difficult to interpret from scientific publications, and therefore, hard to systemically reproduce. Often, the designed hypothesis is tested only once against the acquired data sample and later archived. Interestingly, in empirical sciences such as the biological sciences, it is not uncommon for a hypothesis to yield contradictory results when evaluated on different data samples. In our data-driven world, data that

---

D. Garijo and S. Fakhraei—Co-first author.

© Springer Nature Switzerland AG 2019
V. Gadepally et al. (Eds.): DMAH 2019/Poly 2019, LNCS 11721, pp. 249–257, 2019.
https://doi.org/10.1007/978-3-030-33752-0_18

may be potentially relevant for testing a hypothesis is being continuously generated but is often not studied to its full potential for hypothesis re-evaluation in combination with other related data. The lack of an integrated system to constantly monitor the hypothesis of interest and update the underlying analysis when new data become available, is one of the challenges for automatic hypothesis re-evaluation. Having a framework that can keep such hypotheses alive requires systematically capturing the knowledge about the data and analytics involved in the hypothesis testing, which is often heterogeneous and compartmentalized.

In this paper, we propose a solution to address the above challenges in the neurosciences based on our previous work for Automated DIscovery of Scientific Knowledge (DISK) [1]. We have extended DISK to explore brain-aging related hypothesis and data by generalizing the ability for the system to connect to external knowledge bases, including projects available within the Enhancing Neuro Imaging Genetics through Meta-Analysis (ENIGMA)[1] consortium [2], a neuroscience collaboration where projects span many contributors from different institutions around the world. In our proposed solution we address challenges of *data*, *analytics*, and *hypothesis* complexity. The *data* shared through imaging initiatives such as the ENIGMA consortium includes multiple levels of heterogeneity, and are regularly expanding in volume. The *analytics* related to such data requires the use of dozens of interconnected tools, each of which may require substantial domain knowledge. The underlying *hypotheses* may depend on a range of possible multi-modal technical, neurological, clinical, demographic, and genetic data which could be collected across multiple datasets.

2   Related Work

Two closely related research areas in machine learning are online algorithms [3] (algorithms that revise their models when new data become available), and data-stream specific models [4] (that deal with challenges of reprocessing portions of prior data to scale to large data streams). A major advantage of our work over these methods is that our analytical steps do more than learning from data. For example, some of our steps may include integrating the relevant cohort properties. Another important difference is that our system can react when new kinds of data become available and invoke new analytic tools or algorithms different from the original ones. In addition, distinctive to active agents such as Robot Scientist [5], our method simply listens and reacts to the data that others collect. Moreover, in contrast to other hypothesis evaluation solutions, such as EXPO [6] and HELO [7], our approach represents supporting evidence for hypotheses as reproducible computational components, records their evolution in reaction to new data, and updates their confidence intervals.

---

[1] http://enigma.usc.edu.

3   Background

In this section we describe our domain of focus and the sub-components that we leverage to develop our solution.

3.1   The ENIGMA Consortium

The ENIGMA consortium [8] is an international network connecting researchers in imaging genomics, neurology and psychiatry, in order to understand brain structure and function, based on multi-modal imaging and genetic data collected from various patient populations. One of the major ambitions of the consortium is to combine various datasets made available via its international partners into larger samples necessary to detect minute gene effects on complex traits that are otherwise not confidently identifiable with smaller isolated samples. Major goals of ENIGMA network include: creating a network of scholars with similar interests in brain imaging, genetics, neuro-psychiatry, and ensuring reproducibility of major findings through member collaborations, while facilitating information, algorithms and data sharing.

Members of the consortium constantly share new datasets and/or results, and run experiments and analysis across all available related data. The challenges involved in this global and dynamic collaborative platform, highlights a need to systematically organize its heterogeneous resources to facilitate identification and retrieval of entities of interest. The ENIGMA network would also benefit from a solution to capture the hypotheses under investigation by its members and their related analysis workflows to make them reproducible, especially if such solution could automatically find the related data and dynamically update the analysis results when new data become available. In this paper we layout the overall architecture and components of such solution for the ENIGMA consortium and report on our developed prototype.

3.2   The Organic Data Science Platform

We use the Organic Data Science framework (ODS) [9] and managing information about ENIGMA (ENIGMA-ODS). ODS is built on Semantic MediaWiki, which uses W3C standards such as RDF and SPARQL to represent its contents in a structured manner. Each wiki page represents a different resource (e.g., a researcher, a project, an organization, etc.) and shows the most relevant properties of that resource's class. For example, the wiki page of an organization will have *name* and *address* properties. Wiki pages can be filled out by users, who may contribute to the population and curation of the ENIGMA-ODS knowledge base.

ENIGMA-ODS is structured based on the ENIGMA Ontology[2] [10], which extends standard vocabularies such as Schema.org[3] and includes a representation

---

[2] https://w3id.org/enigma.
[3] http://schema.org/.

for datasets, cohorts, persons, organizations, protocols, instruments, software and working groups together with their more common relationships. However, users may extend the ontology with their own properties and categories whenever necessary. Each dataset has a set of metadata assertions, defined in triples of the form $< subject, property, value >$, where the *subject* identifies the resource being described (e.g., a dataset), the *property* refers to the aspect of the subject we want to describe (e.g., creation date) and the *value* identifies the value of the property for a resource (e.g., creation date is 2-2-2020). The data catalog supports W3C SPARQL queries to specify the desired metadata properties of datasets.

3.3   The DISK Framework

DISK [1,11] is a framework designed to test and revise hypotheses via automatic analysis of dynamic scientific data. DISK evaluates and revises an input hypothesis via continuously examining related data as they become available. It also triggers new kinds of analyses and workflows with the availability of new kinds of data, tracking the provenance of revised hypothesis and its related details. DISK operates based on the description of available ODS metadata, expressed using domain ontologies with the W3C OWL and RDF Semantic Web standards.

A user defines the hypothesis of interest through the DISK GUI. To evaluate a hypothesis, DISK relies on a library of *Lines of Inquiry* (LOI). A Line of Inquiry includes a hypothesis pattern, a relevant data query pattern, a set of workflows to process that data and one or more meta-workflows to combine workflow results and generate revised confidence values or hypotheses. If a user hypothesis matches the hypothesis of a Line of Inquiry, the system will use the LOI query pattern to search for appropriate data to pass to the LOI workflows for execution.

Workflows are executed via WINGS [12], a semantic workflow system for designing scientific computational experiments that specifies the steps and configuration of data processing by software components. The execution results and their corresponding provenance trace are then stored in a Linked Data repository. Finally, the associated meta-workflows explore this repository and revise the original hypothesis, if necessary. DISK was demonstrated for canceromics, and this paper introduces new extensions for neuroscience [1,11].

4   The Neuro-DISK Framework

We have extended DISK for neuroscience data exploration, analysis execution, and hypothesis testing. The framework integrates the ENIGMA-ODS platform for data search, which has access to all available information from datasets, cohorts, protocols and working groups. Our extension enables newly added and curated datasets to ENIGMA-ODS to be used in assessing existing or new Lines of Inquiry. We validate our framework by testing the hypothesis: *"Is the effect size of the number of APOE4 alleles on Hippocampus volume associated with the*

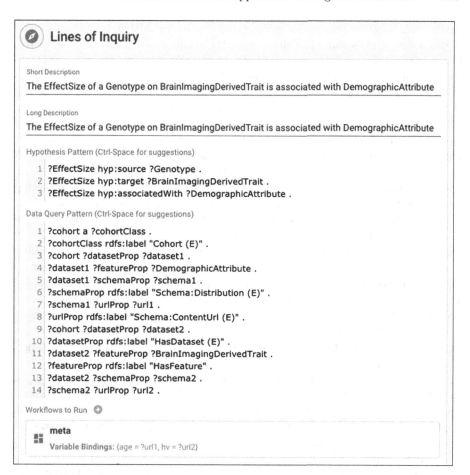

Fig. 1. An example of a line of inquiry for assessing the association between the effect size of a genotype on a brain-imaging derived trait for a particular cohort (or study population), with a meta-level demographic attribute such as age.

age of the cohort?". This hypothesis is important in Alzheimer's disease (AD) studies, which is the most common neuro-degenerative disorder and severely impacts patients' daily behaviors, thinking, and memory over a wide range of ages [13]. The hippocampus, the brain's memory hub, has been shown to be particularly vulnerable to Alzheimer's disease pathology, and is already atrophied by the time clinical symptoms of AD first appear [14]. The e4 haplotype (set of two alleles) of the *APOE* (apolipoprotein E) gene, is the most significant single genetic risk factor for late-onset Alzheimer's disease [15]. At each of two positions in the genome, a possible e4 allele contributes to this genetic risk. However, there have been inconsistent findings in determining whether the e4-risk factor contributes to differences in brain structure, particularly that of hippocampal volume. Several imaging-genetic studies have found a significant correlation between this major genetic risk factor for Alzheimer's disease, and higher rates of hippocampal volume loss [16], while others have found no correlation with volume [17]. Here, by using a meta-regression design, we investigate whether findings attempting to relate APOE4 genotype and hippocampal volume, specifically the effect sizes associated with studies, may be due to the age of the cohorts being studied, and a function of the study sample-sizes.

Our hypothesis triggers the Line of Inquiry shown in Fig. 1, which studies the correlation between *an effect on a brain characteristic* and *a demographic attribute*. This hypothesis meets the requirements listed in the *Hypothesis Pattern* section of Fig. 1, i.e., *APOE4* being the genotype of interest, *Hippocampal volume* a brain imaging derived trait and *age* a meta-level demographic attribute, describing the average age of the cohort. Once the hypothesis pattern is met, Neuro-DISK will aim to find the appropriate datasets to run the workflows associated with the LOI. DISK uses the information under the *Data Query Pattern* section to issue a SPARQL query to the ENIGMA-ODS platform. The query pattern aims to retrieve the dataset URLs (*schema:contentURL*) belonging to the same cohort that contain the target brain characteristic and demographic value. DISK then uses the resulting data URLs as input to the associated workflow in the LOI (i.e., the *"meta"* workflow in Fig. 1). The workflow consists of a sample-sized weighted meta-regression to determine whether the magnitude of the target genetic (APOE4) effect on a phenotype, is driven by the target demographic (age).

The underlying data for this analysis was based on imaging phenotypes and genotypes obtained from publicly available international cohorts, including ADNI-1, ADNI-2, DLBS, and the UK Biobank (application ID 15599). To configure the workflow, we incorporated the data from these independent cohorts with brain imaging and APOE4 genotype information. For each cohort, we ran a fixed-effects linear regression to associate the subjects' number of APOE4 risk-alleles (0, 1, or 2) with the mean bilateral hippocampal volumes derived from Freesurfer v5.3 [18]. Age, sex, and intracranial volume (to control for overall head size) were included as covariates in the regression. The resulting beta-value or un-standardized regression-coefficient and its corresponding standard error, were used to generate a standardized z-score for each cohort; the z-score was then regressed against the mean age of each cohort for the meta-regression, as was done in [19] for genome-wide significant findings. We note that given the sample size of UK Biobank (approximately 10,000 sample points at the time of writing, we split the data according to 5-year age bins). DLBS also had a wide age range from 30 to over 80, so that dataset was split into one younger than 60, and another older than 60 (a roughly even split) for this demonstration.

Figure 2 shows the results of our meta-regression analysis, automatically generated via the Neuro-DISK framework. In this proof of principle analysis with a handful of public datasets, age showed a negative association with the APOE4 effect size on hippocampal volume; should this association hold with more data points, it would suggest that the association between the APOE4 genotype and hippocampal volume may be driven by cohorts of individuals with older mean

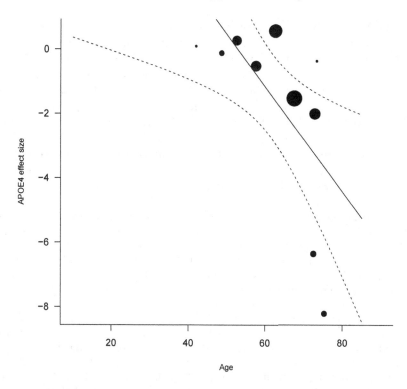

Fig. 2. Meta-regression for age and the effect size of Alzheimer's disease related risk genotype on hippocampal volume (p = 0.011). Age is negatively associated with the APOE4 effect size on MRI-derived hippocampal volume. The size of the points are proportional to cohort size, and dashed lines indicate confidence intervals.

ages, therefore explaining why some studies may not find a significant effect of the most well known Alzheimer's disease risk genotype, with the most well-accepted brain-MRI derived biomarkers for Alzheimer's disease.

5 Conclusions and Future Work

In this paper we described Neuro-DISK, a framework to automatically test hypotheses in the neuroscience domain, specifically in the context of the ENIGMA and international consortium. Our framework integrates the ENIGMA-ODS platform, allowing further testing on previous hypotheses whenever a user contributes new datasets in the system. Note that currently a single hypothesis was tested, and the corresponding variables that were incorporated in the system were selected *a priori*. However, in cases when multiple variables are selected, such as multiple genetic markers, or multiple brain regions, in the same Line of Inquiry, standard multiple comparisons correction techniques including the false discovery rate adjustment are conducted.

Neuro-DISK is still in development, but our current work shows the potential for continuous hypothesis testing in this domain. In this paper, we only used data from four publicly available cohorts. However, as multisite studies are conducted on a larger scale in ENIGMA and other international consortia, upwards of 50 cohorts may be included for evaluating such hypotheses [19]. We are working towards addressing three main challenges: (1) improving synchronization between ENIGMA-ODS and Neuro-DISK to make the system more adaptive to triggering all compatible Lines of Inquiry with the addition of new datasets; (2) designing the query patterns to make them more accessible for users without SPARQL knowledge; and (3) automatically evaluating additional hypotheses based on generated workflow results.

Acknowledgments. We are grateful to the KAVLI foundation for their support of ENIGMA Informatics (PIs: Jahanshad and Gil). We also acknowledge support from the National Science Foundation under awards IIS-1344272 (PI: Gil), ICER-1541029 (Co-PI: Gil), and IIS-1344272 (PI: Gil), and from the National Institutes of Health's Big Data to Knowledge Grant U54EB020403 for support for ENIGMA (PI: Thompson) and High resolution mapping of the genetic risk for disease in the aging brain grant R01AG059874 (PI: Jahanshad). Data used in preparing this article were obtained from the Alzheimer's Disease Neuroimaging Initiative (ADNI) database (adni.loni.usc.edu), phases both 1 and 2. As such, many investigators within the ADNI contributed to the design and implementation of ADNI and/or provided data but did not participate in analysis or writing of this report. A complete listing of ADNI investigators is available online (http://adni.loni.usc.edu/wp-content/uploads/how_to_apply/ADNI_Acknowledgement_List.pdf). We also used the DLBS (http://fcon_1000.projects.nitrc.org/indi/retro/dlbs.html) dataset and the UK Biobank in this study. This research was conducted using the UK Biobank Resource under Application Number '11559'.

References

1. Gil, Y., et al.: Automated hypothesis testing with large scientific data repositories. In: Proceedings of the Fourth Annual Conference on Advances in Cognitive Systems (ACS) (2016)
2. Thompson, P., et al.: ENIGMA and global neuroscience: a decade of large-scale studies of the brain in health and disease across more than 40 Countries, July 2019
3. Shalev-Shwartz, S., et al.: Online learning and online convex optimization. Found. Trends Mach. Learn. **4**(2), 107–194 (2012)
4. Gama, J.: A survey on learning from data streams: current and future trends. Prog. Artif. Intell. **1**(1), 45–55 (2012)
5. King, R.D., et al.: The automation of science. Science **324**(5923), 85–89 (2009)
6. Soldatova, L.N., King, R.D.: An ontology of scientific experiments. J. R. Soc. Interface **3**(11), 795–803 (2006)
7. Soldatova, L.N., Rzhetsky, A., De Grave, K., King, R.D.: Representation of probabilistic scientific knowledge. J. Biomed. Semant. **4**, S7 (2013)
8. Thompson, P.M., et al.: The ENIGMA consortium: large-scale collaborative analyses of neuroimaging and genetic data. Brain Imaging Behav. **8**(2), 153–182 (2014)

9. Gil, Y., Ratnakar, V., Hanson, P.C.: Organic data publishing: a novel approach to scientific data sharing. In: Second International Workshop on Linked Science: Tackling Big Data (LISC), Held in Conjunction with ISWC, Boston, MA (2012)
10. Jang, M., et al.: Towards automatic generation of portions of scientific papers for large multi-institutional collaborations based on semantic metadata. In: CEUR Workshop Proceedings, vol. 1931, pp. 63–70 (2017)
11. Gil, Y., et al.: Towards continuous scientific data analysis and hypothesis evolution. In: Thirty-First AAAI Conference on Artificial Intelligence (2017)
12. Gil, Y., et al.: Wings: intelligent workflow-based design of computational experiments. IEEE Intell. Syst. **26**(1), 62–72 (2010)
13. Alzheimer's Association, et al.: 2018 Alzheimer's disease facts and figures. Alzheimer's Dement. **14**(3), 367–429 (2018)
14. Jack, C.R., et al.: Tracking pathophysiological processes in alzheimer's disease: an updated hypothetical model of dynamic biomarkers. Lancet Neurol. **12**(2), 207–216 (2013)
15. Lambert, J.-C., et al.: Meta-analysis of 74,046 individuals identifies 11 new susceptibility loci for Alzheimer's disease. Nat. Genet. **45**(12), 1452 (2013)
16. Schuff, N., et al.: MRI of hippocampal volume loss in early alzheimer's disease in relation to ApoE genotype and biomarkers. Brain **132**(4), 1067–1077 (2009)
17. Lyall, D.M., et al.: Is there association between APOE e4 genotype and structural brain ageing phenotypes, and does that association increase in older age in UK Biobank? (N = 8,395). bioRxiv (2017)
18. Fischl, B.: FreeSurfer. NeuroImage **62**(2), 774–781 (2012)
19. Hibar, D.P., et al.: Novel genetic loci associated with hippocampal volume. Nat. Commun. **8**, 13624 (2017)

DMAH 2019: Knowledge Discovery from Unstructured Biomedical Data

Training Set Expansion Using Word Embeddings for Korean Medical Information Extraction

Young-Min Kim[✉]

Hanyang University, 222 Wangsimni-ro, Seoul, South Korea
yngmnkim@hanyang.ac.kr

Abstract. Entity recognition is an essential part of a task-oriented dialogue system and is considered as a sequence labeling task. However, constructing a training set in a new domain is extremely expensive and time-consuming. In this work, we propose a simple framework to exploit neural word embeddings in a semi-supervised manner to annotate medical named entities in Korean. The target domain is the automatic medical diagnosis, where disease name, symptom, and body part are defined as the entity types. Different aspects of the word embeddings such as embedding dimension, window size, models are examined to investigate their effects on the final performance. An online medical QA data has been used for the experiments. With a limit number of pre-annotated words, our framework could successfully expand the training set.

Keywords: Medical information extraction · Training set · Word embeddings · Korean

1 Introduction

With the growth of digital assistants, goal-oriented dialogue system has become one of the main concerns of natural language processing applications [4]. Recent studies have started to introduce end-to-end neural architectures, which produced promising results compared to the traditional rule-based systems [2,15]. Most of the studies concentrate on the development of a better framework in traditional domains for dialogue system such as movie reservation or restaurant search [4,8]. There are few previous works in other domains than reservation or recommendation [6,14]. On the other hand, building a dialogue system in a new domain is much more difficult because we need to start from designing the overall conversational process as well as intent and slot definition.

Slot filling is an important task of a dialogue system and is usually defined as a sequence labeling task [2]. Once we have defined slots, which are domain-specific named entities to detect, we first need to build a training set for entity recognition. However, building a new training set is one of the most challenging parts when constructing a real-world application [12]. Previous studies have tackled this problem mainly via semi-supervised learning [3,11,17] or crowdsourcing [1,13].

© Springer Nature Switzerland AG 2019
V. Gadepally et al. (Eds.): DMAH 2019/Poly 2019, LNCS 11721, pp. 261–274, 2019.
https://doi.org/10.1007/978-3-030-33752-0_19

In this work, we are interested in facilitating training set construction for named entity recognition in a new application field, medical diagnosis. We propose to expand a partially labeled training set using neural word embeddings. The source language is Korean and a large set of online QA data is used for the training of word embeddings. The main idea is simple. From a small number of pre-annotated words, we find k-nearest words for each annotated one using word embeddings. The found words are then tagged with the source word's label. Instead of using embeddings as a supplementary representation for input instance like other semi-supervised frameworks [5,16], we directly utilize the semantic relationship encoded in the trained word embeddings to annotate words. This automatically expanded set can be a first version of the training set for NER before manual correction. Although this first version includes errors, it can greatly reduce manual effort during training set construction.

Word, character or context-based neural embeddings have become standard input formats in many NLP tasks [7,10]. However, the use of those embeddings is usually limited to the representation of input data. The main reason is the nature of the distributed word representation that reflects different contextual information of the word. Therefore, if we directly use the embedding similarity to label instances like our approach, there can be a risk of mixing together the different aspects. In our approach, we suppose that the medical diagnosis domain can be an exception. The medical named entities occur in a limited context, which is the medical diagnosis. Therefore, similar expressions are repeatedly found around the semantically related entities in the training set. For example, the words, "감기 (cold)" and "독감 (flu)" both frequently occur with "걸리다 (caught)".

The main contribution of this work is to investigate in detail the effects of neural word embeddings on training set expansion for medical information extraction. Here we suppose that our approach is effective especially for automatic medical diagnosis because formulaic phrases occur much more frequently than in other applications. Different aspects of word embeddings, such as methodology, embedding dimension, and window size, are tested. We examine two representative neural word embedding methods, word2vec(CBOW) and FastText, and show that the former is greatly better than the latter. The source data for word embeddings is an unlabeled diagnosis data collected from an online medical QA forum. We use 347K QA answered by medical specialists. We also manually annotate a part of the collected data to verify the quality of auto-tagging. Two different embedding models are trained for a question set and an answer set.

2   Dataset Construction for the Medical Named Entity Recognition

The first obstacle we face when building a dialogue system is to find source data. There is almost no real-world data in medical diagnosis domain except one of a recent work [14]. However, their dataset provides only a set of detected symptoms and target disease for each user instance but not the raw conversation data. An instance corresponds to a series of conversation between a user and a doctor in a Chinese online community. The slot filling itself is not a matter of concern in their work.

Automatic medical diagnosis via dialogue system is our final goal and this work corresponds to the entity recognition for slot filling stage. Despite the potential of the automatic diagnosis, collecting proper dialogue data is very difficult because of the domain expertise and patent privacy. Inspired by the recent success of transfer learning, we instead try to collect online diagnosis data in QA form. The main difference from usual conversation data is that there is no interaction but only a pair of question and answer exists for an instance. A trained model on the QA data would be further used for the dialogue system.

2.1   Online Diagnosis Data

We choose a Korean online QA service[1] data instead of real diagnosis conversation. It is the biggest Korean QA platform provided to a web portal users. The uploaded questions are categorized into different hierarchical subjects. We collected the medical section QA data answered by medical specialists from Jan. 2009 to Aug. 2018. Among 24 medical department subsections, we selected 12 departments, which are likely appropriate for automatic diagnosis. Two medical specialists who wrote the most the answers per department have been selected. Total 347K QA pairs are collected after a preprocessing and an answer consists of 8 sentences on average except greeting messages. The collected data is used to train word embeddings and a selected part is used for the training set expansion.

After a detailed analysis of the characteristics of the collected data, we select four different departments most relevant for the automatic diagnosis. These are the department of neurology, neurosurgery, internal medicine, and otorhinolaryngology. The source data for the training set expansion is collected from the four departments. The statistics of the collected data is shown in Table 1.

Table 1. Statistics of the collected QA dataset

	Word embeddings	Medical entity recognition
# instances	347K	536
# departments	12	4
# authors	24	8

2.2   Characteristics of Diagnosis Data

To define an appropriate set of entities for automatic diagnosis system, we need to investigate in detail the QA data. We found several remarkable properties of the data as follows.

---

[1] https://kin.naver.com.

First, the questions can be categorized into several types. The most frequent one is to seek the overall expert advice given symptoms. Disease name or the cause of the current state are given or not. Another is to detect disease or to ask whether a suspicious disease would be correct given symptoms. There are also questions for decision making such that which department to go or if surgery is necessary.

Second, symptoms and diseases are not perfectly separable. When disease names are used as final diagnoses for users, they do not need to be represented by official names. Therefore, it is not easy to decide if a term refers to a disease or to a symptom. Moreover, certain symptom names with a modifier indicate disease names such as "peripheral dizziness".

Third, sentences in the answers include more refined expressions than that of the questions. The answers are written by medical doctors who tend to clearly express their opinions. They usually summarize the symptoms, which have been worded in a long-winded way in the questions. On the other hand, question-ers tend to write in a colloquial style. The expressions about symptoms in the questions frequently include mimetic words.

Fourth, maybe the most interesting property is that the terms refer to the diseases or symptoms are likely in a closed set. Unlike named entities, there are not many newly coined words if a benchmark dataset is sufficiently large. This property supports our choice of using word embeddings trained in a large dataset.

Considering these properties, we selected useful entity types for medical diag-nosis such as symptom, body part, medical history, duration of symptom, related disease, etc. To reduce annotation complexity, we keep three essential types only: symptom, disease and body part. We interpret disease in a broad sense including specific symptoms and syndromes that should be judged by medical specialists.

2.3   Training Set Annotation

Four different medical departments have been selected for the training set of medical entity recognition as mentioned above. We first randomly selected 150 QA instances for each department. After eliminating duplicated answers and unnecessary questions such as MRI reading or military service exemption issue, we obtain 536 instances to be annotated. We only annotate answer data because the expressions are much more clear than questions. The entities in question part could further be extracted via a transfer learning. The definition of three entity types to be annotated are given in Table 2.

Table 2. Entity definition for medical diagnosis system

Entity type	Tag	definition
Disease	DZ	disease name used for final diagnosis
Symptom	SX	symptom which can be felt by users
Body part	BP	body part where the symptom occurs

Three annotators discussed the annotation guidelines. Each instance is annotated by one annotator and reviewed by another annotator. We repeatedly modified the guidelines and re-annotated the data to obtain a more accurate result as the annotation progresses. The main guidelines are as follows:

- Frequent informal disease names such as "허리 (waist) 디스크 (disc)", which means "lumbar herniated intervertebral disc", are considered as a disease.
- Symptoms are usually nouns but can be a combination of adjective and symptom when the expression is very common. For example, " 저린 (benumbed) 증상 (symptom)".
- Body tissues such as muscle, ligament or bone are not the target but organs such as stomach, liver, or brain are because we can specify the location of a given symptom.

Training set annotation consists of two stages. First, we auto-tag the data using predefined dictionaries for each entity type. The auto-tagging errors are then manually corrected. This initial set is used as a seed training set, which will be expanded via our proposed framework. Second, we manually annotate the rest of the data. The manual annotation result will be used for the evaluation of our training set expansion method.

Table 3 shows the characteristics of the annotated data. The number of annotated unique terms and that of total terms is given in the first two rows. Manually annotated cases are given in the following rows.

Table 3. Characteristics of the annotated data

	DZ	SX	BP
# unique terms	297	228	199
# terms	915	1,267	1,010
# manually tagged unique terms	186	189	151
# manually tagged terms	417	480	637

3   Set Expansion with Word Embeddings

In this section, we describe our framework for training set expansion. Figure 1 shows the overall process. We first (a) train word embeddings with the question set or answer set. Continuous bag-of-words(CBOW) model of word2vec and FastText are used for the training. Given raw data, we then (b) auto-tag the entities using dictionaries for each entity type: disease, symptom, and body part. After this step, tagged entities and untagged ones coexist in a data instance. The word embeddings are used to (c) find the candidate tokens for each entity type by searching k-nearest tokens of each auto-tagged entity in the previous step. Morphological analysis is followed to filter out inappropriate words. In the final step, we (d) annotate each candidate token with the previously found label to expand the training set. Post-processing can be conducted to enhance accuracy.

3.1   Word Embeddings

Our intermediate goal is to find terms semantically similar to each of the auto-tagged entities using neural word embeddings. However, we cannot guarantee that the neural representation trained on the diagnosis data reflects well the representative properties of the predefined entity types. We instead suppose that medical diagnosis domain is more suitable than the other application domains to directly exploit word embeddings.

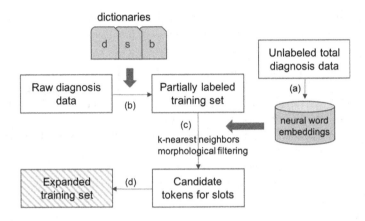

Fig. 1. The overall process of the proposed framework for the training set expansion for medical entity recognition

As we discussed in the previous section, disease names and symptoms are not much scalable. They are usually used in limited circumstances such as medical diagnosis. Therefore, terms occurring near to them, tend not to be diverse. Moreover, formulaic expressions, which are used to express diseases or symptoms, are repeatedly found. This property of diagnosis data is working to the advantage of our framework.

We choose to use word embeddings instead of the other embeddings to keep well the word-level properties during training. We even do not apply morphological analysis at this point because many of disease names are compound words, which can be easily decomposed when applying morphological analysis. The simply tokenized words by whitespace are the input of the embedding models.

Embedding models are separately constructed for two different subsets of the QA data. The first subset is Answer set, which includes diagnosis data written by medical specialists. The second one is Question set, which includes symptom data written by users. These models are further used for the expansion of entity recognition training set. Meanwhile, source data of medical entity recognition is extracted from the Answer set.

3.2   Finding Candidate Terms by Similarity

The candidate words for each entity type are found by searching k-nearest neighbors of each auto-tagged entity. Table 4 shows two examples of found words given a disease name, "폐결핵 (pulmonary tuberculosis)" and a symptom, "소화불량" (dyspepsia). The cosine similarity between a source word and found one is shown just right side of the word.

Table 4. Found top six words via cosine similarity given a disease name or a symptom

source	found words
"폐결핵" (pulmonary tuberculosis)	"식도암(esophageal cancer)": 0.73 "폐렴(pneumonia)": 0.71 "위궤양(gastric ulcer)": 0.69 "기관지염(bronchitis)": 0.68 "결핵(tuberculosis)": 0.68 "천식(asthma)": 0.67
"소화불량" (dyspepsia)	"속쓰림(heartburn)": 0.86 "위염(gastritis)이라고": 0.81 "신물(acid reflux)": 0.77 "복부(abdomen)": 0.67 "작열감(purosis)이": 0.67 "불쾌감(displeasure)의": 0.65

There are two major issues when labeling directly the found words with the corresponding tag. First, we should eliminate unnecessary part of the words such as postposition. In Korean, postpositions are usually attached to a noun to represent its grammatical case. By introducing a morphology analyzer, we detach postpositions if exist and keep the separated tokens for the following three cases:

- common nouns only
- common nouns followed by a proposition
- noun ending at the end

In Table 4, all the words in the first row are tagged as DZ and three words without postpositions in the second row are tagged as SX because they are all common nouns. "작열감 (purosis)" and "불쾌감 (displeasure)" are tagged as SX whereas "위염 (gastritis)" is not, because the first two correspond to the second case but the last one does not correspond to any of the cases.

The second issue is that the current framework aims at unigrams only. This is problematic because many real-world terms of all three entity types are n-grams. To overcome this issue, we may also train a bigram or a trigram model. For now, we do not take into account this in modeling. However, our framework can indirectly detect n-grams by separately detecting successive tokens. The conflict among tagged tokens would be handled in a manual correction.

4   Experiments

In order to evaluate the quality of the proposed framework, we compare the expanded training set with the manually annotated golden standard. Using traditional metrics for named entity recognition is excessive because our result needs a manual correction and further would be used as a training set for entity recognition. Therefore, we use a relaxed metric similar to [9]'s proposition, which have been employed for biomedical information extraction. The relaxed recall is calculated by the proportion of true positive tokens in the golden standard for each entity type as follows:

$$\text{Recall} = \frac{\text{\# true positive tokens}}{\text{\# tokens in the golden standard terms}}$$

Similarly the relaxed precision can be also calculated as:

$$\text{Precision} = \frac{\text{\# true positive tokens}}{\text{\# predicted tokens}}$$

In the results, precision is much lower than recall because no post-processing has been applied after matching automatically all the candidate terms for each entity type. We expect further enhance the precision with some post-processing.

4.1   Experimental Settings

The experiments consist of two parts: first, model training for word embeddings and second, expanding the training set for medical entity recognition.[2]

Word2vec and FastText modules in gensim python package are used for the experiments. The entity dictionaries have been collected from health information sites such as the "National Health Information Portal" and hospital homepages. The number of terms in the dictionary is 2,191 for disease names, 142 for symptoms, and 139 for body parts. Some conflict terms between disease and symptom are preprocessed before experiments.

Different aspects of word embeddings are verified: embedding size, window size, dataset, and model. Embedding size varies between 200 to 600 and window size does between 3 and 7. Both the Answer and Question sets are used to verify the effects of the dataset. Words occurring less than five times in the whole set are eliminated. The experiments are repeated five times for a setting with different initialization of embedding model. Therefore recalls and precisions are averaged ones for the five different experiments.

We check the top "k" most similar words to find the candidate words for each pre-tagged term with dictionaries. The optimal number of "k" has been found during pre-experiments before the evaluation. The value is 15 for disease names and symptoms, and is 10 for body parts.

---

[2] The trained model and the annotated dataset will be soon available.

4.2   Effects of Embedding and Window Size

We first check the influence of embedding size and window size. Figure 2 represents the experimental results for CBOW model trained on the Answer dataset. Once we have trained an embedding model, we find the candidate tokens for each tagged entity in the partially labeled training set for the medical entity recognition. The recall and precision are then computed for each entity type.

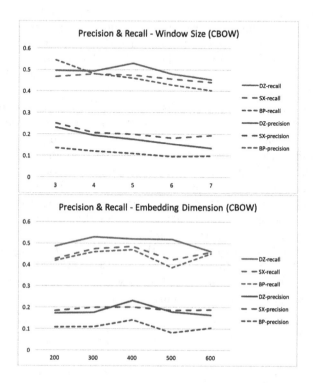

Fig. 2. The effects of window size(left) and embedding dimension(right) for CBOW. Recall(blue lines) and precision(red lines) for each entity type is represented. (Color figure online)

Recalls are represented in blue lines and precisions are in red. Best recall for DZ is 0.53 when the window size is 5. SX recall and BP recall curves decrease with window size. There were few changes in recalls for SX when window size increases from 3 to 5. BP recall rapidly decreases compared to the others especially from size 3 to 4. Considering that disease name and symptoms are more important indicators than body part to diagnose, we pick window size 5 as best one.

All the precisions decrease when window size increases. For our objective, precision is less important than recall because we can enhance precision with a simple manual verification on the found candidate terms. As our goal is to facilitate training set construction, applying this manual verification step is reasonable.

In the case of embedding sizes, recalls decrease from size 500. Embedding size 300 provides a slightly better result than size 300 in DZ recall, but not in SX or BP. As disease name is an important entity type in medical information extraction, we choose 300 as best embedding size.

4.3   Effects of Dataset and Model

Table 5 shows the performance comparison of our proposed method using word embeddings trained with the Answer and Question sets. The embedding size and dimension are fixed with five and 300 respectively. We expected that Answer set would significantly outperform the other because dataset for the entity recognition had been extracted from Answer set. However, the result is somewhat different from what we expected.

The recalls for DZ and SX of Answer set model are better than that of the Question set. The values are 0.53 and 0.47 for Answer set and 0.51 and 0.40 for the Question set respectively. The reason for a large gap in symptom recall is the difference in language use between doctors and questioners when describing symptoms. Questioners use a lot of mimetic words to express their conditions while doctors use more refined expressions. Therefore, the trained word embeddings on the Question set could not effectively extract symptoms.

On the other hands, the BP recalls are 0.46 for the Answer set and 0.62 for the Question set. Surprisingly, the Question set much outperforms the Answer set. We suppose that the reason is also the difference in language use because questioners tend to detailedly express their symptoms using terms for specific body parts. Therefore, there are more diverse words indicating body part in the Question set and the words are frequently found in the set.

Table 5. Evaluation result of our proposed training set expansion framework (CBOW on Answer)

Embedding	Measure	DZ	SX	BP
CBOW (Answer)	Recall	0.53	0.47	0.46
	Precision	0.18	0.20	0.11
	# found unigrams	30	39	24
	# found bigrams	14	3	12
CBOW (Question)	Recall	0.51	0.40	0.62
	Precision	0.20	0.27	0.16
	# found unigrams	23	29	33
	# found bigrams	15	3	9

In the case of precision, the Question set rather outperforms the Answer set for all entity types. It is understandable for BP because its recall is also much better than that of Answer set. When we looked in detail the results for DZ and SX, we found that there are many identical words in the candidate words. Therefore, the total number of predicted words is comparably small after eliminating overlapping words. This finally leads to higher precisions.

Besides two metrics, we also provide the number of correct unique terms detected by our framework. Although our method aims at unigrams, there exist also continuing tokens with the same tags detected separately. The number of found bigrams are counted only when the bigram itself corresponds to an entity. When each token in a bigram term is correct but not the whole span, it is not a correct term. The Answer set outperforms the other in terms of both unigram and bigram for DZ and SX. This result partially supports the reason for the higher precision of the Question set.

When repeating experiments, we sometimes found trigrams also when using Question set. The trigrams are usually disease names, such as "근막 (myofascial) 동통 (pain) 증후군 (syndrome)", which is usually used as a compound word, "근막동통증후군". An interesting thing is that the compound word does not exist in the dictionaries and even not in the manual annotation. Our framework could detect the trigram term from different sources of seed words.

Finally, we represent the effects of the word embedding models in Fig. 3. The CBOW model shows much better results than the FastText model in recalls. As FastText tokenizes words into subwords for training, words with the same root can be more similar to each other than in CBOW. This property becomes a drawback in our framework because we need to find as various words as possible to find many candidate tokens. For the precision, FastText outperforms CBOW

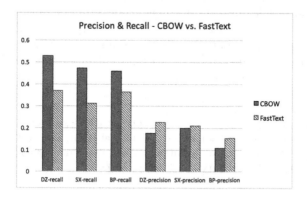

Fig. 3. Performance comparison of two word embedding models, CBOW and FastText

because the found words sharing the same root with its source word would be correctly tagged ones. However, the number of found unique unigrams or bigrams is much smaller than when using CBOW.

5 Conclusions

This paper proposes a simple framework of training set expansion for Korean medical entity recognition in a semi-supervised manner. The target area is medical diagnosis domain and a training set was constructed from a real-world QA data. After a detailed investigation of the source data, we defined the essential entity types for this area. The main idea of our approach is to directly utilize the potential of neural word embeddings to detect semantically related terms for medical diagnosis domain.

Different aspects of word embeddings such as embedding dimension, window size, models, are examined to find their effects on the performance. We empirically showed the effectiveness of the proposed method by obtaining an average recall of 0.49 for three pre-defined entity types using CBOW. It is an encouraging result considering that the source data is real-world one and the target entities are numerous. This simple framework would be an interesting starting option when building a dialogue system in a new domain. Moreover, we can further easily enhance the performance by adding a manual verification step just after finding candidate words. With this manual verification, we can expand the number of neighbors to verify that will leads to better recall.

One of the major drawbacks of our method is we need a manual correction after the training set expansion. There are conflicts among the found entities, and some terms with one syllable need an exception handling. As future work, we are first interested in simplifying the manual correction process by refined postprocessing. Further direction is to build a dialogue system on the constructed data. We will start with defining the diseases to diagnose by the system and with matching the related symptoms to each disease. Reinforcement learning will be a good option for the dialogue system.

Acknowledgments. This work is partially supported by two projects, Smart Multimodal Environment of AI Chatbot Robots for Digital Healthcare (P0000536) and the Project of Korean Management of Technology Specialists Training (N0001611) funded by the Ministry of Trade, Industry and Energy (MOTIE).

References

1. Bontcheva, K., Derczynski, L., Roberts, I.: Crowdsourcing named entity recognition and entity linking corpora. In: Ide, N., Pustejovsky, J. (eds.) Handbook of Linguistic Annotation, pp. 875–892. Springer, Dordrecht (2017). https://doi.org/10.1007/978-94-024-0881-2_32

2. Chen, H., Liu, X., Yin, D., Tang, J.: A survey on dialogue systems: recent advances and new frontiers. SIGKDD Explor. Newsl. **19**(2), 25–35 (2017)

3. Dai, A.M., Le, Q.V.: Semi-supervised sequence learning. Adv. Neural Inf. Process. Syst. **28**, 3079–3087 (2015)

4. Li, X., Chen, Y.N., Li, L., Gao, J., Celikyilmaz, A.: End-to-end task-completion neural dialogue systems. In: Proceedings of the Eighth International Joint Conference on Natural Language Processing (vol. 1: Long Papers), pp. 733–743 (2017)

5. Luan, Y., Ostendorf, M., Hajishirzi, H.: Scientific information extraction with semi-supervised neural tagging. In: Proceedings of the 2017 Conference on Empirical Methods in Natural Language Processing, pp. 2641–2651 (2017)

6. Mo, K., Zhang, Y., Li, S., Li, J., Yang, Q.: Personalizing a dialogue system with transfer reinforcement learning. In: AAAI (2018)

7. Mrkšić, N., et al.: Counter-fitting word vectors to linguistic constraints. In: Proceedings of the 2016 Conference of the North American Chapter of the Association for Computational Linguistics: Human Language Technologies, pp. 142–148 (2016)

8. Mrkšić, N., OSeaghdha, D., Wen, T.H., Thomson, B., Young, S.: Neural belief tracker: data-driven dialogue state tracking. In: Proceedings of the 55th Annual Meeting of the Association for Computational Linguistics (vol. 1: Long Papers), pp. 1777–1788 (2017)

9. Nguyen, A.T., Wallace, B., Li, J.J., Nenkova, A., Lease, M.: Aggregating and predicting sequence labels from crowd annotations. In: Proceedings of the 55th Annual Meeting of the Association for Computational Linguistics (vol. 1: Long Papers), pp. 299–309 (2017)

10. Peters, M., et al.: Deep contextualized word representations. In: Proceedings of the 2018 Conference of the North American Chapter of the Association for Computational Linguistics: Human Language Technologies, vol. 1 (Long Papers), pp. 2227–2237 (2018)

11. Radford, A., Sutskever, I.: Improving language understanding by generative pre-training. In: arxiv (2018)

12. Ratner, A.J., De Sa, C.M., Wu, S., Selsam, D., Ré, C.: Data programming: creating large training sets, quickly. Adv. Neural Inf. Process. Syst. **29**, 3567–3575 (2016)

13. Kondreddi, S. K., Triantafillou, P., Weikum, G.: Combining information extraction and human computing for crowd sourced knowledge acquisition. In: IEEE 30th International Conference on Data Engineering (2014)

14. Wei, Z., et al.: Task-oriented dialogue system for automatic diagnosis. In: Proceedings of the 56th Annual Meeting of the Association for Computational Linguistics (vol. 2, Short Papers), pp. 201–207 (2018)

15. Wen, T.H., et al.: A network-based end-to-end trainable task-oriented dialogue system. In: Proceedings of the 15th Conference of the European Chapter of the Association for Computational Linguistics, vol. 1, Long Papers, pp. 438–449 (2017)

16. Yang, Z., Cohen, W.W., Salakhutdinov, R.: Revisiting semi-supervised learning with graph embeddings. In: Proceedings of the 33rd International Conference on International Conference on Machine Learning, ICML 2016, vol. 48, pp. 40–48 (2016)
17. Yang, Z., Hu, J., Salakhutdinov, R., Cohen, W.: Semi-supervised QA with generative domain-adaptive nets. In: Proceedings of the 55th Annual Meeting of the Association for Computational Linguistics, pp. 1040–1050, July 2017

DMAH 2019: Blockchain and Privacy-Preserving Data Management

Intelligent Health Care Data Management Using Blockchain: Current Limitation and Future Research Agenda

Alevtina Dubovitskaya[1,2]([✉]), Petr Novotny[3], Scott Thiebes[4], Ali Sunyaev[4], Michael Schumacher[5], Zhigang Xu[6], and Fusheng Wang[7]

[1] Lucerne University of Applied Sciences and Arts, Lucerne, Switzerland
[2] Swisscom, Bern, Switzerland
alevtina.dubovitskaya@hslu.ch
[3] IBM T.J. Watson Research Center, Yorktown Heights, NY, USA
[4] Karlsruhe Institute of Technology, Karlsruhe, Germany
[5] University of Applied Sciences and Arts, Western Switzerland, Sierre, Switzerland
[6] Stony Brook University Hospital, Stony Brook, USA
[7] Stony Brook University, Stony Brook, USA

Abstract. Health care is undergoing a big data revolution, with vast amounts of information supplied from numerous sources, leading to major paradigm shifts including precision medicine and AI-driven health care among others. Yet, there still exist significant barriers before such approaches could be adopted in practice, including data integration and interoperability, data sharing, security and privacy protection, scalability, and policy and regulatory issues. Blockchain provides a unique opportunity to tackle major challenges in health care and biomedical research, such as enabling data sharing and integration for patient-centered care, data provenance allowing verification authenticity of the data, and optimization of some of the health care processes among others. Nevertheless, technological constraints of current blockchain technologies necessitate further research before mass adoption of blockchain-based health care data management is possible. We analyze context-based requirements and capabilities of the available technology and propose a research agenda and new approaches towards achieving intelligent health care data management using blockchain.

Keywords: Blockchain · Health care · Intelligent data management

1 Introduction

The accelerating digitization of the health care sector has led to the creation of large volumes of sensitive data stored online in multiple formats and representations, including electronic health records, medical images, genome sequences, sensor data from monitoring devices, payer records, clinical trials data, and more.

© Springer Nature Switzerland AG 2019
V. Gadepally et al. (Eds.): DMAH 2019/Poly 2019, LNCS 11721, pp. 277–288, 2019.
https://doi.org/10.1007/978-3-030-33752-0_20

Once these data are properly combined, they can be leveraged by data analytics and machine learning techniques to advance the medical, pharmaceutical, sports, and other domains of health care-related research and applied medicine. This possibility to leverage healthcare data has inspired a shift of health care to precision medicine and AI-driven health care.

To provide the required data input to the intelligent health care data-management systems, it is crucial to ensure interoperability between different data sources that often store and process the data in multiple formats. Due to the volumes of the data that are continuously being produced, the difficulty to extract the required information is apparent. The task is further complicated by the intricacies of the highly-regulated heterogeneous health care environment.

Regulations in Europe and the United States, such as the GDPR [1] and HIPAA [2] advocate patient's privacy. Accordingly, patients have the right over their health information and can set rules and limits on who can access and receive the health information, as well as the right for when their data are ought to be erased. The Office of the National Coordinator for Health Information Technology in the US (ONC) recently announced a proposed rule on interoperability and information blocking, with a strong focus on patients' ability to access their own electronic health record (EHR) at no cost [3]. Achieving interoperability and privacy simultaneously seems contradictory and hence presents a significant challenge. How to guarantee that data can be easily exchanged and are available when required, while at the same time preserving patients' privacy (i.e., patients are still able to control who can access their data for which purposes)? How can we explicitly prove that patients have given their consent in an efficient manner?

Ecosystems for health information exchange (HIE) aim to ensure that the data from EHRs are securely, efficiently and accurately shared nationwide. However, HIEs have limited adoption, and there is a lack of standard architectures or protocols to ensure security and enforcement of the access control specified by patients [4].

The possibility of using emerging blockchain technology for health care data management has recently raised major attention in both industry and academia [5–8]. Blockchain technology can be employed to give way for users' complete control over their data and privacy without a central point of control, which will help accelerating and enhancing the privacy-preserving data sharing in health care. In case of chronic diseases, such data sharing is particularly important due to the multiple-medication intake (therefore, drug-to-drug interaction and management of the prescriptions and reimbursements), diagnosis and treatment conducted at multiple hospitals (due to the specialization of centers, required "second opinion", and the mobility of the patients) [5,9,10]. Employing blockchain technology can contribute to the optimization of the pharmaceutical supply-chain processes, including clinical trials, and medical research in general [11–13]. Yet, regardless of ongoing academic research and high interest from the industrial perspective, blockchain-based health care data management systems are not yet in place.

Contributions: In this paper, we (i) *define domain-specific requirements* from the perspective of intelligent health care data management (in Sect. 2); (ii) introduce blockchain technology and focus on the selection of the *health care processes that can benefit from applying blockchain technology*, providing a high-level description of the existing approaches, in Sect. 3. In Sect. 4, we analyze the limitations of existing works in, often related to the technological restraints of the blockchain or underlying technologies. Trying to bridge the gap between the domain-specific requirements and technical capabilities, in Sect. 5, we (iii) propose a *research agenda and new approaches for intelligent health care data management using blockchain*. Section 6 concludes the paper.

2   Health Care Requirements and Goals

Patients need to provide their caregiver with the data required for the best treatment outcome. Yet, patients also have a right for privacy. Therefore, data need to be shared with different entities but following the "privacy-by-design" principle: inline with the patients' will, and not revealing more than required.

The amount of health care related data corresponding to a single person has seen dramatic increases over the past years. Reliable systems for data storage and management, agnostic to the number of records are required to ensure that a person can maintain a life-long history of their health care data.

For the system to comply with the regulations governing personal data (including health care data) management in EU or US, each patient needs to provide a consent to share his or her data for both primary care and research purposes, which they can revoke any time.

Moreover, for primary care, the following security properties are essential: availability of the data, data integrity, and data confidentiality. These properties can be defined as follows:

- *Availability* refers to the ability to use the information or resource when requested. Availability is an important aspect of reliability, as well as of system design [14].
- *Integrity* refers to the trustworthiness of data or resources, and it is usually phrased in terms of preventing improper or unauthorized change. Integrity includes data integrity (the content of the information) and origin integrity (the source of the data, often called authentication) [14].
- *Confidentiality* refers to preventing the disclosure of information to unauthorized individuals or systems [15]. Although confidentiality refers to the data, privacy, as defined above, refers to the person and his right to decide to keep his personal data confidential.

Data anonymization can be an alternative to consent management when data are shared for research purposes. In practice, in addition to interoperability and compliance with legislation and policies that regulate management of the personal data and, in particular, protected health information, traceability is required.

Traceability of the data can be defined as the ability to retain the identities of the origin of the data, the entities who accessed the data, and the operations performed on the data (e.g., updates) [16]. Data traceability will be particularly useful in legal cases, in an audit of care practices, as well as for patients, in defining and enforcing their access-control policy, in allowing meaningful data aggregation for research purposes, and in enabling reproducibility of research.

Based on the domain specifics and taking into account the sensitive nature of the health care data, we can define the following required functionalities of a health care data management system:

- Ensure that patients can control and access their information at any time.
- Ensure that patients must not lose access to their data, or in case it happens, are able to recover access.
- Define mechanisms for the health care stakeholders, in particular, care providers to access the data in the framework of multiple scenarios: (i) consent is provided by the patient and is easy to verify (for both primary care and research purposes), (ii) an emergency situation occurs, and the consent is impossible to obtain, (iii) research is based on only anonymized data (no need for consent), (iv) traceability and audit.

3   Applications of Blockchain in Health Care

In this section, we first provide a short introduction to blockchain technology, then, based on the available scientific literature and industry manifesto, we provide a high-level summary of health care scenarios and processes, where applying blockchain has been proposed. For each process, we depict the goals and motivations to apply blockchain technology, mainly focusing on the characteristics and aspects of the current processes that can potentially be improved by employing blockchain: data availability and accessibility, immutability, transparency, security, and privacy, as well as patient involvement in clinical research.

3.1   Blockchain Overview

Blockchain is a peer-to-peer distributed ledger technology that provides a shared, immutable, and transparent append-only register of all the transactions that happen in the network. It is secured using cryptographic primitives such as hash functions, digital signatures, and encryption algorithms [17]. The data in the form of transactions are digitally signed and broadcasted by the participants, and then grouped into blocks in chronological order and time-stamped. A hash function is applied to the content of the block, which forms a unique block identifier that is stored in the subsequent block. Due to the properties of the hash function (the result is deterministic and can not be reversed), by hashing the block content again and comparing it with the identifier from the subsequent block, one can easily verify if the content of the block was modified. An ordered sequence of the blocks forms a blockchain ledger.

The blockchain ledger is replicated and maintained by every participant in the network. With this decentralized approach, there is no need for setting up a single trusted centralized entity that manages the registry. Participants can immediately notice malicious attempts, aiming to tamper with the information stored in the registry and reject it; hence the immutability of the ledger is guaranteed. The technique of adding a new block to the existing ledger is defined by the consensus protocol employed in the blockchain technology. Based on how the identity of a participant and its permissions to participate in the consensus are defined within a network, one could distinguish between permissionless and permissioned blockchain systems [18].

Different platforms are employed in the aforementioned approaches. A recent review [19] provides an extensive list of studies and ongoing projects that focus on using permissionless blockchains in health care settings. The authors also discuss potential problems and challenges to be considered when adopting permissionless blockchain technology (e.g., speed and scalability, confidentiality, the threat of a 51% attack, management of the transaction fees and "mining"). Moreover, the analysis of network traffic can lead to inferring patterns of treatment from frequency analysis of the interactions with the ledger [5].

Membership mechanisms employed in permissioned blockchain platforms allow to control participation in the blockchain network and access to the ledger. While this architecture allows to avoid some of the disadvantages of permissionless platforms, permissioned network is more centralized by construction and may thus introduce a threat of single point of failure. Some of the challenges and potential benefits associated with employing permissioned blockchain platforms in health care, can be found in Krawiec et al. [20] and in the white paper from IBM [21].

3.2   Blockchain Health Care Scenarios

Below, we focus on health care scenarios where blockchain-based approaches and/or applications have already been proposed. We also reference several notable publications that refer to a more detailed description of the blockchain-based applications within specific clinical data management processes. (For a complete overview of the use of blockchain in health care, we refer an interested reader to the recent relevant and extensive systematic literature reviews [7,8]).

1. *Connecting health care stakeholders and maintaining complete history of patient's health care data:*
   Blockchain technology can be used to ensure traceability and immutability of patients' health care data without putting medical records on the blockchain, but keeping the metadata only, that can also include patients' consent. The voluminous and sensitive health care data can be stored within individual nodes on the network, while their intelligent representations will be stored on-chain [5]. An alternative approach is to use compliant cloud-based services for temporal storage and data exchange (i.e., time frame defined by the patient) [10]. FHIRchain [9] is a blockchain-based approach for data-sharing

that encapsulates HL7 Fast Healthcare Interoperability Resources (FHIR) standard for the clinical data. Efficient on-chain consent management and enforcement of access-control policy expressed by the consent will speed-up and facilitate data sharing for primary care in a privacy-preserving manner. Better treatment control can be achieved by connecting patients, multiple health care providers, health insurer/insurances, and pharmacies and providing them with the specific types of data. One of the barriers for establishing "connected health" is a lack of interoperability. Peterson et al. [22] presented a system design based on the permissioned blockchain platform (MultiChain), and discussed how FHIR integration into such system can address the interoperability issue. The proof of interoperability proposed in [22] is based on conformance to the FHIR protocol, which requires verification that the messages sent to the blockchain can get converted to other required formats. Transparent execution of smart-contracts will enable fast, automatized, trustworthy, and bias-free processes reimbursements and claims.

Additionally, it is necessary to ensure compliance with the regulations related to health care data management. Magyar in [23] in their theoretical work, based on the principles of the HIPAA regulation, suggests a list of cryptographic tools that can be potentially applied to ensure data privacy and security. Traceability, the authenticity of the data (and sources), and interoperability between data sources will enable a possibility to build and maintain a complete life-long history of health care data.

2. *Pharmaceutical supply-chain:* Blockchain-based use cases in supply-chain are emerging, including using traceability and immutability properties of the blockchain to combat counterfeit medicines, securing medical devices, optimizing functionality of health care IoT devices, and improving the public health supply chain [24], ensuring control over returned drugs to the pharmaceutical company. In a recent review, Scott et al. demonstrate how blockchain technology can provide functionality that benefits supply chain management in general and traceability of pharmaceuticals in particular [25]. Compliance in pharmaceutical supply-chain, verification of the transportation and storage conditions are of a high importance, (e.g., medications can loose their efficiency, if the conditions of storage or transportation are violated). Addressing this issue, Bocek et al. proposed to use smart contracts deployed on the Ethereum blockchain for compliance verification based on the sensor data (i.e., temperature measurements. from a sensor placed in strategical points of the shipment) [13].

3. *Medical research and its reproduceability:* Clinical trials are conducted in order to evaluate new technologies and drugs. Coordination between multiple centers enables to aggregate higher volumes of more heterogeneous data in a shorter period of time, compare to the clinical trials conducted in only one medical institution. Also, involvement of multiple centers bring independent evaluation. However, such trials are more complex in terms of coordination [26]. Employing blockchain technology can facilitate management of multicenter clinical trials, improve transparency, traceability of the consents in clinical trials, quality and reliability of clinical trials' data, and therefore

increase patient involvement and adherence to the treatment [27,28]. Keeping track of all the actions of data-sharing can be used in order to evaluate a threat to infer more information about a patient, by combining anonymized datasets that contain the information about the same patient, and estimate the potential risks of infringing patients' privacy [29].

4 Limitations of Blockchain for Health Care

In this section, we analyze the limitations of the existing approaches, including some that have been already proposed in the related works.

Limited Availability of the Data. The data are required to be available from anywhere at any time, yet compliant with the access-control policies specified by the patient. At the same time, the access-control policies might be expressed differently at various locations and across different types of data. Therefore, it is a challenge to define unified rules for the global reachability of the data. One issue with permissioned blockchains is that due to its (consortium-oriented) nature, it is likely to be impossible to make it global (i.e., create a single consortium with unified governance).

Vulnerability of the Immutable Data. While, from the medical perspective, it is of high importance to ensure the immutability of the health care data, it is not desirable to have all the data immutably stored on the blockchain, even if encrypted, due to the highly sensitive nature of such information. For example, advances in quantum computing can represent a threat to most of the world's cryptographic infrastructures [30] in the future. Moreover, the availability of certain types of data may present unexpected side-effects, such as the decision to store genomics data on the blockchain can affect a patient's relatives. To this end, design of on-/off- chain data structures, interoperability mechanisms between the ledger and off-chain data storages, and privacy-preserving protocols are of high importance.

Lack of Guarantee of Consistency of the Distributed Ledger at Any Point in Time. Blockchain technology cannot guarantee that every peer in a network has a valid (shared by the majority) state. The peer may have an invalid state due to a software or hardware fault, or malicious attacks. Yet, the peer may still participate in the network albeit having an intermittent or permanent failure. Thus, it is important to ensure that the client (user) obtains valid information from the blockchain even in case of the presence of faulty nodes. Policy and additional mechanisms for querying the blockchain nodes are required in order to ensure obtaining and interpreting reliable answers from the blockchain.

Introduction of a Single Point of Failure. In case of employing off-chain data storage (either for data storage or for running computations over the health care data) and membership service (in case of permissioned blockchain), the risk of creating a single point of failure exists. To mitigate this limitation the following approaches can be employed: applying cryptographic techniques (including symmetric and asymmetric encryption, digital signature, threshold encryption, and homomorphic encryption), decentralization of the data-storage and membership service, and involving trustful independent parties [10,23,31].

Capabilities of Current Blockchain Technologies. Requirements from the health care perspective may not be easily satisfied by applying the technology "out-of-the-box". Thus, bridging the gap between practical needs and technology capabilities may be required. Distributed ledger technology is developing fast, yet multiple limitations have already been identified by the research community, including the limited number of transactions that can be processed, limited data storage capabilities, concerns related to the immutability of the distributed ledger, the legal requirements of allowing opt-outs of data, and the need for standardization.

Verification of the Correctness of the Smart-Contract. Design and verification of the smart-contract business logic cannot be performed in a fully automatic manner, and thus a human must be involved. This person is required to have both expert domain knowledge, as well as technical competence (i.e., one has to make sure that the rules are defined according to the use-case scenario). Moreover, verification of the correctness of the smart-contract implementation is of high importance to guarantee all mandatory tenets.

5   Research Agenda for Blockchain-Based Intelligent Health Care Data Management

In an attempt to bridge the gap between the listed domain-specific requirements and current technology implementations, while taking into account the analysis of the existing approaches and their limitations, we propose the following research agenda in the area of applying blockchain technology for intelligent health care data management. We present it in the form of research objectives (RO) encompassing technical, social, and legal aspects.

RO-1: Ensure privacy-preserving distributed and globally-reachable data. The challenge of building a framework that ensures globally reachable data and enforcement of patient's access control policy is not trivial: data availability and interoperability requirements can interfere with patients' privacy. HIE principles can serve as a building block for such a framework, but suffer from the limitations, already mentioned above. As suggested in [32], blockchain technology can be applied beyond HIE to shift the trusted intermediary role away from a single hospital to the blockchain network and provide the link between physician credentials and patient identity. Yet, the following question remains: is it possible to define a harmonized and standardized set of basic rules that can be built into the health care data management architecture based on the international laws and regulations, preserving different sensitivity levels of the data, and ensuring adherence to such rules without a centralized authority?

RO-2: Ensure truthfulness of the data. Blockchain is not concerned with truthfulness; it guarantees the immutability of data once recorded, regardless of the content. To ensure data quality, in permissioned blockchains, different approaches for the authentication of the users, the data providers, can be applied. One can employ cryptographic primitives (hash/digital signature) and store the output on the blockchain to ensure the immutability of the data that are stored off-chain. To establish the truthfulness, multiple independent oracles, or verifiers, can be involved (i.e., the data are considered genuine only after being approved by multiple parties). There exist some technology solutions, that can be directly paired with blockchain (e.g., IBM verifier [33]).

RO-3: Enable intelligent data-management. How to design privacy-preserving hybrid data storage for machine learning tasks and artificial intelligence techniques (e.g., to use on-chain storage only for the statistical data avoiding storage of sensitive data on the blockchain)? Can we decouple the query from the execution by defining the queries and parameters to be stored on the blockchain, which will be then executed only by trusted entities or data owners (doctors, patients)?

RO-4: Attain multi-ledger interoperability. A plethora of existing blockchain platforms and various prototypes built on top of the technologies can aggravate the problem of the lack of interoperability between health care systems. Thus, ensuring interoperability between different blockchain platforms is of high importance. Moreover, due to custom privacy requirements and individual needs of different patients, one can think of a multiple-ledger design: a patient-specific, or even a case-specific ledger [34]. Data then can be replicated among multiple ledgers and locations, creating the network of networks [35]. Depending on the context, different requirements to access the data will have to be fulfilled. However, it is still unclear how patients will be able to manage their ledgers, as well as how to set up such infrastructure in real-world settings.

RO-5: Educate and involve the patients. Before patients have full control over their data, the patients must be informed and educated about data- and consent- management practices, as well as about existing laws and regulations. Moreover, it is very challenging to ensure that identities and login data (i.e., credentials), as well as cryptographic keys, are appropriately managed by the patients. Yet, this is of a paramount importance in order to prevent external adversarial attacks, (e.g., impersonating a legitimate user, or malicious data access/injection).

RO-6: Assist patient with data-sharing decisions. How to ensure that all the necessary data are shared in case of treatment of a specific condition? Smart systems for data-sharing decision making, which are based on ethics, law, and contextual medical requirements, are needed to guide and yet not to overwhelm someone already occupied with his/her treatment. These systems will be extremely useful for both primary care and secondary use of health care data, therefore advancing personalized medicine, and facilitating better treatment.

RO-7: *Guarantee emergency data access.* In the health care domain, emergency situations, urgently requiring health care data, occur regularly. An access-control policy can be defined such that only the patient can access (is authorized to access) his data, and no caregiver from the medical institution (where the patient was delivered in an emergency situation) has permission to access any data about the patient. In the case when the patient is unconscious, it is impossible to grant access to the data to the caregiver. Robust and secure "break-glass" mechanisms for emergency situations are therefore required to address this limitation.

RO-8: *Enable data analysis and research.* Having a complete, curated and trusted data set is critical for ensuring accurate results in analysis and research. For example, once complete and accurate data of oncology patients' history are systematically stored with the use of blockchain with consent from the patients, the data can be leveraged in advancing oncology research and treatment options. Currently, analytical, compliance and research tools are actively researched and developed [6]. These tools will extend analytical and treatment capabilities; for example, having a detailed history of drug tolerance and side-effects on patients combined with their genetic profiles or markers can help to improve the selection of patient treatment options.

6   Conclusion

Blockchain technology increasingly attracts attention in multiple health care-related contexts, including patient-centric data management, pharmaceutical supply-chain processes or medical research. Blockchain "promises" to address various inefficiencies of health care-related processes, by enabling better traceability, transparency, and efficiency. However, existing blockchain platforms can offer only limited capabilities and solutions from technical, legal, and social perspectives. The technology is in the early phases of evolution and development, yet, a variety of platforms and their applications in health care settings already exist. This leads to the following paradox: recent attempts to address interoperability between different health care stakeholders already resulted in the creation of multiple blockchain-based prototypes built on top of different blockchain platforms, which themselves are incapable of seamless data exchange and integration. Moreover, due to some of the fundamental properties of blockchain technology (such as immutability), ensuring compliance with existing laws and regulations is challenging.

Starting from the health care context-based requirements, basic principles of the blockchain technology, and focusing on processes that can benefit from applying blockchain, we analyzed existing approached and listed their limitations. Based on this analysis, and taking into account the health care requirements, we emphasize the need for further research directions to be followed towards attaining blockchain-based intelligent health care data management.

References

1. Directive (EU) 2016/680 of the European Parliament and of the Council of 27 April 2016 on the protection of natural persons with regard to the processing of personal data by competent authorities for the purposes of the prevention, investigation, detection or prosecution of criminal offences or the execution of criminal penalties, and on the free movement of such data, and repealing Council Framework Decision 2008/977/JHA. http://data.europa.eu/eli/dir/2016/680/oj. Accessed 05 May 2019
2. Health Information Privacy U.S. Department of Health & Human Services. http://www.hhs.gov/hipaa/. Accessed 04 May 2019
3. Conceptualizing a Data Infrastructure for the Capture, Use, and Sharing of Patient-Generated Health Data in Care Delivery and Research through 2024. https://www.healthit.gov/sites/default/files/onc_pghd_final_white_paper.pdf. Accessed 04 May 2019
4. Draft Trusted Exchange Framework 2018. https://www.healthit.gov/sites/default/files/draft-trusted-exchange-framework.pdf. Accessed 05 May 2019
5. Azaria, A., Ekblaw, A., Vieira, T., Lippman, A.: MedRec: using blockchain for medical data access and permission management. In: 2016 2nd International Conference on Open and Big Data (OBD), pp. 25–30. IEEE (2016)
6. Dillenberger, D., et al.: Blockchain analytics and artificial intelligence. IBM J. Res. Dev. 63(2/3), 5:1–5:14 (2019)
7. Hölbl, M., Kompara, M., Kamišalić, A., Nemec Zlatolas, L.: A systematic review of the use of blockchain in healthcare. Symmetry 10(10), 470 (2018)
8. Vazirani, A.A., ODonoghue, O., Brindley, D., Meinert, E.: Implementing blockchains for efficient health care: systematic review. J. Med. Internet Res. 21, 2 (2019)
9. Zhang, P., White, J., Schmidt, D.C., Lenz, G., Rosenbloom, S.T.: Fhirchain: applying blockchain to securely and scalably share clinical data. Comput. Struct. Biotechnol. J. 16, 267–278 (2018)
10. Dubovitskaya, A., Xu, Z., Ryu, S., Schumacher, M., Wang, F.: Secure and trustable electronic medical records sharing using blockchain. In: AMIA Annual Symposium Proceedings, vol. 2017, p. 650. American Medical Informatics Association (2017)
11. Haq, I., Esuka, O.M.: Blockchain technology in pharmaceutical industry to prevent counterfeit drugs. Int. J. Comput. Appl. 975, 8887 (2018)
12. Hackius, N., Petersen, M.: Blockchain in logistics and supply chain: trick or treat? In: Proceedings of the Hamburg International Conference of Logistics (HICL), pp. 3–18. epubli (2017)
13. Bocek, T., Rodrigues, B.B., Strasser, T., Stiller, B., Blockchains everywhere-a use-case of blockchains in the pharma supply-chain. In: 2017 IFIP/IEEE Symposium on Integrated Network and Service Management (IM), pp. 772–777. IEEE (2017)
14. Bishop, M.: Computer Security: Art and Science. Addison-Wesley Longman Publishing Co., Inc., Boston (2002)
15. Sattarova Feruza, Y., Kim, T.-H.: It security review: privacy, protection, access control, assurance and system security. Int. J. Multimed. Ubiquit. Eng. 2(2), 17–32 (2007)
16. De Lusignan, S., et al.: Key concepts to assess the readiness of data for international research: data quality, lineage and provenance, extraction and processing errors, traceability, and curation. Yearb. Med. Inf. 20(01), 112–120 (2011)
17. Nakamoto et al., S.: Bitcoin: A peer-to-peer electronic cash system (2008)

18. Sompolinsky, Y., Zohar, A.: Secure high-rate transaction processing in bitcoin. In: Böhme, R., Okamoto, T. (eds.) FC 2015. LNCS, vol. 8975, pp. 507–527. Springer, Heidelberg (2015). https://doi.org/10.1007/978-3-662-47854-7_32

19. Kuo, T.-T., Kim, H.-E., Ohno-Machado, L.: Blockchain distributed ledger technologies for biomedical and health care applications. J. Am. Med. Inf. Assoc. **24**(6), 1211–1220 (2017)

20. Krawiec, R., et al.: Blockchain: opportunities for health care. In: Proceedings of NIST Workshop Blockchain Healthcare, pp. 1–16 (2016)

21. Attili, S., Ladwa, S., Sharma, U., Trenkle, A.: Blockchain: the chain of trust and its potential to transform healthcare-our point of view. In: ONC/NIST Use of Blockchain for Healthcare and Research Workshop. ONC/NIST, Gaithersburg, Maryland, USA (2016)

22. Peters, A.W., Till, B.M., Meara, J.G., Afshar, S.: Blockchain technology in health care: a primer for surgeons. Bull. Am. Coll. Surg. **12**, 1–5 (2017)

23. Magyar, G.: Blockchain: Solving the privacy and research availability tradeoff for EHR data: a new disruptive technology in health data management. In: 2017 IEEE 30th Neumann Colloquium (NC), pp. 135–140. IEEE (2017)

24. Clauson, K.A., Breeden, E.A., Davidson, C., Mackey, T.K.: Leveraging blockchain technology to enhance supply chain management in healthcare. Blockchain in Healthcare Today (2018)

25. Scott, T., Post, A.L., Quick, J., Rafiqi, S.: Evaluating feasibility of blockchain application for dscsa compliance. SMU Data Sci. Rev. **1**(2), 4 (2018)

26. Friedman, L.M., Furberg, C.D., DeMets, D.L.: Fundamentals of Clinical Trials. Springer, New York (2010). https://doi.org/10.1007/978-1-4419-1586-3

27. Dubovitskaya, A., Calvaresi, D., Schumacher, M.I.: Essais cliniques multicentriques: transparence et contrôle de la qualité grâce à la blockchain et aux systèmes multi-agents. Swiss Med. Inf. **34**, 667–668 (2018)

28. Andrianov, A., Kaganov, B.: Blockchain in clinical trials-the ultimate data notary. Applied Clinical Trials, p. 16 (2018)

29. Dumas, M., Hull, R., Mendling, J., Weber, I.: Blockchain technology for collaborative information systems (dagstuhl seminar 18332). Schloss Dagstuhl-Leibniz-Zentrum fuer Informatik (2019)

30. Mosca, M., Roetteler, M., Sendrier, N., Steinwandt, R.: Quantum cryptanalysis (dagstuhl seminar 15371). In: Dagstuhl Reports, vol. 5, no. 9. Schloss Dagstuhl-Leibniz-Zentrum fuer Informatik (2016)

31. ZShae, Z., Tsai, J.: Transform blockchain into distributed parallel computing architecture for precision medicine. In: 2018 IEEE 38th International Conference on Distributed Computing Systems (ICDCS), pp. 1290–1299. IEEE (2018)

32. Gropper, A.: Powering the physician-patient relationship with hie of one blockchain health it. In: ONC/NIST use of Blockchain for healthcare and research workshop. ONC/NIST, Gaithersburg, Maryland, USA (2016)

33. Balagurusamy, V., et al.: Crypto anchors. IBM J. Res. Dev. (2019)

34. Dubovitskaya, A., Xu, Z., Ryu, S., Schumacher, M., Wang, F.: How Blockchain could empower ehealth: an application for radiation oncology. In: Begoli, E., Wang, F., Luo, G. (eds.) DMAH 2017. LNCS, vol. 10494, pp. 3–6. Springer, Cham (2017). https://doi.org/10.1007/978-3-319-67186-4_1

35. Hardjono, T., Lipton, A., Pentland, A.: Towards a design philosophy for interoperable blockchain systems. arXiv preprint arXiv:1805.05934 (2018)

Keynotes

Transforming Unstructured Biomedical Text to Structured Knowledge

Wei Wang[✉]

University of California, Los Angeles, CA, 90095, USA
weiwang@cs.ucla.edu

Abstract. Unstructured data constitute a unique, rapidly expanding type of biomedical data and a treasure trove of undiscovered biomedical insights. However, the giant volume of these data sets presents a herculean challenge for the biomedical research community to parse through, as scalable methods to index and discern their content do not exist. In this talk, we will present our latest research on natural language processing and machine learning models and algorithms that can accurately recognize entities corresponding to concepts and events, determine their optimal types and relationships using distantly-supervised learning guided by existing ontologies and taxonomies, and minimize human annotation. Our goals are to extract, organize, and learn from biomedical concepts within unstructured text, and translating into a unified knowledge representation supporting efficient inference, integration, and interpretation.

Keywords: Text mining · Health informatics

V. Gadepally et al. (Eds.): DMAH 2019/Poly 2019, LNCS 11721, p. 291, 2019.
https://doi.org/10.1007/978-3-030-33752-0

Privacy-Protecting Predictive Analytics for Medicine and Healthcare

Lucila Ohno-Machado[1,2,✉]

[1]UCSD Health Department of Biomedical Informatics
University of California, San Diego, CA 92093, USA
[2]Division of Health Services Research and Development,
VA San Diego Healthcare System, La Jolla CA, 92161, USA
lohnomachado@ucsd.edu

Abstract. It is well-known that the identities of individuals whose data are part of so-called "de-identified" data sets can be revealed by an attacker who has auxiliary information about target individuals [1]. In the USA, the Health Information Portability and Accountability Act (HIPAA) [2] has specific instructions on how to "de-identify" electronic healthcare data, but this is insufficient to protect the patient privacy. In the European Union, "anonymization" is mentioned in the General Data Protection Rule [3] as a necessary step before data can be shared, but the specifics on what constitutes "anonymized" data are unclear. Given the high stakes involved in sharing clinical data, these definitions are critical.

In this presentation, I discuss both technical and policy-based measures to protect the privacy of electronic health records (EHRs) when they are used for research. On the technical side, I present how we develop HIPAA-compliant multivariate models in a decentralized fashion for a large clinical data research network, and how we collaborate in developing sound methods to prevent privacy breaches. I also present what we have learned about patient preferences towards sharing specific portions of their EHRs with various research institutions: Not only sharing according to patient preferences for particular categories of data is feasible, but it also removes the burden of deciding, on behalf of others, what constitutes sensitive information and results in improved patient satisfaction.

Keywords: Privacy · Predictive analytics · Healthcare · Medicine

References

1. Rocher, L., Hendrickx, J.L., Montjoye, Y.: Estimating the success of re-identifications in incomplete datasets using generative models. Nat. Commun. **10**, 3069 (2019)
2. Health Insurance Portability and Accountability Act of 1996, 18 USC §264 [Internet] (1996). https://www.govinfo.gov/content/pkg/PLAW-104publ191/pdf/PLAW-104publ191.pdf. Accessed 31 July 2019
3. https://eugdpr.org. Accessed 31 July 2019

V. Gadepally et al. (Eds.): DMAH 2019/Poly 2019, LNCS 11721, p. 292, 2019.
https://doi.org/10.1007/978-3-030-33752-0

Author Index

Printed in the United States
By Bookmasters